The Chairman:
John J. McCloy; The Making of the American Establishment (1992)

The Color of Truth:
McGeorge Bundy and William Bundy; Brothers in Arms (1998)

Hiroshima's Shadow:
Writings on the Denial of History and the Smithsonian Controversy (1998)
Co-editor with Lawrence Lifschultz

American Prometheus:
The Triumph and Tragedy of J. Robert Oppenheimer (2005)
Coauthored with Martin J. Sherwin

Crossing Mandelbaum Gate

Coming of Age Between the Arabs and Israelis,

1956–1978

Kai Bird

SCRIBNER

New York London Toronto Sydney

Scribner
A Division of Simon & Schuster, Inc.
1230 Avenue of the Americas
New York, NY 10020

First Scribner hardcover edition April 2010

SCRIBNER and design are registered trademarks of The Gale Group, Inc.,
used under license by Simon & Schuster, Inc., the publisher of this work.

For information about special discounts for bulk purchases,
please contact Simon & Schuster Special Sales at 1-866-506-1949 or
business@simonandschuster.com.

The Simon & Schuster Speakers Bureau can bring authors to your live event.
For more information or to book an event contact the Simon & Schuster Speakers
Bureau at 1-866-248-3049 or visit our website at
www.simonspeakers.com.

Book design by Ellen R. Sasahara

Manufactured in the United States of America

1 3 5 7 9 10 8 6 4 2

Library of Congress Control Number: 2009052243

ISBN 978-1-4165-4440-1
ISBN 978-1-4391-7160-8 (ebook)

Illustration Credits
Pages x, xi, 9: Maps by J. Del Gaizo, © Kai Bird; pages 1, 3, 5, 18, 21, 65, 76, 84, 99,
109, 226, 246, 295, 302, 331, 332, 341, 342, 347: Bird Family Archives; page 38:
Before Their Diaspora: A Photographic History of the Palestinians, 1876–1948, Walid
Khalidi, Institute for Palestine Studies; pages 44, 55, 63, 87, 123, 125, 153, 165, 167,
173, 190, 203, 243, 248, 290, 293, 364: Getty;
page 94: Royal Geographic Society; pages 96, 98, 131: Saudi Aramco;
page 146: Corbis Bettmann; pages 237, 239: Carleton College Archives;
pages 343, 349: Becky Kook; page 345: Edward Sorel.

Dedicated to Joshua
Who will invent his own identities

Contents

Book III: Jews, Israelis and the Shoah

Author's Note on
Memoir and History

This book is a meld of personal memoir and history, fusing my early life in Jordan, Israel, Saudi Arabia, Egypt and Lebanon with an account of the American experience in the Middle East over the last half century. I am aware that my autobiography has little intrinsic interest—except for its often Zelig-like presence at the epicenter of the evolving Middle Eastern tragedy. I was simply here and there, a happenstance observer. As memoir, this book is my attempt to understand what was happening around me as I grew up in the Arab world. Parts of this narrative are liberally sprinkled with passages from my parents' correspondence. As a memoirist, I have written a story that is mine. But as a historian I have not hesitated to grapple with the difficult issues, the forgotten history and the controversial counternarratives that plague this part of the world. This history may startle some readers and offend others. But it will, I hope, stimulate a conversation.

K.B.

The Middle East Prior to the June 1967 War

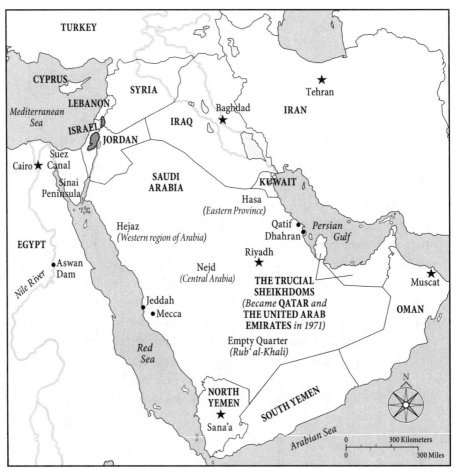

▓▓▓ *Occupied by Israel since June 1967*

Israel–Palestine

Tyre

LEBANON

Golan
Heights

SYRIA

Haifa

*Sea of
Galilee*

*Mediterranean
Sea*

Jordan River

Dawson's Field

Tel Aviv ★

West Bank

Amman ★

Allenby Bridge

Jerusalem ●

Bethlehem

Gaza

*Dead
Sea*

JORDAN

Gaza Strip

*1949 Armistice Line
(Green Line)*

ISRAEL

N

EGYPT

0	40 Kilometers
0	40 Miles

Preface

～

My newborn son, just nine days old, was lying on the dining-room table, swaddled in his soft blue-and-white-striped birthing blanket. A bearded stranger with a knife stood over him. It was a Sunday, my son's *bris* day. The Torah commands, *On the eighth day, [the child's] foreskin shall be circumcised* (Leviticus 12:3). But we nevertheless had the *mohel* (the circumciser) come on the ninth day. Already we were altering tradition—but no matter, it was only Leviticus.

When I told my mother that we intended to have a *bris,* Yiddish for "circumcision," she was astonished. She had never been to a *bris*; neither had I. When I was born, Mother had a doctor circumcise me in a hospital. My father was similarly circumcised at birth. We were Christians, and this allegedly hygienic procedure had been practiced for two generations in our family. But a *bris* was something else, something strange and Old World. A *mohel* would come to our house with his *izmel* (lancet) and before an audience of friends and family cut off the foreskin of our darling boy's infant penis. This primordial ritual would permanently mark my son with the identity of a Jew—and in this case, a Diaspora Jew. To the rabbis, he would have a Hebrew name: Yehoshua Avigdor ben Yonah.

For me, my son Joshua's *bris* was a simple but firm acknowledgment of his mother's Jewish heritage, a nod in the direction of tradition. Like her, he would be Jewish, because according to Judaic law, a child's Jewishness is defined by his mother's identity. But I also realized that the world of the *goyim* would in any case always regard him so. All Jews had been bound by a covenant since the time of Abraham:

"To you and your offspring I will give the land where you are now living as a foreigner. The whole land of Canaan shall be [your] eternal heritage, and I will be a God to [your descendants]." God [then] said to Abraham, "As far as you are concerned, you must keep My covenant—you and your offspring throughout their generations. This is My covenant between Me and between you and your offspring that you must keep: You must circumcise every male. You shall be circumcised through the flesh of your foreskin. This shall be the mark of the covenant between Me and you." (Genesis 17: 8–11)

My parents came to Joshua's *bris* and held him in their arms before the ceremony. Father read a poem he had written for the occasion. When the time came, my wife's cousin Robert was designated by the *mohel* to hold Joshua's tiny limbs firmly while he wielded the *izmel* to cut the foreskin. Blood flowed. With his little finger, the *mohel* then flicked a single drop of soothing red wine into Joshua's mouth. It was all over in seconds.

Afterwards, I spoke a few words to explain our baby boy's name: "We have chosen a strong Hebrew name like Joshua because he is descended on his mother's side from a family of Holocaust survivors. We hope he too will become a survivor of life's adversities and that like his warrior namesake he will take life's journey strong in body and mind. But unlike the biblical Joshua, we hope he is never forced to become a warrior and that when he someday visits Jerusalem, the city of his father's earliest memories, he will find all the peoples of that ancient place at peace."

Joshua has yet to visit Jerusalem, and alas, the city is far from peaceful. This book—part memoir and part historical narrative—will explore why this is so.

This is not a 9/11 book, but it explores the history behind the passions, the fears, the hatreds and the anger that prompted nineteen young Arab men to plow commercial airliners into the Twin Towers, the Pentagon and an empty field in Pennsylvania. Neither is it about the current crisis in Palestinian-Israeli relations. I have written this book in large part to understand why the Middle East of my childhood seems stuck in endless conflict. Only history can offer any insights into this question.

My father was a career Foreign Service officer, a diplomat and an Arabist who spent virtually all of his career in the Near East, as it was called in the U.S. State Department, from 1956 until 1975. So I spent most of my childhood growing up amongst the Israelis and the Arabs of Palestine, Lebanon, Saudi Arabia and Egypt. I went back for a year in 1970–71 to study at the American University of Beirut. I went back again in my twenties as a freelance reporter. I had many adventures. For instance, in September 1970 Palestinian *fedayeen* hijacked a British airliner flying from Bombay to Beirut on which my high school sweetheart was a passenger. She was held hostage on an abandoned desert airfield in northern Jordan for four days.

I know the dangers and the seductions of the Middle East. It is part of my identity. I grew up amongst a people who routinely referred to the creation of the state of Israel as the Nakba—the disaster. And yet I fell in love with and married a Jewish American woman, the only daughter of two Holocaust survivors, both Jewish Austrians. Gradually, over many years of marriage, I came to understand what this meant. One can't live with a child of Holocaust survivors without absorbing some of the same sensibilities that her parents transmitted to her as a young girl. It is an unspoken dread, a sense of fragility, a surreal anticipation of unseen horrors. The children of survivors are inevitably saddled with an existential guilt. Their parents remind them every day how "lucky" they are, how privileged not to have lived in those dark years. And yet, however fortunate their life in America—or Israel— these children of the Holocaust cannot help but wonder whether, as Henry James put it in his short story "The Beast in the Jungle," they are "being kept for something rare and strange, possibly prodigious and terrible, that was sooner or later to happen." I can't count the number of occasions on which my beautiful wife has quietly, insistently intimated that there really is a beast lurking in the jungle, waiting to pounce and destroy her privileged existence in the Diaspora. I am the *goy* who reassures her that it is not so—that the beast is a phantasm. But I know where the beast comes from. It comes from history. So the Holocaust—or, to use the more accurately descriptive Hebrew term, the Shoah—well, it too has become a part of my own identity.

The Nakba and the Shoah. The bookends of my life. In my twenties I came to the conclusion that I did not wish to spend my entire life forlornly trying to rectify the injustices of the Nakba and the Shoah. So I refrained from writing about the Middle East and all its wars. It was an abdication.

Instead, I wrote three biographies of leading figures in the American foreign policy establishment, John J. McCloy, McGeorge Bundy and J. Robert Oppenheimer. (The last of these—*American Prometheus: The Triumph and Tragedy of J. Robert Oppenheimer*—was coauthored with Martin J. Sherwin.)

These books all explored how power worked in twentieth-century America. This meant I had to write a great deal about America's acquisition of the atomic bomb and its use on Hiroshima and Nagasaki, about the postwar nuclear arms race and various aspects of the Cold War—such as how close we came to waging nuclear war during the October 1962 Cuban Missile Crisis. I also co-edited an exhaustive anthology about the decision to use the atomic bomb, *Hiroshima's Shadow*.

Thus, instead of the Nakba and the Shoah, much of my career as a biographer and historian has been obsessed with things atomic. I am not unaware here of a certain personal irony: having decided to avoid the grimness of the Nakba and the Shoah, I spent years writing about an apocalyptic weapon.

Thirty years have passed since I left my childhood haunts in the Middle East. And only now do I feel compelled to grapple with the difficult history of a most troubled land. I write about the Nakba—the story of Palestinian dispossession. But I also tell the Shoah story of my mother-in-law's dispossession and survival in war-torn Italy as a spy for the Italian resistance. I write about the Saudis of my youth, and the American oilmen who made a Faustian bargain with the Wahhabi kingdom. I write about Arab intellectuals such as George Antonius and secular Arab nationalists such as Egypt's Gamel Abdel Nasser. I write about the wars that have defeated Arab modernity and given rise to the Islamists. The Suez War. The June War. Black September. The October War. In my childhood and youth I experienced all these wars. I was evacuated from Jerusalem during the October 1956 Suez War, and evacuated again from Egypt just before the June 1967 War. During the September 1970 hijackings and the subsequent Jordanian-Palestinian civil war, I was in Beirut. And I was in Yemen and Saudi Arabia just before the outbreak of the October War in 1973. I write about the region's descent into violence, terrorism and a seemingly endless cycle of retaliation. Along the way, I discover for myself a historical record of all the doors not opened, the roads not taken to peace. Finally, I write about the Palestinian hijacker Leila Khaled and the "Hebrew Palestinian" Hillel Kook—living symbols of my "bookends," one for the Nakba, the other for the Shoah.

My story begins in Jerusalem—a city where apocalyptic literature was born and nurtured. I encountered in Jerusalem and elsewhere on this idiosyncratic journey all sorts of people: Jewish Americans, Jewish Austrians, Jewish

Hungarians, Palestinian Americans, Jewish Israelis, Jewish Egyptians, Arab Israelis, Hebrew Palestinians, Palestinian terrorists, Israeli terrorists, Sunni Wahhabi Saudis, Shi'ite Saudis, Coptic Egyptians, Armenian Palestinians, Jewish Turks who now call themselves Israelis, Christian Palestinians, Muslim Palestinians, Hasidic Israelis, secular Israelis, and at least one boy whose identity is half Jewish German-Polish and half Sunni Palestinian. All of these people have more than one identity. Or rather, their identities are composites of many strands of history, ethnicity, religion and place. They have what the Lebanese-French writer Amin Maalouf calls "multiple allegiances." So this book is also necessarily about the fundamental issue of identity. It is a voyage through the world of the "other."

Only now do I realize that it is also a book about my own expatriate identity. It is about a boy born in Oregon who travels to Jerusalem and grows up amidst the Arabs and Jews in the tribal mosaic that is the Middle East. I was forced from an early age to develop what the Jewish American writer Leon Wieseltier calls a "stranger's wakefulness" to what was going on around me. So this is a story about a four-year-old boy whose mother overhears him telling a friend that the difference between "this country" and "Washington" was that this was "a place where men got angry at each other and started fighting and now everyone had to go around being a soldier." He can see and hear all around him violence committed in the name of identity. It is about the boy who becomes keenly aware of the borders drawn on maps and globes. He knows these borders divide people into one identity or another. In Jerusalem, however, this privileged little boy is allowed to pass every day back and forth through Mandelbaum Gate, the one passageway permitted between the Arabs and the Jews. It is given to him to see both sides.

Book I

Arabs

The Old City of Jerusalem

1

Jerusalem

Mother, Kai, Father and Nancy, 1958

On the eve of the Suez War in 1956, soon after we arrived, my father observed in a letter to his parents: "Once more we can cross freely through Mandelbaum Gate and once again every day we remark about the contrast between an energetically determined Israel and a stubborn, colorful and slowly progressing Jordan. . . . One side is willing and capable of doing the job. The other is still almost feudal, clannish and with a 'baksheesh' (personal charity approaching graft) mentality."

My parents came to Jerusalem as blank slates. My father and mother spent their formative years in Eugene, Oregon, a town of fewer than 20,000 people. Oddly enough, my father was named Eugene, although everyone called him "Bud." The Great Depression hit his parents hard. My paternal grandparents had met in Montana, where they had laid claim to separate, neighboring tracts of land under the Homestead Act. For seven years they scratched out a living growing wheat, until its sinking market price forced them to sell the land and move to Oregon. During the Depression my grandfather worked for the local dairy in Eugene—owned by the family of the novelist Ken Kesey.

My father graduated from high school in 1943 and was lucky to be chosen by the Navy for officer training—and by the time he was commissioned, the war was over. He had known my mother, Jerine, in high school, but they didn't start dating until after my mother's fiancé died when his Navy ship was sunk in a Pacific typhoon. By then, Bud and Jerine were both enrolled at the University of Oregon.

My mother's father, Chad Newhouse, had survived gassing in World War I, and spent his working life as an accountant and insurance salesman. His wife, Bernice Haines, worked for two decades at Quackenbushes, the local hardware-and-housewares store. I remember as a child marveling at the old-fashioned wire pulley contraption which the cashier used to send customers their change from a second-floor cage. Bernice—or "Bee," as we called her—could remember a time when Indians on horseback still roamed the plains of eastern Washington where she grew up. Chad had a family Bible that had come across the Oregon Trail in a covered wagon.

They were all pretty ordinary, small-town Americans. They worked hard, and had very little money. My mother went to a Disciples of Christ church and sang in the choir. My father was raised a Christian Scientist. But in 1948 a Baptist minister married them in the Congregational church. After years of shopping around, they eventually became Episcopalians. I was born in Eugene on September 2, 1951. Father named me after Kai-Yu Hsu, a refugee from Communist China whom he had befriended at the University of Oregon. "Kai" means "mustard" in Mandarin Chinese, and "Kai-Yu" suggests someone who adds "spice" to life.

Father was boyishly handsome. When he grinned, he exposed his one physical flaw—the badly crooked teeth of an adolescent too poor to go to the orthodontist. In high school he had edited the school newspaper and joined a local chapter of the Sea Scouts, so he learned to sail on nearby lakes and up north in Puget Sound. When he began dating Jerine at the University of Oregon, he'd often take her out sailing—and bring along his best friend, Bob Naper, who later joined the CIA.

Jerine had that scrubbed, open-faced look of the 1940s, with wide, trusting eyes and brown curly locks. She had played the piano on the local Eugene radio station at the age of seven, and in her university days she regularly played the organ at her local church. She had lived in California as a young child, but that was the full extent of her travels until she married Bud—when he then took her to Stockholm on a year abroad for his graduate studies in history. My parents had nothing in their upbringing to prepare them for the Middle East.

After finishing his master's in history at the University of Oregon in 1952, my father was awarded a Rockefeller Internship with the State Department. That autumn we moved to Washington, DC—and Father passed the Foreign Service exam. But by 1952 the Republican senator from Wisconsin, Joe McCarthy, had forced a hiring freeze at the State Department, charging that "pinkos" from Harvard and Yale had infiltrated the Foreign Service. Two years passed before Father was finally offered an appointment to the Foreign Service.

Mother and Father, 1951, the year I was born

In the meantime, the Department had by sheer chance assigned him to serve his internship on the Israel-Jordan desk. He worked under a veteran Arabist, Donald Bergus. With fewer than 600 officers, the Foreign Service was an elite "old boy" institution, the civil service of the American foreign policy establishment. Most of Father's colleagues were bluebloods from the East Coast: white, male and Anglo-Saxon Protestant. Many had been schooled at Phillips Exeter Academy or similar preparatory schools and had then attended an Ivy League college. And within this elite institution the area specialists, particularly those who specialized in difficult languages like Arabic, were a select group.

In the spring of 1956, Father was appointed vice-consul at the American consulate in the Jordanian-controlled part of Jerusalem. His job would be to handle visa and consular affairs for Americans visiting Jordan—and to report on the Jordanian monarchy's activities in both Jerusalem and the West Bank. We would live among the Arabs of East Jerusalem. To his innocent eyes, Jerusalem was the Holy Land. He wrote home to his parents about the wonderment he felt walking the same streets where the historical Jesus had walked two thousand years earlier.

Father was young and filled with an innate optimism about the postwar world. Just before leaving for Jerusalem, he spent three days observing a meeting of the Security Council at the United Nations. After listening to the speeches with a headphone over his ears, he waxed philosophical in a letter home: "It seems to me the world is so closely linked together that there shouldn't be any cause for war or even misunderstandings." But then he saw evidence that this was not true: "Our little five-foot, mustachioed ambassador from Jordan refused to sit next to Israel's ambassador, Abba Eban. He kept an empty seat between himself and the Jew at the conference table."

At thirty-one, my father was garrulous and charmingly informal in manner. He was also very much a married man. "I know that I love you," he wrote Jerine after his arrival in Jerusalem, "when there is a feeling of relief and a single sharp jab of joy when your letters are handed to me." (He had gone ahead to find a house.) Mother hated to be separated from him, and her own letters could be equally passionate: "The love thoughts tumble out too quickly to capture with pen and paper. I can only say, I love you, lover." In their few weeks of separation he complained about his "gay but monkish existence." He was, in fact, a shameless extrovert. "This life is no place for one who does not thoroughly enjoy meeting people," he warned my slightly more shy and sheltered mother. One evening after dinner at the Greek consul general's home he played charades with a French newsman, a balding British diplomat and the widow of the man who earlier that spring had been hanged for the 1951 assassination of Jordan's King Abdullah. "She is German," Father wrote, "has adopted the Muslim religion, is thoroughly opportunistic, and apparently well liked. . . . She also is about the most seductive looking blonde one will encounter anywhere. I have placed on the shelf her kind offer to help me look for a house." (Someone—presumably Mother—had underlined in pencil the words "on the shelf.")

Even then, as a lowly vice-consul on his first posting, he took delight in crossing social boundaries. "The life here may seem hectic to you," he warned Mother. "But if we can regulate ourselves to the slightly madcap atmosphere and refuse to be disturbed by rank consciousness—I am by far the best antidote against that this society has seen in a long while—nor by snippy old ladies and slinky young ones, it will be a charming existence."

Mother arrived a few weeks later, bringing my little sister, Nancy, and me. The three of us flew from Washington, DC, to Beirut aboard a twenty-one-seat Pan American Airways DC-3, a propeller plane with a cruising speed of 180 miles per hour. After spending one night in Beirut, we boarded a smaller aircraft and flew into Jerusalem's tiny Kalandia Airport. Every time a plane landed or took off, police had to stop the traffic on the road from Jerusalem to Kalandia because the runway crossed the road. Father met us with a consulate car and drove us to the American Colony Hostel, then a quaint bed-and-breakfast lodge in East Jerusalem's Sheikh Jarrah neighborhood. Now it is a luxury boutique hotel and boasts the favored bar and restaurant for East Jerusalem's expatriate community of diplomats and journalists.

The American Colony was our home that first summer of 1956 in Jerusalem. My earliest memories stem from this stone building and its rose garden. From that day to the present, the Colony has always been my Jerusalem. To live there was to partake of its history as a way station, a genteel expatriate haven in the midst of Arab Jerusalem. We had a two-bedroom suite with daily maid service and three meals a day delivered to our rooms—or we could eat in the Colony's grand dining room. In the late afternoons and evenings dozens of expatriates and Palestinian intellectuals mingled in the "big salon," sitting in overstuffed armchairs under an elaborate Damascene ceiling hand-painted with gold leaf. In the flagstone courtyard there was a water fountain surrounded by palm trees, potted plants, ivy geraniums and pungent jasmine.

This lovely courtyard remains one of the most serene spots in Jerusalem. A high rock wall stretched from Sheikh Jarrah all the way to Mandelbaum Gate, dividing the city. But from the second- and third-story windows of the American Colony one could gaze across an open field of no-man's-land and into Israel. For some reason that summer the Israelis decided to clear a nearby minefield dating from the 1948 war. This meant blowing up as many as eighteen large antitank mines daily. On one occasion hot iron landed in the garden across the street.

*   *   *

The American Colony was run by Mrs. Bertha Spafford Vester, a seventy-eight-year-old American matriarch. The image of this formidable woman presiding over the Colony's dinner table constitutes one of my earliest memories. Vester had come to Jerusalem in 1881, when she was three years old. Her father, Horatio Gates Spafford, a well-to-do lawyer from Chicago, had moved his family to Jerusalem, seeking a simple religious way of life. Together with sixteen other Americans and a handful of Swedish-American immigrants, the Spaffords founded what the local population came to call the American Colony. Their intent was to live a spare, austere life, sharing everything in common. They called themselves the Overcomers, and they believed the Second Coming of Christ was at hand. As evidence, they cited the increasing numbers of Jews then flocking to Palestine—in their view, a fulfillment of the biblical prophecy that the Jews would return to their land shortly before the Second Coming.

At that time, in the 1880s, the total population of Jerusalem was no more than 35,000, and nearly everyone lived inside the walled Old City, whose gates were closed at sunset and reopened at sunrise. By the turn of the century, the city had grown to about 50,000, of which a slight majority were Jews, with the remainder being evenly split between Christian and Muslim Arabs.

Though a Holy City to three major religions, Jerusalem was in reality a bleak, inhospitable stony landscape. Its harsh bright light reflected all that stone. When Herman Melville visited in 1857, he noted in his diary, "Stones to right and stones to left . . . stony tombs; stony hills & stony hearts." In 1867 another visitor, Mark Twain, called Jerusalem "the knobbiest town in the world, except Constantinople." Even the ancient olive trees, planted amid row after row of stone terraces, seem covered with limestone dust. Living conditions, moreover, were anything but pristine. Open sewers stank, garbage and filth lined the narrow stone streets, and most of the city's residents lived in cramped and squalid quarters.

Still, at the beginning of the last century Jerusalem's skyline must have been magnificent. Every rooftop appeared to have at least one and sometimes as many as a half-dozen dirty white plastered domes made of stone. Seen from the east, from atop Mount Scopus, the Old City gleamed not only with its gray-white city walls but also from the golden hue of the seventh-century Dome of the Rock and the turquoise tiles of the shrine's octagonal

Divided Jerusalem, 1948–1967

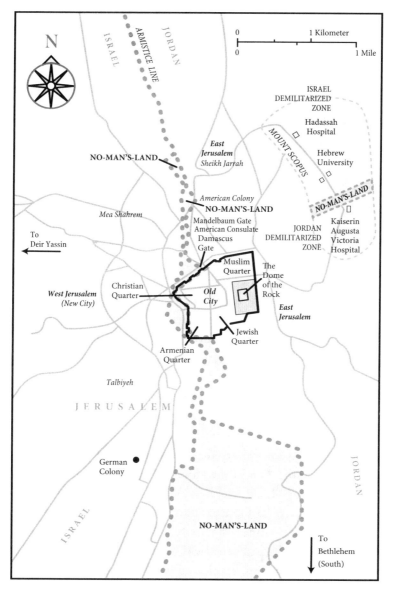

outer walls. Outside the city walls, in the valley of Gethsemane, sat a Russian Orthodox church with its distinctive onion-shaped domes. Elsewhere on the stony skyline stood Christian bell towers, Muslim minarets and the arched remnants of ancient Roman and Crusader ruins.

The Spaffords rented a large home just inside the Old City. They opened a butcher shop, a bakery, a metal shop and a photographic business. The Colony was run as a Protestant commune. By the turn of the century, it was home to more than 120 men, women and children. Eventually, the community bought a cluster of handsome stone houses at 26 Nablus Road, about a half mile north of Damascus Gate. A wealthy merchant, Rabah al-Husseini, had built the main property in the years 1865–1876. Husseini and his four wives occupied the two-story mansion until his death in the 1890s. The Husseini clan then leased, and later sold, the property to the Spaffords.

By then, the Spaffords and their American Colony had become an integral part of Jerusalem's social and political life. It was neutral ground, the one place in the city where intellectuals and clerics of any creed might meet with other Christian sects or Palestinian Muslims or Jews. Over the decades the Colony organized numerous charitable ventures, including an orphanage and hospital in the Old City. In 1920 an American reporter described the colony as: "A noble band of American men and women [living in] a lonely outpost of American civilization in a strange far-off land . . ." The Spaffords' daughter, Bertha, married another member of the Colony, Frederick Vester—a German-Swiss national born in Palestine.

In the 1920s Bertha Vester took control of the Colony and, distancing herself from her parents' idiosyncratic religious views and the messianic outlook in which she had been raised, focused instead on "good deeds." Bertha would wield enormous influence over Jerusalem society throughout the following decades.

In the early years, the Overcomers had strong and diverse ties to Jerusalem's Jewish community. Indeed, their religious millennialism made them early promoters of the Zionist dream of a Jewish homecoming—though, of course, they also believed, like today's Christian Zionists, that the Jews would have to convert to Christianity to be saved when Christ arrived. Horatio Spafford often visited the Western Wall (or "Wailing Wall"), and encouraged various rabbis to drop by the Colony's "Big House" to discuss religion. One frequent nonrabbinical visitor was Eliezer Ben-Yehuda, the Jewish scholar who spent decades creating a lexicon for modern spoken Hebrew. But gradually the American Colony and its social milieu became critical of the Zionist project, objecting to its "self-segregation." Why, the second-generation Vesters would ask, are the Zionists building hospitals, schools and welfare agencies to which only Jews are welcome?

By the end of World War I, the Vesters had converted part of the Colony into a refined "hostel" where distinguished visitors to the Holy Land sought lodging. T. E. Lawrence, Field Marshal Lord Allenby, Lowell Thomas, Gertrude Bell, John D. Rockefeller and many others spent time in the Colony. It only ceased to be a religious community in the early 1950s, and thereafter Bertha Spafford Vester ran it as an upscale boutique hotel, catering to wealthy American and European tourists.

I remember her as a kindly but formidable old woman. She had an unabashedly dominating personality—which perhaps explains why she appeared not once but twice on the television show *This Is Your Life*. She was a "brooch lady," meaning her dresses were invariably adorned with intricate silver or gold brooches. She wore her stark white hair in a Victorian-style bun. Everyone deferred to her loud, striking voice. Bright, blue-eyed and a clever conversationalist, Mrs. Vester rarely hesitated to speak her mind. She liked my parents and frequently invited us to go swimming in an old sugar-mill pond, a rock quarry–like structure that she owned near Jericho.

In 1948, just eight years before we arrived in Jerusalem, the road outside the American Colony had been the scene of a horrific massacre. Bertha Vester wrote about it in her possessively titled memoir, *Our Jerusalem*, published in 1950. Every expatriate living in Jerusalem in those years inevitably had a copy, and I know my parents read and admired the book. "After the Deir Yassin massacre [of April 9]," Mrs. Vester wrote, "the Arabs became frantic and on April 13 attacked a convoy going to the Hadassah Hospital. The road passes the American Colony and about one hundred and fifty insurgents, armed with weapons varying from blunderbusses and old flintlocks to modern Sten and Bren guns, took cover behind a cactus patch in the grounds of the American Colony. Their faces were distorted by hate and the lust for revenge. They were blind and deaf and fearless; only one obsession dominated them. I went out and faced them. I said the American Colony had served them for more than sixty years. Was this our reward? I told them. . . . 'To fire from the shelter of the American Colony is the same as firing from a mosque or a church.' . . . Some of the men listened for a minute and then threatened to shoot me if I did not go away. I said, 'Shoot me if you want to, but I must protest against your using the grounds of the American Colony as a cover.'"

The insurgents turned their backs on Vester and resumed firing on the Jewish convoy. The ambush had begun at 9:30 a.m., when a convoy of two ambulances, two cars, several trucks carrying medical supplies and foodstuffs, and three buses inched their way through Sheikh Jarrah. The windows of the buses were covered with metal plates to deter sniper fire. Aboard were 112 doctors, nurses, professors and students bound for Hadassah Hospital on Mount Scopus. Most were unarmed. As the convoy rolled past the villa owned by Grand Mufti Haj Amin al-Husseini, a land mine exploded under the lead vehicle. Simultaneously, the convoy was hit by a hail of gunfire from both sides of the road. Grenades and Molotov cocktails were thrown. A few vehicles escaped, but most of the convoy was trapped. And even though British military forces were stationed just two hundred yards down the road, they did nothing to stop the slaughter. The Palestinian insurgents went on firing for six hours. Around 3:00 p.m. they succeeded in dousing two of the armored buses with gasoline; the buses caught fire, burning alive the few remaining survivors. Seventy-seven Jews were killed that day. Among them were prominent medical doctors, a physicist, a professor of psychology, a scholar of Jewish law and a well-known linguist. This murderous ambush of unarmed doctors and scholars would not be forgotten.

As a boy I was unaware of this tragedy that had taken place on my doorstep. When I was five to six years old, a similar convoy of Israeli armored buses and personnel carriers rolled past the American Colony every other Wednesday on its way to resupply Mount Scopus. The adults around me always stared nervously at the convoy; they knew what had happened on this road. I only remember feeling oddly frightened by the eyes of the drivers as they peered through the slits of their armored windows.

There was some sort of awful explanation for what the Palestinians had done that day. Only four days earlier, on the morning of April 9, 1948, a force of some 130 Jewish insurgents, members of two radically militant Zionist factions, the Stern Gang and the Irgun, had attacked the Palestinian village of Deir Yassin, just three miles west of Jerusalem. Machine gunners from the Haganah provided cover fire as the Stern and Irgun forces stormed the village. According to Israeli accounts, "the conquest of the village was carried out with great cruelty. Whole families—women, old people, children—were killed, and there were piles of dead." One Israeli intelligence officer, Mordechai Gichon, visited the village six hours later and reported the next day, "The adult males were taken to town in trucks and paraded in the city streets, then taken back to the site and killed with rifle and machine-gun fire." Scholars today estimate that over a hundred Palestinians were killed that day. But at the time, the figure of 254 killed was circulated by both Jewish and Arab sources. In any case, news of the massacre was publicized widely—and persuaded thousands of frightened Palestinians to flee their homes in succeeding weeks.

I grew up knowing that Deir Yassin was a rallying cry among Palestinians. And, of course, every Israeli schoolchild is taught to remember the massacre of the seventy-seven Jews killed in the convoy to Mount Scopus. A monument to the victims now stands just down the road from the American Colony.

After living in the American Colony for nearly two months, we shifted temporarily to a "dingy little apartment" in West Jerusalem, "furnished with frogs, cracked bowls and a Philco refrigerator." Only on September 11, 1956, did we finally move to permanent quarters. Our new home was a half mile from the American Colony, in the Sheikh Jarrah district of East Jerusalem, on a hill overlooking the stretch of "no-man's-land" that bordered Israeli-controlled Mount Scopus. (Sheikh Jarrah takes its name from a mosque named after Saladin's surgeon.)

Ours was a small house, newly built of Jerusalem's famous gleaming white limestone, hand-chipped into rough-hewn rectangular blocks. "Jerusalem is built in heaven," so goes a medieval hymn, "of Living Stone." And in fact, when the British arrived in 1917, they quickly mandated that all new housing had to be constructed of this chalky white stone, mined from a local quarry. Even in 1956 this law was still being observed on both sides of divided Jerusalem.

"We love our house," Mother wrote home to Oregon. The front porch was glassed in, and both the small living room and the dining room had a fireplace. We had sea-shipped from the States virtually all of our furniture, including beds, bureaus, a sofa and a dining room table Father had built himself from two hollow plywood doors. Mother had bought a new refrigerator, a stove and a washing machine in Washington and added these appliances to the shipment. She had been forced to take out a loan from the State Department credit union to pay for them. Contrary to Father's instructions, however, the sea shipment landed at Tel Aviv instead of Beirut, necessitating long negotiations with both the Israelis and the Jordanians on how to transport the goods to East Jerusalem. Normally, no large trucks were allowed to cross Mandelbaum Gate—the one heavily guarded passageway from Israeli-controlled West Jerusalem into Jordanian-controlled East Jerusalem. After considerable delay, the Israelis agreed that the large wooden packing crate could be trucked to the Gate, where it was opened, and porters were allowed to carry its contents piece by piece into East Jerusalem.

Oddly, the house never had a phone. And during Jerusalem's cold, damp winters it was heated by the fireplaces and by small portable kerosene space heaters that we moved from room to room. Mother bought cheap Damascus brocade in the Old City's souk to make drapes for the house's fourteen windows. She was delighted to learn that she could borrow a shiny black upright piano from the consulate. With a piano in the house, it felt to her truly like home.

My parents slept in the master bedroom, with its balcony that overlooked Mount Scopus. My sister, Nancy, and I shared the only other bedroom. From the roof terrace one could also see the Mount of Olives and the imposing tower of Augusta Victoria Hospice, a massive structure atop Mount Scopus, built by the German Kaiser at great expense from 1906 to 1910 and modeled after some picture-perfect medieval castle. In our back garden there was an ancient Roman cistern.

Mother was upbraided by other consular wives for refusing to have more than one servant (plus the part-time gardener who came with the house). Most diplomatic households were staffed with a cook, a maid, a gardener and a nanny. Mother thought such a bevy of servants was somehow un-American. Father reported to a friend, "My wife and one other American here have declared war on having servants or light conversation only at cocktail parties."

At least part of the problem, truth to tell, was that Mother couldn't afford servants on Father's annual salary of $4,200 (about $33,000 a year in today's dollars). But eventually she hired a cook named Youssef, who often slept on a cot under the back stairwell. Mother didn't think much of his cooking, but he was honest and completely reliable. He did much of the shopping in the vegetable market in the Old City and helped with the laundry—though hanging the laundry out to dry was beneath his station. More importantly, he could be on duty in the evenings when my parents were often out on the cocktail and dinner-party circuit. We paid him 42 Jordanian dinars, or about $42, per month.

Scorpions were everywhere. One day my mother discovered a rather large, four-inch-long one in my bedroom. The gardener was called, and I remember watching with astonishment as this white-haired old man stomped on it with his callused bare foot. Thereafter, Mother placed tin cans filled with kerosene beneath the legs of each bed—to discourage scorpions from climbing into the beds. I learned to be always on the lookout for the little creatures. Each morning I knocked my shoes on the floor to make sure nothing had crawled inside.

Jerusalem in those years was a small town that echoed with the braying of donkeys, the ringing of church bells and the Muslim call to prayer. We awoke every morning to the sounds of roosters crowing and dogs barking. I gawked whenever camels strolled down the street, carrying loads of wood. Flocks of sheep and goats grazed on the surrounding brown hills. In the evenings, as the sunset's last rays reflected off Mount Scopus, we could often glimpse a few armed Israelis patrolling the perimeters of Hebrew University and Hadassah Hospital—built in 1938 and now abandoned. If we looked carefully, we could also make out the three domes atop the hospital's entrance.

Our rented house was a stone's throw from the 1949 armistice line, and Mount Scopus was but an island of Jewish property in a sea of Arab territory, patrolled by Israeli police under the nominal command of a United Nations chief of staff. But, in violation of the armistice, the Israelis refused to allow this U.N. official to inspect the grounds. Mount Scopus conveniently overlooked all the roads leading from Jordan into East Jerusalem, so the Israelis were eager to assert de facto sovereignty over the strategic hill. Much to the annoyance of both the Jordanians and the United Nations, the Israelis were constantly observed digging trenches, building sandbagged foxholes and smuggling in small arms.

On some nights I could hear the random, not-so-distant tapping of machine-gun fire. "War and rumors of war seem to be the habit around here," my father wrote, "and waking up in the night to hear rifle fire is almost an every night occurrence." That first summer several United Nations "blue helmet" observers were wounded by sniper fire—whether from Israeli or Jordanian shooters was unknown. My parents gave standing instructions to Youssef that in their absence—and in the event of heavy firing—he should place my little sister, Nancy, and me inside the bathtub.

One evening my parents arrived for dinner at the British consul general's home just as a machine-gun battle erupted near Mandelbaum Gate. "I don't know whether we should be coming or going," stammered my mother. The consul general ushered them inside and then went to his telephone—the only open telephone line to West Jerusalem. "I say, old boy," he said to his Israeli counterpart, "your chaps are shooting at our chaps over here. Could you call this off?" Remarkably, a few minutes later the firing ceased.

Some evenings my father would haul out his heavy night-vision Navy binoculars and peer up at Mount Scopus. Often he could see Israeli "police" digging trenches. Late at night he sometimes heard the drone of a small one-engine airplane flying overhead and soon afterwards would spot parachutes drifting down to the grounds of Hadassah Hospital. In violation of the armistice, the Israelis were resupplying their troops in the enclave.

Oddly enough, in these uncertain circumstances the Israelis maintained a small zoo up on Mount Scopus, which they called the Biblical Zoo, featuring animals mentioned in the Torah. Most of them had been relocated in 1948, but for some reason a lion was left behind. So the convoy to Mount Scopus always included food for him—the carcass of a mule. We knew when it was time for the convoy because from across the ravine in no-man's-land we could hear the roar of a hungry lion.

Initially, my parents felt overwhelmed by Jerusalem society. "I think we are the most common clods," he wrote to his former history professor at the University of Oregon, "to penetrate the stratums of Arab and Israeli society in some time." But in time, they entertained or went out nearly every night. "I have never seen such a small big town before," he wrote. "The eligible society is restricted to about 150 people of all shades, including some questionably fascinating ones. As one handsome young Greek advised me, 'You must acquire a reputation, any reputation at all.' "

Soon after arriving in Jerusalem, Father was introduced to Katy Antonius, a formidable woman and certainly one of East Jerusalem's "eligible 150." He described her as "something out of Eliot's Cocktail Party. . . . she is gossipy, easy to charm and thoroughly affected." A Greek Orthodox of Lebanese and Egyptian descent, Katy was the widow of George Antonius, a King's College–educated intellectual and Arab nationalist whose 1938 book *The Arab Awakening* had seduced at least two generations of American diplomats. I was to read it when I was fifteen, and later use it as the primary inspiration for a high school senior-year essay on Palestine. It convinced me, as it had my father, that the Palestinian cause was just, legitimate—and terribly misunderstood in the West. The book and the author's widow were to color our family's outlook on the Middle East for years to come.

But before Father had even read the book, or had a chance to charm Katy, he committed a calculated faux pas. Seizing the occasion to "acquire a reputation," he purposefully addressed Mrs. Antonius by her first name. Katy publicly reprimanded him, calling him "cheeky."

Father's boss advised him to write a formal letter of apology. He did so, but in his own way. "Cheeky may express it well," he wrote Antonius. And then he related how in 1950 on his first trip to Europe, "I learned aboard ship about a Swedish social requirement that everyone be addressed by their formal titles and last names—until the oldest person asked the younger person's first name. I was told this while playing bridge with another, older couple, and immediately inquired the first name of the lady. We all laughed and the story was worn threadbare by my wife . . . my sincerest apologies for being presumptuous. I could hardly wish to offend the widow of a man who has made such a major contribution to our understanding of Arabia."

Katy must have been charmed, because soon she allowed him to call upon her at her home, where he "had a merry time apologizing to her. We drank tea and chatted for two-and-a-half hours and she is forever my friend." Thereafter, we spent many hours in her home, part of which she later turned into an upscale restaurant-cum-salon. She called it the Katakeet—named after a gossip column that appeared under that title in a local newspaper. Everyone read Katakeet, and often Katy herself was both the source and the subject of the gossip. "Katy was naughty," recalled another old Jerusalemite. "She was curious about everything. She would start gossip; she was always bringing people together, matching people up. In a small community of 60,000 she was known by reputation to everyone."

Initially, Katy was unimpressed by my mother, and candidly told Father that she didn't understand why he had married that "brown wren." She changed her mind when Mother showed that she too had strong opinions. Katy became a frequent dinner guest and one of my parents' best friends in Jerusalem. The daughter of Dr. Faris Nimr Pasha, a well-known Egyptian newspaper proprietor, she had been nurtured in Alexandria's upper-class society. She spoke fluent French and English. "Katy Antonius was an intelligent, bright, and witty woman, full of humor and charm," said another Jerusalemite, Anwar Nusseibeh. "[She was] always up-to-date on the intricacies of political events, pretty, good-hearted, and generous." She had founded an orphanage in the Old City, called Dar al-Awlad (House of Boys), and she regularly invited some of these boys to her parties. Interestingly, one such boy was the then thirteen-year-old Awad Mubarak, who later became an American-trained child psychologist and an advocate of nonviolent resistance to the Israeli occupation. (He was deported by the Israelis in May 1988—six months after the start of the first Intifada, Arabic for "shaking off.") Katy mentored young Mubarak as a boy, telling him that "people are people, and there is no reason to fear them or their rank." Mubarak later recalled being astonished to hear Katy, as if to prove her point, loudly cursing Jordan's King Hussein for his treatment of the Palestinians.

Katy was a character, part dragon-lady and part flirt. She was always smartly dressed in the latest fashions and often wore a string of pearls. Her black hair was cut fairly short and boasted a distinctive white streak.

Katy Antonius, Jerusalem, 1957

Her parties were elaborate affairs. "Evening dress, Syrian food and drink, and dancing on the marble floor," wrote the English writer and politician Richard Crossman after attending an Antonius dinner. "It is easy to see why the British prefer the Arab upper class to the Jews. This Arab intelligentsia has a French culture, amusing, civilized, tragic and gay. Compared with them the Jews seem tense, bourgeois, central European."

As befitted the widow of George Antonius, Katy was a fierce partisan on behalf of her fellow Arabs, and she hated what the Jewish immigrants had done to her Palestine. In 1946–47, at a time when the British were trying to arrest and hang Jewish terrorists belonging to the Irgun and the Stern Gang, Katy's lover was General Sir Evelyn Barker, whose job it was to stamp out these violent Zionist factions. He had fallen in love with Katy at one of her Jerusalem soirees. We know this today because Katy kept his voluminous love letters until one day in 1948 when Israeli soldiers stormed her house in West Jerusalem. Before blowing the house apart, the Israelis retrieved Barker's letters and stored them in Israel's state archives. They reveal a man deeply in love—but also one consumed with hatred for the Jews. "Katy, I love you so much, Katy," Barker wrote. "Just think of all this life and money being wasted for these bloody Jews. Yes I loathe the lot—whether they be Zionists or not. Why should we be afraid of saying we hate them—it's time this damned race knew what we think of them—loathsome people."

Katy may not have shared Barker's anti-Semitism, but she was beyond doubt bitterly anti-Zionist. "Before the Jewish state," she later remarked, "I knew many Jews in Jerusalem and enjoyed good relations with them socially. Now I will slap the face of any Arab friend of mine who tries to trade with a Jew. We lost the first round; we haven't lost the war."

Jerusalem was very much a divided city. A jarring series of ad hoc fences, walls and bails of barbed wire, running like an angry, jagged scar from north to south, separated East Jerusalem from West. Driving anywhere near the armistice line often meant running into signs in Hebrew, English and Arabic, reading, "STOP! DANGER! FRONTIER AHEAD!"

Often Father had to cross over to what we called "the other side." And if he was delayed, there was no way he could phone my mother. The Birds socialized on both sides of the armistice line. Father commented on the "strange awkwardness of parties held first on one side among the Jews and then on the other among the Arabs." And whichever side he was on, he had to be careful not to speak too freely of friends across the line. He also wrote home about the stereotypes: "The charm and eloquent sincerity of the Arab character, the quick intelligence and clever stratagems of the Israeli. . . ."

As a five-year-old, I observed the events around me with innocent eyes. One evening we were invited to a dinner party at the American Colony, and I overheard an elderly American heiress announce that she would give a million dollars to anyone who could solve this Arab-Israeli conflict. I promptly tugged on my father's sleeve and said, "Daddy, we have to win this prize."

I was keenly aware of the conflict. Once in October 1956, my mother overheard me telling a friend that the difference between "this country" and "Washington" was that this was "a place where men got angry at each other and started fighting and now everyone had to go around being a soldier." And around the same time Father wrote about me to a friend: "Outside of an occasional 'Shalom' instead of 'Ma'assalama' on this side, Kai seems to know these two peoples are somehow *different.* He told Raja Elissa at the party the other night that he 'went to school on the other side' with a big grin. Everyone roared."

To get to West Jerusalem one had to cross no-man's-land, passing through Mandelbaum Gate, the heavily guarded passageway from East to West Jerusalem. The "gate" took its name from a house that once stood on the spot, built by a family of Jewish immigrants from Byelorussia. I crossed through the Gate nearly every day, past the barbed wire and the cone-shaped anti-tank barriers. Men with guns stood guard. The skeletal remains of armored personnel carriers and rusting tanks lay about as constant reminders of lost lives and past conflicts. "Mandelbaum Gate" was a phrase I heard every day, but I knew nothing of its history.

Simchoh Mandelbaum and Esther Liba Mandelbaum came to Jerusalem in the late nineteenth century—and their story is emblematic of the Jewish experience in Palestine. Both Simchoh and Esther were the offspring of rabbis, and Simchoh spent much of his life studying the Torah. The couple had ten children, all born in the Old City. To support their large family the Mandelbaums opened a stocking shop; Esther worked the looms, weaving the stockings, while Simchoh colored them in several large wooden vats of dye. They became known as the "stockinged couple."

Over the years, they outgrew their cramped house in the Old City's Jewish Quarter, and Simchoh decided to buy a plot of land on which to build a new home. One day he inspected a parcel of barren land outside the northern wall of the Old City. Seeing a metallic glint, he bent down and picked up an ancient coin. It was engraved with a cluster of grapes on one side, while on the other were inscribed the Hebrew words "For the liberation of Jerusalem." A local curator told him the coin dated back to the time of the Second Jewish Revolt, when the messianic Jewish general Simon Bar-Kochba briefly reestablished a Jewish state in the years AD 132–135. Sim-

Eugene Bird, 1962

choh thought this a good omen. His friends, to be sure, were telling him he could make more money if he moved his stocking business to Jaffa Street in the growing New City. But according to family lore, Simchoh refused: "If I don't buy it, non-Jews will come along and purchase the lot and build houses all along the road up to the hospital at Har Hatzofim, and will close in around Mea Shearim and Botei Ungarin [two Jewish districts in Jerusalem]. But if other people see that I bought a lot here, they will come too, and Jewish settlement will spread north." Determined to perform what he considered a *mitzvah* (good deed) for his people, Simchoh built his three-story house out of white Jerusalem stone, and it became a visible landmark at the end of Shmuel Hanovi Street. The Mandelbaum household was soon filled with grandchildren, and the family stocking business branched out into the weaving of fine linens and blankets. But instead of attracting Jewish neighbors, Mandelbaum House became a sometimes embattled Jewish outpost. The local Waqf—a Muslim religious charity—owned much of the neighboring land and refused to sell any of it to Jews. By the late 1920s the tensions between the two communities were at a breaking point.

When, in August 1929, Arab rioters went on a rampage, Mandelbaum House was used by the Haganah Jewish militia to turn back the mob at what was becoming a dividing line between the New (Jewish) City and Arab Jerusalem. The American reporter Vincent Sheean wrote that he was shocked by "the ferocity of the Arab anger." Over a period of three days some 133 Jews were killed throughout Palestine, 17 alone in Jerusalem. British police and Jews in turn killed 116 Arabs, many in self-defense.

The worst massacre occurred well outside of Jerusalem, in the West Bank town of Hebron, where an Arab mob formed after photographs were distributed supposedly showing the Dome of the Rock shrine in Jerusalem destroyed by a bomb. The photographs were fake. But the mob brutally murdered sixty-seven Hebron Jews, people whose families had lived there for generations. The sole British police officer in Hebron, Assistant District Superintendent Raymond Cafferata, witnessed an Arab cutting off the head of a Jewish child. He shot him in the groin. Cafferata later testified that he and his small Arab police force had fired their guns into the crowd, but the mob broke through their lines and began attacking the homes of Jews. The most horrific atrocity took place in the home of Eliezer Dan Slonim, the manager of the local English-Palestine bank. Slonim was also the sole Jewish member of the Hebron Municipal Council, and he had many friends in the Arab community. Often on a rainy winter evening, some of Hebron's leading sheikhs had stopped by to play chess and drink coffee in the warmth of the Slonim home. Indeed, Slonim was so confident that the local Arab elders would protect him that the previous day he had refused the Haganah's offer to store weapons in his home. When the mob broke through his door, Slonim was the first to die, butchered with knives. His wife, Hannah, and their son, Aaron, were also stabbed to death, along with nineteen other Jews who had sought refuge in Slonim's home.

A day later a Dutch-born Canadian journalist, Pierre van Paassen, described the scene: "We found the twelve-foot-high ceiling splashed with blood. The rooms looked like a slaughterhouse . . . the blood stood in a huge pool on the slightly sagging stone floor of the house. Clocks, crockery, tables and windows had been smashed to smithereens. Of the unlooted articles, not a single item had been left intact except a large black-and-white photograph of Dr. Theodor Herzl, the founder of political Zionism. Around the picture's frame the murderers had draped the blood-drenched underwear of a woman."

Afterwards, the British forced the remaining Jewish community, numbering several hundred, to evacuate Hebron. They would not return permanently until 1967. The Hebron massacre made headlines around the world and severely traumatized the Yishuv—the Hebrew term for Israel's pre-1948 Jewish settlements in Palestine.

Hebron was gruesome, undeniable evidence that Arab anger over the growing Yishuv posed a deep existential threat to the entire Zionist enterprise. The fact that one of the earliest victims was Slonim, a moderate Zionist who had believed in the possibility of Arab-Jewish dialogue, only strengthened the political hand of the hard-line Revisionist Zionists, who argued that Palestine would have to be conquered and the Arabs expelled.

Moderate voices were being silenced on both sides. The 1929 riots had begun in Jerusalem when wild rumors began circulating to the effect that a Jewish group was planning to take over the al-Aqsa Mosque on the Temple Mount (the Haram al-Sharif). In fact, in mid-August several hundred members of a radical Zionist group calling itself the Committee for the Western Wall—together with members of Vladimir (Ze'ev) Jabotinsky's Revisionist Zionist youth organization, Betar—staged a march on the Western Wall. Escorted by British police, the group arrived at this sacred site shouting "The Wall is ours" and singing "Hatikvah," the Zionist anthem:

> *Our hope is not yet lost*
> *The hope of two thousand years.*
> *To be a free people in our land*
> *The land of Zion and Jerusalem.*

This demonstration provoked a counterdemonstration the next day sponsored by the Supreme Muslim Council. Jewish worshippers at the Wall were assaulted, and some prayer books were burned. The following day a Jewish boy was knifed and killed during an argument at a soccer field, and his funeral turned into a political demonstration. Tensions built until the following Friday when thousands of Arab youth from surrounding villages swarmed onto the Haram al-Sharif for Friday prayers. When rumors flew that two Arabs had been killed by Jews, the worshippers began picking up sticks and stones and proceeded to attack Jewish targets in the Old City. The ensuing riots established a predictable pattern: Arab anger at Jewish encroachments on their land—usually via quiet purchases of land from absentee landlords—would spark an incident on the Temple Mount, followed by another round of violence.

During a later Arab uprising in 1936–39, Mandelbaum House was once again used by the Haganah as a military outpost. By then Esther Mandelbaum was a widow, but she let the Haganah hide weapons in her linen closet. In the spring of 1948 Arab snipers, perched on rooftops in neighboring Sheikh Jarrah, routinely targeted the house. Esther was forced to flee, and the Haganah turned it into a frontline fortress.

On April 14, 1948, Jordanian Legionnaires mounted a major assault on the house. A tremendous explosion finally brought it down, killing thirty-five Haganah soldiers. "I remember that day well," recounts Simchoh Mandelbaum, a grandson of Esther's. "We had left just three days earlier, and since then the house had been captured by Legion forces and recaptured by us four times. . . . It was hard to absorb the fact that 35 Jews had met a terrible death there in the house where we had been born and lived a rich childhood." Although most of the house was flattened, part of a stone archway—the front garden gate—and three walls with arched windows remained standing. For the next nineteen years this grim ruin served as a symbol of the divided city. Just days after East Jerusalem was conquered by Israeli troops in June 1967, Israeli bulldozers obliterated the site. The Israelis wanted nothing to remain of that symbol of division.

In 1956, Father's office in the American consulate was but a stone's throw from Mandelbaum Gate, so it was he who often drove me to school. The "gate" did not open until eight each morning, and since school began at eight, I was always a few minutes late. The few private cars with crossing privileges had to use license plates from someplace other than either Israel or Jordan—ours carried Oregon plates. The "gate" was not really a gate but rather two roadblocks manned by armed soldiers standing behind sandbags. These checkpoints were separated by a stretch of rough cobblestone, pockmarked by ugly cement cones that stood three feet high and served as tank traps. Rolls of barbed wire extended along the road for several hundred meters, separating Israeli-controlled West Jerusalem from Jordanian-controlled East Jerusalem. The no-man's-land between the two was like an ugly scar of abandoned streets and ruined buildings, dividing East from West, Israeli from Arab. Military engineers from both sides mined and periodically re-mined this gash running through the city.

Mandelbaum Gate was the chief focal point of "incidents." It was where Palestinians often tried to cross the "Green Line"—the 1949 armistice line—and where Arabs, Israelis and U.N. observers were frequently wounded or killed. In the early years after the 1948 war the Green Line was porous and brittle. Trespassing was a daily occurrence. The Israeli historian Benny Morris estimates that from 1949 to 1954 there were 10,000 to 15,000 incidents annually. By 1956 this figure had fallen to 6,000–7,000 each year.

Initially at least, many incidents were minor. Although some infiltrators were thieves or smugglers, the majority were Palestinians trying to smuggle themselves back to their former homes and, most often, farmers attempting to harvest crops from their ancestral lands. The armistice line meandered quite arbitrarily through some 300 miles of fields and villages. Often the line cut off villagers from their olive groves or wheat fields, and Palestinian peasants were driven by sheer economic necessity to cross over and harvest their fields. A Palestinian would sneak across the Green Line at night, steal a cow from a kibbutz, and herd it back across the line. Invariably, the Israelis reacted with force. And so, as the years went by, some young men came armed with knives or guns, intent on killing the first Israeli they encountered. Some 200 Israeli civilians and scores of Israeli soldiers were killed in sporadic attacks, usually carried out by one or two infiltrators. The Israel Defense Forces (IDF) always responded with retaliatory raids, which became increasingly bloody.

United Nations observers were authorized to investigate each incident, often an impossible task. One such observer, Commander E. H. Hutchison—a friend of my parents—wrote a small book recounting his growing frustrations. Hutchison tells the story of a young Israeli woman who was abducted and then found in a cave a mile from the Jordanian armistice line. She had been raped and murdered, and her face cruelly mutilated. The Israelis believed that one or more Palestinian infiltrators from the village of Beit Jalla were responsible. Several weeks later an Israeli commando team crossed the armistice line and attacked three houses in Beit Jalla with bombs, hand grenades and Sten guns. A young couple was killed in one house, a pregnant woman was shot in another (she survived, her fetus died) and in the third house a mother and her four children were killed by machine-gun fire and grenade fragments. The Israelis left behind rose-colored Arabic-language leaflets stating that "persons from Beit Jalla killed a young Jewish woman near Beit Vaghan after committing against her a crime that will never be expiated. What we have done here now is recompense for this horrendous crime—we can never remain silent when it comes to criminals. There will always be arrows in our quivers for the likes of these. Let those who would know, beware." No one ever stood trial, either for the murder of the Israeli woman or for the murders in Beit Jalla.

I saw lots of guns on both sides of Mandelbaum Gate. One afternoon Youssef, the gardener at the consulate, took Father to visit his home in nearby Silwan. After serving him a Turkish coffee, Youssef proudly showed him his stash of rifles—rusty old English Enfields—"just in case," he said, "something happens."

Between 1949 and 1956, at least 2,700 Palestinian infiltrators—and perhaps as many as 5,000—were killed by the IDF. A majority of these were unarmed young men. Though the term was not then employed, this low-level conflict had some of the characteristics of what might be called today an *intifada*.

Aside from diplomats and United Nations personnel, only a few foreign dignitaries and religious leaders were allowed to cross the armistice lines. On rare occasions, the Jordanians reluctantly issued permits for tourists to cross Mandelbaum Gate—but only in one direction. No tourist could enter Jordan if they had an Israeli visa stamp in their passport. It was as if Israel were a figment of the imagination. Indeed, the code word for Israel among American diplomats in East Jerusalem was "Dixieland." So Father would sometimes come home from work and casually say, "Oh, tomorrow I have to cross over to Dixieland." The American consulate posted a sign on the Israeli side of Mandelbaum Gate, warning unwary tourists, "In crossing the lines from the Jewish-held section of Jerusalem to the Arab-held, you are advised to be close-mouthed and as non-committal as possible about what you've been doing in Israel. Also carry with you as few souvenirs of obvious Israeli origin as convenient. The Arab authorities do not appreciate any evidence of pro-Israel sympathy on your part. Remember, the Arabs and Israelis are still technically at war."

Despite their proximity, the two peoples had virtually no interaction with each other. And oddly enough, though they were technically at war, each side demonstrated little curiosity about the other. After passing through the gate, few people questioned us about what life was like on the other side. Israelis lived as if they inhabited their own universe instead of a sliver of the Levant. One morning, while passing through Mandelbaum Gate, my father struck up a conversation with one of the Israeli guards. When he mentioned that the 1948 refugees lived in tents, the guard was incredulous: "They're still living in tents?"

My daily journey to school required crossing through the checkpoints of Mandelbaum Gate, where a large blue-and-white United Nations flag flapped in the wind. The "gate" was monitored by U.N. soldiers, with their distinctive blue berets tilted on their heads. Crossing west, one came first to the Jordanian checkpoint. Armed with rifles, their muzzles pointed lazily in our direction, King Hussein's men would inspect my father's distinctive black diplomatic passport and then quickly scan the inside of the car and trunk. The Israeli checkpoint was always more difficult. The young Israeli soldiers were ever alert and bristled with nervous energy. There was nothing cursory about their inspection of our diplomatic passports or the car. This was the everyday routine, coming and going. Everyone was considered a potential threat.

One particular afternoon late in the summer of 1956, we passed the first checkpoint without incident, but as we approached the Israeli soldiers, I felt a sudden rush of panic. "Stop, Daddy, stop," I shouted. My father turned to see his five-year-old son clutching his T-shirt, tugging at a button he had been given by a Palestinian playmate. My memory is that it was a button with an image of Egypt's president, Gamal Abdel Nasser, an immensely popular figure in East Jerusalem at the time but an enemy of Israel. The Israelis would surely have ignored such a button pinned to the shirt of a small boy. But with the naïve clarity of a five-year-old, I was sure that the button and its political message made me a target, as if I were a Palestinian infiltrator trying to slip by.

When there were "incidents," Mandelbaum Gate might suddenly be closed by one side or the other. At one point in the autumn of 1956 I told our neighbor that I wasn't going to school anymore—"unless we could talk the guards at the gate into letting us through."

* * *

My earliest childhood playmate was a neighbor, Dani Bahar, a sandy-brown-haired little boy with hazel eyes.* I played with Dani every day, and through the years we have remained friends. Dani's father, Mahmoud Bahar, was the youngest son of a large Muslim Palestinian clan that had lived in Jerusalem for generations. Dani's mother, Frieda, had been reared in an observant Jewish home in Gdansk and Berlin. Theirs was a most unusual marriage. But if rare, such interfaith marriages between Jews and Muslims were not unheard of prior to the creation of Israel. A number of prominent Palestinian families in Jerusalem—including the wealthy Nashashibi clan—had Jewish daughters-in-law. All of these relationships dated to a time when Jews still mingled in Palestinian society—a time when an Arab might see a Jewish doctor or shop in a Jewish grocery store, a time when Jewish children sat in the same classroom in the Old City alongside Christians and Muslims.

As a young man, Mahmoud—I knew him as Abu Dani, or "father of Dani"—had wanted to study architecture. Lacking the tuition for college, he instead enrolled in Jerusalem's Schneller Vocational School. During World War II he worked for the British army in a metalworks factory. Mahmoud was the kind of man who easily made friends, and though he was Muslim many of his fellow craftsmen were Jewish. One day in the factory he was introduced to a young blond, blue-eyed Jewish woman from Germany.

Frieda had left Germany in 1934, just after graduating from high school. She was the eldest daughter of a linguist and scholar in Berlin who was also active in Agudat Yisrael, the political and social arm of the Haredi, or ultra-orthodox, Jewish community, then and now. Like the fundamentalists of other faiths, Haredim believe literally in the divine inspiration of their sacred texts, and of the commandments and rules governing all spheres of life prescribed by those texts, which include first and foremost the Torah—the first five books of the Hebrew scriptures—and the Talmud's rabbinical commentaries preserved in the Mishna and the Gemorra. Dani's devout grandfather did not live to see his daughter marry a Muslim. In the early 1940s, he and his wife were deported by the Nazis to the Lodz ghetto and were never heard from again.

---

*"Dani" is an alias—he is highly reluctant to be named, so I've changed some details of his story to protect his identity. I have also used pseudonyms for other members of his family.

By then, Frieda was living on a kibbutz in Palestine. Curiously, it was her father who had sent her to Palestine in 1934, when she was only nineteen. Perhaps she had rebelled against her father's intense piety, or had simply become an ardent Zionist. In any case, she did not end up in a death camp. Instead, this young woman of Haredi background fell in love with Mahmoud Bahar. The couple was separated, however, during the 1948 war, when Mahmoud found himself stranded in East Jerusalem, across the armistice line from Frieda. For a time he managed to send messages to her through Mandelbaum Gate via United Nations personnel he had come to know. Eventually, in 1952, they managed to meet in Paris. Mahmoud proposed marriage; Frieda accepted. They were wed in a civil ceremony in Paris, and then Mahmoud took his bride back, via Amman, Jordan, to East Jerusalem. There, he opened a small business. By the mid-1950s, he had saved enough to start building a new home.

Dani was born in the early 1950s, and in the eyes of his father's fellow Muslims he was a Palestinian Muslim. And yet, because in Judaism one's identity is determined by the mother's lineage, Jews could regard Dani as one of their own. He is an anomaly—a Palestinian with a Muslim father and a Jewish mother. Even today, Dani somehow defies any labels. He was educated at an Israeli university and speaks fluent Hebrew, Arabic and English. He loves classical music and the theatre. He is a secular intellectual. Even so, when his Jewish mother died in the late 1990s, he made sure she was buried in a Jewish cemetery with Orthodox rites. And on her gravestone he added the names of his grandparents and two uncles lost to the Shoah. But Dani considers himself a Palestinian, and he deplores what the Israelis have done to his Jerusalem. He has a Jerusalem identity card, but like the vast majority of Palestinians in the city he has refused to take Israeli citizenship.

Though very young, I was aware of Dani's mixed heritage. I remember Frieda as a tense, high-strung woman who doted on her only son. In East Jerusalem at the time there were only a half-dozen other Jewish women married to Palestinians. Dani's mother had few friends; but East Jerusalem was a small town in the 1950s and she was well known to shopkeepers. Dani remembers many a long afternoon trailing after her as she went from shop to shop. Not surprisingly, her life centered on her son and husband. "Poor woman," my mother wrote, "she is so isolated, living here among the Arabs."

Dani didn't mean to do it, but one afternoon he killed my white Easter rabbit. The unfortunate animal was hiding at the time under a child's rocking chair. Dani sat down and started rocking vigorously, unaware of either the rabbit or the fact that a long nail was sticking out from under the seat. The poor rabbit was stabbed to death. The only reason I remember this incident is that it inspired me to organize an elaborate Jerusalem-style funeral procession, complete with palm branches waving in the wind. After marching a couple of blocks down the street, Dani and I, and a few other neighborhood kids, buried the rabbit in a shoebox in a nearby field. I was obviously inspired by the religious processions I had seen in the narrow Old City alleys outside the Church of the Holy Sepulchre.

My father's job in the East Jerusalem consulate entailed a variety of duties, including the vetting of visa applicants. One such applicant was a twelve-year-old boy, Sirhan Sirhan, a Christian Palestinian who emigrated with his family to California in 1956. Twelve years later Sirhan assassinated Robert Kennedy. Afterwards, Father was informed by the State Department that his name graces Sirhan's visa application. Father, who in his time had processed hundreds of such applications, had no memory of the Sirhans.

Vice-Consul Gene Bird worked on the ground floor of the consulate, just around the corner from Mandelbaum Gate. His office was large, drafty and stone-floored. Outside, mufti-uniformed Jordanian soldiers stood guard with heavy rifles. They wore oddly shaped pith helmets with a sharply polished spike protruding from the top. Just four months prior to Father's arrival in 1956, these same Legionnaires had fired into a crowd of angry young Arab men protesting the Eisenhower Administration's heavy-handed attempt to persuade King Hussein to join the newly formed Baghdad Pact, a military alliance of Britain, Iraq, Turkey and Pakistan designed to "contain" the Soviet Union's influence in the Middle East. This was at the height of the Cold War, when America viewed the entire globe through its singular obsession with containing Communism and the Soviet Union. For Washington policy-makers small countries like Jordan were mere pawns in this great game. But in the Middle East itself, the Pact was a farce from the moment it was created. It served only to remind the Arab street that American priorities were not Arab priorities. Far from rallying Arab opinion against Communist propaganda, the Pact was immediately perceived as a Trojan horse for either old British colonial interests or America's new imperial ambitions.

In January 1956, anti–Baghdad Pact protesters attempted to storm their way inside the U.S. consulate, and rifle fire from Jordanian Legionnaires killed six young men. My father's predecessor as vice-consul, Slater Blackiston Jr., panicked and, displaying extraordinarily bad judgment, fired into the crowd with his own rifle. He was rumored to have wounded a young girl. Blackiston, a former Marine, claimed he was defending his family, who were living in an upper-story apartment in the consulate. When the crowds gathered in the street below, he hid his two young sons in a closet. If news of Blackiston's involvement had spread, it could easily have created a major diplomatic incident. The State Department ordered his immediate evacuation. Back in Washington, however, the Foreign Service's "old boy" network stepped in to save his career. Instead of a reprimand, Blackiston was given a medal. And to my father's dismay, he was the one asked to write the citation that accompanied the medal. Several years later, Blackiston, with whom my father never got along, would become his boss in Cairo.

I was too young to know of such happenings at the time, but as I grew older the stories slowly tumbled out. I used to play in the lovely rose garden that surrounded the walled consulate—the very place where those six young men had been shot. Just around the corner, out in the street, was the spot where in 1948 the U.S. consul general, Tom Wasson, was shot dead one day—apparently by an Israeli sniper hidden in an abandoned building in no-man's-land—as he was walking toward the consulate's garden gate entrance. Well aware of the danger, Wasson was wearing a bulletproof vest, but the bullet struck him at the top of his shoulder, hit the vest from the inside and ricocheted back into his chest. He died three hours later.

Father had few opportunities to do much in the way of political reporting. He was assigned to report on the arcane politics of the Old City's rapidly shrinking Christian religious hierarchy. To this end he had meetings with the various bishops and archbishops of the Armenian, Greek Orthodox, Russian Orthodox and Anglican churches. These black-robed gentlemen were constantly feuding over church prerogatives, territory and money. "Jerusalem office hours are not too long," Father wrote home in January 1958, "but visitors take up most of my time and then there have been parties, too many parties, during the past few weeks. I feel as if I need to get away for a day or two from this atmosphere of tension, suspicion and distrust, with its fine coating of smiling officials and well-dressed women. People are too diplomatic sometimes to be believable."

Father was particularly popular with the Russian nuns who controlled the Russian Orthodox Church of Mary Magdalene, located on the Mount of Olives, near the Garden of Gethsemane. On one of his first visits to this iconic church, built in 1886 by Czar Alexander III, he had let the nuns know that he had had something to do with the CIA slipping the nuns $80,000 for the repair of the church's seven gold-leaf onion domes. Why, one might wonder, would the CIA have wanted to fund roof repairs at the Church of Mary Magdalene? Well, the Cold War was waged in Jerusalem just as ardently as in the back alleys of Berlin, also a divided city. In this instance, Father had convinced the CIA that if they didn't fund the roof repairs, the Soviets might step into the breach.

The Soviets had been the first to recognize the new state of Israel, and so in the 1950s the Soviet ambassador to Israel was the "dean" of the diplomatic corps. Consequently, after 1948 the Israelis handed over the "Russian Compound" and all Russian Orthodox Church properties to the Moscow-based, Soviet-controlled church hierarchy.* A Soviet Ecclesiastical Mission operated in West Jerusalem, led at the time by a Russian "priest" who in reality was a Soviet KGB colonel whose previous assignment had been as an adviser to the North Koreans during the Korean War. But in East Jerusalem, Jordanian authorities had given control over Russian ecclesiastical properties to the anti-Communist Russian Orthodox Church headquartered in New York. Thus, there were two Russian Orthodox hierarchies in divided Jerusalem—and naturally, the CIA wanted all the world's pilgrims to the city to see that the anti-Communist version was exercising good stewardship over such landmarks as the Church of Mary Magdalene.

The consulate had one CIA officer serving under diplomatic cover who arrived in Jerusalem about the same time as Father did—and this caused some locals to conclude that Father was the CIA man. Unfortunately, this agent persuaded Father to pass an unmarked envelope to a Palestinian gentleman who appeared once a week on his doorstep. Inside the envelope was a certain amount of cash: payment for information rendered. As a Foreign

---

*A building in the Russian Compound later became the Moskobiya Detention Center, where to this day Palestinian detainees are interrogated by the Shin Bet, Israel's domestic intelligence bureau.

Service officer, Father shouldn't have agreed to do something that might easily have compromised his diplomatic status. But, naïvely, he did. He stopped the arrangement only when a local Arabic-language newspaper reported, incorrectly, that Eugene Bird was the CIA's representative.

Jerusalem then was a small town, but it attracted a colorful cast of characters. On their busy social circuit my parents met the mistress of a well-known religious leader, a prominent business leader known to be a homosexual, a "Communist who has also had close relations with people from the 'other side' and may be a spy," a bachelor diplomat who came from his previous posting with a silver tray inscribed "To the night club attaché," and a consul general who regularly stood on his head in order to relax.

Father loved his job. He loved meeting the local journalists. He easily won the trust of the businessmen, lawyers and landowners who constituted Jerusalem's Palestinian aristocracy. And he brashly spoke his mind, even to those above him in rank. All of this made him slightly suspect to his superiors: "I am finding," he wrote a friend back in Washington, "that in the present situation you may do yourself harm with the 'ins,' but there are always the 'outs' who applaud. The trick is a balanced understanding and a truthfulness about the internal politics which is bound in the long run to leave one who talks with you the impression that you are sincere and frank." I can't help thinking that while Father was seen as charming, cheeky and exuberant, he was also thought of as wildly naïve. He would never make ambassadorial rank.

He liked to gently provoke people and challenge their preconceptions. In the early autumn of 1956, Father attended a reception at Orient House, a large stone mansion near the American Colony. Built in 1897 by the al-Husseini clan, Orient House later became for a time the PLO's headquarters in Jerusalem. But in 1956 the al-Husseinis were running it as a luxury hotel. Standing in the receiving line that evening was Anwar Nusseibeh, a prominent Palestinian lawyer and judge who had lost a leg during the 1948 battle for Jerusalem. As they were introduced, Father remarked that he had just visited one of Jerusalem's sprawling refugee camps. Nusseibeh responded, "Mr. Bird, you must think we Palestinians are so primitive, still living in tents." Father shot back that he thought the Palestinians were only about "thirty years behind America." He then explained that as a boy he too had once "lived like a refugee" in a tent for a while in the midst of the Great Depression. A startled Nusseibeh would always remember the young vice-consul who had once lived in a tent. Father was exaggerating only slightly. His family had been extremely poor in those years, and they had indeed spent a few weeks one summer living in a tent in Oregon. What the aristocratic Nusseibeh did not know was that even then the vice-consul who stood before him was in debt and living from paycheck to paycheck. In July 1956 Father had a bank balance of only $300—of which Mother had budgeted $270 for day-to-day expenses.

Along with the al-Husseinis, the Nashashibis, and the Jarallahs, the Nusseibehs were one of Jerusalem's four or five leading families. They were thoroughly Anglicized. Anwar Nusseibeh had obtained a law degree from Cambridge in 1936. While practicing law in the courts of British Mandate Palestine he wore the powdered white wig and black cloak of a British barrister. On weekends he played a very good game of tennis and went for long horseback rides in the desert. The Nusseibehs were our neighbors, living in a lovely stone house across the street from the American Colony. Father had them to dinner occasionally, and he often encountered Anwar in the course of his official and unofficial duties.

One of Anwar's sons, Sari Nusseibeh, was just two years older than I. Like the children of many aristocratic families of Muslim heritage, young Sari attended a Christian English-language school, St. George's School in East Jerusalem. His bedroom window gave him a view of no-man's-land. "I could also look down on a shoot-to-kill zone that separated the Jews from the Arabs," he wrote in his memoirs. "It was a good perch from which to spy on the other side." He could see as well a slice of everyday life in Israel—he called it the "Zionist entity"—where strange black-clad men sporting long beards and dangling curly sidelocks walked about the narrow streets of the Jewish neighborhood of Me'a She'arim. "Sometimes the bearded creatures looked back at me," Sari wrote. "It was almost like being in a dream." Much later, he became a Cambridge-educated philosopher and president of al-Quds University in Jerusalem. In the late 1980s, during the first Intifada, Sari was the anonymous author of many of the weekly underground leaflets that directed the protests. Even today, he remains one of Jerusalem's most articulate and decidedly independent intellects.

As a lowly vice-consul, Father didn't normally deal with heads of government. But on one occasion he attended a small conference at the Jewish

Agency and listened as Israel's founding prime minister, David Ben-Gurion, fielded some questions. "He has hair whiter than even his pictures show," Father wrote, "somewhat a halo effect, and tiny blue eyes. He is extremely expressive with his face, his answers almost reflected in his expression before he gives them. He leaves the impression of deep intellectual and moral power, quick, and would be described as cunning by those who disliked him."

Initially, my parents were decidedly neutral in their attitude towards the Israeli-Palestinian conflict. In mid-July 1956, just two months after arriving in Jerusalem, Father wrote home, "Jerri and I are both completely objective still about the conflict. We can sympathize with the Arabs and their lost lands, but we think they should recognize that it is a lost cause and that life can and must go on within the context of the present armistice." On the other hand, my mother observed that same week that "It is difficult not to become prejudiced on one side or the other. I find that most people are prejudiced for the side on which they live."

Sometime during his two-year tour in Jerusalem, Father began to contemplate the notion of becoming an Arabist, a specialist in Arabic language, culture and politics. But back in the 1950s, after the founding of Israel, the term also came to mean a diplomat whose sympathies in the conflict lay with the Arabs. As the writer Robert Kaplan noted in his book *The Arabists,* the word was used by some critics of the State Department to describe someone "assumed to be politically naïve, elitist, and too deferential to exotic cultures." Even today it remains for some a pejorative, a cutting label applied to a Foreign Service officer who "intellectually sleeps with Arabs." Francis Fukuyama once described the Arabists he encountered in the Reagan Administration's State Department as "a sociological phenomenon, an elite within an elite, who have been more systematically wrong than any other area specialists in the diplomatic corps. This is because Arabists not only take on the cause of the Arabs, but also the Arabs' tendency for self-delusion."*

This seems overly harsh. But it is certainly true that my father and his fellow Arabists invariably developed a deep admiration for the language and the culture from which it comes. Arabic is a very hard language to learn. I remember, as a young boy, seeing my father sitting for hours on end with a

---

*Elite or not, the State Department trained very few Arabists. Between World War I and World War II the Department had only six qualified Arabists. Interestingly, in the spring of 2002, right after 9/11 and about a year before the Iraq War of 2003, the Department still had only six officers proficient in Arabic.

headset over his ears listening to Arabic-language tapes on a large reel-to-reel tape recorder. Memorizing the vocabulary was hard enough, but getting the cadence just right was equally important. And to study classical Arabic means inevitably encountering texts steeped in the history, culture and religions of the Levant. Not surprisingly, those who invested thousands of hours in these studies often became strongly attached to the people and culture.

Father decided to become an Arabist after reading George Antonius—Katy's late husband. In fact, it may well have been Katy who prompted him to read the book; she was very proud of it. When it was published in 1938, the U.S. consul general in Jerusalem, George Wadsworth, ordered extra copies for all members of his staff. Wadsworth gushed that the book contained "all that is known about the Arab world." Another American diplomat wrote, "If you read the book of Antonius you will need nothing more to guide you in your work in the Near East."

Why has this book held such appeal for American Arabists? Well, one reason is that they are flattered to learn from Antonius's narrative that the "Arab Awakening" was catalyzed by Americans. Antonius argues that it was idealistic young American missionaries who first planted the seeds of what became modern Arab nationalism. He recounts how on December 3, 1866, Daniel Bliss, a New England Congregationalist, opened the doors of the Syrian Protestant College in the seaside town of Beirut. He had sixteen students, all from Greater Syria, then a province of the Ottoman Empire. Five years later Bliss bought a piece of land on a lovely escarpment in West Beirut, overlooking the Mediterranean. His college eventually was renamed the American University of Beirut, and it has provided an American-style liberal arts education to generations of Arabs from across the Middle East. Significantly, Bliss and his colleagues used Arabic as their language of instruction for the first seventeen years. As Antonius observed, "The educational activities of the American missionaries in that early period had, among many virtues, one outstanding merit: they gave the pride of place to Arabic, and, once they had committed themselves to teaching in it, they put their shoulders with vigor to the task of providing an adequate literature. In that, they were the pioneers; and because of that, the intellectual effervescence which marked the first stirrings of the Arab revival owes most to their labors."

In 1875, five young graduates formed a secret society dedicated to the cause of Arab unity and nationalism. Antonius argues that the 1916 Arab

Revolt against the Ottoman Empire emerged from these secret societies. His book then goes on to document how the British broke their promises to the Arabs for self-determination and majority rule in an independent Palestine.

If *The Arab Awakening* remains a classic history, at least in English, of the rise of Arab nationalism, I nevertheless today find the book less interesting than its author. Antonius's life story personifies the enduring controversy over the question of Palestine. It is alluring, mysterious and ultimately tragic.

As a Greek Orthodox Christian of mixed Egyptian-Lebanese parentage, Antonius favored a secular, multicultural Arab society where Christians, Muslims, Druze and Jews would live together in a nonsectarian state. He was himself the product of a multicultural childhood, born in 1891 in Dayr al-Qamar, a small trading town in the Chouf mountains of central Lebanon. His father was a cotton trader. The people of Dayr al-Qamar were largely a mix of Druze and Christians. But through hundreds of years of intermarriage the Levantine culture of Greater Syria became a multireligious, multicultural hybrid. The people of the Levant were a potpourri of ethnic and religious heritages—including Christian Maronites, Druze, Sunnis and Shi'ite Muslims and Greek Orthodox Christians. What all these people shared, however, was not religion but a common language. It was Arabic that united them culturally. On the whole, sectarian violence was relatively rare, but when it occurred, it could be brutal. During the civil war of 1859–60 more than 2,200 Christians were massacred in Dayr al-Qamar in a single day. But during the years of Antonius's youth the Chouf was a peaceful reserve.

When Antonius was ten years old, his family settled in Alexandria, Egypt, another multicultural seaside city, where he attended the prestigious Victoria College. In 1910, he began his studies at Cambridge University, where he earned a degree in engineering. He spent the years of World War I back in Alexandria, where he befriended E. M. Forster and helped the future author of *A Passage to India* to write a guidebook on Alexandria. In the early 1920s he settled in Jerusalem, obtained Palestinian citizenship and went to work for the British Mandate government. The British valued this suave Arab intellectual, a man fluent in both Arabic and French—and who spoke his English with a refined Cambridge accent. "No one that I have ever met . . . so admirably combines the passion of the Syrian patriot," wrote one British official, "with the lucidity of the Cambridge don in stating his patriotic beliefs." When he visited London for a few months in late 1920 and early 1921, Antonius had the opportunity to spend several hours with T. E. Lawrence. He was singularly unimpressed and came away with the feeling that this British officer had no comprehension of how egregiously London had reneged on its wartime promises of independence for the Arabs.

Back in Jerusalem, Antonius chafed in the bureaucracy; he was eager to play a role in shaping the political future of Palestine. In 1930 he persuaded an American think tank, the Institute of Current World Affairs, to appoint him a fellow with a generous stipend and an assignment to write regular reports on Middle East politics.

George Antonius, author of *The Arab Awakening*, 1938

In 1927 Antonius married Katy Nimr. The couple initially lived in a spacious, high-ceilinged apartment in Jerusalem's Austrian Hospice. They lived as Palestinian aristocrats. Their living room was lined with bookshelves, and Persian carpets were strewn about on the walls and stone floors. (Over the years of their marriage they acquired a personal library of 12,000 books.)

In the early 1930s they rented a beautiful old white stone house in the Sheikh Jarrah district. The house was owned by Haj Amin al-Husseini, the controversial Grand Mufti of Jerusalem, a position created by the British mandatory authorities in 1921. As Grand Mufti, Husseini was nominally in charge of Jerusalem's Islamic sites, but the position gave him a prominent political status. Husseini was a mercurial, charismatic leader—but he would also prove himself a demagogue. When the American journalist Vincent Sheean encountered him in 1929, he found the Mufti "an extremely level-headed, deliberate man, mild-mannered and thoughtful." But even then, Sheean noted, "Nothing but death could have kept him from opposing Zionism by every means in his power." Husseini once wrote of Jews, "They have no pity and are known for their hatred, rivalry and hardness, as Allah described them in the Koran." During World War II he would flee to Nazi Germany, where he met with Adolf Hitler and urged the Nazi leader to prevent Jewish emigration to Palestine.

Husseini was always a fanatical Palestinian nationalist, and exactly the wrong man at the wrong time to lead the Palestinians. But during the prewar years Antonius became his friend and informal adviser. The well-known British travel writer Freya Stark later wrote that Husseini "had bewitched George Antonius as securely as ever a siren did her mariner, leading him through his slippery realms with sealed eyes so that George—whom I was fond of—would talk to me without a flicker about the Mufti's 'single-hearted goodness.'" George was a naïve man, at heart a romantic intellectual.

Sheean visited Jerusalem in 1929, armed with a letter of introduction to Antonius from E. M. Forster. He quickly became an ardent admirer of his new acquaintance: "His intelligence never seemed to be altogether harnessed to one subject, as was the case with everybody else I met in that part of the world. . . . Antonius was remarkable in many ways, but most remarkable because he kept an even keel, and remembered his obligation as an intelligent and cultivated human being not to lose his head."

Surrounded by piles of archival documents and deep-red Bokhara carpets, Antonius began writing what was to become his Arab manifesto—while his sharp-tongued wife quickly became Jerusalem's most sought-after hostess. Antonius thought of himself as "a bridge between two different cultures and an agent in the interpretation of one to the other."

In Palestine, his chosen homeland, he believed there was room for a thriving Jewish community—but no room for an exclusively Jewish state. As early as 1929, he told Sheean that he "believed the Zionist programme was unfair to the Arabs without offering any solution to the Jewish problem; he [Antonius] was convinced it would lead to serious, recurring troubles." Nevertheless, under British rule Jewish refugees from Europe were smuggling themselves into the region in rising numbers. In 1918 the population of the Palestinian Yishuv numbered around 57,000, or only 8 percent of the total population. By 1929 there were probably 750,000 Arabs and 150,000 Jews. But in 1935 alone some 62,000 Jews arrived in Palestine. Most of these immigrants were seeking refuge from Hitler's Germany, and Palestine's gates were still at least partially open. America, by contrast, was accepting very few Jewish refugees. By 1939 there may have been as many as 1,070,000 Arabs and about 460,000 Jews in Palestine. As a consequence, the Zionist leadership believed they were gradually but methodically capturing Palestine, "goat by goat, dunum by dunum."

As early as 1923, Ze'ev Jabotinsky had spelled out the inevitable consequences: "Thus we conclude that we cannot promise anything to the Arabs of the Land of Israel or the Arab countries. Their voluntary agreement [to Jewish immigration] is out of the question. Hence those who hold that an agreement with the natives is an essential condition for Zionism can now say 'no' and depart from Zionism. Zionist colonization, even the most restricted, must either be terminated or carried out in defiance of the will of the native population. This colonization can, therefore, continue and develop only under the protection of a force independent of the local population—an *iron wall* which the native population cannot break through. This is, in toto, our policy towards the Arabs. To formulate it any other way would only be hypocrisy." Jabotinsky's *iron wall* was essential to the Zionist enterprise. Without it, there would be no Jewish state. The leading mainstream Zionist leader, David Ben-Gurion, was no less uncompromising: "There is a fundamental conflict. We and they want the same thing. We both want Palestine. Were I an Arab . . . I would rise up against immigration liable sometimes in the future to hand the country . . . over to Jewish rule." In 1936 Ben-Gurion made his intentions even more explicit in a private letter to his son: "We will expel the Arabs and take their place."

That same year the Palestinians rose up, first with a general strike organized by the Arab Higher Committee, an elite group of six notables led by the Grand Mufti. Initially, their protests were entirely nonviolent. They demanded free elections, based on majority rule, to create a national assembly. Zionist leaders rejected this proposal, citing the Balfour Declaration, which promised a Jewish homeland. The British rebuffed the Arab Higher Committee. Obviously, if elections had been held, any such assembly would have voted to restrict Jewish immigration.

As the months rolled by, strikes and peaceful demonstrations gave way to escalating violence. A British official was assassinated in the Galilee, and the

British foolishly responded by banning the Arab Higher Committee, whose members were exiled without trial to the Seychelles. The Grand Mufti managed to escape abroad disguised as a woman, dressed in an *abaya*. Deprived of their traditional leaders, Palestinian peasants and villagers took to waging guerrilla warfare against the British and the Jews. Over the next three years the British brutally repressed the rebellion, killing as many as 6,000 Palestinians and incarcerating another 6,000.

Antonius was horrified by the British response to the rebellion. "Their policy has turned Palestine," he wrote, "into a shambles, they show no indication of a return to sanity, that is to say to the principles of ordinary common sense and justice which are held in such high honor in England." When the Arab general strike first took hold in April 1936, Antonius met three times with Ben-Gurion, then chairman of the Jewish Agency, to explore the possibilities, if any, for a peaceful solution. The Palestinian peasantry, Antonius explained, saw themselves being displaced from the land they had tilled for generations. ". . . in the entire 18 years of British rule," he complained, "not a single step had been taken by the Jews that gave the Arabs the impression that the Jews were interested in their goodwill." Ben-Gurion insisted that a Zionist state would not "dominate" the Palestinians. To the contrary, he told Antonius, they would be liberated by being exposed to the Zionist example of "women's equality under the law and hard work." Antonius ignored this patronizing remark and replied that it was quite evident that the Zionist goal was to create a state where "all of this country would be handed over to Jewish rule, with the Arab merely tolerated; the state would be sovereign and separate, and none of the Arabs would have any share in it." The two men understood each other all too well.

Antonius published his book in late 1938, just after *Kristallnacht*—Nazi Germany's infamous general pogrom against its Jewish population—and a decade before the establishment of the state of Israel. It quickly became a manifesto for the Arab nationalist cause. He took his title from a line in a poem by the nineteenth-century Lebanese poet Ibrahim Yazeji, "Arise, ye Arabs, and awake."

On the critical question of Palestine, Antonius was blunt and passionate. He condemned Arab violence against Jews and Jewish violence against Arabs. He invoked "common sense and justice" and concluded, "There is no room for a second nation in a country which is already inhabited, and inhabited by a people whose national consciousness is fully awakened and whose affection for their homes and countryside is obviously unconquerable. . . . Once the fact is faced that the establishment of a Jewish state in Palestine, or a national home based on territorial sovereignty, cannot be accomplished without forcibly displacing the Arabs, the way to a solution becomes clearer." Palestine should become an independent Arab state, he wrote, "in which as many Jews as the country can hold without prejudice to its political and economic freedom would live in peace, security and dignity, and enjoy full rights of citizenship." Such a multinational, secular state, Antonius argued, "would enable the Jews to have a national home in the spiritual and cultural sense, in which Jewish values could flourish and the Jewish genius have the freest play to seek inspiration in the land of its ancient connection. . . . No other solution seems practical, except possibly at the cost of an unpredictable holocaust of Arab, Jewish and British lives."

The Arab Awakening was widely praised by reviewers in both Britain and America. The *New York Times* reviewer called Antonius "an eloquent advocate" of Arab nationalism. Antonius did not write as an "Orientalist" but rather as a critic of the Western imperial adventure in the Middle East. In 1938 such criticism was quite unusual. The book nevertheless was cited for decades by historians in the West and did much to shape visiting journalists' explanations of the rising tide of Arab nationalism in the postwar era. Its influence was on American and British policy-makers and observers—and Arab intellectuals—but not the Arab masses.

Although Antonius opposed the creation of an exclusively Jewish state in Palestine, in the late 1930s he was by no means insensitive to the plight of the Jewish people in Fascist Europe. "The treatment meted out to the Jews in Germany and other European countries is a disgrace to its authors and to modern civilization," he wrote. "But posterity will not exonerate any country that fails to bear its proper share of the sacrifices needed to alleviate Jewish suffering and distress. To place the brunt of the burden upon Arab Palestine is a miserable evasion of the duty that lies upon the whole of the civilized world. . . . No code of morals can justify the persecution of one people in an attempt to relieve the persecution of another. The cure for the eviction of Jews from Germany is not to be sought in the eviction of the Arabs from their homeland."

Antonius wanted to create a democratic, multiethnic state in which the Jewish minority would assume "the rights of ordinary citizens" within a pluralistic civil society. "All the elements in Palestine should work together, the only divisions being those of party alignment working in the common interest and not on a sectional or communal basis."

On the eve of World War II, Antonius found his life unraveling. In 1939, his friend and mentor at the Institute of Current World Affairs, Charles Crane, died. Antonius himself fell into bouts of ill-health. He had expected his book to sell more widely than it did; depressed, he fell behind on his work for the Institute, and in late 1941 the Institute terminated his contract. To his distress, he was left without even a pension. His personal life was also falling apart. He and Katy had always had somewhat of an open marriage, but now Katy demanded an end to it. By then Antonius was hospitalized in Jerusalem with a perforated duodenal ulcer. It may have been cancerous, but in any case, he died suddenly on May 21, 1942. He was only fifty years old. A week or two earlier, Katy had obtained a divorce. She kept the house in West Jerusalem.

Antonius was buried in the Greek Orthodox cemetery on Mount Zion. His name is engraved in both English and Arabic on a simple gravestone. The brief epitaph was the line he quoted in his book: "Arise, ye Arabs, and awake."

Antonius died far too young. And his Arabs did not awaken, at least not in the manner he would have desired. Had he lived, would his cultured voice and reasoned arguments have persuaded the Arabs and Jews of Palestine to take a different direction than war? Probably not. But perhaps the world outside Palestine would have seen the conflict from a different perspective. Without Antonius there were few Arab intellectuals capable of explaining the case for a multicultural Palestine to the West. Furthermore, Antonius died just three months after the 1942 Wannsee conference in which Hitler's top aides fashioned a plan for "the complete annihilation of the Jews." When the horrors of the Holocaust became fully known in 1945 the fate of the six million would persuade many that the Zionist cause in Palestine was not only just but necessary.

Albert Hourani, a future Oxford don, was disheartened when he learned of his friend's sudden death. "Antonius died at the moment when he was most needed—at the moment for which his whole life had been a preparation." Visiting Jerusalem shortly afterwards, Hourani could see that the two peoples were on a collision course and that there were few men capable of changing the internal dynamics of the conflict. Antonius might have been one such man. He might have been the bridge.

2

On the Road to Suez

President Gamal Abdel Nasser, Port Said, December 1956

Even our child-play centered on the city whose name I pronounced as "Rusalem."

"You should hear them play when they think they are not being noticed," Mother wrote. "It is all about war, getting shot, very realistic bombs and explosions and then proper moans and groans of the wounded, even play about getting through gates, hiding from bad soldiers, protecting the good ones. . . . They even remember here to say only the right (Arab) words and use no Hebrew."

Two peoples. One land. They might have shared it like a Byzantine mosaic—an arrangement that would have been highly ornate and complicated but would at least have been a decidedly indigenous solution. In this scenario there would have been no Jewish state, only a Jewish homeland within the Palestinian mosaic. Or perhaps, as the Jewish Austrian Israeli philosopher Martin Buber envisioned in the 1920s and '30s, the Jews and

Arabs of Palestine would have created a formal binational state. It was not to be. This was the Holy Land, so it had to be fought over endlessly.

"I feel closest to the Bible scenes," Mother wrote, "when out in the open air, in the brown hills, among the poor Arab population, walking the streets of the Old City." My parents occasionally drove the six miles to Bethlehem on Sundays to attend services at the Church of the Nativity; Mother practiced her Bach on an organ in Jerusalem's Lutheran church in the Old City. As a family, we often attended Sunday services at St. George's Anglican Cathedral, just 600 yards up the road from our Sheikh Jarrah home. We lived as Christian Jerusalemites.

One Palm Sunday, Father drove us all down to Bethany for a sunrise service. In the distance we could see the Dead Sea and the Hills of Moab and Mount Nebo, "where," Father wrote, "Moses is supposed to have been buried within sight of the Holy Land on the west side of the River Jordan. . . . The sun rose later than predicted and we stood and sat about the ruins of an old Crusader or Byzantine church that has only two large corners sticking above ground on foundations of what looked like masonry from Christ's time. . . ." On the drive back, "Jerusalem burst into sight, just at our feet, with the Haram al-Sharif, where Solomon's temple and Herod's great structure during the time of Christ had been built. We stopped half way down in a field of olive trees that was already laced with trenches, for this is highly valuable ground militarily speaking, and held our last little service."

Father was fascinated by the archaeologists he met, Israelis and others, who every day seemed to dig up new artifacts that authenticated the stories of the Bible. After visiting a new archaeological dig in the ancient village of al-Jeeb, just five miles outside Jerusalem, he bought a Bible and announced that he was going to read it from cover to cover. His interest was more historical and political than religious. He thought the archaeologists' discoveries "give us more of a claim on the Holy Places, more of a reason for my being here . . . such close attachments to the Holy Land make it important for us to continue our efforts to have governments friendly to us and to our ideals." Father seems not to have noticed the irony that his Christian "claim" to the Holy Land echoed that of the Jews. Everyone had a claim to the Land.

Often on Friday afternoons, just before the start of the Jewish Sabbath, we drove to a bakery in Jewish West Jerusalem to buy a warm loaf of challah.

Not infrequently, Mother would pack us into our old Chrysler sedan, drive through Mandelbaum Gate and then take the narrow, winding two-lane road down to Tel Aviv's sandy white beaches. Israel was then still very much a developing country; the infrastructure was Spartan and there was plenty of poverty. But it nevertheless felt like a Western country. And seen through the eyes of expatriate Americans like my parents, these Westernized Israelis were clearly the "foreigners"—or, at best, they were people of largely European ancestry making a "home" in a stranger's land. They were building a Jewish homeland, and doing so with vigor. But they were nevertheless strangers in a strange land. And it wasn't that they were strangers in Palestine because they were Jewish. After all, Sephardim Jews had been part of Jerusalem's mosaic for centuries. They were not strangers per se in Palestine. But recent Ashkenazi immigrants seemed to be strangers precisely because they did not consider themselves any longer to be Jews of the Diaspora. They were no longer in exile. Men like Ze'ev Jabotinsky had openly proselytized Diaspora Jews to renounce the Diaspora. Eight years after the creation of Israel, David Ben-Gurion and other mainstream Zionists insisted that their goal was to persuade all Jews everywhere to live in the one Jewish state called Israel. Having denied their Diaspora identity, they claimed to belong to this place.

I knew very well that *I* was a stranger, an expatriate. To my child's eyes, living amongst the Arabs of East Jerusalem, it seemed only natural to walk down the street and see men in kaffiyehs sitting in sidewalk cafés sucking on their gurgling water pipes. This was their world. What seemed foreign, or somehow out of place, was when we crossed Mandelbaum Gate on a hot summer day and suddenly saw Orthodox Ashkenazic men, young and old, wearing long black coats and black hats lined with fur. The Orthodox Ashkenazic were clearly from some other time and place—but so too were the bustling crowds of secular, nonpracticing Jewish Israelis who seemed so modern, so Western. My perspective was privileged. I could cross Mandelbaum Gate and they could not.

Mother took the occasion of her first Rosh Hashanah—the Jewish New Year—to explain to her parents the nature of Judaism in Israel. "It is complicated," she wrote. "The Jews here are very divided in religious beliefs. The only church allowed (the only Jewish one, I mean) is the Orthodox. . . . I would say that the majority of the Jews here are not practicing Orthodox, but the laws require nominal observance of Orthodox rules, such as no wheels on the Sabbath." By the late 1950s, the Orthodox communities, particularly in Jerusalem, were aggressively trying to impose their religious observances on a largely secular citizenry. Most Jewish Israelis did not attend Shabbat services and did not observe the kosher dietary laws in the privacy of their own kitchens. In public, however, the Orthodox tried to make everyone conform to their rules. Sometimes this led to incidents in which Orthodox men threw stones at Jewish drivers breaking the Sabbath. "Police have had to hose them [the Orthodox enforcers] when they got violent," Mother wrote. "It is a peculiar situation to me; for once again you see intolerance on the part of the very people who came here to escape intolerance and persecution. Will we ever learn!"

Early in their two-year Jerusalem tour, my parents made a point of crossing Mandelbaum Gate on a regular basis to attend parties in West Jerusalem. In the warm summers, when people were wearing short-sleeved shirts, Mother was disconcerted to see Israelis with numbers tattooed on their arms. By 1949 close to 350,000 Holocaust survivors were living in the new Jewish state—nearly one-third of the Jewish population of Israel. The rest either had come from Europe prior to the war or were immigrants from Arab countries.

They became friends with an architect named Ben-Dor, who lived in what he called an "Arab house" not far from Zion Square in West Jerusalem's "New City." Israelis valued the aesthetically attractive old Arab homes of Talbieh, Katamon or the German Colony, with their high ceilings, archways and wrought-iron gates. Whenever guests came to his house, Ben-Dor always showed them a mortar shell that had landed in their house but had fortunately not exploded. It was hard to socialize in the evenings with Israelis because Mandelbaum Gate closed at sunset. Mother complained that this made for a "quite one-sided affair, for our Israeli friends must always invite us and we can never return the hospitality." One of the impressions they gathered from their early morning coffees or afternoon teas in West Jerusalem was that few Israelis had any view of what life was like on the "other side." This was not surprising, given the isolation that all Israelis accepted as a matter of course. Nine years after the 1948 war, they found themselves living in a small state from which they could travel only by plane or via boat through Cyprus. The armistice that had ended the battles had not ended the state of war. All their neighbors—Lebanon and Syria to the north, Jordan to the east and Egypt in the west—treated Israel as an illegitimate pariah. Cut off from any contact with the Arab world, most Israelis had a peculiar, even contradictory, view of their predicament. Though the Arabs were no match for the Israel Defense Forces, many Israelis felt besieged and lived with a fear of what lay across the horizon. At the same time, they dismissed the Arabs, and especially the Palestinians, as a simple and primitive people. The fear was quite understandable in a psychological sense—particularly if you had a tattoo on your arm. But the combination of these fears with a sense of superiority over the people on the "other side" made political compromise with the Arab enemy seem both unthinkable and unnecessary.

The State Department considered Jerusalem to be a "hardship post" and therefore paid its employees there a 10 percent bonus. What with the nightly shootings and occasional explosions my father believed he was earning that 10 percent. "We are happy, if somewhat jumpy when the stone-shippers next door drop one with a bang." He then signed off this October 9 letter to his parents with a jaunty, "Yours until Evacuation Day." He had every reason to suspect that troubles lay ahead. All summer long a crisis had been brewing in Cairo, Egypt, that would soon change our lives.

Four years earlier, on July 23, 1952, Colonel Gamal Abdel Nasser and a small number of fellow army officers had come to power in a virtually bloodless coup. Instead of shooting the alcoholic and ineffective King Farouk, Nasser persuaded his fellow coup-plotters to send him into exile. Nasser hoped to clean up a corrupt bureaucracy and put Egypt on the road to a modern, developed economy. He thought of himself as a reformer, a secular modernist and a pan-Arab nationalist. He defined his Egyptian identity as part of the larger Arabic-speaking Arab world. He was an anticolonialist, and he resented what remained of British colonial influence in Egypt—primarily the joint British and French ownership of the Suez Canal, which also entailed the continued stationing of British troops on Egyptian soil in the Canal Zone.

Nasser may have seized power through the army, but he was genuinely popular, and in June 1956, just before the Suez Crisis erupted, he was elected president of Egypt with a decisive mandate. His most deadly political enemy at home was the Muslim Brotherhood, a party founded in 1928 by a schoolteacher, Hassan al-Banna, who was highly critical of secularism and believed that Muslims should live in a state governed by Islamic "Sharia" law. Before it was banned in 1948 by King Farouk's regime, the Brotherhood may have had as many as 100,000 members. Al-Banna was assassinated in 1949, but his followers flourished politically in the years that followed, and soon after Nasser came to power in 1952 they condemned the new regime for its Westernized secular outlook. On October 26, 1954, a Muslim Brotherhood agent nearly assassinated Nasser as he was delivering a speech in Alexandria.

One might think that Nasser's having such enemies should have persuaded the Americans to regard him as a reasonable political partner. But President Dwight D. Eisenhower confused the Egyptian leader's populism and anticolonial flourishes with neutralism—and in Ike's book, neutralism translated into naïveté in the face of the Communist threat. Eisenhower viewed everything through the prism of the Cold War, and his Middle East policy had one primary goal: to keep Arab oil in American hands and away from the Soviets. Early in 1953 he approved National Security Council document No. 5401, which boldly declared, "United States policy is to keep the sources of oil in the Middle East in American hands and defend them at all costs, and deny them to the Soviet Union, even if this led to a confrontation or to the destruction of these resources by the Americans themselves."

This policy took no account of local interests; even a peaceful settlement of the Arab-Israeli dispute was to be pursued only in order to keep the Soviet Union out of the region—and away from that oil.

Nasser had other concerns. When, in the spring of 1953, Secretary of State John Foster Dulles visited Cairo and first met Nasser, he attempted to persuade the Egyptian leader of the need to form a military pact against the Soviets. Nasser brushed this off: "I must tell you in all frankness that I can't see myself waking up one morning to find that the Soviet Union is our enemy. We don't know them. They are thousands of miles away from us. . . . I would become the laughing-stock of my people if I told them they now had an entirely new enemy, many thousands of miles away, and that they must forget about the British enemy occupying their territory."

Eisenhower and Dulles could be sympathetic to an anticolonial argument, if only because they understood that colonialism gave the Soviets propaganda points. So the following year, Dulles pressured the British to remove their troops from the Canal Zone by 1956. But there were limits to what the Americans were willing to do for Nasser. In February 1955 the Israelis launched a major raid into the Egyptian-controlled Gaza Strip, killing twenty-eight Egyptian soldiers. Nasser always regarded this as a major turning point. "The smoke of the attack on Gaza on February 28, 1955," he later explained, "revealed a dangerous truth: that Israel is not only the stolen territories behind the armistice lines, but also the spearhead of imperialism. . . ." And yet, the Israelis had launched their Gaza raid in retaliation for what they saw as a rising number of violent incidents in 1954–55 along their southern border. These small-scale attacks on Israeli soil came from loosely organized, armed Palestinians who were caught infiltrating Israel from Gaza. From Ben-Gurion's perspective, Nasser was responsible. From Nasser's perspective, the Israelis had so far refused to deal in any way with the refugee problem, which after all was the root cause of all the border incidents. They had also refused to negotiate final borders. Nasser believed their policy of mounting massive retaliatory attacks in response to relatively small incidents demonstrated that they still had larger territorial designs on both Gaza and the Sinai. Finally, he feared the Israelis might even wish to remove him from power.

Each side acted methodically to fulfill the other's worst fears. The Israelis had no intention of compensating refugees, let alone repatriating them. And Prime Minister Ben-Gurion firmly believed that disproportionate force was the only way to respond to border incidents. Not only that, but Ben-Gurion began to think that Nasser's ambitions might require Israel to launch a preemptive war.

Outraged by the Gaza carnage, Nasser responded in two ways. First, he allowed Palestinians in Gaza to organize irregular guerrilla units called *fedayeen*—"self-sacrificers." By the summer of 1955, *fedayeen* were causing the number and scale of border incidents to escalate. In late August 1955 the Israelis retaliated by overrunning two Egyptian army posts. And in response, a *fedayeen* unit slipped into Israel from Gaza and went on a road rampage for four days, getting as far as ten miles south of Tel Aviv. Eleven Israeli civilians were killed. Two days later, the Israelis attacked a police station at Khan Younis in the Gaza Strip and killed seventy-two Egyptian soldiers. Within hours, United Nations observers persuaded both sides to observe an informal cease-fire.

Soon after the February 1955 Gaza attack, Nasser turned to Washington and asked for an arms shipment. He was quickly and firmly rebuffed. Nasser's recourse was to go elsewhere. On September 27, 1955, to the Eisenhower Administration's shock, Nasser announced that he had negotiated a major deal to buy Soviet arms through Czechoslovakia.

To the Israeli defense establishment such an arms deal could mean only one thing: Nasser intended to launch a "second-round" fight for Palestine and the elimination of Israel. In mid-October, even the usually moderate Abba Eban, Israel's ambassador in Washington, had signed onto a near-apocalyptic memo: "We must assume that the Soviet arms [supply] will be massive, effective and uninterrupted, accompanied by technical advisers to instruct the Egyptians in its use. We are faced with the bleak prospect of our enemy's reinforcement with the support of the second greatest power on earth. We are consequently confronted by a degree of danger which we have never known." He then recommended "that Israel opt for a plan of action to overthrow Nasser's regime, be it on our own or jointly with the Western powers." Similar sentiments were expressed in the Israeli press. "The arms were purchased solely for planned aggression against Israel," editorialized *Davar,* a moderate newspaper aligned with the Labor Party.

Nasser was a pragmatist. In December 1955, he told Eisenhower's private envoy, the Texan banker Robert Anderson, that the Arabs could live with an Israeli state—but a "fixed frontier must be drawn between the Israeli state and the Palestinian state . . ." and the Palestinians "ought to be able to return to their homes, and that is what the majority will certainly want, or where this is impossible, they ought to receive compensation." Nasser's critics, both in Israel and in the West, have repeatedly claimed that he intended to "throw the Jews into the sea." To be sure, he wasn't happy with the Israeli state—but no one has ever been able to cite a single one of his private or public utterances to support such a charge. It is a canard.

In retrospect, there is no evidence that Nasser had any plans to initiate a war; most likely he regarded his arms purchases as merely a necessary step toward modernizing the Egyptian army and so enabling it to defend Egypt's borders effectively. But he completely misunderstood how the Israeli public would regard the Czech arms deal—let alone how it would be seen by men such as Ben-Gurion and his army chief of staff, General Moshe Dayan. Details of the arms deal began to emerge after a couple of months. The purchases included 170 T-34 medium tanks, 60 Stalin-3 heavy tanks, 200 armored personnel carriers, 100 mobile antitank guns, 134 antiaircraft guns, 100 MiG-15 jet fighters, 48 Ilyushin-28 jet bombers, 20 transport planes, 2 destroyers and 6 submarines. The sheer scale of these armaments shocked the Israelis and confirmed their worst fears.

Up until 1955, the Israelis had only 50 jet fighter planes and some 130, mostly World War II era, tanks. If Nasser took delivery of his purchase, Egypt would have a three-to-one advantage over Israel in arms. General Dayan consequently favored "an early engagement with the hostile Egyptian regime . . . in order to either topple it or force it to change its policies." Dayan didn't use the term "preemptive war," but that was what he advocated. In November 1955, he wrote Ben-Gurion, "I think we must bring about a major confrontation with the Egyptian army as quickly as possible. . . ." An equally alarmed Ben-Gurion nevertheless had his doubts. He thought a nakedly unprovoked attack on Egypt would cost Israel dearly in terms of world public opinion. And it would also jeopardize Israel's attempts to persuade the Americans and Europeans to sell armaments to Jerusalem.

Ben-Gurion eventually decided on a two-track strategy. He would seek fresh armaments from the French and the Americans. But he would also allow General Dayan to draw up a contingency plan for provoking Nasser into taking the first steps towards war. If the "Egyptian tyrant," as Ben-Gurion called him, could be seen to have fired the first shot, then the Israel Defense Forces (IDF) could march on Cairo.

Throughout the winter and spring of 1956 "incidents" occurred all along the 1949 armistice line between Israel and Egypt. Dayan refurbished his troops, and Ben-Gurion succeeded in persuading the French to supply them with new jet fighters and armor. The Israeli press openly debated not if, but when, war was likely with the Egyptians. The pervasive sense of anxiety was existential; the common Israeli citizen felt a deep sense of victimhood. Independence in 1948 had not brought with it security, but instead an endless series of violent clashes. The Jewish homeland was small and surrounded by a hostile population that seemed intent on destroying it. And now, suddenly, an Egyptian leader had emerged who seemed able and ready to realize that intention.

The Israeli politician Moshe Sharett noted in his diary that spring, "Again I asked myself if putting flesh on the assumption that we are on the brink of war and repeating it incessantly to the public was not liable, by force of inertia, to ultimately contribute to actually bringing war down on our heads." But the iconoclastic Sharett was among the very few voices of reason within the Israeli political establishment. Because most Israelis sensed a palpable imminent danger, Ben-Gurion had little trouble in mobilizing his people for a preemptive war.

*   *   *

Throughout 1955 and early 1956, Washington had continued to negotiate with Nasser. If not armaments, Nasser wanted American and World Bank financing for an ambitious development project, the Aswan High Dam. Nasser argued that such a dam would control the Nile River's annual flooding and simultaneously provide Egypt with the electrical power necessary to industrialize. Initially, the Eisenhower Administration indicated it would give a green light to the project. But Eisenhower began to have second thoughts. On March 8, 1956, he wrote in his diary: ". . . the Arabs . . . are daily growing more arrogant and disregarding the interests of Western Europe and of the United States in the Middle East region." And then Nasser did something truly unpardonable in Eisenhower's eyes: on May 16, 1956, he recognized Communist China. Eisenhower had had enough. On July 19, 1956, Nasser learned from reading the morning newspapers that Washington would no longer honor its pledge to help fund the Aswan High Dam. The Egyptian president, for his part, interpreted this as a supreme act of Western deceit.

Four days later, Nasser spoke on national radio and fiercely condemned the Eisenhower Administration: "Let them die in their fury, for they will not be able to dominate us or control our existence. We shall continue on our chosen road in spite of them, the road of honor, freedom and dignity."

And then, on July 26, 1956, Nasser broadcast another speech, this time before a crowd of a quarter million cheering people in Alexandria's Mancia Square. Prior to the speech he had instructed a select team of Egyptian commandos to occupy the offices of the British- and French-owned Suez Canal the moment they heard him speak the name of Ferdinand de Lesseps, the Frenchman who won the initial concession for building the Canal in 1855. Half an hour into his three-hour speech, Nasser mentioned de Lesseps and then stunned his audience by announcing that he had, as of that very moment, nationalized the Suez Canal Company. Over the next weeks and months, convoys of freighters continued to traverse the Canal, demonstrating to the world that Egyptian engineers and pilots were perfectly qualified to operate the Canal. Nationalization was extremely popular with the Egyptian masses—and with Arabs everywhere.

Overnight, Nasser was heralded as the embodiment of the idea of the

Arab nation. The ideal of a unified nation encompassing all the Arabic-speaking peoples carried powerful appeal. Nasser gave hope to all elements of the Arab kaleidoscope, from the Maghreb to the Euphrates—whether they were Sunni, Shi'ite or Christian—that unity would usher in an era of prosperity and genuine independence from the former colonial powers, Britain and France. He also gave hope to the refugees of Palestine that this resurgent Arab nationalism would somehow bring them back to their home-land. Nearly two decades earlier George Antonius had invoked a line from Ibrahim Yazeji's nineteenth-century poem: "Arise, ye Arabs, and awake." With Nasser, the Arabs finally seemed to be awakening. And that made him, in the eyes of his enemies, at least, a very dangerous man.

Nationalization may have been politically popular, but Nasser had sound economic reasons as well to take control of the Canal. Absent American financing, he now needed the Canal revenues to finance the Aswan High Dam. Under British and French ownership the Suez Canal Company had been earning about 39 million English pounds annually—and paying Egypt a paltry 800,000 pounds. And there were considerations of personal and national feeling as well. Nasser was personally offended and angered by the manner in which he had learned that financing for the High Dam would not be forthcoming. Dulles flatly told reporters that Egypt could not afford such a large undertaking. And then he leaked an aide-mémoire to the press on the subject. One newspaper published a cartoon of Nasser playing chess with Dulles—who was saying "Checkmate!" Dulles thought he was sending both Nasser and the Soviets a strong message. He seemed to believe that the Soviets couldn't afford to fund both their promised arms sales to Nasser and the High Dam project. He was wrong. Even Vice-Consul Gene Bird knew this, and a generation of Foreign Service officers would cite Dulles's blunder as a major turning point in America's relationship with Nasser and with the entire Arab world.

Dulles didn't understand that he was dealing with a highly intelligent, and quite rational, chess-player. That summer Nasser quietly extracted promises from the Soviet Union to fund the Aswan High Dam project. So now Nasser had both the Suez Canal under full Egyptian sovereignty—and the promise of a billion-dollar loan from the Soviets at a mere 2 percent interest. Checkmate!

Needless to say, the French and British immediately threatened to seize back the Canal with military force. The Canal, they protested, was their

President Nasser playing chess

asset. For the next three months the "Suez Crisis" became the topic of newspaper headlines around the world. By early September the French and British were quietly formulating plans to unseat Nasser's regime. They did so, however, entirely behind Eisenhower's back. As Britain's recently retired prime minister, Harold Macmillan, bluntly stated in a speech on September 22, 1956, "He [Nasser] must be stopped somehow. There is much more to this than a disagreement over the Suez Canal." What Macmillan meant was that the future of European colonial-era economic interests was at stake. The problem the French and British faced, however, was finding a politically palatable pretext for initiating a full-scale invasion. The Eisenhower Administration was making it clear that it could not condone an intervention against Nasser so long as the Canal was operating smoothly. And it was.

In early September, to overcome this obstacle, the British discreetly sought out Ben-Gurion. The approach was made by a private citizen, Robert Henriques, a member of an aristocratic English-Jewish family. Henriques later wrote that he had passed on the following message: "At all costs Israel must avoid war with Jordan. But if, when Britain went into Suez, Israel were to attack simultaneously, it would be very convenient for all concerned. Britain would denounce Israel's aggression in the strongest possible terms; but at the peace negotiations afterwards, Britain would help Israel to get the best possible treaty."

Ben-Gurion had his own motives for colluding with the British and French. He too, of course, regarded the nationalization of the Canal as disturbing evidence of Nasser's overreaching ambition. But he was even more concerned about the Egyptian-Czech arms deal. War with Egypt, he thought, was inevitable. It would be all for the better if it happened with allies.

Beginning in late September, the parties to this subterfuge choreographed their war plans down to the smallest detail. Ben-Gurion agreed to drop paratroops deep into the Sinai, seeming to threaten the Canal; in response the British and French would issue an ultimatum to both the Israelis and the Egyptians, demanding that the Israelis withdraw their troops— and that the Egyptians allow Anglo-French forces to occupy key positions along the Canal. When Nasser rejected the ultimatum, which they were confident he would, the British would destroy Egypt's air force—leaving the Israel Defense Forces free to seize the whole of the Sinai. After securing the entire Canal Zone, the British and French forces would turn west, attack Cairo and replace Nasser with a more pliant and pro-Western ruler.

Ben-Gurion insisted on written guarantees that the British would eliminate Nasser's forty-eight newly delivered Ilyushin-28 bombers, which he feared could be used to bomb Israel's cities. So on October 22, 1956, Ben-Gurion, Shimon Peres, director general of Israel's Ministry of Defense, and General Dayan slipped into a villa in Sèvres on the outskirts of Paris and met with the French foreign minister, Christian Pineau, and Patrick Dean, a high-ranking British Foreign Office official. The resulting accord was signed in triplicate two nights later, and on October 25, the Israelis flew back to Tel Aviv. Everyone was satisfied. The French and British would be given a pretext for war by the Israelis—and the Israelis had guarantees that the British would take out the feared Egyptian bombers. As Dayan wrote in his diary: ". . . in the early phases we can give our [Sinai] operation the character of a reprisal action, and . . . the Egyptians are not likely to recognize it as the opening of a comprehensive campaign, and will not rush to bomb civilian targets in Israel."

My parents were not oblivious to these rising tensions. On August 6, 1956, Mother wrote of what she called the Arabs' "rather excitable temperament." There were demonstrations in the street, and she observed that "rumors of war seem to be the habit around here." She nevertheless decided that she was "already quite blasé about it and I have long since decided that if we are to be here for two years there is no use in getting excited about incidents that might be something but have been happening for years. . . ."

Still, they were struck by the fact that in September the British announced the evacuation of all their dependents. My father saw no reason to follow the British move: "We have no real fear because, after all, open military intervention by the West could only occur if Nasser shuts down the Canal—and he would be foolish to do that. I think a good formula will be worked out without too much difficulty." Father was wrong.

That autumn, just as we were settling comfortably into Jerusalem society, the "incidents" along no-man's-land began to escalate. On September 12 and 13, the Israel Defense Forces struck in the Jordanian villages of Rahwa and Gharandal, killing thirty Jordanians. Ten days later a Jordanian soldier whose brother had been killed at Rahwa suddenly fired his Bren gun at a group of one hundred Israelis visiting an archaeological dig just across the armistice line. Four Israelis died. Two days later the IDF retaliated on the village of Husan and thirty-nine Jordanians died. "For some reason," Mother wrote, "the 'incidents' have been more numerous and the 'reprisals' very heavy. Neither side is 'right' but Israel's policy of retaliation simply keeps the fire going. It is openly acknowledged that for every (Israeli) life lost in a border incident, the Israelis will kill in return and usually many, many more. An eye for an eye has turned into twelve for one or better."

In early October the Israelis launched three heavy attacks, destroying four Jordanian police stations and killing over a hundred men. Only later would these attacks against Jordan be recognized for what they were: an attempt to lull the Egyptians into thinking that the Israelis were going to turn east, that they were stoking a war in which they intended to seize the Jordanian West Bank and unite Jerusalem.

Meanwhile, in the United Nations Nasser's diplomats made all the concessions necessary for a real negotiation to end the crisis over the Canal's status. This, of course, was a source of worry, not satisfaction, for the British and French: "They knew their military schedule would be disarranged," observed one American diplomat later, "if they became entangled in drawn-out procedures in New York." In short order, an Anglo-French rider was introduced making further demands on Nasser—demands they knew he would reject. The U.N. negotiations collapsed.

On October 22, in a further provocation, French intelligence agents hijacked a Moroccan airliner and diverted it to French-occupied Algiers. Aboard the aircraft were the Algerian resistance leader Ahmed Ben Bella and four of his comrades. Nasser had been lending material aid and political comfort to Ben Bella—which was another reason why the French wished to unseat the Egyptian president. (Ben Bella would spend the next six years in a French prison, until he became premier of an independent Algeria in 1962.) In the meantime, the Arab street exploded in rage against this act of French perfidy. Dozens of French citizens in Morocco were dragged from their cars and burnt alive. A general strike was declared for October 28 across the Middle East.

On that day Bill Wilson, the British consul, invited us for lunch at his home in Israeli West Jerusalem. He also invited the French consul's family. Wilson knew that his government was about to move against Nasser, and he did not want us to be in Jordanian East Jerusalem on that day. As we drove to Mandelbaum Gate, we could hear the *shebab* (young men) demonstrating in the Old City. During the course of the luncheon Wilson received a phone call from East Jerusalem. (The British had the only functioning phone line between East and West in the divided city.) He was informed that smoke was rising from the French consulate—and that the French consul himself was inside the besieged building. Wilson excused himself, saying that he and my father were going to play a game of tennis.

Instead, they rushed back to Mandelbaum Gate, from which they could view the French consulate through a pair of binoculars. It stood in Sheikh Jarrah, a three-story building just a block from our house. Black smoke was pouring from the windows and balconies, and three Frenchmen appeared on the roof. In a gambit to appease the crowd, they tore down the French flag and threw it to the ground. Shots were fired from within the building, but the mob did not fall back. Finally, Jordanian police intervened. To Father's surprise, no one was killed. But that night we all slept at the home of Colonel Leary, an American military officer attached to the United Nations who lived in West Jerusalem.

Mother was appalled by the Arab mob violence. "For the first time," Father wrote, "Jerri was disgusted with the Arabs and well she might be."

Word came that evening that the State Department had issued the first of three progressively more serious alerts for dependents. The first alert suggested that dependents could leave if they wished; the second strongly advised all dependents to leave; the third required the immediate evacuation of all dependents. War had not yet broken out, but the State Department had received intelligence that the Israel Defense Forces were mobilizing. The Israelis, in fact, had been secretly and gradually mobilizing 100,000 reservists for days. Mother announced that she was not going—or at least she would wait for the third, mandatory evacuation order. Should it come, American dependents were being sent to Athens or Beirut. "I didn't want to go," she later said. "I had never checked into a hotel alone, and had no confidence that I could manage with two little children on my own in a strange city."

That evening, at 9:00 p.m., a Tel Aviv radio station broadcast an official bulletin that Israeli troops had moved into the Sinai, allegedly to attack some Palestinian *fedayeen* bases. Four hours earlier Israeli paratroopers had been dropped at the eastern end of the Mitla Pass, deep inside the Sinai. It was these troops that would trigger the full-scale invasion of Egypt's Canal Zone by the British and French.

On October 30, Father found himself stuck in West Jerusalem—with his family on the other side of Mandelbaum Gate. That same day the French and British delivered their long-planned ultimatum to the Egyptians and the Israelis. As expected, Nasser rejected it. The next day the British began bombing Egypt.

The first atrocity of the war occurred on the evening of October 29. As the IDF pushed into the Sinai, the Israel Border Police imposed a curfew on Arab-Israeli villages inside the armistice line. Having announced a curfew at 4:30 p.m., police warned that anyone found outside after 5:00 p.m. could be shot. For an hour that evening just outside the village of Kafr Kassem, police set up roadblocks and detained Palestinians returning from their fields. And then they machine-gunned them in batches. By 6:00 p.m. forty-eight civilians, including six women and twenty-three children, lay dead. News of the massacre was suppressed until weeks after the war was over. Ben-Gurion himself revealed what had happened in a statement before the Knesset. Eleven of the police involved in the massacre were eventually indicted, and eight were convicted; but no one spent more than three and a half years in prison.

In the minds of most Palestinians, Kafr Kassem was another Deir Yassin, another cold-blooded attempt to frighten them into abandoning their homes. And yet, for Israelis, it remains even today a morality tale, to be studied carefully by Israeli soldiers, of when a manifestly illegal order should be disobeyed. To Israelis, the massacre was a tragic aberration. To be sure, any number of Israeli commanders in other sectors instructed their troops to ignore orders to kill curfew violators. And yet, such murders can only take place in an atmosphere already tainted by hatred. As General Dayan noted in his diary at the time, there was a feeling among his officers that the war was "an opportunity to settle accounts . . . when at last there can be a release for the pent-up bitterness they have harbored for the eight years . . . of Arab threats to destroy Israel."

My parents did not learn of Kafr Kassem until December—but it and the war itself hardened their growing dislike for Israeli policies. Such attitudes were common among expatriates living in East Jerusalem. They had walked through a number of the refugee camps right outside Jerusalem and Jericho, and it was easy to see that the Palestinians were the underdogs in this conflict. They lived in tents or crude shacks with no running water or modern sewers. Eight years had passed, but they all believed that someday they would be going back to their homes. Father wrote home to his parents in Oregon, "The depth of the Arab refugee attachment to Palestine, their dedication to solving the problem with Arab honor and prestige restored, well, the Gods still slumber. . . ."

Even after the outbreak of open warfare, my mother refused to leave. The day after the war began, she steeled herself to drive alone through Mandelbaum Gate, the car full of such heirlooms as the Newhouse family Bible and her mother's rocking chair, for safekeeping in the consulate general on the Israeli side. Israeli soldiers were everywhere, with their guns pointed at the crossing point. Once through, she had to negotiate streets in West Jerusalem's "New City" alongside Israeli tanks.

The next day, the State Department finally issued the mandatory evacuation order. The moment he heard it, Father sent a consulate driver to our Sheikh Jarrah house—which still had no phone—with a message to Mother: she had two hours to pack our bags. The driver drove us first to the consulate, where we said a quick good-bye to Father, and then to Kalandia, the small airport adjacent to Ramallah, on the northern outskirts of East Jerusalem. We caught the last plane out, leaving Father behind. Mother told us that we would not be long and would soon be reunited with Father in Jerusalem. "I did not like at all the prospect that something might happen in the Jerusalem area," Father wrote. He feared the Israelis intended to attack and seize East Jerusalem and the rest of the West Bank. This, however, would not happen for another eleven years, during the June 1967 War.

That last plane out of Jerusalem took us to Beirut. After landing, we were walking across the airport tarmac when Mother saw a reporter with a television camera filming us. When she instinctively smiled, the reporter stopped filming and snapped, "Quit smiling, lady, don't you know this is a serious situation?" Mother wanted to slug him, but she had three-year-old Nancy in her arms and me nervously holding on to her skirt. Instead, we took a taxi to the Eden Roc Hotel, a lovely establishment right on the beach. After checking in, Mother took us to the American Embassy, thinking she would find assistance there. Here she was in a foreign city, alone with two young children; she had very little cash and, needless to say, no credit cards. But when she nervously introduced herself, a young consular official asked her where her husband was. When she said, "Jerusalem," he responded that was impossible because the Consulate General was closed. "No," she insisted, "the consulate is open and my husband is working there, working to get American tourists caught in the area out of Jordan." When she asked what she should do now, the befuddled officer invited her to sign the visitors' book. We stayed at the Eden Roc Hotel only a few days before moving into cheaper quarters. Mother expected we'd all be going back to Jerusalem within weeks, so she didn't bother to send us to school.

As things turned out, we did not return to Jerusalem until July 1957.

The war lasted only eight days, from October 31 to November 7. The Jordanians imposed a blackout on East Jerusalem. Father had to hang blackened sheets across all the windows in our Sheikh Jarrah house. "I admire the iron nerves of both sides," Father wrote, "who can live with this situation without any outward evidence of fear. During the blackout there was the deepest, deepest silence for a town of 75,000 that you can imagine. Not a soul stirred, not a person ventured out, and the only lights were those from Israel-Jerusalem." Father was convinced that his office telephone conversations were being "monitored constantly," presumably by the Jordanians.

* * *

What the British called Operation Musketeer Revise was a military success—but political folly. The British bombed Port Said for five days, and then on November 5 22,000 British and French troops, ferried in by amphibious landing craft and helicopter, landed on the beaches at the northern end of the Canal, just outside Port Said and Port Fuad. They easily overwhelmed the Egyptian defenders. By then Israeli forces had seized control of the entire Sinai Peninsula, as well as the heavily populated refugee camps in the Gaza Strip. But if the invaders' objective was to secure the Canal, ostensibly their main goal, they failed in their mission. After British planes flying from Malta and Cyprus bombed Cairo's aerodrome, Nasser ordered the sinking of all forty ships—flying under a dozen different flags—then traversing the Canal. This effectively closed the Canal until April 1957.

The British lost sixteen men, and French fatalities numbered ten. One hundred seventy-one Israelis were killed—most of them when lightly armed paratroopers under the command of Colonel Ariel Sharon rashly, and without orders, assaulted entrenched Egyptian troops at Jebel Heitan near the Mitla Pass. Rough estimates suggest that 1,000 Egyptian soldiers and civilians were killed in the fighting over Port Said. Much of that city lay in ruins or was burning. As many as 2,000 more Egyptian soldiers lost their lives in the Sinai. The invaders won all the battles—and then on November 6 they lost the war.

On that day President Eisenhower forced first the British and then the French to comply with a U.N. Security Council cease-fire resolution. He did so by using American financial muscle to threaten a run on the already weak British pound. On the morning of the 6th the British government asked Eisenhower's treasury secretary for $1.5 billion in credits to shore up the pound. But London was told it would get the credits only if it ceased military operations in the Canal Zone by midnight. "It was not exactly blackmail," said one British minister later, "but compliance with the UN was a postulate of American help."

Eisenhower's motives were manifold. The "police action" by the French and British against Egypt came just as the Soviets launched their own "police action" to repress the Hungarian uprising. This was an embarrassment. Furthermore, Eisenhower understood that the actual goal of the invasion was the removal of Nasser. Even though Ike had severe doubts about the Egyptian leader, this naked act of aggression by the two colonial powers had manifestly turned the Egyptian army colonel into a national hero whom it would be impossible to unseat. Finally, Eisenhower was clearly annoyed that Britain and France had misled him with a venture that could only undermine both the United Nations and the rule of law.

For all these reasons, Eisenhower was also determined to force the invaders to withdraw from any territory they had seized. Within a week both Britain and France had withdrawn their troops. "We not only had a little difficulty in getting Britain and France to come out," Eisenhower told the *New York Times* correspondent Kennett Love, "but later we had much more difficulty in getting the Israelis to come out. Finally, we had to be very tough with them, really, but they finally agreed." Father was almost ecstatic: "Everyone wants us back pronto. . . . Americans are rated highly."

On November 7, the very day the war ended, Ben-Gurion disingenuously told the Knesset, "Our forces did not infringe on the territory of the land of Egypt . . . our operations were restricted to the area of the Sinai Peninsula alone." He further proclaimed that the 1949 armistice lines "between us and Egypt are vanished and dead." Clearly, Ben-Gurion intended to keep the Sinai.

Edward R. Murrow interviewing Prime Minister
David Ben-Gurion, May 1956

Eisenhower responded to these brazen assertions with a stern note to Ben-Gurion warning him that such a stance was certain to bring about a "condemnation of Israel as a violator of the principles as well as the directives of the United Nations." Ike also authorized Undersecretary of State Herbert Hoover Jr. to pass on an oral warning to Golda Meir, Israel's foreign minister: if Israel did not withdraw from the Sinai, the Eisenhower Administration might impose economic sanctions. The very next day, a stunned Ben-Gurion immediately reassured the American president that he had no intention of annexing the Sinai. And then, a few hours later, he told the Israeli people in a radio broadcast, "None of us knows what the future of the Sinai Desert will be."

For more than four months Ben-Gurion procrastinated in the hope that over time Eisenhower would relent and allow the Israelis to keep all or part of the Sinai. In February 1957 Ben-Gurion told Secretary of State Dulles that a withdrawal was opposed by "our entire people," implying that American Jewry supported Israel's claim to the Sinai. Eisenhower dismissed this kind of pressure, telling the *New York Times*'s Kennett Love, "We thought the American Jew was an American before he was a Jew. . . ."

Meanwhile, we—Mother, Nancy and I—were stuck in Beirut. In late November and again in December, Dulles told the Israelis that the crisis would not end until all Israeli troops were withdrawn from the Egyptian Sinai. Until this happened, he warned, the dependents of American officials evacuated from the region would not be allowed to return to their posts in Israel, Jordan and Egypt.

Mother hated being separated from her husband. She kept writing him, "Never again." When the war ended on November 6 she thought we'd be returning in a matter of days. So did Father. But he also felt that Washington had to hold firm with the Israelis: "We have won a position," he wrote to another Foreign Service officer back in Washington, "and all we need to do is stubbornly hang onto it to make people once again believe in us."

When Father informed Mother that we'd be spending Christmas in Beirut, she called this the "crowning blow." Early in December she moved us into a small pension in Ras Beirut called the Staff House Hotel. Guests ate their meals together, summoned by a gong. Or we could walk a short distance to my favorite restaurant, Uncle Sam's, appropriately named for its American fare of cheeseburgers, French fries and milk shakes. But life seemed to be on hold. There was nothing much to do except wait for Father's occasional phone calls from Jerusalem. Mother desperately needed these phone calls. But they were expensive, and uncertain. It often took as long as four hours to "place" a call through the hotel's reception desk.

One afternoon we came back to the room and Mother learned that she had just missed a call from Father. For the first time since the evacuation she suddenly broke down and began sobbing. "Kai was such a sweet little man about it," Mother wrote to Father. "He asked me why I was crying and I told him it was because I was lonely for you and I had missed your call. So when Nancy asked what was wrong he answered her—just that way." I was by all accounts an overly serious and sensitive child. Instead of talking—my younger sister Nancy did all the talking—I stared and listened.

Kai in Jerusalem, 1956

My own memories of these Beirut months are of dark, rainy days filled with boredom. I spent a lot of time studying maps. I needed to know where I had been and where I was. At five years of age I could find Jerusalem, Beirut, Egypt, France, Oregon, England and Washington, DC, on the globe. And I could point to China because I knew my name was Chinese.

Early in the new year of 1957 we moved out of the pension and rented a fifth-floor apartment with a balcony from which one could see a small patch of the blue waters of the Mediterranean. We lived in the heart of Ras Beirut, meaning "Cape" Beirut, the most Westernized and upscale commercial part of the city. When we walked the busy streets, we heard Arabic, French and English being spoken. The Arab souk was a long *service* taxi ride downtown. (The *service* taxis ran a set route, like a bus, but the *services,* usually a four-door Mercedes sedan, stopped and picked up passengers anywhere along the route for a small fixed fee.) Ras Beirut boasted fashionable Hamra Street with its French clothing boutiques and its bookstores. The American University of Beirut, with its sprawling garden campus overlooking the ocean, was just a ten-minute walk down the street—as was the beautiful ocean-side *corniche,* and the beach below it. Sidewalk cafés served grilled *shwarma* (lamb) sandwiches in pita bread and toasted chicken sandwiches with a savory white garlic sauce. The cinemas played the latest movies from Hollywood, but also films from France, Italy and Egypt. In 1957, Ras Beirut was on the cutting edge of postwar modern civilization. It was a cosmopolitan oasis populated by Europeans, Americans and Lebanese expatriates who had made their money in Latin America, Africa or Asia and then returned to their homeland. By comparison, Jerusalem was a small-town backwater.

But for us, having come from Jerusalem, where Father remained, the "conflict" was ever-present. Even our child-play centered on the city whose name I pronounced as "Rusalem." "You should hear them play when they think they are not being noticed," Mother wrote. "It is all about war, getting shot, very realistic bombs and explosions and then proper moans and groans of the wounded, even play about getting through gates, hiding from bad soldiers, protecting the good ones. . . . They even remember here to say only the right (Arab) words and use no Hebrew." No doubt, in my childish mind the "bad soldiers" were the Israelis.

By February 1957, Mother was learning that she could cope. The separation had revealed the depths of her resiliency. "I have learned a very good lesson—that I can do some things I thought I couldn't do." In one of her many love letters she told Father that the separation had strengthened their marriage. But still, she hated it—and she blamed Israel for her predicament: "It really sounds like Israel is going to make more trouble and won't back down. And how strong will Eisenhower be on this thing . . . if they let Jewish pressure and sympathizers bring too much pressure to bear on them and give in, we are finished in this area, and it would never be safe for us to get back [to Jerusalem]." She had changed, she wrote to a good friend back in America: "Whereas when I came out my bias was undetermined, or if anything slightly leaning toward the Israeli side, I now find it difficult to understand the refusal of the Israelis to regard themselves as the aggressor."

In Mother's view, Israel had fired the first shot in this war, unprovoked by "any armed military attack." She meant that no Arab *state* had attacked Israel. She knew that the Israelis cited the hundreds of "incidents" along the armistice lines as provocation enough. But the "incidents," she thought, were both inevitable and not sufficient to justify preemptive war. "They surely cannot hope that the thousands of refugees who sit outside of their homeland can be completely kept in check. If you had lived in tents, in the bitter cold winters since 1948, seeing your homes occupied by outsiders, you might be better able to understand that sporadic, isolated attempts to strike back are inevitable." Both she and my father were adamant that Israel should not profit territorially. That was a moral imperative. Only after Israel was forced to retreat within its borders could the various parties negotiate the underlying issues. They were thus in sync with Eisenhower's own position that aggression should not be rewarded.

"We are going to have to get diplomatically tough before this is finished," Father wrote. "The State Department might keep all dependents away until people on both sides recognize that it is up to them to reach a settlement."

In early February 1957 the Israeli cabinet defied a unanimous vote in the U.N. General Assembly and voted not to withdraw from Gaza. "I personally believe," Father wrote, "that Eisenhower is going to have to move in with our strength and force them out. . . . Perhaps Ben-Gurion will fall in the resulting mess, and frankly peace will be closer if he does. . . . He has been a great Jewish leader, perhaps the greatest, yet his lack of statesmanship in the present period is amazing."

Finally, Ben-Gurion caved. The last Israeli soldier left the Sinai and Gaza on March 16, 1957—and we were allowed to return to Jerusalem. Eisenhower had indeed been very tough with the Israelis. It was one of the few times an American president imposed his will upon an Israeli prime minister.

Wars have unintended consequences. Far from destroying the Egyptian regime, this war elevated Nasser to new political heights. For a short time, the Americans looked as if they had positioned themselves to take advantage of the prevailing winds of anticolonialism: Eisenhower had punished the European aggressors. But the Americans squandered this political capital. Instead of engaging with Nasser, the Eisenhower Administration made it clear that it regarded his appeals to Arab unity with suspicion and disfavor.

So Suez was ultimately a disaster for the West. The war destroyed what diplomatic cachet the British had remaining in the Arab world. Both the British and French lost control over the Suez Canal. The Israelis gained no territory. Instead, their collusion with the Europeans marked them as collaborators with the former European colonizers—not a smart thing at the end of the colonial era. In the short run, the Israelis won access to a reliable pipeline of French arms. But in the long run, this did nothing to enhance Israeli security.

Most Israelis accepted the withdrawal from the Sinai with resignation and melancholy. Many had thought the war would liberate much more than the Sinai's waterless plains—that it would end Israel's virtual isolation. As a character in Amos Oz's novel *My Michael* says, "There is going to be a war. This time we shall conquer Jerusalem, Hebron, Bethlehem, and Nablus. . . . The Holy Places will once again be ours." But in this preemptive war nothing was gained; and worse, something special was lost. "Instead of being a light to the nations," remarks one of Oz's characters, "we have become just one of the nations, and who can say whether it is for better or for worse?"

In the autumn of 1957 I was sent to a private all-boys multilingual school in the Christian Quarter of the Old City. The Collège des Frères, founded in 1876 by a Catholic monastic order, the La Salle Brothers, occupied a large four-story walled compound near the New Gate. It was one of the two or three most elite private schools in East Jerusalem. It offered a very Catholic education. But the aristocratic and up-and-coming bourgeois Muslim families of Jerusalem sent their sons to Frères or the St. George's Anglican School. Prior to the creation of Israel, there were also Jewish students at these elite schools—and afterwards only a handful. By 1957, Frères's student body was largely Muslim. But in those days religion was a private affair. I don't think most of these Palestinian boys thought about whether their classmate was a Muslim or Christian. A common language defined their identity. What mattered was class—and the fact that they were all Arabs and spoke Arabic.

Classes were taught, in consecutive trimesters, in three languages: first Arabic, then French and finally English. My teacher was a Catholic Palestinian. I spoke no Arabic or French, and I was the only American, indeed the only non-Arab, in my class—and as I had been a late talker, I was not terribly articulate even in English. Father observed that I was "the shy type in large crowds . . . definitely not an extrovert." We sat on dark wooden benches attached to little desks designed with lids that when lifted revealed a place to store your papers and books. The desk had a round inkwell carved into one corner. I remember learning the Arabic alphabet and numerals by rote memorization. I was not a good student.

One day I was called to the front of the classroom, where the teacher sat at a desk on a raised platform. I had been caught writing with my left hand—a breach of etiquette in the Arab world because the left hand is associated with the toilet—and now the teacher had me present my left hand, knuckles upward—whereupon he smacked it with a wooden ruler. I learned quite a bit of Arabic that autumn.

I felt very much out of place and grew to hate the school. It got to the point where each morning Father had to stuff me kicking and screaming into the school's minibus. These are some of my earliest, vivid and most unpleasant memories. In January 1958, my parents gave up on Frères and pulled me out. "Kai was not in his element," wrote the principal diplomatically to my father, "because of the language difficulties and lack of communication with his fellow classmates." Very shortly, I was back to my daily journeys across Mandelbaum Gate, to the Anglican Mission School in West Jerusalem.

Six weeks after our return to Jerusalem, Father committed a diplomatic gaffe. In Ramallah, he ran into Antoine Albina, a businessman who owned a travel agency. Albina was also a member of the Jordanian parliament, and his cousin owned the building in East Jerusalem that housed the American consulate. Despite his modest prominence, Albina was somewhat mercurial. Whenever he learned that an American congressman or senator was in town he'd picket the consulate, shouting, "Give us back our lands." In the course of their brief encounter on that day, Father apparently lost his patience and quipped, "Mr. Albina, yesterday you were a pussycat in Jerusalem, but today in Ramallah you are a mad dog." Father was making a poor joke—but in the Arab world, dogs are considered unclean, and to call someone a dog is extremely insulting. The next day one of the local newspapers reported that Vice-Consul Eugene Bird had called Deputy Albina a "mad dog."

Shortly thereafter, Albina circulated an open letter in which he denounced Father by name as a "Jew-lover." In the streets of East Jerusalem this was libel.

Albina—whose travel agency specialized in bringing Russian pilgrims to Jerusalem—believed that Father was too friendly with the people across

Mandelbaum Gate. Mother regarded Albina as a "known crank," but to her and Father's dismay similar sentiments also echoed from "the throats of those we thought friends." Mother found this "heartbreaking," and she also feared that in a place like Jerusalem a written assault "only precedes the physical attack." Only a week earlier a man from Hebron had been found in possession of six sticks of dynamite; he was arrested just outside the consulate.

"If bias we have," Mother wrote home, "it has surely been in favor of the Arab cause, but there is no rhyme nor reason to a people torn with emotion." Albina's attack on Father resonated among a citizenry simultaneously embittered with the Israelis and chafing under Jordanian rule. President Eisenhower had single-handedly forced the Israelis to withdraw from the Sinai, but America was still resented for its sheer power, and particularly for its influence over Jordan's King Hussein. America had saved the Arabs from the colonial powers, but it was thought to have bought Jordan cheap from Hussein's former British colonial masters. Most Palestinians, and particularly our Palestinian neighbors in East Jerusalem, disliked the twenty-one-year-old king.

King Hussein bin Talal was constantly reshuffling his cabinet, and in the mid-1950s his regime was widely regarded by the Arab street as reflexively pro-American. He maintained a firm hand on his throne. Any opposition was met with repression. The once popular and sometimes incendiary Grand Mufti, Haj Amin al-Husseini, was kept in exile, and his vocal followers were periodically imprisoned. Officers in the Arab Legion and the intelligence services were well paid and invariably recruited from the king's Hashemite constituency and the Bedouin tribes of eastern Jordan.

The Jordanian monarch never would have survived had it not been for the material and political support he received from Washington. A majority of his subjects were Palestinian—and this remains true today, even excluding the occupied West Bank. The Hashemites had come to Jordan from western Arabia in the course of World War I. In 1921 Winston Churchill, then London's colonial secretary, and T. E. Lawrence offered Hussein's grandfather Abdullah the throne of Transjordan—the name given at the time for that portion of British Mandate Palestine that lay east of the River Jordan. They gave King Abdullah an annual budget of 150,000 English pounds, but in return for this princely subsidy Abdullah had to recognize the British Mandate over Palestine and, implicitly, the Balfour Declaration, which expressed the British government's approval for the establishment of a "Jewish national home" in Palestine. The Arabic-speaking British intelligence agent Harry St. John Philby—father of Kim Philby—was appointed Abdullah's "adviser." Abdullah, though a clever and pragmatic ruler, was essentially a British puppet. In 1921, his father, the Sharif Hussein, still controlled the Hejaz, including the holy cities of Mecca and Medina. But by 1924 the Sharif and his clan—known as the Hashemites—would lose their domain to a rival tribe from central Arabia led by the formidable Abdul-Aziz ibn Saud.

It made no sense, except to Churchill and his Colonial Office bureaucrats, to place Abdullah, a Hejazi, and his Bedouin tribesmen in charge of Transjordan, a comparatively settled society of small tradesmen, shopkeepers and farmers living in small towns. For Churchill, it was simply a way of perpetuating de facto British control and postponing independence and self-determination for the indigenous peoples on both sides of the River Jordan. Not surprisingly, relations between the Hashemites and the Palestinians were always tenuous. Rumors, probably true, circulated that Abdullah was also taking money from the Jewish Agency.

After the 1948 war, King Abdullah conducted secret talks with Golda Meir and other Israeli officials, exploring the possibilities for an overall peace settlement. Inevitably, he came to be seen as a self-aggrandizing collaborator. On July 20, 1951, Abdullah was praying at Jerusalem's al-Aqsa Mosque with his grandson Hussein at his side when a twenty-one-year-old Palestinian tailor's apprentice got close enough to fire three bullets. Abdullah was killed instantly with a bullet to the ear. One of the other two bullets bounced off a medal pinned to Prince Hussein's chest, and he survived. Jordanian prosecutors later charged that ten Palestinians, led by Colonel Abdullah Tell (a former military governor of Jerusalem) and Dr. Musa Abdullah al-Husseini (a member of the exiled Grand Mufti's clan) had planned the assassination. Four Palestinians were hanged for the murder, but Colonel Tell and Dr. al-Husseini escaped to Egypt. Abdullah's mentally unstable son, Talal, became king, but a year later he abdicated in favor of his own son, seventeen-year-old Hussein.

Hussein remained highly distrustful of his Palestinian citizenry, and rightly so, because the current political tides were moving against the Hashemite monarch. Most of his subjects found political inspiration in Nasser's brand of pan-Arab nationalism. As evidence of this, on October 21, 1956, Jordanians voted decisively in the country's first democratic elections for a center-left coalition led by Suleiman Nabulsi. A graduate of the American University of Beirut, Nabulsi was a nominal socialist and Arab nationalist in the mode of Nasser.

In early April 1957, the Nabulsi government sponsored antiroyalist demonstrations, and for a moment it seemed as if the monarchy would be forced to give way to a full parliamentary democracy. But Nabulsi was unprepared for Hussein's next move. After first getting an explicit green light from President Eisenhower and Secretary of State Dulles, the king, having personally rallied the Bedouin troops of his Arab Legion, dismissed Parliament and declared martial law on April 25. Hussein claimed to have uncovered a plot by Palestinian army officers to seize power. The "free officers" accused of coup-plotting were all identified as Nasserites. Hussein described a "deeply laid, cleverly contrived plot to assassinate me, overthrow the throne and proclaim a republic." But the real coup was the one King Hussein executed against his own duly elected Parliament. Much of the operation was plotted and managed by a CIA agent named James Russell Barracks, who had started planning the coup soon after the October 1956 elections. In a demonstration of support, the Eisenhower Administration hastily dispatched the U.S. Sixth Fleet to the eastern Mediterranean. All political parties were now banned, the press was censored, and for all practical purposes Jordan became a police state. Even months later, King Hussein's Legionnaires would periodically close all the gates to the Old City for a day or two while they went door-to-door, searching for a Communist, a too-vocal Nasserite or some other perceived enemy of the king.

Soon after the coup, the Central Intelligence Agency placed King Hussein on its payroll. Starting that spring, a young CIA operative known as "JD" showed up at the palace each month with a brown manila envelope containing 5,000 Jordanian dinars, or about $14,000. These covert payments were code-named "Operation NOBEEF." Hussein used these funds at his personal discretion to bribe political opponents, secure the loyalty of key army officers and clan leaders and hire personal bodyguards. Hussein also began to hold regular meetings with the CIA's station chief in Amman, Frederick W. Latrash. (The thirty-one-year-old Latrash's previous posting had been in Guatemala, where he had a hand in overthrowing the elected president, Jacobo Arbenz.) The NOBEEF payments continued for decades, through five U.S. administrations, and increased from $168,000 a year in 1957 to $750,000 in 1976. In return, Hussein gave the CIA permission to run a large and active station in Jordan's capital, Amman. "JD" became part of Hussein's inner social circle; the relationship was personal and highly discreet. None of this was public knowledge at the time. (The details of these arrangements were only disclosed by Bob Woodward in the *Washington Post* in February 1977.)

With the obvious encouragement of his new American backers, King Hussein had thus saved his country from the pitfalls of a constitutional monarchy. Thereafter, the Americans invariably referred to Hussein as "our plucky little King." Far from criticizing him for deposing an elected government, President Eisenhower told Foster Dulles that "the young King was certainly showing some spunk and he admired him for it." Washington believed that a Nasserite coup could easily have led to an invitation to the Egyptian president to unify his country with Jordan. From the perspective of the Americans, Arab unity was something to be avoided at all costs—even though a majority of Hussein's subjects would have preferred either Nasser or the chaos of democracy.

Palestinians also naturally resented King Hussein's unstated but obvious policy of "Jordanization." By the mid-1950s, Palestinians on both sides of the River Jordan outnumbered the "Transjordanians" in the East Bank by two to one. (From 1948 to 1967 the West Bank was a part of Jordan.) But power resided in Amman—and Jerusalem was treated more or less like a provincial townlet. This particularly irked Palestinians at a time when the Israelis were claiming West Jerusalem as their capital. King Hussein rarely visited Jerusalem. Father and Mother were in the receiving line at Jerusalem's Kalandia Airport in 1957 when he visited the city for the first time since his grandfather's assassination. Hussein piloted the small plane himself, and when he stepped out of the cockpit my parents were in the receiving line to greet him. Mother was struck by how short the monarch was—and how young! Hussein charmed my parents, as he was to charm many foreigners. But in these years, and for many years to come, he was not beloved among the Palestinians, who thought he had neither the interest nor the ability to get back their lands.

Hussein gradually became an astute politician, learning to pit the various Palestinian clans against each other. He elevated leading members of the old aristocratic Jerusalem families to positions of power. Men like Anwar

Nusseibeh, Aref al-Aref and Dr. Husayn Fahkri al-Khalidi were from time to time named to various cabinet posts. But they could be dismissed on a whim—and were. Hussein himself, of course, remained, denying the Palestinians any real semblance of self-determination.

In the late 1950s, Hussein was no constitutional monarch but a boy-king in the pocket of the Americans. In reality, the Hashemite regime was a wholly artificial political entity. Hussein survived only because he was an authoritarian. So it was no surprise that some Palestinians felt compelled to harangue Vice-Consul Bird about his government's complicity with the Hashemites—and, of course, with the Israelis. "Most of the time I feel like telling Jews and Arabs alike," Mother wrote, "that the best thing the U.S. could do is leave them their silly pile of rocks to fight over—for we couldn't care less! The Arabs say, 'It is Truman's fault that Israel was created and thus we lost our homes' and the Jews say 'It is the fault of Eisenhower that we are left to suffer repeated attacks from the Arabs' . . . and on and on they go!"

Gradually, Father restored relations with his network of Jerusalemites. He punned and joshed his way through Jerusalem's cocktail circuit, and within a few months the Albina affair was largely forgotten. But it was a sobering lesson on how deep ran the passions of this divided city. Mother once called it "this indescribably intense place—Jerusalem."

One local couple in particular had stood by them during the affair. Vicken and Ada Kalbian were their closest friends and neighbors, who lived a hundred yards down the hill, right on the edge of the strip of no-man's-land facing Mount Scopus. Dr. Vicken Kalbian was our family doctor and in fact the doctor for almost everyone in the American consulate. An Armenian Christian Palestinian, he was the same age as my father, born in 1925 in Jerusalem's German Hospital. After graduating from St. George's Anglican School in 1942, he went to the American University of Beirut, where he studied medicine as his father had before him.

The Kalbians' ancestors had lived in Jerusalem for many generations. During World War I, the city's Armenian population had swelled with survivors of the Turkish massacres. After the Young Turks came to power in Istanbul in 1915, the new regime turned on the Armenians of the former Ottoman Empire; thousands were forcibly expelled, and as many as 1.5 million Armenians were systematically massacred in the twentieth century's first holocaust. Vicken's grandfather was among those killed, a fate his father missed only because he happened to be studying medicine in Beirut at the time.

In 1918, in the midst of this unfolding tragedy, an American named Edward Blatchford (1868–1956) turned up in Jerusalem and voluntarily organized an Armenian orphanage. A graduate of Amherst College, Blatchford fell in love with Jerusalem. After the war he was appointed the American vice-consul for religious affairs. He spoke fluent Arabic, French and Turkish—and he knew everyone in Jerusalem society, including the Grand Mufti, Haj Amin al-Husseini. Other American diplomats came and went, but Blatchford remained for decades, paid as a "dollar-a-year-man." His closest friend and confidant was Vicken Kalbian's father, Dr. Vahan Kalbian, who had volunteered his services at the Armenian orphanage. Naturally, Kalbian Senior became the American consulate's medical doctor, and Vicken inherited this position when his father retired in 1950.

In 1923, when the Armenian orphanage shut its doors, one of the last remaining orphans was a thirteen-year-old girl, Baidzar, who was taken into the Kalbian home. Baidzar had witnessed the murder of her parents by the Turks but had managed to make her way to Jerusalem. She and thousands of other children had walked from Konya in Anatolia to Jerusalem—a distance of several hundred miles—with very little food or water. For the next half century, Baidzar would serve two generations of Kalbians as the family nanny.

In 1954, Vicken married Ada Haddad, a Roman Catholic Jerusalemite who had grown up in the German Colony suburb, just south of the New City. It was a love union, at a time when marrying outside the Armenian community was unusual. Ada's father, who owned lumberyards in Haifa and Jerusalem, had built a beautiful stone house in Jerusalem with marble floors. In addition to his business, he worked for the Spanish consulate, and at some point he had acquired a Spanish passport. Ada, whose grandmother was of Italian ancestry, finished her secondary education at a school in Haifa.

My parents saw the Kalbians almost every day. "I do not remember any consul," Vicken recalled of Father, "who was as gregarious, as curious, or as vital. He held weekly Thursday stag luncheons at his house to which he invited journalists, lawyers, and the occasional politicians. And he wouldn't hesitate to try to present the Israeli point of view, if only to get a good discussion going. He and I would sometimes stay up until three in the morning."

Father was nothing if not provocative. Ada once overheard him telling a Palestinian, "Well you know, you're not the only refugees in the world." That was taken, said Ada, "very, very badly."

Father and Dr. Vicken Kalbian, Jerusalem, 1956

The Kalbians were affluent and cosmopolitan Arab-speaking Jerusalemites. Their story of what happened both before and after deeply influenced my parents. Even today, the Kalbians mourn for the Jerusalem of their youth.

"When I was growing up in the twenties and thirties," Vicken said, "we did not differentiate between Arab and Jew. I would go to a Jewish dermatologist, a Jewish podiatrist, a Jewish tailor, without thinking twice. Things hadn't heated up like they did in the late 1930s, when people started boycotting and you couldn't shop in Jewish shops. In my class at St. George's there were at least five or six boys out of twenty who were Jewish. My best friend was a Jewish boy, Lucian Meysels. His father was the art critic for the *Jerusalem Post*. Lucian and I were at the top of our class. We used to play chess together. After 1967 I asked about him, but no one knew where he was. They were Viennese Jews who had come in the 1930s. I had another friend, Rousseau. . . . They were probably North African Jews. "

Vicken Kalbian grew up in a handsome Jerusalem stone home at Number 4 Balfour Street. A brass plaque identified it as *Kaza Kalbian*. A beautiful wrought-iron gate opened onto the front garden. The Kalbian "kaza" stood just behind the YMCA in the lovely garden neighborhood of Talbieh. Inhabited mostly by middle-class Christian Arabs, Talbieh nevertheless was also home to some Jews and Muslims.

When the British Mandate government began to unravel in 1947–48, Vicken Kalbian was just finishing his medical degree at the American University of Beirut. The British had announced that their mandate would end no later than May 15, 1948, after which Palestine would be divided between a Jewish and a Palestinian state in accordance with the United Nations' November 29, 1947, partition plan. Under that plan, Jerusalem was supposed to remain united as an international enclave. But within days of the UN's decision, the city descended into sectarian brutishness and outright anarchy. Jews in once-integrated neighborhoods such as the German Colony, Katamon and Talbieh fled to mainly Jewish districts such as Rehavia. Terrorist attacks became more frequent. On January 5, 1948, a bomb planted by the Haganah (the Jewish underground army) in the Semiramis Hotel killed twenty-six Palestinian Christians, including the Spanish consul. Despite other attacks carried out by both Jewish and Arab partisans, the Kalbians remained in their Talbieh home until a Jewish woman was killed in the neighborhood in mid-January. Soon afterwards, the Haganah sent trucks mounted with loudspeakers through the streets of Talbieh, demanding that all Arab residents leave immediately. The Kalbians identified themselves as Christian, Arabic-speaking Armenians whose home was Palestine. The Haganah regarded them as non-Jews and therefore Arabs.

The Kalbians decided it was prudent to comply. When they left on February 1, 1948, they thought they'd be coming back in a few weeks. They packed a few small suitcases and, together with Nanny Baidzar, boarded a plane at Lydda Airport bound for Beirut. "My father had a man stay in the house, a Mr. Garabed," Vicken recalled. "He witnessed the pillaging of the house; the Jews locked him into the bathroom and then looted the house, taking away everything in a truck. But foolishly, they failed to tie down the piano, so when the truck started to move, the piano slid off, breaking into pieces. The only thing they did not take was the chandelier in the dining room. I guess it was too high to reach."

The Kalbians spent much of the years 1948–50 in Beirut, waiting and hoping to be allowed to return. Vicken initially obtained an immigration visa for America, but his father soon convinced him that his medical skills were sorely needed in East Jerusalem. So in July 1950 Vicken returned and became the chief resident at the 500-bed hospital on Mount Scopus, Augusta Victoria, a hospital funded by the Lutheran World Federation. Most of his patients were poor Palestinian refugees, many of whom lived in tent cities on the outskirts of Jerusalem.

Vicken returned to a city much divided. "After '48, people forgot what Jerusalem had been. Now a Jew was the person on the other side of Mandelbaum Gate shooting at our soldiers, and we were shooting at them."

Ada's family had a similar experience growing up in Jerusalem. Like Vicken she too had had many Jewish friends: "My piano teacher was a Jew, my dressmaker was Jewish. We invited Jewish friends to dinner. There was a Jewish girl I used to play with. There was no enmity between us. On the contrary, Palestinians helped so many refugee Jews who came from Nazi Germany because they felt sorry for them. So why did they take Palestine? Honestly, why didn't they take it out on the Germans?" Early in 1948, she too heard the sound trucks warning all Arabs to leave their German Colony neighborhood. In early April 1948, Ada was sent to her grandmother in Italy. Her parents left for Lebanon later that month. Because Ada's father had a Spanish passport they arranged for a Spanish consul to stay in the house together with Ada's brother. But one day the two men went to the Old City and found that they could not get back. "Unfortunately," Ada said, "they had not put up the Spanish flag on the house; they just locked the door and left, leaving behind all my parents' possessions, silver, rugs, paintings, everything. We lost everything. My mother only managed to bring out her jewelry. They stayed in a village in the mountains of Lebanon for six months. My father applied as a Spanish national to go back to Jerusalem, but the Israelis refused, because Spain had not recognized Israel at the time."

Nineteen years later, after the Israelis annexed East Jerusalem in the wake of the June 1967 War, the Kalbians finally had a chance to see their old family homes. Three weeks after the war ended, Vicken crossed over to Talbieh and knocked on the door of Number 4 Balfour Street. A stranger opened the door. "He was a Jewish Turk who had come to Israel in 1948," Vicken said. The man wasn't particularly friendly, but he had been expecting a Kalbian to show up. The brass Kalbian nameplate was still affixed to the house. He said, "I'm glad you came; all our neighbors have been expecting you." Vicken saw he had a young daughter.

It was unclear whether the Turk was renting the house or had bought it from someone. "He was very casual," Vicken said. "He obviously didn't believe he was doing anything wrong by living in the house. We didn't have any deep conversation." Vicken saw that his parents' chandelier still hung from the dining room ceiling.

Vicken went back again in 1999, to show the house to his grown daughters, Aline and Maral. (By then, they could visit Israel as American citizens.) "We opened the heavy iron gate and went into the garden. I was telling my daughters which room was mine, when the door opened and this woman came out . . . she was the girl I had seen in 1967, and now she was married and living there with her husband.

"She said, 'Dr. Kalbian.'

"And I said, 'How did you know?'

" 'Oh,' she replied, 'I heard you talking in English to your daughters . . . who else would know the history of this house?' "

The Israeli woman guided her visitors up to the attic, where she opened a dusty box containing some Kalbian family photos and an old clock. The woman graciously gave them the clock and photos.

After they walked through the old house—which had been turned into a number of apartments—the woman offered the Kalbians lemonade and candied apricots. Pointing to the apricots, she said, "This is from your tree."

Startled, Vicken said, "From my tree?"

"Yes," she replied, "everybody knows the story of how the young Kalbian boy decided that he would plant an apricot seed. Of course, people laughed at him and tried to explain that this was not how you get an apricot tree to grow. You need a seedling, not just a seed. But young Kalbian insisted his seed would take root."

And indeed, behind the kitchen was an apricot tree—and yes, Vicken remembered planting the apricot seed back in the late 1930s. "My daughters started to cry," Vicken said. And so did he.

Ada had a slightly more surreal encounter when she went back, with Vicken, to the German Colony in 1967 after the June war. Upon approaching the house, they saw two women and a boy standing on the balcony. One of the women nodded and said, "Shalom."

In reply Ada blurted out, almost defiantly, "I'm the owner of this house!"

"Oh, please come in," said the Israeli, "we didn't know why no one had come."

"They took us to the living room," Ada recalled, "which had been my parents' bedroom. They had made the house into two apartments. And then the young Jewish boy said, 'You know, you Arabs are terrible. You destroyed all our cemeteries.' I said, 'Would you like to talk about cemeteries? I just came from Mount Zion, and you people destroyed my grandfather's grave.' The Jewish boy replied, 'Maybe we should speak of something else.'

"As we were leaving one of them said, 'By the way, we bought the house.' I said, 'Excuse me, but I never sold this house. Who did you buy it from?'

"'We bought it from the Israeli government,'" she replied.

"I said, 'It didn't belong to them.' And then we marched out. I was so angry."

In 1967 the Kalbians took their property deeds to an Armenian lawyer in Jerusalem. He determined that their two homes were indeed registered with the Israeli Department of Absentee Property. Under Israeli law due compensation could be paid to the rightful owners—but only if they had not fled to a "hostile" nation like Lebanon, Jordan, Syria, Egypt or, indeed, anywhere in the Arab world, with the exception of Libya (because Libya's King Idris had not gone to war with Israel in 1948). The Israelis also handed any such absentee owners a bill for back taxes plus inflation and interest. The Kalbians' lawyer said they would have no case in an Israeli court. Vicken knew of only one fellow Palestinian who had retained his property, and that was a family who had fled to Libya and had rented their home to the Belgian consul. Disheartened by the Israeli occupation of Jerusalem, and resigned to their losses, the Kalbians eventually emigrated to America in 1968. "One day in 1968 I went to the Old City," Ada said, "and I happened to leave my identity card with Vicken. An Israeli soldier stopped me and demanded to see my papers. When I said that I didn't have them, he shoved his Uzi in my face and yelled at me. I just snapped; I screamed at him, 'Go ahead, shoot me.' I have nothing against the Jews, but I have a lot against the Israelis. I don't think there is ever going to be any peace."

My parents could not hear such stories without acquiring strongly partisan views. We saw the Kalbians nearly every day in East Jerusalem, and they were to remain among our closest friends for the next five decades. Eighteen months into their Jerusalem tour, my parents had long since thrown their sympathies entirely to the Palestinians.

"The situation here seems impossible," Mother wrote in 1957, "unendingly hopeless and without solution. I feel no sympathy for Zionism whatsoever and none for the Israeli society, and it is a thing which you almost have to see and feel for yourself to understand." The longer she lived in Jerusalem, the more indignant she became. For most Americans, and for much of the world, the Israelis appeared to be the victims. This infuriated Mother, who had come to believe that the Israelis had seized much of Palestine "by threat, murder, pillage—all the methods that we ascribe to the men who have persecuted the Jews. No Arab can see why he should be turned out of his home just because Nazis persecuted Jews, and neither can I. Yet the Arabs continue to lose their case in the public eye. . . ."

The evolution in my mother's views was not uncommon. Most expatriate diplomats or United Nations staff stationed in East Jerusalem arrived with an inclination to admire the energetic Israelis and their aspirations for a new homeland. But many soon had a change of heart. As the Israeli historian Mordechai Bar-On writes in *The Gates of Gaza,* the officers sent by the U.N. to monitor the armistice lines tended to side with the Arabs. One reason they did so, Bar-On suggests, was that the "local Arabs' almost colonial subservience was so much preferable to the aloofness, standoffishness, and outright disdain with which the Israelis treated them."

But as Bar-On points out, the Israelis' disdain was easily explained. In Israeli eyes, these U.N. officers were interlopers constantly interfering with Israeli efforts to defend their borders. "Only eight years ago we got rid of the British army and repulsed the attack of the Arab armies," said an Israeli officer who served as a liaison to the U.N. mission, "and now once again we have foreign soldiers wandering around to whom Israeli law does not apply."

Fundamentally, the U.N. observers and the Israelis had inherently conflicting goals. The Israelis wanted real, genuine peace—on their terms, of course—with the Arabs, and short of that they were determined to exercise sovereignty over every inch of territory under their control. And when an incident occurred, they were determined to retaliate with overwhelming force. Both the Arabs and the U.N. observers regarded the armistice lines as temporary—while the Israelis jealously guarded them as if they were sovereign borders.

In the autumn of 1957 tensions mounted over Mount Scopus when it became clear from U.N. aerial photos that the Israelis were fortifying what was supposed to be a demilitarized zone; they also barred U.N. observers from inspecting it. All of this was in violation of the Mount Scopus armistice agreement of July 7, 1948. In response, in mid-November, the Jordanians refused to allow the Israelis to send their twice-monthly resupply convoy through Mandelbaum Gate up to Mount Scopus. On a previous occasion, U.N. observers had caught the Israelis trying to smuggle guns inside oil drums filled with gasoline. This time an armed standoff ensued at Mandelbaum Gate and lasted for nearly two weeks. Father was deeply involved in the negotiations, together with U.N. and Israeli officials. "Such situations all seem ridiculous," he wrote home, "but behind the refusal of either party to give in on sending up a few barrels of gasoline lies the whole dispute." The convoy was finally allowed to proceed up to Mount Scopus only after the Secretary General of the United Nations, Dag Hammarskjöld, flew out to Jerusalem and met with Ben-Gurion and King Hussein. The U.N., in existence a little more than a decade, was nevertheless playing a crucial role in trying to keep the peace.

Most U.N. observers could not help but condemn the Israelis for the disproportionate number of casualties inflicted in the course of their retaliatory raids. By the midfifties, the lack of trust was palpable. U.N. officers were wounded or killed during encounters between the Israel Defense Forces and Jordan's Arab Legion. My parents often socialized with Lieutenant Colonel George Flint, a Canadian army officer who led the U.N.'s Israeli-Jordan Mixed Armistice Commission. Mother was a friend of his wife, Audrey, and their two teenage daughters. Everyone knew Flint had been badly wounded in July 1956 when a land mine exploded as he attempted to investigate a sniper incident on Mount Scopus. But then, in May 1958, a sporadic battle broke out on the slopes of Mount Scopus between Israeli and Jordanian army patrols. Four Israelis were killed and two wounded. Accompanied by Jordanian army officers, Lieutenant Colonel Flint attempted to impose a cease-fire so that the wounded Israelis could be evacuated. His party was carrying a white flag when shots rang out, apparently from the Jordanian side of the border. Flint, age forty-seven, was hit, and he bled to death before medics could reach him. He was the thirteenth U.N. representative to have been killed since the 1948 war.

Flint was probably killed by Jordanian sniper fire. But notwithstanding this, the U.N. personnel resented the Israelis for their stubborn determination to hold on to Mount Scopus, the scene of repeated bloody incidents. Inevitably, the growing animus between the Israelis and the U.N. filtered back to U.N. headquarters in New York, where even Hammarskjöld found the Israelis exasperating. Upon his return from Israel in the spring of 1956, Hammarskjöld told another U.N. official that "the underlying state of mind of the Israeli leadership was a combination of an inferiority complex and a fatalistic conviction that violence was their only weapon for survival. This was a very unhealthy, pathological attitude which was far more dangerous than the 'madness' of the Arabs. The Israelis were doomed as Oedipus. The Arabs were just plain crazy."

On April 24, 1958, the Israelis celebrated their tenth anniversary of independence with a big parade in West Jerusalem. "There is plenty of excitement in the air and more than a little tension," my mother wrote. "But I can now hear a big boom in the middle of the night, wonder sleepily if the Jews are shooting from Mount Scopus, decide it isn't worth investigating and go back to sleep."

Mother was by now thoroughly tired of the whole situation, and she looked forward to a new posting away from the conflict. "I would not welcome another tour in this part of the world," she wrote home that winter. Even Father seemed to be resigned to his own ineffectiveness. He wryly called himself a "feeble fireman . . . trying to alleviate tensions out here." Jerusalem was infecting my parents with its deeply entrenched sadness; it was a sectarian battlefield, no longer the "Holy City." No one could live very long in this brooding city of ancient hatreds without breathing in its tragedy and its melancholy. As Amos Oz wrote in *My Michael,* his novel set in 1950s Jerusalem, "Jerusalem is a remote city, even if you live there, even if you were born there."

Travel orders arrived from the State Department in the spring of 1958. We were to be posted back to Washington, DC, later that summer. "Kai was exuberant," Father observed.

In the early autumn of 1958, just after arriving back in Washington, I developed a near-fatal case of nephritis. My kidneys were failing. I was hospitalized for a month, while at the same time Mother was in another hospital with hepatitis and my sister Nancy was in yet another hospital with a bad case of measles. Poor Father spent his days running from one hospital

Kai, Giza, Egypt, 1958

to another. I vividly remember being tortured by the presence of a large clock on the wall above my hospital bed—every twelve hours precisely at ten o'clock the nurses were instructed to give me an injection of penicillin in the buttocks. I fought the nurses; it took three or four of them to hold me down.

Late that summer I was thought to have recovered—and so the State Department gave Father new travel orders. Now we were scheduled to move to Turkey in November. But before this could happen, I had a severe recurrence of nephritis. My kidneys swelled dangerously, and the doctors decided to operate—but they warned my parents that they didn't think they could save me. Fortunately, the day before the operation the surgeon ordered one more X-ray, which revealed that my kidneys had mysteriously shrunk back to normal size. The operation was canceled. I was out of danger but terribly weakened. For more than a year my physical activities were limited and closely monitored. Mother claims this brush with death at the age of six led to a character change; I became, if anything, more shy and introspective than ever.

Because of my bout with nephritis, we spent more than two years in Washington. My memories of America in these years are suburban. We lived in a two-bedroom ranch house in Springfield, Virginia, just across the Potomac

River from the capital. It was a new housing development, and nearly every house looked "ticky-tacky" like every other house. Our neighbor had an atomic bomb shelter dug in his backyard. It was fully stocked. "Where would *we* go when the Soviets fired their missiles?" I wondered. My public elementary school on Braddock Road routinely conducted atomic bomb "duck and cover" drills as did every other elementary school in America. It seemed like a pretty lame exercise.

One day in late 1959, Father received a call from an assistant to Under Secretary of State Loy Henderson. They were looking for a handsome young Foreign Service officer to be featured in a full-page advertisement about the attractions of a career in diplomacy. Father evidently filled the bill. A few weeks later, he posed in the courtyard of the recently built mosque on Massachusetts Avenue in downtown Washington. The photographer lent him his own leather briefcase as a prop. The photograph later appeared in *Life, Look* and the *Saturday Evening Post.*

Soon after this initiation in public relations, Father was designated to "defend" the State Department on David Garroway's *Today Show.* A political novel by Eugene Burdick and William Lederer, *The Ugly American,* had recently become a national best-seller, and the State Department thought the depiction of Foreign Service officers in this *roman à clef* about a fictional Asian country (a thinly veiled Vietnam) sullied the department's reputation. Father did his best to deny that Foreign Service officers were "ugly Americans." He read the book, and drawing on his own experience in Jerusalem, he tried to suggest that his colleagues worked hard to integrate themselves into foreign cultures, often in difficult circumstances. Alas, the interview segment included footage of a Foreign Service officer in Latin America complaining that she couldn't buy Kleenex in the embassy commissary. Case closed.

In September 1960, my sister Shelly was born. That same year, Father applied to study Hebrew at the Foreign Service Institute. He wanted to specialize in the Middle East, and he thought he'd like to be posted to Israel. But only one other FSO applied for Hebrew-language training, so the class was canceled and Father was instead assigned to Arabic. The two-year program entailed studying the language in Washington the first year, while the second year was spent in Beirut, Lebanon. So late in the summer of 1961 we shipped out on an American Export Lines passenger ship, the SS *Excalibur,* bound for Beirut. That year, we lived on the third floor of the U.S.

Embassy building, right across from the *corniche*. I attended fifth grade at the American International School, which was just a ten-minute walk down the *corniche*. On weekends, we'd swim in the blue-green waters of the Mediterranean and perhaps have lunch at St. George's Hotel, where Kim Philby and numerous other spies and journalists drank whisky in the evenings. That winter we went skiing in the mountains. Occasionally, I bought delicious *shwarma* sandwiches (thinly sliced grilled lamb) from street vendors. For a treat, Mother would take us to my favorite hamburger joint, Uncle Sam's. Beirut had everything.

After nearly two years of language study, Father was finally given a new posting, in the heart of Arabia.

3

The Magic Kingdom

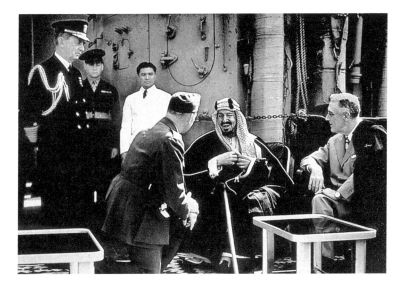

Colonel William A. Eddy, kneeling, translating for King Abdul-Aziz
al-Saud and President Franklin Roosevelt, aboard a U.S. warship in
the Great Bitter Lake, February 1945

*I gather the Chiefs also wonder whether this flea-bitten part of the world
is one where we should get involved. I'm afraid we are involved here
long since—even though it may have been a mistake in the first place.
But remember oil.*

McGeorge Bundy, National Security Adviser to
President Kennedy, January 11, 1963

On July 28, 1962, we boarded a brand-new Boeing 720B jetliner in
Beirut bound for Dhahran, Saudi Arabia. Aside from the crew and
three other passengers, the plane was empty. It was a new route for Saudi
Airlines, operated by the American airline TWA, and the crew was delivering the aircraft to Arabia. Less than two hours later we landed in Dhahran
on a tarmac built by the American military in 1945–46. The cabin door

opened, and a rush of wet, hot air assaulted us. For a few seconds I thought it was the heat exhaust from the jet engines. It was like stepping into a humid sauna. In the summer months the normal daytime temperature in the Kingdom of Saudi Arabia, as measured in the shade, hovered at 120 degrees Fahrenheit. It wasn't dry heat either; because the Arabian Sea was just a few miles to the east, the humidity could often rise to 80 percent. My mother called it "the Arabian oven."

Waiting for us inside Dhahran's lovely white airport terminal were several members of the consular staff. The pleasantly air-conditioned terminal, built in 1961, had been designed by the famous Japanese-American architect Minoru Yamasaki, who then went on to design the Twin Towers that would be taken down by the 9/11 hijackers—fifteen of whom were Saudis. We were driven just four miles down the road to the compound of the American consulate. This little community contained a dozen single-family homes and the office quarters of the U.S. consulate general. Built in the years 1947–51 at a cost of $600,000, the compound occupied fifty-five acres on the northeastern slope of a gently sloping hill. (It was also the site where Abdul-Aziz ibn Abdul al-Rahman al-Saud, the founder of the Saudi Kingdom, had pitched 350 tents in April 1939, when he and his royal retinue, some 2,700 strong, first visited the newly discovered oil wells in Dhahran.)

From the consul general's two-story residence on top of the hill, one could see the sparkling blue glimmer of the Arabian Sea and beyond it in the haze, the island of Bahrain. About a mile to the north stood the "American Camp" of the Arabian American Oil Company (Aramco). In 1933, Standard Oil Company California (Socal) had won a concession to explore for oil. A few years later, Socal formed a consortium with Texaco, Exxon and Mobil to manage the concession. Oil was first discovered in March 1938 at Jebal (hill) Dhahran. A quarter century and millions of barrels later, oil wellhead Dammam No. 7 was still producing over a thousand barrels of oil per day. Clearly, we were there—and the consulate existed—only because Aramco was pumping oil and shipping it to America.

A four-foot-high rock wall enclosed our compound, but often the desert winds would pile up so much sand against the outer side that camels and goats could walk right over the wall. In the spring and summer the northern sky would suddenly turn dark brown, or burnt orange, signaling the onslaught of a *shamal,* a fierce sandstorm that blew in hot northwesterly winds with stinging sand for two or three days at a time. *Shamal*s were often so thick that visibility was reduced to a few feet. They could sting the paint off automobiles. In the winter these sandstorms blew colder winds and were called *samoum*s. The house was always a bit sandy.

The consulate compound had its own generator for electricity, its own septic system and water tower and well. Every building except for the workshop was efficiently air-conditioned. From the glassed-in porch of our small stone-block two-bedroom house all we could see for miles was flat desert interspersed with the occasional *jebel* and a bit of scrubby vegetation. The only greenery in the compound was a few scrawny eucalyptus trees and two dozen baby Washington palm trees, planted the previous year, that lined the one paved road up the hill from the consulate to the consul general's residence. A solitary thirty-foot date palm—resembling the Saudi national emblem—stood in the circular driveway in front of that residence. Scattered about the compound were a few bougainvillea bushes that added a touch of color in the winter months—the only time it ever rained. Gas flares burned night and day in the surrounding *jebel*s. The distinctive whiff of sulfur was often in the air. A previous vice-consul, Frank Melloy, had jocularly labeled the flares "The flames of Hell!" (Melloy was later ambassador to Lebanon— where he was assassinated in 1976 during the Lebanese civil war.)

Dhahran was a "true hardship post," my mother explained to a friend back in Oregon. Our home—House No. 6—had two bedrooms for a family of five. Groceries—even bread—were difficult to find on the local market. Lettuce and other vegetables had to be washed in warm water and detergent. The stone-and-cement house was furnished with dilapidated ten-year-old furniture and a tiny refrigerator. Unlike our home in Jerusalem, the house had a phone, and its number was simply "thirty-four." There were no locks on the doors. When Mother asked the consulate's administrative officer for locks, he blithely answered that no one had locks, there was virtually no crime in Arabia. But he promised that new furniture was on order—and my mother was very glad she had shipped a freezer from Beirut.

Father was to be paid a 25 percent hardship allowance. Eight Foreign Service officers lived in the compound; as "economic officer," Father was ranked number three, after Consul General Jack Horner and the political officer. Across the street lived Robert Ames, a tall, strikingly handsome young CIA officer who operated under the cover of the "reserve" Foreign Service. He liked to wear hand-tooled cowboy boots. Like my father, Ames was learning Arabic. (He would die twenty-one years later in the April 1983 bombing that wiped out the entire CIA station in the American embassy in Beirut.) Together with a squad of five U.S. Marines, support staff, code clerks, and all their dependents, the compound housed some thirty-five Americans and their families.

We felt like we were living on another planet. Mother called it the "last frontier of the Arab world." The nearest town, al-Khobar, was six miles south, a tiny ramshackle port that Mother described as "just a lot of scrubby buildings in the middle of the sand and hot." In the sixties—unlike today— foreign women did not have to cover themselves with the black *abaya* or wear a scarf to cover their hair. When Mother went to al-Khobar, she wore short sleeves and dresses that covered her knees. She never had any unpleasant encounters with the bamboo-wielding religious police, the Mutawah, officially known as the Committee for the Propagation of Virtue and the Prevention of Vice.

What made our existence feel truly surreal was the piece of Texas down the road. Aramco's "American Camp" was a one-square-mile compound surrounded by a high chain-link fence. Company guards carefully monitored the one gate in and out of the compound. No one was allowed to enter without an Aramco identity card that featured both a photograph and a thumbprint. Inside you might as well have been in a Dallas suburb— except that daily life here was demarcated by the periodic blasts of company sirens, announcing the beginning of the workday, the lunch hour and the end of the workday at 5:00 p.m. The "Aramcons" lived in ranch-style one-story stone or white-clapboard homes with pitched red roofs and screened porches. There were also some simple "portables" and dormitory-style housing for bachelors. The homes were uniformly landscaped with green lawns, jasmine shrubbery and pink oleander hedges. Black asphalt streets were laid out in semicircles. In the hub of this pristine suburban town lay Aramco's main administrative building—nicknamed the "Kremlin." There were an elementary and junior high school, a commissary, swimming pools, a movie theatre, a bowling alley and a baseball field on "King's Road." There were tennis courts, a horse stable and a golf course—where the putting green was sand sprayed with oil. When Mary Eddy, the wife of the veteran OSS and CIA officer Bill Eddy, first saw the American Camp, she wrote home, "The oil town at Dhaharan [*sic*] is just like a bit of USA. . . ."

The Saudis refused Aramco permission to build any churches, so Aramcons attended services in a large auditorium. Three denominations—Catholic, Episcopalian and Baptist—shared an altar that could be folded up and hidden away like a Murphy bed. We went to the Episcopalian services; Mother directed the choir and played the organ. The Saudis permitted a Catholic priest, an Episcopalian minister and a Baptist preacher to live in the American Camp. Their Saudi visas identified them as "educators," and they did not wear their priestly collars or other clerical garments except inside the auditorium. My sister Nancy and I were both confirmed by the Episcopal archbishop of Jerusalem, who was permitted a discreet visit to the Kingdom in 1964.

"It was like the TV show *Mayberry*," recalled one longtime Aramcon. People socialized a lot, freely dropping by one another's homes—which all looked alike. Children ran about the camp unsupervised. Women were allowed to drive inside the camp—though not outside. There were lots of ten- and fifteen-year-old Chevys and VW Bugs, all rusted out from the Arabian Gulf's humidity and their paint battered from sandstorms. Aramcons called them their "camp cars." The company went to extraordinary lengths to provide normal social activities. When the local Girl Scouts went on a camping trip, the company sent along a refrigerator truck to keep their food cold. It also sponsored a Little League season, bowling tournaments and sailing regattas at Half Moon Bay. On Christmas, Santa Claus arrived in camp on a donkey or camel. "Dhahran was a utopia," said Carolyn Daily, a longtime resident of the camp.

Foreigners served jailtime or were expelled if caught trying to bring a bottle of scotch into the country, but walk into any Aramcon's home and invariably you could smell the distinctive whiff of home brew, whether beer, wine (made from canned blackberries) or, more often than not, something that would pass for vodka, distilled in the bathroom or garage, using large pressure cookers, coils of copper tubing and huge glass crocks. New residents were handed a leaflet titled *The Blue Flame*—named for the blue flame that heats a still—which listed the safety precautions necessary for operating a still without blowing it up. If there was a fire or explosion, Aramco would allow the Saudi police to enter the camp—but it was understood that they would try to delay the police as long as politely possible so the guilty parties had a chance to clean up the evidence. Aramcons called their home brew *sadiki*—Arabic for "my friend."

My parents, for their part, had no need of a still. As the number-three man in the consulate, Father had as one of his duties that of flying every few weeks to Bahrain and returning the same day with a large suitcase jammed with two dozen bottles of Johnnie Walker Black. His black diplomatic passport permitted him to bypass any customs inspection.

King Abdul-Aziz had banned alcohol from his realm in 1953, when a Saudi prince shot and killed a British expatriate in Jeddah during a drunken rage. But by the sixties, the Saudis were turning a blind eye toward the hundreds of stills operating in Dhahran and the two other Aramco towns, Ras Tanura and Abqaiq. As one Aramcon later wrote, the Saudis must have realized that "without booze, there would be no Americans, and without Americans, the oil would remain in the ground."

With a population of some 2,500, Dhahran's American Camp represented the world's single largest concentration of overseas Americans. In some ways, it was modeled after the sterile company mining towns of the American West. But here there were no old people, and no children older than fourteen; Aramcons sent their teenagers to boarding schools in Europe or America. There were no dogs, because Saudis consider them unclean and therefore banned their importation. (They made an exception for their native breed, the Saluki, a sleek hunting dog the Bedouin used to chase down gazelles.) There were no maids—but some Aramcons hired Yemeni or African houseboys. There were no real restaurants or grocery stores. There were no billboards or advertising of any kind. There was a company cafeteria, and snack bars at the swimming pools. There were no widows, orphans or handicapped people. Neither were there African-Americans or Jews. (Nora Johnson, who later wrote a memoir of her time in Dhahran, claimed that anti-Semitic jokes were "freely" told at Aramco parties.)

In the autumn of 1963 an American sociologist, Thomas F. O'Dea, produced a report for Aramco on social change in Saudi Arabia. O'Dea wrote that although "Americans were foreigners and the Saudis were citizens of a politically independent country, the Americans were in an effective sense those who occupied the positions of power." By 1963 Aramco had promoted some 70 Saudis out of nearly 12,000 Saudi workers to senior staff positions. O'Dea bluntly observed that "there is a general resentment of Americans all having Senior Staff status, and of their residence in a fenced-in area. . . ."

O'Dea's interviews in Dhahran unearthed specific resentments against the rising number of U.S. Air Force personnel. Saudis told him they thought the American airmen were in Dhahran to protect the royal family and not the average Saudi. Aramco's executives were so shocked by O'Dea's conclusions that they suppressed his report.

Saudi laborers worked the oil fields alongside their American counterparts, but they were confined to bachelor barracks outside the compound. Naturally, the Aramcons called it the "Saudi camp"—and the racists among them derisively referred to the Saudis as "coolies." In the 1950s, signs were posted reserving various public toilets and water fountains for Americans only. In the early 1960s, only a handful of Saudis, educated in America or Beirut, were qualified by rank to live in the American Camp—but even these often chose to live outside.

By the time our family arrived in Dhahran in 1962, the apartheid-like culture of the American Camp had lost its rougher edges. I never saw signs saying "Americans only." I never heard Saudis referred to as "coolies." But then, my parents socialized with Aramco's intellectuals, men like Dr. George Rentz (1912–1987), a company historian who immersed himself in the history and culture of the Arabian Peninsula. As one Aramcon memoirist later wrote, "The intellectuals of Dhahran put up with the town and cherish the Muslim culture and the barren challenge of the land; the less inspired ones cherish, with equal fervor, the startling efficiency with which the oil company has imported all the comforts and mediocrity of home—the fact that Dhahran is more Statelike than the States—and they consider the Arabs repulsive."

Sometimes on weekends Father would drive us out across the desert. We had a Nash Rambler station wagon equipped with "double tires"—meaning there were two inflation valves and no inner tube. This made it possible to deflate part of the tire, turning it into a wide-tread sand tire. Our objective was to find a collection of burial mounds dating back to the Roman Empire. We'd have a picnic on the desert floor and then walk around the mounds, looking for bits of ancient Roman glass or coins. One Aramcon couple, Bert and Marnie Golding, calling themselves amateur archaeologists, spent their weekends scouring the desert floor, searching for various artifacts. Over the years they amassed a prized collection of pottery, ancient coins and other pieces of pre-Islamic art—much of which they donated to Dr. Abdullah Masri, Arabia's first professional archaeologist.

Occasionally, during these day trips across the desert, we'd come across an encampment of the "White Army"—descendants of the Ikhwan, the legendary Wahhabi shock-troops used by King Abdul-Aziz ibn Saud to unify the Kingdom. These present-day Ikhwan (the Brethren) were always on the move, pitching their emblematic white tents by the hundred. They dressed in white *thobes,* billowing robes cut short above the ankle, because they believed the Prophet himself had decreed that garments that touched the ground were pretentious. They covered their long black hair with white muslin turbans or the traditional Bedouin red-and-white-checkered *ghutra.* But they eschewed the *iqal,* the thick black rope that usually held the *ghutra* in place, because this was also thought to be pretentious, as the Prophet was not known to have worn an *iqal.* They grew their beards long and jammed curved *jambiyah* knives into leather bandoliers. Each man carried a long, often ancient rifle. They still rode camels—though they also had a fleet of trucks and jeeps to carry their supplies.

The Ikhwan had begun in 1912 as a simple Wahhabi revivalist movement in the bleak village of al-Artawiya, 160 miles northeast of Riyadh. Hearing of their zealotry, Abdul-Aziz encouraged the Ikhwan to grow, drawing new recruits from various Bedouin tribes. This served two purposes for him: one,

Abdul-Aziz al-Saud's camel cavalry, central Arabia, 1911

to domesticate the Bedouin and end their wanton raiding parties; and two, to provide him with the shock troops he needed to unify a main part of the Arabian Peninsula under his rule. By the end of World War I, the Ikhwan had grown to a ruthless force of some 60,000 men. Over the next dozen years, they massacred thousands of men from recalcitrant tribes—and gave Abdul-Aziz a kingdom. But then in 1928–29, the Ikhwan turned on Abdul-Aziz and challenged his authority. He brutally suppressed this rebellion, using armored motorcades and modern machine guns to kill thousands. In the aftermath of one battle, some 250 captive Ikhwan were mercilessly beheaded. By the end of 1929, Abdul-Aziz had vanquished the rebels.

By the 1960s, a reconstituted "White Army" was being folded into a newly established National Guard. These hardened Bedouin warriors have remained both an ally and a lingering threat to the House of Saud. Their uncompromising fundamentalism persists as a powerful cultural influence. Needless to say, we always avoided driving into their encampments.

When I visited the Aramco camp, I sometimes felt like the foreigner. These were not the kind of Americans I had encountered in Washington, DC, or as an expatriate in Jerusalem or Beirut. Most of the Aramcons were oil-drillers, chemists, engineers or corporate managers. And most were from the flat-lands of Texas, Oklahoma or the Midwest. They were latter-day American cowboys who had come to the desert Kingdom for a few years or even a decade or two to earn the high salaries Aramco paid. Some wore jeans with silver buckles, cowboy hats and boots. They called Arabia the "Magic King-dom." "They were a rough, proud, stubborn and hard-drinking race," wrote an Aramcon in his memoirs. Some of these roughnecks called the Saudis "ragheads." (The Saudis referred to the Americans as "Nasranis"—followers of the man from Nazareth—an accurate, though to them equally disparag-ing label.)

If the Aramcons saw themselves as "cowboys," bringing modern civiliza-tion to the "Indians" of Arabia, it was the Saudis who kept the "cowboys" confined as much as possible inside a reservation. "You Americans don't understand," one Saudi prince told an Aramco executive, "the fence around Dhahran wasn't built to keep Saudis out. It was built to keep you Americans in." Saudi authorities feared that the "cowboys" might arouse the ire of the Wahhabi *ulema* (clergy).

King Abdul-Aziz and Crown Prince Saud, Riyadh, October 1951

King Abdul-Aziz ibn Saud had agreed to admit the American oil explorers into Arabia in 1933 in exchange for an initial payment of $175,000 in gold sovereigns. Eighteen months later, Abdul-Aziz would get another $100,000, and if oil was discovered the oil companies promised an immediate loan of $500,000, and a 50 percent royalty on the sale of any crude oil. The concession agreement gave Aramco a monopoly on oil production for sixty years. It was the beginning of a long and profitable partnership between America and the House of Saud. In 1933, Abdul-Aziz desperately needed the gold to pay off his debts to local merchants and to buy the loyalty of his tribesmen. (He was also hoping the geologists might find water as they drilled for oil.) Initially, a half dozen American geologists broke up into teams of two men each to scour the desert in trucks with bloated sand tires. Abdul-Aziz made sure that a guide and an escort of a dozen Bedouin troops accompanied each pair. This was for their protection, but also to make sure that his subjects were not exposed to forbidden—*haram*—behavior. These scouting parties kept to the vast empty desert and avoided the towns and villages where Wahhabism was most fiercely practiced.

Initially, it was easy for Abdul-Aziz to hide this handful of Americans from his subjects. His desert realm was vast, nearly the size of America east of the Mississippi, with barely three million people. But after the Americans struck oil in March 1938, suddenly hundreds and then thousands of foreign unbelievers began to arrive.

Abdul-Aziz insisted on excluding the Nejd—the Wahhabi heartland—

from Aramco's concessionary territory because he feared that his Wahhabi tribesmen might revolt at the presence of heathen geologists. Even in the early 1960s very few foreigners were allowed to travel to the Kingdom's capital, Riyadh, and even fewer were permitted to live there. Foreign legations were confined to the more liberal Hejazi port city of Jeddah.

But while King Abdul-Aziz wanted his Americans to discreetly segregate themselves and their strange culture from his people, he did not expect them to treat Saudi oil workers as second-class citizens in their own country. The decision to build a "company town" surrounded by barbed-wire fences and housing Americans exclusively was Aramco's preference. And, as the political scientist Robert Vitalis argues in his book *America's Kingdom,* it was a preference grounded in the culture of American mining towns. But as the American Camp at Dhahran grew and its living conditions became the envy of disgruntled Saudi workers, the king's men made it clear to Aramco that they were unhappy with such disparities. As early as 1948, the king's finance minister, Abdullah Sulaiman, "pressed the point that living conditions of the Arab employees must approach that provided for the Americans. . . ." Sulaiman told Aramco executives that they should plan their camp layouts "so that eventually senior Arab family housing will merge into the American camp." Aramco didn't listen.

Father's work was particularly demanding in this harsh environment. Within weeks of our arrival he was dealing with Aramco officials, Persian Gulf political agents and Saudi businessmen. In August 1962, he was summoned to his first *majlis* with the emir of the Eastern Province, Saud bin Jiluwi, a second cousin of the late King Abdul-Aziz. The emir had ruled Hasa Province (recently renamed the Eastern Province) since 1935 with an executioner's sword. He was universally known as the "head-chopper." He was also Arabia's second-largest slaveholder and landowner after the king himself. (Many, though not all, of these slaves were black Africans.) On this occasion bin Jiluwi roasted several sheep, which were served on heaping mounds of rice. The U.S. consul general, Father and several Aramco officials sat cross-legged on deep-red Bokhara carpets. Father was ceremoniously offered the eye of a lamb. He popped it into his mouth and gamely swallowed it. Afterwards, Father wrote that he couldn't help being impressed by "the tremendous dignity of these people."

Emir Jiluwi, governor of the Eastern Province and
Consul Gene Bird, 1964

After two years of study, Father's Arabic was adequate for street conversations, but problematical for any serious political negotiations. A few weeks after arriving in Dhahran, he wrote home, "The Saudis are among the most difficult of the Arabs to work with." His job as economic officer required him to learn the oil business, and that meant getting to know a wide cast of characters in the American Camp. By 1962, Arabia was all about oil, and with its monopoly on Saudi oil production, Aramco was driving the country's economy. So far as Saudis—both royals and commoners—could see, Aramco was America. The cultural divide between them and their American guests was both wide and deep. Too often Aramcons were culturally deaf and ignorant of Saudi history and social mores. Arabia was not only a distant and strange place, it was in another time.

Aramco's chief executive officer and president in the 1960s was Tom Barger. My parents got to know Tom and Kathleen Barger quite well. Father played handball with Tom once or twice a week, and I went horseback riding with their daughters nearly every day. The Bargers were an extraordinary couple. Tom, born and raised in North Dakota, was trained as a mining engineer and geologist. He taught engineering at the University of North Dakota, worked as a mining engineer in the Arctic Circle and finally, in the midst of the Depression, was reduced to taking employment as a gold miner in Montana. He was only twenty-eight years old in 1937 when he became one of a dozen geologists recruited for a three-year contract for the California Arabian Standard Oil Company—a subsidiary of Standard Oil of California (Socal). His pay was $300 a month plus expenses, a good wage at the time. Before flying off to Arabia, Barger married Kathleen Ray, the coquettish daughter of a North Dakota rancher, and an expert horsewoman in the local rodeos. (Because his parents disapproved of Kathleen, Tom had to marry her in secrecy.) On December 1, 1937, Barger took a steamship from New York to Southampton, and from there he boarded a flying boat to Alexandria, Egypt. In Alexandria he transferred to a four-engine biplane that flew to Bahrain Island in the Persian Gulf. Two weeks after leaving New York, Barger sailed twenty miles in a dhow from Bahrain and landed on a half-finished pier in al-Khobar. That afternoon he happened to catch a glimpse of Crown Prince Saud, who was on his way to Bahrain to pick up a brand-new Studebaker.

Tom Barger, president of Aramco, and Mother, 1964

For the next three years Barger traveled all over Arabia in a Ford station wagon, accompanied by several Bedouin soldiers and a couple of other American geologists. In his first letters home he referred to these Arabs as "coolies," but his letters soon conveyed a deepening admiration for their survival skills in a forbidding environment. Barger learned enough Arabic to have simple conversations with Bedouin he met on these mapping expeditions. Weaving between sand dunes that sometimes towered 200 or

300 feet, he learned to appreciate the patience and resilience of his Bedouin guides. He was also helped by his reading of *Travels in Arabia Deserta,* the 1875 book by the great British explorer Charles M. Doughty. Barger was a perfect corporate envoy to the Saudis. Some called him the "conscience of Aramco."

Barger was well aware of Saudi sensitivities. In 1939 he was appalled one day to learn of an incident involving Crown Prince Saud ibn Abdul-Aziz. The prince was visiting the Eastern Province and showed up unexpectedly at a well site. He explained to "Ed," the American oil-rigger in charge, that he wanted to see the drill rig in operation. It happened then to be shut down, and, though it would have been easy enough to give the emir a demonstration, Ed refused and rudely walked away. "To Ed, the Prince was just another Bedouin bothering him," Barger wrote his wife. Saud was offended, and later that evening he sent forty troops to the American encampment and seized all the barrels containing their drinking water. "Some Americans here," Barger observed, "forget whose country this is and that we are here on the sufferance of Ibn Saud."

One of Barger's early mapping expeditions, in 1939, took him into the Rub' al-Khali, the great desert expanse known in English as the Empty Quarter. Only two other Western explorers—Bertram Thomas in 1930 and Harry St. John Philby in 1932—had crossed this desert, both of them on camels. Barger did it by station wagon and truck. Often the Bedouin he encountered had never seen an automobile. By the time my father made a similar trip by Land Rover in 1963, the Bedouins he met often had pickup trucks as well as camels. These were people who often went for months with very little water, surviving on camel's milk, dates and occasionally goat or sheep.

The arrival of Americans in some parts of Arabia was something akin to science fiction stories of human encounters with aliens from another planet. In his 1984 *Cities of Salt,* the Saudi novelist Abdelrahman Munif described the American arrival through Saudi eyes: "With the first light of dawn, huge iron machines began to move. Their deafening noise filled the whole wadi. So gigantic and strange were these iron machines that no one had ever imagined such things even existed. . . . When the machines stopped, small windows and doors opened up in them and dusty men came out and looked around them. A bewildered silence reigned: Where had these men been? How had they entered and come out of these machines? Were they men or devils? Why were they there, and what would they do? These yellow iron hulks—could a man approach them without injury? What were they for and how did they behave—did they eat like animals, or not?"

Munif's books were surprisingly popular with Saudis—though officially banned. When *Cities of Salt* was initially published in Arabic, black-market copies were selling in Riyadh for nearly $200. The royal family was outraged by the author's veiled depiction of Saudi princes as hypocritical, corrupt and pliant agents of the American infidels. To be sure, some of Munif's descriptions of these first American-Saudi encounters were novelistic exaggerations. The Bedouin were, in fact, often surprisingly adaptable in the face of the new machinery. By the early sixties, a common sight on the roads around Dhahran was a Bedouin driving a small Chevy pickup with a large camel kneeling in the flatbed, evidence of Saudi adaptation to modern ways.

Munif was born in Jordan, but his father was a merchant of Saudi origins. Educated in Cairo and Belgrade, he earned a doctorate in petroleum economics. But he then turned to writing, and his massive novels are drenched in the politics of radical Arab nationalism. His fiction also mourns the sullying of an ancient heritage; oil, he believed, had corrupted a whole way of life. "Before the oil the desert man was thin as a stick," Munif said in a 1985 interview, "now he is as round as a barrel of oil. This is against the law of nature. Man in that desert world used to follow his camel all day long and be content with a little bit of milk and dates. He would stay strong and lean, able to handle the adversity of the physical world around him. This enabled him to survive and adapt. How are we to compare that man of days past with what we have today?"

Munif's "desert man thin as a stick" was no doubt an overromanticized portrayal; the Bedouin were thin, after all, because they were always hungry. But in Munif's view, if the desert Arab had been rescued from the cruel adversities of his natural environment, this had come at a severe cost to his dignity and independence. The explorer Wilfred Thesiger, writing in his 1959 book *Arabian Sands,* echoes this romantic theme: "Now it is not death but degradation which faces them." Driven from the desert into the consumer culture of the cities, these Bedouin Arabs find jobs working for foreigners extracting oil. Now they have money but no freedoms or political rights. The climax of Munif's *Cities of Salt* lies in a fictionalized account of a Saudi labor strike against Aramco in the 1950s. The royal family found the book to be hostile to both the House of Saud and Aramco. In 1963—long before any of his books were published—Munif was one of a handful of dissidents who were exiled and stripped of their Saudi citizenship.

The stark contrast in culture, religion and living standards between the Americans and the Saudis led to resentments—and outright conflict. In May 1953 a dozen Saudi workers submitted a petition signed by 154 "intermediate skilled" Aramco employees demanding better housing and higher salaries. Their leader was a young man named Abdul-Aziz Abu Sunayd who had started working for Aramco as an office boy. Sunayd had worked his way up and taken advantage of the company's numerous training programs. In 1951, he had been sent to the American University of Beirut, and he then spent a year in Long Island, New York, teaching Arabic to Aramco employees bound for Arabia. But when he got back to Dhahran, Sunayd chafed at Saudi societal restrictions and became increasingly disaffected from both the monarchy and Aramco. "The government is for princes," he told an American Aramcon. "And the company is for Americans. . . . I am no longer a Saudi. But also I am nothing else."

Such existential angst was more common than the Aramcons realized. Arabia was literally undergoing modernization in one generation. And Sunayd's disaffection was quite clearly inflamed by the company's segregation policies. In May 1953, Sunayd wrote to Aramco's president to complain that he had been turned away at the American Camp's movie theatre—he had wanted to see Charlie Chaplin's *Limelight*—and this had only reminded him of how he had been treated when he visited Washington, DC, still then very much a segregated Southern city. Shortly afterwards, Sunayd rashly decided to challenge Aramco—and by extension, the al-Sauds.

At the time, Aramco was paying its Saudi workers about $110 a month, which compared quite favorably to some European pay scales in those years. But what mattered to the Saudis was the vast social and economic gulf between them and the Americans. William Eddy, a CIA asset who was employed by Aramco's Arab Affairs Division, attributed the labor unrest to "workers who compared this primitive land of low pay, slaves, eunuchs and harems to the comfortable conditions of U.S. residents in Dhahran, plus probably Red stimulation." When negotiations with Sunayd and his fellow coworkers stalled in mid-October, Saudi authorities imprisoned eleven of the leading protesters. The next day angry demonstrators attacked the police station and stoned Aramco vehicles. Crowds marched on the American consulate. Within days 17,000 out of 19,000 Saudi employees of Aramco were on strike. In response the government dispatched 1,000 troops into the Saudi worker camps; they arrested hundreds, and some fifty workers were deported to Riyadh. On October 27 the strike collapsed. Aramco nevertheless agreed to raise wages and improve housing conditions. But the government sentenced Sunayd and his comrades on the strike committee to ten years of internal exile in their respective villages. Sunayd was lucky to be left alive. On November 1, 1953, he was stripped of his citizenship and expelled across the Iraqi border.

The strike revealed disturbing fissures in Aramco's position in the Kingdom. The striking workers had legitimate labor grievances, but they were obviously influenced as well by the winds of Arab nationalism blowing in the region, and their resentments were also fueled by the condescending behavior of Aramcons, most of whom blamed the strike on the Saudis' supposed ignorance. "Of course," wrote one Aramcon housewife, "the poor ignorant [Arab workers don't] even know what is what about anything, so [are] very easily led by things." In 1955 Tom Barger wrote that the "growing dislike for Americans . . . in some instances has been justified by the attitude and behavior of some of our own people."

It was about this time that Barger launched a campaign within the American Camp to discourage the use of racist or disparaging labels. But he also realized that some level of disgruntlement was inevitable. "No matter what we would do," wrote one of Aramco's Arab experts, "the Saudis in the front of development will be unhappy. Although they are leading their fellows in progress, they are accordingly all the more keenly aware that they are not receiving the benefits, and are not treated by most Americans, the same as an American employee. . . . The apparent leaders of this strike (and I'm sure there are others undercover) are the bright boys who we have been able to bring along fastest. They are the intelligentsia. Tom Barger tells me that [the historian Arnold J.] Toynbee says the intelligentsia always are unhappy and discontented."

There was also the Shi'a factor. Because Aramco had traditionally drawn its labor force from the Eastern Province, a large number, perhaps a majority, of its workers were Shi'ite Muslims, and the Shi'ites in general always felt themselves discriminated against by the Kingdom's Sunni Wahhabi majority. The emir of the Eastern Province, the much-feared "head-chopper,"

Saud bin Jiluwi, routinely referred to the Shi'ites as "dogs." When Aramco was hit with another strike in the spring of 1956, the emir arrested some two hundred workers and had three of them publicly beaten to death. Thereafter, the king banned all strikes.*

By the time we arrived in Dhahran in 1962, Aramco's Saudi workforce had shrunk nearly 50 percent from its high mark of 24,000—and many of those let go were Shi'ites. Hundreds of Palestinian refugees, suspected of being under the sway of secular Arab nationalism, were also fired during these years. In the summer of 1964 disgruntled Saudi workers briefly boycotted Aramco facilities, charging that the "average Saudi employee" lacked any future in the company. When interviewed by an Aramco Arabist, they "complained that Mr. Barger is a Jew [which he wasn't], in the sense that he is tight-fisted and *bakhil* (a miser)." As a boy of twelve, I was blissfully unaware of this history, but I do remember visiting the squalid shantytowns in the largely Shi'a port town of Qatif.

Royalist Arabia was home to vast oil reserves—so it also attracted the notice of intelligence agents, analysts and government relations experts. Mike Ameen arrived in Dhahran in 1953 at the age of twenty-eight. A former Marine and FBI agent, he had grown up in a family of Lebanese-Americans in Massachusetts. While working on an FBI case involving a car-theft ring in Saudi Arabia, Ameen was introduced by the Saudi ambassador to an Aramco official. Aramco promptly recruited him and sent him to work in Aramco's Government Relations Department. From 1958 through 1971 he was one of the few Americans living in Riyadh, serving in effect as Aramco's ambassador to the king. Speaking fluent Arabic, he seemed to know everyone and everything. "He was a diplomat, a master of bunkum, hokum and flattery," wrote an Aramco official. "He was a smooth talking man who could minimize the sound of a negative." Ameen saw the king, the crown prince and other influential royals and commoners on a daily basis. If a royal needed something, it was his job to provide it.

------

*The leader of this strike, Nasser Said, was exiled to Beirut, where he formed a dissident group that called itself the Arabian Peninsula People's Union. A relatively minor thorn in the regime's side, Said was nevertheless kidnapped by Saudi intelligence agents in December 1979 and shipped to Riyadh in a crate. He languished in prison there for many years.

Diplomats like my father envied Ameen's access to the royal family. While Father liked the very likable Ameen, who in the right circumstances could be a garrulous, profane and entertaining raconteur, what rankled was the fact that the Saudis accorded Aramco executives like Ameen prerogatives normally reserved for the diplomatic corps. American ambassadors to Saudi Arabia invariably complained that the king and his ministers had grown used "to dealing with Aramco as they would with representatives of a foreign government." Saudi royals knew that if they wanted something done quickly and discreetly, Aramco was the place to go. "I am no socialist," my father wrote in October 1962, "but when an American corporation earning a clear profit of a million dollars a day has the attitude these people have towards American government representatives it galls me. The company is well-run, efficient, and as coldly calculating about the operation as one could find anywhere."

Even worse, the Aramcons learned that if they desired something from the U.S. government, they had to go to the CIA, not the State Department. During the Cold War, it was not unusual for the CIA station chief in any particular country to have more cachet than the ambassador. More often than not, the "spooks" operated under diplomatic cover, but they reported directly back to CIA headquarters. They had separate communications and, inevitably, a far larger budget, for both salaries and expenses.* "We always found ourselves in the strange position," Mother recalled, "of knowing who the CIA types were—even the deep-cover ones—because in many cases they didn't do very well at their cover." It bothered Mother that her husband was frequently mistaken for a CIA agent, just because he didn't stand on ceremony and was far from circumspect. "There were often rumors," Mother said, "but inevitably, it was very clear—we were so poor! And there were no lavish parties and no envelopes with cold, hard cash."

It is an open secret that career Foreign Service officers around the world have long resented the CIA. Father euphemistically referred to his CIA colleagues as the "fellows from the other side of the house." Still, he understood that in Saudi Arabia, given the peculiar history of the Kingdom, it was no surprise that the CIA had forged a particularly close "special relationship" with

---

*In the aftermath of the first great oil crisis of 1971–73, the CIA's resident station chief, Ray Close, another scion of an American missionary family in the Middle East, took early retirement and immediately went to work for a company owned by Prince Turki ibn Faisal al-Saud, the twenty-eight-year-old head of Saudi intelligence.

the oil company. Traditionally, a number of the key Aramcons staffing the company's Department of Government Relations were, in fact, undercover CIA officers. Through the late 1940s and the 1950s, William A. Eddy was one such. The son and grandson of Presbyterian missionaries in Syria, Eddy spoke fluent Arabic. Naturally, in February 1945, when President Franklin Roosevelt met with King Abdul-Aziz aboard the USS *Quincy,* anchored in the Great Bitter Lake (the saltwater lake that lies between the north and south portions of the Suez Canal), it was Eddy—then a colonel in the Office of Strategic Services (OSS)—who served as translator. After World War II, he moved to the newly established CIA—and to Aramco as well.

Another CIA veteran was Ronald Irwin Metz. A tall, ruddy, gregarious man with a hearty laugh, Metz became a close family friend whom I would see off and on over the next forty years. In my eyes, even at the age of twelve or thirteen, he seemed to be so alive, so vibrant and so full of stories. And for good reason. Born in Nebraska in 1921, Metz graduated in 1944 from the University of California at Berkeley with a degree in Chinese and Far Eastern Studies. That year he was recruited by the OSS and parachuted behind enemy lines into China. By the end of the war he spoke good Mandarin Chinese and was awarded a Bronze Star. As an OSS veteran he soon found himself, like Eddy and others, folded into the fledgling Central Intelligence Agency, where he reported as an undercover agent in the Far East and Washington. While teaching a training course on interrogation techniques he fell in love with a pretty, blond-haired CIA recruit, Helen Chapin, the daughter of the U.S. ambassador to the Netherlands. When they married at The Hague in 1951, they rode to the cathedral in a horse-drawn carriage; the guests at the elaborate ceremony included Queen Juliana. In the attendant publicity Ron Metz's CIA cover was supposedly blown.

Whether his intelligence career ended or merely took off in a different direction is open to debate. In any case, after his marriage Metz moved to Beirut, where he studied Arabic and received a master's degree in Middle Eastern studies from the American University of Beirut in 1954. Upon graduation he was hired by Aramco's Government Relations Department and sent to Riyadh as the company's liaison with King Saud, eldest son and successor of the Kingdom's founder, Abdul-Aziz ibn Saud, who had died in 1953. Ron and Helen lived in a traditional red clay brick villa in the old city. In Riyadh during the mid-1950s Metz quickly became one of the new ruler's drinking companions and quite probably his closest foreign confidant. When Ron visited, often at King Saud's request, he would be greeted effusively by the king in his audience chamber. Servants would bring trays of sweet black tea. Saud would dismiss the servants, toss the tea and pull out a bottle of scotch.

One evening Metz was suddenly called by the king's German doctor and told that His Majesty needed an emergency blood transfusion. Saud's blood type was O-negative—the same as Metz's. So Metz rushed over to the palace and the doctor performed a "live transfusion." Saud was now stable enough to be transported to the airport for a flight to Dhahran's hospital—but in the absence of an ambulance, Metz called his wife and told her to drive their station wagon to the palace. Helen Metz always kept a *ghutra*—the red-and-white-checkered headscarf worn by Saudi men—in the closet for just such an emergency. Wrapping it around her head, she jumped in the car and drove off to the palace. (This was the only time in all her years in Arabia that Helen drove a car.) The king was then transported to the airport in the back of the Metzes' station wagon.

Some weeks later, after a full recovery, King Saud spotted Ron Metz in a crowd at the palace and called him over. He said that he understood he had helped to save his life, and he wanted to know if he could do anything for him. Metz, an intensely devout Christian, said yes, he would like permission to import some red wine for use in the Eucharist, the Christian ceremony commemorating the Last Supper. The king gave his assent but warned Metz not to make this public.

It was Metz's job to report back to Aramco on the royal family—its behavior, lifestyle and palace intrigues. One of his best sources on life inside the palace was the king's cook, José Arnold, a Swiss-American who had formerly supervised Aramco's Dhahran cafeteria and had subsequently been assigned by Aramco to organize the palace kitchen in Riyadh. From Arnold, Metz learned who was seeing the king, and even the complexities of Saud's harem.

In 1958, King Saud was forced by his critics within the royal family to take a long leave of absence abroad. Led by Crown Prince Faisal, this faction privately accused the king of profligacy and incompetence. This began Faisal's slow rise to power. Sensing which way the winds were blowing, Aramco quickly decided it needed a new face in the Saudi capital. They sent Mike Ameen to Riyadh and transferred the Metzes to Dhahran. We'd see them in the American Camp's Episcopalian services every Sunday.

By the time our tour was up in 1965, Ron was making arrangements for another career move. He had decided to get a divinity degree from Yale. He was ordained in 1969 as an Episcopalian priest and then posted to Jerusalem, where he spent the next six years serving as the Anglican archbishop's troubleshooter, interceding on behalf of his Palestinian parishioners with the Israeli occupation authorities. Metz was indefatigable, and he became obsessed with the plight of the Palestinians in East Jerusalem. By then— on the assumption that the Agency doesn't use the Church as cover for its agents—he was presumably off the CIA's payroll. He died in August 2002.

Only employees' children were allowed to attend Aramco's well-equipped school. Our first year in Saudi Arabia, Nancy and I, aged nine and eleven, respectively, were homeschooled by my mother, using materials from the Calvert Correspondence School. Mother was an exacting teacher. Every few weeks Nancy and I mailed batches of homework and tests back to Kansas. Weeks later we would receive our scored-up homework. It was not an ideal arrangement. The next year, Mother and other non-Aramco expatriates established a school within the consulate compound. They persuaded Aramco to donate a used "portable"—a prefabricated wooden hut—to house the school. Mother hired a certified public school teacher from New Jersey as headmaster, Mr. Preston. Soon I was in the company of about forty other students, ages five to thirteen, representing fifteen different nationalities. It was a two-room schoolhouse, and each of the two rooms held multiple grades. Mother taught music, and Mr. Preston taught everything else.

Mother and the school's other founders decided to call it the Dhahran Academy.

I loved to be outdoors. Every morning I would rise early before school and walk for a mile across the desert to the oil company horse-stables. They called it the "Hobby Farm." The stables abutted what they called "Imhoff Gardens"—an oasis of greenery only made possible by the fact that the site was also the location of Aramco's sewage pond. "Imhoff Gardens" was a "sewage garden"—but it seemed like a little piece of paradise to me. The "farm" was a quite elaborate affair, with a clubhouse, a large gymkhana field, training rings and a grandstand for spectators. The Aramcons had scores of beautiful Arabian horses in these fine stables, but they always needed extra hands to exercise the horses. I became an eleven-year-old jockey and trainer. If I showed up at six in the morning, I could ride for an hour and everyone benefited—the horses, the owners, the stable hands and me. I learned English show-riding and Western rodeo-style events, and competed in both.

Kai racing Frosty, Dhahran, 1965

One day, I was taking my horse through its paces with a team of other riders when an Aramcon mother sitting in the stands called the gymkhana director over and demanded that I be kicked off the team. I was a "consulate kid," she pointed out, and the Hobby Farm was for Aramco employees. She insisted that an Aramcon child should take my place. An argument ensued, but in the end the gymkhana director felt compelled to acquiesce; he apologized but told me I would have to leave the team. I was stunned and embarrassed, though also angry. I began to make connections about the unfairness of exclusion. I had long since become aware that Father's black diplomatic passport bestowed certain privileges and status, in which Mother, Nancy and I were included. When we traveled, that passport expedited our passage through customs. It announced that Father's family was special. And yet, here in Saudi Arabia we were not so special. The Aramcons had the privileges, and they could tell us what we could have and what we were denied. I resented being "ghettoized" in the consulate compound, and suddenly I saw what it was like to be stigmatized as the "other."

Fortunately, another Aramcon, Mrs. Virginia Brown, who owned a beautiful white Arabian stallion named Frosty, had witnessed my expulsion and made a mental note to help me. If I was barred from the gymkhana team, I was nevertheless not barred from the gymkhana's individual competitions, so long as I was riding a horse owned by an Aramcon. The following season Mrs. Brown asked me if I would like to jockey her horse in the upcoming races. Frosty was without a doubt one of the strongest, most seasoned horses on the Hobby Farm. He knew exactly what his rider expected of him. Like a Western quarter horse, he could rise on his hindlegs and in an instant spin around 180 degrees. That year I rode him in both the Western racing events (pole bending, "keyhole" and barrel racing) and English show-riding. We took blue ribbons all year long, and I won the year-end championship trophy. Frosty taught me persistence, discipline and the patience to work alone at something for hours on end. I thought that my triumph that year, at age thirteen, was a "consulate kid's" comeuppance to the Aramcons and their exclusionary rules.

In our family, politics was always a welcome topic for dinner-table conversation. I was a child of the Cold War, and living abroad made that conflict a visceral experience. I knew Father was a foot soldier in our ideological competition with the Soviets. I remember the tension in our house in October 1962, when President John F. Kennedy announced a naval blockade of Cuba. A month later, long after the crisis was over, the consul general invited everyone in the compound and a few Saudis to a screening of Kennedy's speech announcing the blockade. It had taken that long for the 16mm reel of the speech to arrive in Dhahran. I was mesmerized by Kennedy's somber Boston Brahmin voice. And then a year later, Father woke me up in the middle of the night. "What do you think is the worst thing that could happen to America?" he asked me. I thought he meant a nuclear war. But then he explained that Kennedy had been assassinated.

Arabia was a man's world—an ideal playground for an adolescent boy. I played first base for the Steelers, a Little League team sponsored by Aramco. For a time I was in the Boy Scouts but quit when they segregated all the non-Aramcon boys into one squad. I had some Aramcon friends—Johnny Pendleton was one—but most of my friends were non-Aramcons in the Dhahran Academy. Nobuo Atsumi, a stocky Japanese boy, was in my eighth-grade class. He was a whiz in math; I was not. One classmate, Paul Chiramel, was a Christian Indian from Bombay. There were kids from Iceland, Britain, Africa, Taiwan and a half dozen other nationalities.

The Saudi government prohibited its nationals from attending the academy—but there were a handful of exceptions. Sheri and Mona Wahba were the two charming granddaughters of Sheikh Hafiz Wahba, the Saudi ambassador to London. Sheikh Wahba was an Egyptian, but he began serving as King Abdul-Aziz's ambassador to London in 1934—and he was still there in the 1960s. His son, Mustafa Wahba, was a Cambridge-educated economist who married a woman from Graz, Austria. For a time in the late 1950s Mustafa worked for Aramco; he and his family were among the few Saudis to live within the American Camp. In 1960, he was appointed the deputy minister of finance for economic development, and many regarded him as a liberal reformer. In 1962, due to his association with a faction of the royal family who favored a constitutional monarchy, he was dismissed by Crown Prince Faisal. In the years 1962–65—when my parents knew Mustafa—he had a consulting business. Aramco would not employ him because of his liberal political associations. Neither was he permitted to send his daughters to the Aramco school. But because his wife was Austrian, he was allowed to enroll them in the Dhahran Academy.

Another exception was Faiza Saleh Ambah, one of the daughters of Dr. Saleh Ambah, the director of the College of Petroleum and Minerals in Dhahran. My parents were very good friends of Dr. Ambah and his wife, Aisha al-Fassi. Dr. Ambah had received a doctorate from the University of Southern California in 1963, and he was a strong advocate of universal education, for both men and women. Initially, Faiza Ambah was enrolled at an Arabic-language girls' school in al-Khobar—but her parents pulled her out when they learned the teachers there were authorized to use rulers to whack the fingers of unruly students. Because Faiza had been born in California and was therefore technically an American, the Saudi government allowed her to enroll in the Dhahran Academy. She graduated from the academy in 1973 and was then sent to a boarding school in Switzerland. Eventually she earned a graduate degree from the University of Southern California, and today she is a reporter for the *Washington Post,* living in Jeddah. Her father's promising career was suddenly derailed in February 1970, when he was arrested and thrown into a Riyadh prison, the not uncommon fate of such highly educated Saudis if they came to be seen as pushing too hard on the doors of political reform.

* * *

At the end of 1963, our family of five suddenly became six when we adopted my fourteen-year-old cousin, Christina. I was the only son, and the eldest child. But now, at the age of twelve, I suddenly had an older sibling. Christina's father—my father's elder brother—had drowned in a fishing accident on the McKenzie River in Oregon in 1953, and her mother was incapable of providing for Christina and her three brothers and sisters. So for a few years my grandparents in Eugene raised these cousins, until finally in 1963 my parents decided to adopt Christina. (My father's sister adopted her brother Jim, and the other siblings by then were in college or working.)

Christina was a free spirit and we got on well. She introduced me to Elvis Presley, the Beatles and rock-and-roll. She was now a part of the family, but there was no school for her to attend in Dhahran. The Academy only went up to the eighth grade. After a winter of homeschooling, she was sent away to the Schutz American School, a missionary boarding school in Alexandria, Egypt.

My other sisters, Nancy and Shelly, were, for the most part, too young to notice the limitations of being female in Arabia. Yet Shelly vividly recalls an encounter in Jeddah with a Mutawah, a member of the religious police. She was walking with Father in the souk one day when suddenly she heard the snap, snap of a bamboo stick hitting the ground inches from her heels. She was wearing knee-length baggy shorts—culottes—which the Mutawah thought inappropriate for a young girl. Father turned around and quickly confronted the man. A diplomatic "incident" might have ensued; instead, the Mutawah backed off. As I've said, Arabia was for the boys.

I had a zoo of animals. We seemed to have inherited a black gold-speckled cat that we named Zayt—Arabic for "oil." She gave us many kittens. We had a rabbit hutch—though some of the poor creatures died in the intense summer heat. I had a baby goat I had bought from a Bedouin family who had camped not far from the consulate compound. Though I remember bottle-feeding it religiously, it soon died. We had another burial—like the one for my poor Jerusalem Easter rabbit.

Best of all, I had a dog. When I was eleven, Father returned from a trip to Sharja on the Trucial Coast with a Saluki. The sheikh of Sharja had given him this sleek, golden-haired hunting dog. He told him she was called Zahra—"blossom" in Arabic. Zahra was a beautiful creature, graceful, gentle and the most dignified, even aloof, dog I have ever encountered. In Arabic, "dog" is *kalb*, a term that is always a pejorative. But Salukis are not considered to be *kalb*s and instead are always called "Salukis." Zahra was a "feathered" Saluki: her long curved tail was adorned with long hair so that when she stood in the wind the tail formed a perfect funnel of "feathers." She could patiently sit at your feet for hours with her paws crossed and her long, pointed snout held aloft. Salukis are sight hounds, and DNA testing has established that they have been around for about 7,000 years, making them the oldest breed of domesticated dog. The Bedouin still use Salukis, in tandem with falcons, to chase down gazelles for their meat. I often took Zahra for desert walks, and occasionally we would take the Nash Rambler for a drive in the desert and watch with delight as she raced behind us across the sand. She could run as fast as thirty-five to forty miles per hour. Zahra would be my companion until I left home for college.

After the school day ended, if I had no riding, I fled to the swimming pool operated by a small contingent of U.S. Air Force enlisted men at the nearby air base, built by the U.S. War Department in 1945. They sometimes put ice blocks into the pool to keep it from getting too warm. When we rode or played tennis in 120-degree heat, we'd pop salt tablets to avoid getting dehydrated.

Due to Saudi sensitivities about the presence of foreign soldiers, King Saud had officially closed the air base in 1962. But American fliers continued to live there, under an agreement to provide "training" to their Saudi counterparts, and the facility remained a valued American military asset. The U.S. Air Force used it as a key communication hub between its military base in Libya and Clark Field in the Philippines. It also served as a refueling port and haven for tired fliers. "The very presence of United States military personnel in Saudi Arabia," the State Department noted in 1961, "even though unarmed, has long disturbed Saudi and Arab nationalists." Washington knew the air base was a political liability for the Saudis—but the American military presence in the Kingdom nevertheless grew ever larger over the coming decades.

When I was twelve years old, we rented a dhow, a large wooden sailing vessel, and sailed out from the port of Qatif, twenty-five miles north of Dhahran, into the Persian Gulf. (The Saudis called it the Arabian Sea.) This was a two-day expedition. We spent the night at sea, sleeping on the open deck. It was pearling season, so we encountered small fleets of pearl-fishing dhows anchored above fresh oyster beds about fifty feet below the surface. Anchoring our own boat, we sat on wooden deck chairs and watched the pearl divers. They used the "stone" method, holding a large, weighty stone tied to a sturdy rope over a hundred feet long. Standing on the edge of their dhow, they'd take a deep breath and jump feetfirst into the blue-green waters. The weight of the stone would plunge them to the seafloor, where they had no more than a minute or so to scour the oyster beds for pearls. Pearl fishermen had earned their livelihood from this trade for hundreds of years. It was dangerous work—they gambled their lives for a share in each boat's profits. Usually, the boat's owner received one-fifth of the pearl profits, another fifth went to the fisherman who pulled the diver back up to the surface, the remaining three-fifths went to the diver. I remember being transfixed by the scene, watching the pearl divers disappear into the sea for what seemed like an impossibly long time, only to burst suddenly through the surface, wearing a small cloth bag around their necks filled with oyster shells. This ancient livelihood was even then dying out, a victim of the Japanese cultured-pearl industry. But, like many things in Arabia, tradition stubbornly held on.

Women were not allowed then, and are not allowed today, to drive in Saudi Arabia. There were two exceptions: Aramcon women could drive inside the American Camp; and a dispensation was given by the Emir bin Jiluwi so that the seven or eight wives of diplomats who lived in the consulate compound could drive. They were restricted to an eight-mile stretch of paved road between the airport and the Aramco compound. (In the spring of 1974, my mother violated these restrictions and drove all the way to Riyadh, wearing a kaffiyeh wrapped around her head so passing drivers might mistake her for a man.) Mother was a strong, capable and independent-minded woman. She knew there could be trouble if she got caught. "Should we have any kind of accident," she wrote in 1962 to friends back in Oregon, "there is some doubt as to our fate—jail or what (possibly the husband would be permitted to take his wife's place in jail!)." But she had also learned that many Saudi Bedouin women drove the family pickup trucks when they were out in the desert, away from urban centers like Riyadh or Dhahran.

Three weeks after our arrival on July 28, 1962, Mother taught a sewing class for wives of middle-ranking Saudi employees of Aramco. Ten young women arrived for the class heavily veiled. Once inside, however, they threw off their black robes and veils. "It must be terribly hot," Mother wrote, "and I find it very depressing to see." She was shocked to discover that these young women, many of whom were daughters of al-Khobar merchant families, were completely illiterate. Some had been betrothed when as young as nine or ten. Their husbands might speak some English and worked in the oil industry, but these "gay, lively girls" lived much as their grandmothers and great-grandmothers had before them. "These women wear very shabby imitations of Western-style dresses under the black robes but continue to henna their feet and hands, wear nose buttons, twine herbs in their hair, and many haven't even a notion about how you hold a needle and thread." And yet, my mother found herself oddly admiring of these Saudi women. "There is a dignity about these people," she wrote home, "which always impresses a Westerner. . . . I found myself feeling that it was I who was the curious one, and found them looking at me with a bit of amusement."

Even in the early 1960s, we knew that Arabia had the world's largest reservoir of "liquid energy" on the planet—the estimates ran to some 350 to 500 billion barrels of oil. You could literally smell the oil in the air. But it was still a very poor country. Infant mortality was high, and life expectancy hovered at around forty years. Trachoma, the eye disease that had nearly blinded King Abdul-Aziz himself in his later years, was widespread. Of the three million Saudis, roughly 10 percent were literate. Mother's letters home noted "the tremendous wealth of the royal family . . . and at the other extreme the pitiful tin shanty towns surrounding each boom town. You see Cadillacs in abundance, but also the donkey just as frequently."

There were also some 4,000 to 10,000 slaves. The slave trade in Arabia dated back hundreds of years. Most, though not all, were black Africans. King Saud, the eldest son of Abdul-Aziz, owned hundreds. His father had banned the import or export of slaves in 1936. But the number of slaves nevertheless continued to grow, slowly augmented by African pilgrims coming to Mecca on the Haj. Some of these pilgrims could not afford to pay their way home. Others sold themselves into slavery to pay off debts. Mother remembers seeing slave women from Ethiopia with Christian crosses tattooed on their foreheads. Even in the early 1960s, a young, healthy slave in the oasis of Buraimi could be bought for $900. The Saudi *ulema* (theologians or preachers) insisted that the Koran sanctioned slavery.

The *ulema* also staunchly defended some of the more draconian aspects of Sharia (Koranic) law. Crime was practically nonexistent, but we all knew that the punishment for thievery might entail the culprit's hand being chopped off, though such a verdict was imposed only after three offenses. And if the thief was a Saudi Aramco employee, the deed was performed at the company's main gate at quitting time, to ensure a large public audience. The severed hand would then be draped across the top of the camp fence for all to see.

Murder called for an executioner wielding a sword. My friend, the writer and Arabist Peter Iseman, once witnessed a public beheading in Jeddah's Bab al-Jadid business district, adjacent to an old mosque:

A police squad car arrives with the victim, a Yemeni dressed in skirt and sandals who has killed his sixteen-year-old wife. A few minutes later a Pontiac Cabriolet arrives with the executioner. He is about six feet tall, charcoal black, and elegantly dressed in white with a black bandolier and sash. The executioners all come from one family of ex-slaves, my friend explains. The Yemeni, chained and blindfolded, is guided to a piece of cardboard on the street, where he obediently drops to his knees. The black executioner stands about three steps behind him with a polished, double-edged sword about three and a half feet long. His assistant, an apprentice perhaps, stands behind the kneeling Yemeni with a sharp stick. When the signal is given, he jabs him in the side and the Yemeni's bowed neck stiffens by reflex. The executioner is already moving and everything is soundless. He takes a few tiny ballet steps and then one long stride as the blade rises and drops through a perfect arc, severing the head in one majestic stroke. The head rolls forward, the neck spurts blood over the street, and the body topples backward. The executioner's apprentice fetches the head and puts it on a stretcher, and sound returns. The crowd roars once in exclamation and disperses.

Wahhabism dictated every aspect of Saudi life. Muhammad ibn Abdul-Wahhab (1703–1792), an itinerant revivalist preacher, founded the sect in the eighteenth century. Abdul-Wahhab preached that the tribes of Arabia were no longer observing the tenets of Islam as originally ordained and practiced by the Prophet Muhammad in the seventh century. Abdul-Wahhab singled out for special condemnation the domed tombs that had been erected over the graves of famous Islamic saints and scholars. He labeled such honorific tombs a sacrilege and charged that Muslim pilgrims visiting these graves were in effect worshipping pagan idols. For Abdul-Wahhab, the essential doctrine of *Tawhid,* meaning the absolute uniqueness and unity of God, required the destruction of all such tombs. His followers called themselves Muwahiddun—perhaps best translated as "Unitarians"—and rejected the term "Wahhabism" as derogatory.

Abdul-Wahhab was not a reformer; Islam, he said, was already complete and wholly perfect. It was only necessary, he said, to return to seventh-century fundamentals. "Praise be to God," he is supposed to have proclaimed, "we are followers, not innovators." His favorite hadith (spoken word) of the Prophet was: "In *bid'a* [innovation] is Hellfire." He was in every sense of the word a perfect fundamentalist. The only basis for Islam, he argued, were the Koran and the Sunna, the Prophet's sayings. He rejected the rich theological literature of medieval Islamic scholars, arguing that Muslims needed no one to interpret their faith for them. It was, he emphasized, the individual responsibility of each and every Muslim to study the Koran and learn its divine message. As the Koran says, "Every man and every woman must determine the truth (or 'black from white') for himself or herself." On its face, this notion might suggest tolerance for a multitude of interpretations; but in practice Abdul-Wahhab's eighteenth-century followers insisted that the only righteous way for a Muslim to live was exactly how the Prophet's followers had lived in seventh-century Arabia. In their view, modernity was the enemy of virtue.

The intellectual origins of Abdul-Wahhab's ideas are necessarily murky, but he appears, while studying at Medina, to have fallen under the influence of the fourteenth-century writings of Ibn Taymiyyah, one of the first Islamic theologians to advance the then quite novel notion that "deviant" Muslims in some circumstances could be treated as infidels and put to death. Ibn Taymiyyah tentatively labeled both Sufis and Shi'ites as pagans. Such teachings inevitably encouraged the worst kind of intolerance.

Abdul-Wahhab moved back to the Nejd (central Arabia) and began preaching an even more extreme, and far less nuanced, version of Ibn Taymiyyah's doctrines. He became violently anti-Shi'ite. And he placed a strong emphasis on an ascetic and puritan lifestyle. Whereas the Prophet had sanctioned many earthly pleasures, Abdul-Wahhab created an entirely new and highly revisionist code of personal conduct. Other than Ibn Taymiyyah's writings, Abdul-Wahhab's definition of Islam had few historical antecedents; it seems to have sprung naturally from the Spartan landscape of the Nejd. Neither was Abdul-Wahhab much of a scholar—he compiled several small volumes of the Prophet Muhammad's hadiths with virtually no commentary of his own. But he relentlessly condemned all non-Abdul-Wahhabi Muslims as apostates from the faith of the one unitary God.

He made his first public mark when he ordered the execution of a woman who had allegedly confessed to adultery. After miraculously producing four male witnesses, as required by the Koran, Abdul-Wahhab had the woman stoned to death.* By one account, he participated personally in the stoning.

The historian in me is quick to point out that only a few decades earlier the elders of the Puritan colony in Salem, Massachusetts, were hanging men and women for the quite preposterous crime of "witchcraft." A few brave Puritans objected to this injustice at the time—and so too did many of Abdul-Wahhab's fellow tribesmen object to the stoning death of this alleged adulteress in the name of religion. Abdul-Wahhab had to abandon his abode and seek new frontiers. His own brother, Sulayman, denounced him in what must have been the first written refutation of Wahhabism. This might have been the end of the story, but Abdul-Wahhab soon found himself a powerful benefactor. In 1744, Abdul-Wahhab moved to the village of Dariyah, just outside of Riyadh, where he met an ambitious tribal sheikh named Muhammad ibn Saud.

Abdul-Wahhab and Muhammad ibn Saud soon entered into a pact. The sheikh would enforce Abdul-Wahhab's strict interpretation of Islam—and Abdul-Wahhab blessed Muhammad ibn Saud's tribesmen as they conquered much of the Arabian Peninsula. They did so with a missionary zeal. This Wahhabi-Saudi compact is the origin of the House of Saud. For a time the Wahhabi warriors even challenged the Ottoman Empire. In 1802 a Wahhabi force conquered Ottoman-ruled Karbala. Because it was populated by Shi'ites—whom the Wahhabis considered heretics—some 2,000 to 4,000 residents were slaughtered. The Ottomans dispatched an army to Arabia, but the Saudi regime survived until 1818, when its capital was razed by Ottoman troops.

Muhammad ibn Saud's descendants established a second Saudi state later in the nineteenth century, only to lose it again, in 1891, to the Rasheeds

---

*The Koran actually requires the four male witnesses to attest that they were not able to pass a string between the copulating couple.

of Hail. This time the clan—including the young Abdul-Aziz ibn Saud—fled to Kuwait. They did not return until 1902, when Abdul-Aziz ibn Saud stormed Riyadh and subsequently restored the Saudi kingdom. By then the House of Saud had heavily intermarried with the descendants of Abdul-Wahhab, known today as the Al as-Shaykh ("the family of the sheikh"). The Saud family's right to rule was thus inextricably linked to Wahhabism as defined by these theologians. The *ulema* had direct access to the king, meeting with him by tradition every Thursday. To this day their opinions on education policy, religious practices and a whole range of social issues are not easily ignored by the al-Sauds.

When Aramco's early geologists began exploring for oil in the 1930s, they needed to import radiotelephones. But the Wahhabi clergy, the *ulema,* forbade this on the ground that such devices were the work of the devil. King Abdul-Aziz knew Aramco needed the radiotelephones—and he even wanted one for himself. But he also knew that every innovation had to be introduced as authentically Islamic. He set up a demonstration of the phones, stationing one in Mecca and another in Riyadh. He then placed a call from Riyadh to a group of *ulema* in Mecca. The *ulema* confirmed that this was indeed ibn Saud's voice—but this only proved that the sinful king had been seduced by the devil. The king then began reciting portions of the Koran and asked if these were not the words of Allah. The *ulema* had to agree that perhaps the device was not the devil's work. Aramco got their radio phones within weeks.

By the early 1960s there were local radio stations, and a woman's voice was heard on Radio Mecca for the first time in 1963. When the *ulema* complained about this to Crown Prince Faisal, he cited as precedent the fact that the Prophet himself had listened to poetry recited by the legendary seventh-century woman al-Khansa, known for her poetic laments for the deaths of her brothers in battle. Television was practically nonexistent until Aramco received permission to install a low-wattage broadcast station in Dhahran.* The consulate compound was close enough to pick up this weak signal. They broadcast highly censored (no kissing), commercial-free episodes of *I Love Lucy, Father Knows Best* and *Perry Mason*—all dubbed in Arabic. These black-and-white shows were broadcast for two or three hours each evening, and

---

*The first television signals reached the Eastern Province from Bahrain. And in the 1950s, the U.S. air base briefly had a low-wattage station for their troops.

then the station would sign off with a static picture of an American Indian chief. By 1965, Aramco's broadcasts were attracting a couple hundred thousand viewers in the Eastern Province each night. I watched *Bonanza* with the voices of the Cartwright boys dubbed into Arabic. (The English audio track was broadcast simultaneously on the radio.) *Bonanza* later became a quite popular show when Saudi television went peninsula-wide. I recently learned from Lawrence Wright's book *The Looming Tower* that Osama bin Laden's favorite show as a boy was also *Bonanza*.

By the time we arrived in Arabia, Saudi society was on the precipice of monumental changes. The pressures of mid-twentieth-century modernity were inexorable. "We are talking about a place," wrote the Saudi anthropologist Saad Sowayan in 2006, "that until the dawn of the 20th century had practically been living in the prehistoric age." The Kingdom's founder, Abdul-Aziz ibn Saud (1880–1953), emerged from central Arabia, the Nejd, and proclaimed himself king in 1932 of all the lands that constitute present-day Saudi Arabia. He is sometimes described today as "the unifier," but he did so by the sword, forcing the submission of numerous other tribes. Religion gave a cloak of legitimacy to the Saud enterprise. And yet, while the House of Saud unified Arabia in alliance with the ultraconservative Wahhabi *ulema,* the Sauds were themselves agents of change. This had been true under Abdul-Aziz, and it would be true under the sons who succeeded him. As the royal family sanctioned the introduction of technological innovations, modern transport and, most importantly, literacy, it risked undermining the social compact. Politically, the royal family was engaged in a delicate balancing act, gradually introducing the benefits of modernity to its people while preserving the Abdul-Wahhabi social fabric. By the early sixties, these tensions precipitated a power struggle within the royal family. It was during these momentous years that the House of Saud entrenched itself as a conservative absolute monarchy—and turned off the road to a democratic constitutional monarchy.

When Abdul-Aziz died in 1953, his eldest living son, Saud, succeeded him. Born in 1902, Saud had been designated Crown Prince as far back as 1933. (Abdul-Aziz had forty-five sons—as did Saud!) Upon ascending the throne, the portly, six-foot-four-inch-tall Saud promptly went on a spending spree, both personally and on behalf of his Kingdom. He issued a royal decree instructing Aramco to raise the salaries of its Saudi workers by as much as 20 percent. In addition, the oil company would henceforth pay 20 percent of the cost for Saudi employees' family housing. Aramco would also subsidize food and clothing for its workers—and install 550 new watercoolers. Under Saud, Aramco was compelled to treat its Saudi workers better.

Saud spent millions on new palaces, including an enormous one-square-mile complex of buildings in Riyadh. When completed, Nasriyah Palace was enclosed by a seven-mile-long blush-pink wall; inside was a garish, Disney-like complex of palaces, villas, swimming pools, gardens and water fountains. A virtual royal town, Nasriyah reportedly cost nearly $50 million. (In 1963 Father took us up to Riyadh on the train—built by Bechtel and paid for by Aramco—and we got a private tour of this ostentatious compound. When we were ushered into the royal *majlis* meeting hall, my nine-year-old sister, Nancy, ran to the front of the room and sat on the king's gold-leaf throne. The guards quickly shooed her away.)

Saud also handed out millions of dollars to tribal leaders, a traditional means of winning their fealty. He spent millions to renovate the Grand Mosque in Mecca and the buildings surrounding the Prophet's Tomb in Medina. A building contractor from the Hadramaut in South Yemen, Mohammed bin Laden, landed the contract for the work in Mecca—which was the beginning of the Bin Laden fortune.

The royal family's personal finances were always mercurial, but by March 1958, Saud's government was grappling with a debt of $480 million, or about $3.2 billion in current dollars. Either the Kingdom was spending way beyond its means—or it was not being properly compensated by Aramco. Sixty percent of the country's oil income, moreover, was being spent exclusively on members of the royal family. Some members of the family had doubts about Saud's mental or moral fitness to rule. His addiction to "irritating liquids"—a polite euphemism for his favored Cointreau—had begun to affect his health. And some suggested that his fondness for an exceptionally large stable of concubines was not within the bounds of Wahhabi good taste. Saud further alienated his own constituency within the family by his friendship with Id Ibn Salem, a commoner who had started out in the palace garage as a mechanic and had risen to become the king's personal assistant and gatekeeper. Saud depended upon Ibn Salem to procure him both women and alcohol.

His half brother, Crown Prince Faisal, had by contrast a reputation for personal austerity and competence. Faisal was born in Riyadh in 1904 or 1905, the third son of Abdul-Aziz ibn Saud, and he had served as his father's foreign minister ever since 1932. Faisal disliked his brother Saud and distrusted his political instincts. In April 1958 the crown prince persuaded key elements in the royal family that he should be given additional government responsibilities beyond his position as foreign minister—in fact, placed in overall charge of the Kingdom. A critical catalyst to this development was a group of liberal princes led by Prince Talal ibn Abdul-Aziz al-Saud, the twenty-third son of the late king. As a young man Prince Talal had served King Abdul-Aziz as minister of communications, and in 1955–57 he was King Saud's ambassador to France and Spain. He returned in 1957 and began promoting democratic notions. "Eventually," he told the press, "this country will become a constitutional monarchy." So it was that in April of 1958, King Saud was handed an ultimatum demanding that he transfer all executive powers to Faisal. Saud reluctantly acceded and temporarily left the country for "medical treatment" in Switzerland.

For the next two years Crown Prince Faisal ruled the Kingdom, introducing an austere budget and streamlining the government. He banned the import of Cadillacs, and he cut the annual allowance for individual princes—fixed by Saud at $30,000 a year plus "expenses." Henceforth, the royal family's privy purse was set at no more than 18 percent of government revenues. In 1960 he abolished censorship, and soon press reports began to be published suggesting that the Kingdom was moving towards a constitutional monarchy. The liberal, foreign-educated princes led by Prince Talal pushed for the creation of a national assembly. But though Faisal was thought by some observers to be a modernizer, Prince Talal gradually realized that the crown prince was more royalist than the king. Faisal was in fact opposed to any real democratization.

So too was the American government. In June 1960, Prince Talal sought a meeting with the American chargé d'affaires in Jeddah to express his concerns about U.S. policy in Arabia. Talal explained that the current political turmoil was a struggle between a "constitutional monarchy versus absolute autocracy." He asked that the U.S. government stand with the democrats. When the diplomat politely demurred, saying that the United States could not involve itself with the internal politics of the Kingdom, Prince Talal asked, if that was the case, then why was Colonel Bill Eddy constantly meeting with the king? The American asked, by way of response, why that should matter—Eddy, after all, was Aramco's representative. No, Prince Talal replied, he "believed Eddy was now working for [CIA chief] Allen Dulles." Eddy's reporting to the CIA is still classified, but he was undoubtedly urging King Saud to reject Prince Talal's demands—and to iron out his rocky relationship with Crown Prince Faisal.

Prince Talal al-Saud, 1950

By 1960 Prince Faisal was in a quandary; his austere budget had cut funds for any economic development, and a stagnant economy was not a recipe for popularity. Soon the U.S. Embassy was reporting back to Washington, "The feeling is growing that Prince Faisal remains a bottleneck to progress. . . ."

At the end of 1960, King Saud once again reasserted his prerogatives and Faisal was forced to retreat. Then, in a stunning move that seemed to ally him with the liberal reformers, Saud reshuffled his ministries and appointed a number of well-known liberals to the cabinet. The key post of minister of finance and national economy was given to Prince Talal, who told a Beirut newspaper that the new government would soon implement major reforms, including the creation of a national assembly, two-thirds of which he said would be elected. The new government alarmed Aramco's Tom Barger, who called it "the biggest political poker game in the history of the kingdom."

For the first time, Aramco executives had reason to believe they might lose the oil concession to nationalization.

The London-based *Economist* reported that King Saud "has chosen to join sides with the forces of revolution . . . making a bid for the kind of popular support which the deposed monarchs of the Middle East never enjoyed."* In late December 1960, the American Embassy in Jeddah cabled Washington that a bright forty-one-year-old Saudi technocrat named Abdul-Aziz al-Muammar had emerged as King Saud's closest adviser. Aramco's Ron Metz reported that al-Muammar was a "man who knows very well that he is in possession of power and influence." Some Aramcons thought of him as a radical or even a Communist, but Metz more accurately described his ideas about planning and development as something akin to Ba'ath Party socialism. Metz was astonished that such a man had become the gatekeeper for the king. Al-Muammar himself explained to Metz that "His Majesty said that now that he had all he could possibly desire in the way of palaces and other luxuries, the only further desire in his life is to accomplish something for the people. . . ."

Born in 1919, al-Muammar came from a prominent Hejazi family; his father had been an aide to King Abdul-Aziz ibn Saud, and al-Muammar had a degree in economics from the American University of Beirut. He had been a leader of the 1953 Aramco workers' strike. In 1955 he was working for the Ministry of Finance when he was suddenly arrested. Though he was suspected of Communist, Ba'athist or simply antiroyalist sympathies, no charges were pressed and after a few months he was released. Despite this incident, in 1958 he was appointed a counselor to King Saud, and by late 1960 he was thought to be the most powerful commoner in Riyadh. Both U.S. State Department and Aramco officials described him as "fiery" and "idealistic." After interviewing al-Muammar, the Berkeley historian George Lenczowski told a State Department official that he was a "radical and emotionally unbalanced Arab nationalist."

Prince Talal continued to make the case for democratization—and he was not alone. He had the support of several of his brothers, as well as a number of younger princes from other branches of the House of Saud. In

---

*The author of the *Economist* story was none other than Kim Philby—who in early 1963 would defect to Moscow. The son of St. John Philby, the Arabian explorer and confidant of King Abdul-Aziz ibn Saud, Kim had developed numerous contacts within Aramco and among Saudi expatriates living in Beirut.

addition, he had attracted support from educated commoners in Arabia's major cities.

One important ally was Abdullah al-Tariki, a commoner from the Nadji oasis of Zilfi. His father had been a camel-herder. He was born in 1917, and his early education took place in Kuwait and Cairo. In 1940, he earned a degree in petroleum engineering from the University of Texas, making him one of the first Saudis to earn an American college degree. Tariki had served as a translator for King Abdul-Aziz in his dealings with Aramco, and by the mid-1950s he was a key adviser to King Saud on petroleum issues. Tariki soon became an influential critic of both Aramco's labor practices and its shady accounting of oil royalties. Though Aramco had agreed in 1950 to split its oil profits fifty-fifty with the Kingdom, it was in fact selling much of its oil at a special discount to the company's corporate owners. This reduced the Saudi regime's own take to 32 percent. By Tariki's calculations, Aramco owed the Kingdom millions of dollars.* "We are the sons of the Indians who sold Manhattan," he once quipped. "We want to change the deal."

Abdullah Tariki, founder of OPEC, 1961

Tariki began to build a genuine political base amidst the Kingdom's growing middle class. In 1960 he was appointed minister of petroleum and national resources, and in September of that year he engineered the creation

---

*Aramco was also avoiding U.S. taxes by calling the oil profits it paid to the Saudis a "tax" instead of a "royalty." This allowed the company to deduct hundreds of millions of dollars of "foreign tax" from its U.S. tax bill.

of the Organization of Petroleum Exporting Countries (OPEC) and advocated renegotiating the terms of all oil company concessions throughout the Arab world. Some Aramcons speculated that his criticisms of the company stemmed from the bigotry he encountered in the 1950s when he was initially barred from living in the American Camp. "I was the first Arab to penetrate into the tight ARAMCO compound," Tariki told *Time* magazine in 1959, "and I never saw such narrow people . . . It was a perfect case of an Arab being a stranger in his own country." Tariki was neither anti-American nor, as some Aramcons whispered, a Communist. He had married an American woman and showed no animus towards American culture. He was an Arab nationalist who thought Arabs should benefit from and control Arab natural resources.

Prince Talal and Tariki pushed for real political reform, specifically, a proposal for a constitution and an elected assembly. They had many allies in the country, including a young economist named Mustafa Wahba, the son of Sheikh Hafiz Wahba, the king's ambassador to London. Mustafa Wahba had joined the new government as deputy minister of finance under Prince Talal. Wahba told a consulate officer that "for the first time in the history of the country, people were taking intelligent interest in politics and paying real attention to the promises being made." Wahba was brimming with confidence that concrete steps would be taken to develop the economy and create democratic institutions. (Wahba's daughters were my schoolmates at the Dhahran Academy in 1964–65.)

Wahba's confidence was sorely misplaced. Early in September 1961, King Saud fired Talal and several other liberals in the cabinet. Ron Metz reported to his Aramco colleagues that Talal's dismissal signaled an escalation in the "struggle for leadership" between Saud and Faisal.

On December 24, 1961, Radio Mecca reported that Prince Talal's draft constitution had been formally submitted to the king. Within days, however, it became clear that King Saud had no intention of ceding executive powers to an elected body. Saud referred the proposal to the *ulema*—who deemed it un-Islamic. The Kingdom, they said, already had a constitution and it was called Sharia law.

Tariki survived until March 1962, when he was abruptly dismissed by Crown Prince Faisal, who was then once again in control. Faisal had a personal reason to purge Tariki: The previous autumn the petroleum minister had persuaded the Kingdom's Council of Ministers to void a contract with a Japanese company on the grounds of corruption. He had submitted evidence that 2 percent of the company's profits were going to be allocated in perpetuity to Faisal's brother-in-law Kamal Adham. Tariki had even been brazen enough to suggest that Faisal was personally profiting from a nontransparent deal. Tariki went into exile in Beirut and would not return to Arabia until after Faisal's death. (Kamal Adham later became Faisal's much-feared intelligence chief.)

Prince Talal also went into exile in Beirut, where he formed a royal opposition group, al-Umara'al-Ahrar—"the Free Princes." Based in Beirut's luxurious St. George's Hotel, he and his brothers continued to attract the support of educated Saudis. But Talal had essentially burned his bridges, and over time his influence waned until he came to be regarded by the Saudi establishment as merely an irritating gadfly. Aramco executives—and Washington—were, for their part, greatly relieved to see Prince Talal and Tariki dismissed. To Father's bosses in the State Department, Talal and his "Free Princes" offered instability, the expulsion of American military personnel from Arabia and the nationalization of Aramco. Now, these "anti-American" propositions were pushed to the back burner. But the defeat of liberal reformers like Talal, Tariki and al-Muammar would lead to many unsavory consequences for decades to come for both the Americans and the Saudis.

Tariki in exile also became an outspoken critic of the royal family. When a friend asked him how he thought the regime could ever be changed, Tariki replied, "A small army detachment can do the job by killing the king and Faisal. The rest of the royal family will run for cover like scared rabbits. Then the revolutionaries will call Nasser for help." Tariki and Talal and others advocates of radical reform vastly underestimated the determination of Prince Faisal and his conservative blood-allies within the royal family both to survive and to maintain an absolute monarchy.

Saudi liberals were naïve to think that King Saud could be maneuvered into the acceptance of genuine democratic reforms. The Free Princes in fact became pawns in the power struggle between Saud and Faisal. And in the end, they turned out to be backing the wrong man. Real power in the House of Saud was slowly draining away from a weak-minded and physically ill Saud and toward Crown Prince Faisal—who had the clear backing of both Aramco and the U.S. government.

Saud's continued fondness for "irritating liquids" led to a further deterioration in his health. One night in November 1961, determined to demonstrate his virility—and thus to counter the reports of his ill-health—an inebriated Saud insisted on having intercourse with his favorite wife, Umm Mansour. The act was consummated with the assistance of four slave girls. That night he began to cough up blood, and he was rushed to Aramco's hospital in Dhahran. Doctors there initially thought he needed an operation for a bleeding ulcer. Eventually, Tom Barger, by then Aramco's president, arranged for a TWA charter plane to fly Saud out of the country.

Once again Saud was forced to cede power back to Faisal while he flew to Boston for surgery. And when he returned in the spring of 1962, the senior princes of the House of Saud made it clear that Faisal must retain nearly all executive authority. Father was in Riyadh when Faisal was once more elevated to the office of prime minister. Vice-Consul Bird managed to persuade the palace guards to let him station himself at the entrance to the courtyard where the Crown Prince was to appear. He had a new 8mm movie camera, equipped with a pistol grip and a somewhat menacing telephoto lens. At first glance, the camera looked to be a gun. So when Father pointed the camera at Faisal as he emerged, the Crown Prince hesitated, and then smiled thinly and moved on. Later, I saw the film and watched as Faisal walked into a crowd of hundreds of tribesmen, all sporting long rifles, daggers and sabers. The film shows Faisal dancing, in a perfunctory fashion, the *ardha,* the traditional Bedouin sword dance, stabbing the air with his saber.

Faisal formed a new government, recruiting a blend of technocrats of commoner background—like Ahmed Zaki al-Yamani—and some of the more capable and strong-willed princes. And then, on November 6, 1962, he stunned the Kingdom by announcing the abolition of slavery. (Faisal compensated each slaveowner with about $3,000 for each slave freed.) He also pledged to revive a long-moribund Consultative Council (Majlis al-Shurwa). But this never happened. Faisal was a pragmatist; he would implement just those reforms demanded by modernity—and no more. These did not include a popularly elected assembly. Neither would he force Saud to abdicate the throne without the explicit blessing of the *ulema.*

Throughout 1963–64, Faisal gradually consolidated his power. Early in 1963 he appointed his trusted brother Abdullah as commander of the National Guard. Certainly the Kingdom's most cohesive fighting force, the National Guard was largely composed of veterans of the Ikhwan, the fierce Wahhabi tribal warriors who had conquered Arabia for Abdul-Aziz in the first couple of decades of the twentieth century. When, in December 1963, King Saud made yet another feeble effort to assert his control over Faisal, Abdullah's National Guard was deployed around the king's palace. For weeks the atmosphere in Riyadh was tense; some thought the Kingdom was on the verge of civil war. Aramco's political agent, Ron Metz, reported that seventy-two leading princes had coalesced around Faisal and that they were determined to force Saud's abdication. Metz described this group as "a cohesive, purposeful dominant element of power." He also reported that both Saud's loyalists and Faisal's partisans had discussed assassinating their opponent—but both factions had rejected this option.

That spring, Tom Barger was so worried that he ordered all of Aramco's exploratory expeditions recalled from the desert. The American Camp was locked down, and Barger alerted Washington that American troops might be necessary to defend Dhahran and protect the oil fields.

King Saud had hoped that the tribesmen outside Riyadh might rally to his assistance; he had lavished millions of dollars on them in recent years. But by the spring he was not even sure of the loyalty of his own Royal Guards. The best-equipped military force in the Kingdom, the Royal Guards were financed and trained by U.S. military advisers. But their commander, General Uthman al-Humaid, was known to be sympathetic to Faisal. Furthermore, by this time both Aramco's Riyadh representative, Mike Ameen, and the U.S. government were gently pleading with Faisal and his known allies in the royal family to force Saud's abdication. On March 29, 1964, a group of leading *ulema,* after being lobbied by a handful of senior princes close to Faisal, reluctantly issued a fatwa declaring Saud unfit to rule. The next day the *ulema* and sixty leading princes signed a fatwa stripping Saud of his remaining powers and cutting his allowance in half. A confident Faisal sent word to Barger that the crisis had passed. The very next evening, Metz visited Faisal and reported that he seemed to be "relaxed and in excellent humor." Faisal intimated that "it has been difficult, but things will be all right now."

By early April 1964, Faisal had gathered all executive powers into his hands; he was regent, prime minister and foreign minister; but Saud remained king. That autumn King Saud asked the *ulema* to reconsider their fatwa. This convinced his opponents in the royal family that it was time for him to abdicate altogether. On October 29, 1964, more than a score of *ulema* and a hundred senior princes gathered at a hotel near Riyadh airport and reached a consensus that Saud had to go. When the sixty-year-old monarch was informed of this, he holed up in his Nasriyah Palace. For three days he refused to see a delegation of the *ulema*. Finally, the royal family sent to him instead Muhammad ibn Abdul-Aziz, sixth son of the late Abdul-Aziz, who had over the years become a soft-spoken but highly regarded vizier to the House of Saud. Prince Muhammad persuaded King Saud to abdicate on November 2, 1964.

Soon afterwards, the al-Sauds—including Faisal—gathered at Riyadh's airport to see Saud and his full retinue off into exile. Saud flew to Dhahran, where he insisted on seeing his Aramco doctors for a last consultation. Early in January 1965 Father took us all out to Dhahran airport to witness Saud's final departure from the Kingdom. He was in a wheelchair, so a U.S. Air Force sergeant driving a forklift had to hoist him aboard the Saudi Airlines Boeing 720. Father filmed the scene as the plane took off into the dying sunset. Saud spent his final years in one of Athens's seaside hotels.

Even today in Saudi Arabia, the manner of Saud's abdication is a sensitive and controversial affair. At the time and ever since, the al-Sauds have floated the story line that it was the *ulema* who instigated the abdication. But in fact it was Faisal himself and his closest brothers—Muhammad, Khaled, Fahd and Sultan—plus the founding monarch's brother, Abdullah bin Abdul Rahman (otherwise known in Aramco circles as "Uncle Abbie"), who orchestrated what amounted to a slow-motion coup against the brother who they believed was sapping the House of Saud of its power and legitimacy. The coup had the explicit backing of Aramco and the U.S. government. In retrospect, Faisal's rise to power ended the crisis and forged a consensus among these senior princes that was to last for the next four decades. But at the time many observers felt that it would not be very long before Faisal himself would have to give way to real political reform and liberalization. The CIA predicted that "Faysal will find it difficult to win positive support from the small but growing educated class and from urban labor, especially if the country fails to make political progress." They were wrong.

4

Arabia:
"Progress Without Change"

Prince Faisal, King Abdul-Aziz and Crown Prince Saud,
Riyadh, 1951

No one in the family understands why Osama became so religious.

Salem bin Laden, 1979

M y parents' first tour in Saudi Arabia lasted from 1962 to 1965, precisely the years of Faisal's ascendancy. Their second tour came in 1972–75, with Father serving in the embassy in the Red Sea port of Jeddah. They liked Arabia, and after retiring from the Foreign Service, Father arranged a third stint in the "Kingdom" from 1979 to 1982, serving as General Electric's government relations representative in Riyadh. I went back to visit Arabia and Yemen several times in 1973–74, when I was just starting out as a freelance reporter for publications like the *Christian Science Monitor, Worldview,* the *Chicago Daily News* and the *Far Eastern Economic Review.*

Father acquired many Saudi friends and associates throughout these years, including Abdullah Tariki's successor as petroleum minister, Ahmed Zaki al-Yamani; members of the Alireza merchant family in Jeddah; the Bin Laden family; and various royals.

Like many expatriates in the Kingdom, Father associated King Faisal's years in power with the country's rapid economic modernization. Faisal's father, Abdul-Aziz, is known as the "unifier" and founder of the Kingdom, but it was Faisal who made Saudi Arabia what it is today. There was a moment before his slow-motion coup against his elder brother Saud when the Kingdom might have modernized its political system as well as its economic infrastructure. It might have become a constitutional monarchy. But that was a road not taken.

Faisal proved to be an enigmatic and highly autocratic ruler. He was in some ways the most cosmopolitan of the al-Sauds. In 1919, at the age of fourteen, he became the first Saudi royal to visit London and Paris, acting as his father's de facto foreign minister. In 1945, at the age of forty-one, he attended the founding conference of the United Nations in San Francisco. He had seen the industrialized West and understood the attraction of its cosmopolitan pleasures. On occasion, he drank alcohol, until a stomach operation in 1957 led him to forswear it altogether. In 1945 British police saw him emerge from a Bayswater brothel. For most of his life he was a chainsmoker. But aside from a few youthful indiscretions, Faisal was at his core a man of steely character, conscientious in his daily work habits, clever and decisive. With the passing of the years he also became ever more austere and puritanical. Unlike many royals, he never kept concubines. During his lifetime he never had more than three wives concurrently, and after divorcing his first two wives, from 1940 on he lived alone with his third and favorite wife, Iffat bint Ahmed al-Thunayan. She convinced him to allow his daughters to be educated at schools in Riyadh. He sent his sons to the Hun School, an elite preparatory school in Princeton, and then to a variety of Western universities.

In matters of public education, Faisal was a determined modernizer. He built hundreds of new schools—and not only for boys. In 1956 he and Iffat quietly opened a small school for girls in the relatively cosmopolitan city of Jeddah. In 1963 he built another school for girls in the town of Buraydah, in the heartland of the Wahhabi Nejd. Only one girl, the daughter of the teacher, registered. Protests in Buraydah were so fierce that Faisal dispatched the National Guard to keep the school open the first year. It was an extraordinary moment, a turning point akin to President Dwight Eisenhower's decision in 1957 to send the National Guard to Arkansas to defend the right of African-American students to attend a public high school. Faisal was a stubborn man and determined to pursue what he saw as a necessary reform. Within two years, even the tribal leaders of Buraydah saw the benefits of educating their girls. By 1974, a quarter million girls were enrolled in Saudi schools and colleges—and twice that number of Saudi men. In 1970, only about 15 percent of men and just 2 percent of women were literate; twenty years later 73 percent of men and 48 percent of women could read and write. King Faisal deserves credit for all this. But his educational reforms also suggest that Saudi society was far more capable of embracing rapid change than many observers of the Kingdom thought possible.

In his personal tastes and lifestyle, Faisal was perceived as modest and even frugal. One of his first acts as king was to expel Saud's corrupt and sybaritic personal assistant, Ibn Salem, giving him forty-eight hours to leave the country. And he tore down the seven-mile-long pink wall around Nasriyah Palace. He and Iffat lived in a small, relatively unassuming villa outside the grounds of Saud's ostentatious palace.

But if he was a modernizer, Faisal was also a political conservative. With Saud's abdication there was no more talk about introducing a Consultative Council or an elected assembly. Faisal placed senior princes—his closest half brothers—in key cabinet posts. He was a stickler for detail and found it nearly impossible to delegate authority. Far from liberalizing the political process, he gathered all authority unto himself. As he aged, Faisal became increasingly suspicious of a host of perceived enemies: Jews, Nasserites, Ba'athists, Shi'ites—and even the Americans. He made no effort to conceal his deep-seated anti-Semitism; he often lectured foreign dignitaries about the "international Zionist conspiracy," and he routinely handed out copies of *The Protocols of the Elders of Zion,* a nineteenth-century Russian forgery that purported to describe a Jewish conspiracy to dominate the world.

He understood that the Kingdom's rising oil wealth might encourage nonroyals to demand political rights and personal opportunities heretofore reserved for the royal family. Aramco understood this delicate political dynamic. "The appearance of beautiful homes, fancy cars, modern appliances and beautiful dresses, in both Western and Arabic movies," reported Ron Metz to Aramco, "instills a desire in many of the viewers to possess things which they are not able to afford. This has been excellent for business in the Eastern Province in the short term, but may cause considerable social discontent over the long term."

Faisal was prepared to deal harshly with his critics. He had not forgotten Abdul-Aziz al-Muammar's liberal criticisms of the House of Saud. In the spring of 1963, Faisal recalled him from his post as ambassador to Switzerland. Upon his return, al-Muammar continued to speak out against autocracy. Faisal warned him, "Either you stop stirring up trouble, or you go to prison." Al-Muammar's eldest daughter recalls the day in August 1963 when her father was dragged off by soldiers: "I remember my mother's screaming protests, begging not to take him, trying to block the arresting soldiers. Father did not resist." Mother and daughter then obtained an audience with King Faisal and appealed for al-Muammar's release. But Faisal told the daughter, "Forget your father, I am your father now." Al-Muammar remained in prison for nearly thirteen years—until after Faisal's death.

Faisal used his new powers to crack down on what he regarded as suspicious signs of "Nasserism." Nasser's secular ideas resonated among Saudi youth in the 1960s, and Faisal perceived this—rightly from his standpoint—as a threat to the legitimacy and stability of the Kingdom. In July 1964, he arrested scores of Saudis suspected of Nasserite or Communist associations. Censorship of the press was reimposed. The political officer in the U.S. consulate in Dhahran reported that police were raiding cafés in the Eastern Province and picking up anyone caught listening to Nasser's *Voice of the Arabs* radio program. Dozens of young Saudi men were disappearing into Dammam's new prison, a facility the consulate's political officer called an "ominous reminder to everyone" of the regime's "real means of control." An Aramco government relations official observed in 1965 that Faisal seemed to be "running the government by himself with no regard for established lines of authority and the theoretical structure of government."

Even such a well-connected Saudi as Mustafa Wahba—the son of the Kingdom's ambassador to London from 1934 to 1964—discovered that he was not above suspicion. After Prince Talal's exile in 1962, Wahba was never able to shake his association with the "Free Princes." His foreign education and foreign wife made him still more suspect. In 1968 King Faisal gave Wahba twenty-four hours to leave the Kingdom, stripping him and his family of their Saudi citizenship. His daughters, my schoolmates in the Dhahran Academy, never returned to Arabia.

Father's colleague in the embassy, Hume Horan, later argued that Faisal had in effect turned the Saud family into a political party:

> It wasn't so much a family as a political party that ran the country. Or you could say the family was a political party, and an extraordinarily efficient one. This multitude of princes of varying degrees constituted a network of trusted, well placed people throughout the country right down to the lowest "precinct" level. The impedance was zero. Information could flow through those channels of the royal family with a dazzling speed. An Embassy officer once remarked to an ordinary Saudi contact, "When is that King of yours going to drop the weird obsession he has about the *Protocols of the Elders of Zion?*" The very next day we got a call from the Royal Diwan saying, "You had better rein in Mr. so-and-so if he wants to stay in the country." In 24 hours that news had made it to the top and back down again! So, one could say the country was run by a political party that was at the same time a family.

Faisal feared both internal subversion and external threats. In September 1962 a military coup unseated the monarchy in Yemen. Within days of the coup, Nasser dispatched thousands of Egyptian troops to support the new Yemeni "republic"—in reality a military regime modeled after Nasser's regime. "The fuss in Yemen," Mother wrote a few weeks later, "is causing considerable discussion." Faisal was duly alarmed: the Yemeni army officers who had ousted their king were obviously inspired by Nasser's example, and Faisal feared Arab nationalists in his own military might someday attempt a similar coup against the House of Saud. By early 1963, more than 30,000 Egyptian troops were fighting a debilitating war against Yemeni tribesmen loyal to the deposed emir. Faisal stoked the Yemeni civil war by supplying arms to the royalists. That spring Egyptian Ilyushins bombed Saudi towns in southern Asir Province. In response, Faisal authorized American jet fighters to make a show of defending Saudi airspace, and the Egyptians never again bombed Saudi territory. But they slogged on in Yemen for five more years; to Faisal's disappointment, the republic survived.

*   *   *

Throughout the 1960s, the U.S. government and Aramco encouraged the Sauds to strengthen the monarchy in the face of the threat posed by secular Arab nationalists. Aramco's worst nightmare was a military coup d'état by some self-styled Saudi Nasserite or Ba'athist who might then nationalize the oil industry. Precisely this scenario was narrowly averted in the summer of 1969. On June 5, 1969, Faisal's growing intelligence apparatus uncovered a plot by a group of Saudi air force pilots. Saudi security forces arrested sixty pilots, soldiers and police, including the king's personal pilot. The commander of the Dhahran Air Academy, Lieutenant Colonel Dawood al-Romaih, apparently had planned to use fighter planes to shoot down the king's aircraft. All "non-royal" Saudi pilots were grounded and denied live ammunition. The plotters seemed to have some loose connection to the Arab National Movement (ANM), a secular group founded in Beirut in the early sixties by a group of students at the American University of Beirut. Several hundred people were arrested over the next few months, including a good friend of my father's, Dr. Saleh Ambah, the dean of the Dhahran College of Petroleum and Minerals, whose three daughters were attending the Dhahran Academy. Quite possibly Dr. Ambah's only crime was the fact that two of his wife's brothers were allegedly members of the ANM. He and his brothers-in-law spent the next thirty-one months in prison.

King Faisal was shocked by the coup attempt, which led him to question the loyalty of scores of people. The only apparent crime of a Saudi military attaché who was imprisoned was being the brother of Abdul-Aziz al-Muammar. Rumors circulated that some of those arrested had been thrown out of transport planes over the Empty Quarter. In fact, it seems that many of the arrestees were detained in secluded villas, given decent food and access to television. Their families received stipends, and eventually, by the late 1970s, nearly everyone was released.

Father was disturbed to learn of Dr. Ambah's sudden disappearance. He regarded him as an exemplary Saudi intellectual, a man of moderation and good judgment. The future aspirations of the average Saudi citizen depended on making a place for many more Dr. Ambahs. His arrest signaled a step backwards for the cause of Arabian modernity. Father's discreet inquiries about his friend were met with stony silence. There was nothing to be done.

Three years later, in April 1973, Father was sitting in Riyadh's Yamamah Hotel lobby—owned by the Bin Ladens—when he spotted Dr. Saleh Ambah walking down the corridor. "Saleh was most happy," Father cabled the State Department, "to see his old friend from Dhahran, who, he noted frankly, had grown a little fatter." Saleh said that he had been released the previous November and he had just had dinner with King Faisal at his palace for the evening *majlis*. Afterwards, he had walked with the king in the garden and assured him of his loyalty. Father asked him many questions and later wrote a confidential four-page memorandum on Dr. Ambah's ordeal. He wryly entitled it, "The Return of a Prodigal."

Dr. Ambah had been arrested by the Saudi secret police, the Mabahith, on February 9, 1970, just as he was about to board a plane for a business trip abroad. He was taken to Riyadh and confined to two rooms of a residential building. "Yes," he told Father, "there had been a few difficult moments in the first few days." Minister of Petroleum Ahmed Zaki al-Yamani—who had appointed Ambah as the first dean of the College of Petroleum and Minerals—told the American ambassador a month later that Ambah was shackled with "arm and leg manacles and being badly treated." Yamani said he "deplored" the arrest, but he was unable to do anything.*

For the first two years, Dr. Ambah was kept in solitary confinement with nothing to read and no access to television or radio. His wife, Aisha al-Fassi, says that he was kept in chains for several months and denied access to any medical treatment. Every few months General Mas'ud of the Mabahith would come by the house and interrogate him. Ambah told Father that he had no idea why he had been arrested. At times, General Mas'ud's questions took on a menacing tone. But at such moments, Ambah said he "refused to be intimidated by accusations and roughness in talk." During the last eight months of his detention, Ambah went on several hunger strikes, demanding books to read. His jailers finally relented but only gave him old religious books he had already read during his secondary schooling in Mecca. He later told a friend that he had been treated as if he were "the number one enemy of the state."

After Ambah's release, Father observed in his report that he seemed remarkably calm about what had happened to him. Why wasn't he bitter?

---

*Yamani himself was something of a reformer. He complained to U.S. Ambassador Herman Eilts of the "slow pace of internal political and social reform which he acknowledged was 'embarrassing' to him and which he thought the U.S. government should continue [to] push."

Ambah laughed and said some al-Saud princes had asked him the same thing during a recent dinner. He had replied that "a plant which lets itself be placed in acid only draws acid into its own system." He had decided while in prison that if he was ever released, he would not come out of this experience an embittered man.

Father pressed him to talk about his political views and attitudes toward the House of Saud. Ambah replied by pondering whether "the rate of change had been too fast." Perhaps, he said, he had moved too quickly to make the Petroleum College a modern educational institution. Maybe he had expected too much. Maybe the College had been "too great a shock to the Saudi system and they had gone a little too fast in some of their ideas." He had allowed the students to hold elections for a student council, and he had opened up the campus to a vibrant social life that included student theatre, musical bands and even some stand-up comedy. Maybe all these things had set off warning bells with the authorities.

Father observed that "Saudi Arabia would probably continue to be very conservative, resisting deep social change, while maintaining a faster pace . . . so far as the technological social change was concerned." Ambah agreed, but he nevertheless thought Arabia would "have to change more rapidly, especially in a social way, in order to get into the 20th century. . . ."

Father concluded his cable to Washington with this summary: "[Ambah] remains vocally critical of the speed with which the society is changing—making a fine distinction between the policies of those who rule (which he projects a confidence in)—and the ability of the society itself to change or be modified from the top."

Ambah's widow, Aisha al-Fassi, tells me, "My husband firmly believed in reforming his country and fighting rampant corruption." She blames his arrest on "insecure political cronies." But she also describes him as a "fervent Arab nationalist." So too does her daughter, Faizah Ambah, who writes that her father saw his work as "getting generations ready for a modern new world in the 1960s, inspired by a new nationalism. . . ."

Saleh Ambah was a teacher, not a revolutionary. Although he believed change had to come from the bottom, he did nothing to oppose the al-Sauds. But for those in power, his modern expectations were nevertheless highly threatening. As dean of the Petroleum College, Dr. Ambah was in a position to infect many young minds. "He was an inspiration to his students," recalls his daughter Faizah. Dr. Ambah never got his job back at the Petroleum College. Eventually, he moved his family to Jeddah and went into business, starting up a factory to produce pharmaceuticals. He died in Arlington, Virginia, in January 2002 and was buried in his birthplace, Mecca.

Dr. Ambah's story is emblematic. His tenure as dean of the Petroleum College was a liberal moment. But a royal family steeped in historical fears dashed his hopes and dreams for Arabia. They thought it dangerous to move too quickly. Real social change would cause the Wahhabi *ulema* to question the legitimacy of the House of Saud. It was safer to rely on the Mabahith to keep the demands for liberal political reform at check.

The treatment accorded Dr. Ambah became a familiar pattern over the next three decades. Critics of any stripe—liberal reformers, secular nationalists, outspoken Shi'ites or, more recently, Salafists—would suddenly disappear and reemerge months or years later, chastened but ostensibly rehabilitated and "forgiven." Arresting and then "pardoning" the Kingdom's various critics arguably stabilized the House of Saud—but at a cost. While the regime tightened its grip on power, it built no representative political institutions that could convey any larger political legitimacy beyond the royal family. No national assembly, and not even a "consultative" council, was nurtured. In the absence of such secular political institutions, the Wahhabi establishment thrived.

Faisal was a fundamentalist who thought he could use his religion to combat the radical, secular Arab nationalist ideas of Gamal Abdel Nasser. His foreign policy called for the creation of a pan-Islamist bloc. The Americans encouraged Faisal as a counterweight to Nasserism. The king's intelligence chief, Kamal Adham, built a network of "Islamic" agents across the Arab world. He funded anti-Nasserite Muslim Brotherhood cells across the region. Initially, the notion of a "pan-Islamist" bloc had little appeal to most Arabs in comparison to Nasser's secular pan-Arabism. Fundamentalism was out of fashion in the 1960s. But when Nasser stumbled and the forces of secular nationalism were defeated in the 1967 June War, Faisal's brand of pan-Islamist fundamentalism was there to fill the political vacuum. It was under Faisal that Saudi money was first used to build hundreds of madrassas—religious schools that propagated the militant and puritanical Wahhabi brand of Islam all over the Middle East and Asia.

King Faisal tried to co-opt the religious establishment and control it. Traditionally, the *ulema* had depended on charity for their livelihood; in a radical departure, Faisal made them state employees. Doctrinaire Wahhabis were given well-paid positions as high-ranking functionaries. A case in point was Sheikh Abdul Aziz bin Baz, whom Faisal appointed rector of Medina's Islamic University in 1969. Blind since adolescence, bin Baz was a fundamentalist preacher who had a long history of trying to thrust his anti-modernist views on the House of Saud. In the 1940s, he had issued a fatwa (religious ruling) decreeing that the presence of infidels anywhere in Arabia was an abomination. Infidels were banned from the holy cities of Mecca and Medina, but in his fatwa the sheikh proclaimed that they should be banned from the entire Kingdom. He declared it "illicit" for a Muslim to employ a non-Muslim, and argued that the "presence of infidels, male or female, poses a danger to Muslims, their beliefs, their morality, and their children's education." Sheikh bin Baz was still issuing fatwas during Faisal's reign. In 1969 he angered King Faisal by issuing a fatwa that proclaimed that the earth was flat, and that the sun circled the earth in orbit. Faisal ordered all copies of the document destroyed—but he allowed the sheikh to keep his post as university rector.

In the sixties, figures like Sheikh bin Baz were sometimes the object of quiet ridicule. Mother remembers the sheikh turning up one day in 1964 to inspect a nursing school in Dhahran. While he could not prohibit the training of female nurses, he was intent on restricting their behavior. One of Mother's friends was in the room when Sheikh bin Baz entered and abruptly announced that the nurses were inappropriately dressed. When asked how, being blind, he could discern this, he replied, "I can smell their perfume." He further decreed that while the nurses must be veiled at all times, it would be permissible for them to reveal one eye when attending to their patients. At this, Mother's friend reported, the room was filled with incredulous giggles.

Sheikh bin Baz rejected anything that smacked of modernity, objecting to everything from educating women to television. His fatwas deemed both barbershops and cigarettes to be *bid'a*—illicit innovations. Still, King Faisal not only tolerated him but also gave him the assignment of building a Wahhabi missionary organization to indoctrinate young men. It was called the Dawa Salafiya al-Muhtasiba, and some of its members would eventually take up arms against the House of Saud.

Ulema of Sheikh bin Baz's stripe entrenched themselves inside the King-dom's growing bureaucracy. In the late 1970s, Faisal's successor, King Kha-lid, appointed bin Baz chairman of the Department of Scientific Research and Guidance. The post gave Sheikh bin Baz senior cabinet rank, and each week he was now seen on Saudi television sitting with the king, discussing public affairs.

The *ulema* had always exercised a strong influence in the Kingdom, but prior to Faisal's time, they had wielded that influence informally. Under Faisal, however, the conservative religious establishment gained a judicial veto over social mores for the next generation. This institutionalization of Wahhabism nurtured extremist ideas. Faisal also made the Kingdom an asylum for Muslim political refugees from Nasser's Egypt and the Ba'athist regimes in Syria and Iraq. Many of these refugees were members of the Muslim Brotherhood (among them, Osama bin Laden's high school gym teacher). King Faisal ultimately gave sanctuary to thousands of members of the Muslim Brotherhood, and these politically active fundamentalists found common cause with the Wahhabi *ulema*. The seeds Faisal planted in the sixties would in the decades to come bring forth a brand of extremism that would threaten the House of Saud.

By early 1973 Aramco was pumping out eight million barrels of oil per day—and King Faisal was finding it hard to spend the revenue from all this oil. During a visit to Jeddah in the summer of 1973, I could see the King-dom was undergoing a massive makeover. Office buildings and private villas were going up everywhere; highways were being built, and modern super-markets and department stores were selling a wide variety of modern house-hold appliances, electronics, automobiles and other luxury imports. What I didn't know at the time was that earlier that year Faisal had funneled nearly $1 billion to Nasser's successor in Egypt, President Anwar Sadat, to finance a war against Israel. Sadat wanted to restore Egyptian sovereignty over the Israeli-occupied Sinai, and Faisal was determined to use his oil wealth as a weapon on behalf of the Palestinian refugees. Early in the summer of 1973, Faisal paid a secret visit to Sadat. Planning for the war accelerated. In July, Faisal gave a rare television interview in which he bluntly warned, "America's complete support of Zionism against the Arabs makes it extremely difficult for us to continue to supply U.S. petroleum needs and even to maintain friendly relations with America." The Nixon Administration ignored this blunt message. No one in official Washington could believe that the cautious, ultraconservative autocrat could attack American interests in the Middle East.

In the early morning hours of October 6, 1973, 80,000 Egyptian troops stormed across the Suez Canal, and stunned the world by forcing the Israeli army to fall well back into the Sinai. When President Nixon announced on October 19 that the United States was airlifting $2.2 billion worth of emergency armaments to Israel, King Faisal immediately imposed an embargo of all oil shipments to American ports. The embargo punished American consumers, who were soon paying double and triple the prices paid prior to the war for non-Arab oil. Ironically, for a time the embargo turned Faisal into something of an Arab nationalist hero.

But Faisal's embargo failed to change Washington's policies in the Arab-Israeli conflict. The Israelis eventually repulsed the Egyptian army, and on October 26 the war came to an end with an American-brokered cease-fire. The only long-term effect of the embargo was to inaugurate a new era of petrodollars. In 1970, Aramco had paid the Saudis $1.2 billion; four years later, the embargo caused oil prices to skyrocket and they never came down again. In 1974 the Saudis earned a phenomenal $22.5 billion from oil revenues. Father sent a cable back to Washington entitled "The Saudi Spending Machine." He predicted, accurately, that the Saudis would be earning more than $100 billion a year from oil exports by the end of the 1970s.

Faisal believed his kingdom could use this vast new oil wealth to import technology and modern consumer goods without any accompanying cultural liberalization. He wanted "progress without change." He wanted modernization without the Godlessness and individual liberty of Western secular culture. Two public cinemas were discreetly opened in Jeddah in the early 1970s, but elsewhere cinemas remained illegal—both because of the content of the films they might show and because *any* public gathering had potential political overtones. Television, by contrast, could be viewed in the privacy of Saudi homes, so Faisal deemed it an "innocent recreation." In 1965 the king authorized the installation of major television stations in Riyadh and Jeddah. President John F. Kennedy had proposed the idea of a national TV network to Faisal in 1962, believing that the medium would accelerate liberal reforms in the Kingdom. When Kennedy offered to have the U.S. Army Corps of Engineers install stations in Jeddah and Riyadh,

Faisal is said to have replied, "What would a blind person want more than a pair of eyes?" The stations began broadcasting on July 17, 1965. Initially, however, no human forms were broadcast, and even Mickey Mouse was censored when he was about to kiss Minnie.

Still, in September this cautious experiment turned deadly and was to have long-term consequences. A grandson of Ibn Saud, Prince Khaled ibn Musa'id—who had spent time in a mental institution in Europe—led a group of *ulema* and religious fanatics, outraged by this "un-Islamic" innovation, in an attempt to storm the new broadcasting studio in Riyadh. Shots were exchanged, and the demonstrators retreated to Prince Khaled's palace. Faisal issued orders that if the police were fired on again, they should respond with deadly force. Prince Khaled led another demonstration against the broadcast station, and when police blocked their way, he drew a pistol from his robes. A senior police officer shot him dead.

Nearly ten years later, on the morning of March 25, 1975, Prince Faisal ibn Musa'id rose from a night of partying and went to King Faisal's Riyadh palace. The twenty-six-year-old prince was a nephew of the king and the younger brother of Khaled ibn Musa'id, the prince killed during the television protests. The young prince had attended a number of colleges in America, where he learned to smoke marijuana, drink and carouse. The State Department had had to intervene on his behalf when Colorado police caught him in possession of LSD. News of his escapades reached his uncle, and when the prince returned, the king lifted his passport. Perhaps the prince was angered by this ban on his future travel, but he certainly blamed Faisal for his brother's death.

When Prince Faisal ibn Musa'id arrived at the anteroom to the king's office, a television crew was there, ready to film the ruler's meeting with a delegation from Kuwait. The prince happened to know one of the Kuwaitis, and when the doors opened, he walked in with the delegation. With the cameras rolling, King Faisal approached his nephew and moved to greet him with a traditional kiss on the cheek. At that moment, Prince Faisal drew a pistol from his robes and fired three shots. The first shot severed an artery in the king's neck. Another bullet grazed his forehead. Another sliced through an ear. King Faisal died an hour later in a hospital.

Within hours, Faisal's younger brother, Crown Prince Khalid, was proclaimed his successor. Three months later, Faisal ibn Musa'id was taken to Riyadh's main square and beheaded before 20,000 onlookers.

Soon after Faisal's assassination, King Khalid released Abdul Aziz al-Muammar—the reformer of the early 1960s who had advocated a constitutional monarchy—and paid for him to go to America for medical treatment. Likewise, Dr. Saleh Ambah's two brothers-in-law were finally amnestied, together with scores of other political prisoners.

I was living in San'a, North Yemen, working as a freelance reporter, when I heard of Faisal's assassination. That spring I profiled him for *Worldview*, a monthly American magazine. "If Faisal was an enlightened man of his generation," I wrote, "he was still an uncompromising autocrat." I think of that equation a bit differently today. Faisal now seems to me more the autocrat and less the enlightened man. Shortly before Faisal's death, Father took a California congressman in to meet the king. During the course of their short conversation, Faisal casually remarked that he "hoped to have congressmen for the Kingdom someday." But in his eleven years of absolute power, King Faisal never took one step towards democratizing his realm. To the contrary, he entrenched the monarchy and postponed the process of liberalization for decades.

Saudi Arabia remains one of the most closed societies of the twenty-first century. Paradoxically, it is also an extreme example of globalization. King Faisal's eleven-year reign made it possible for the House of Saud to retain a firm monopoly on political power. But after 9/11 the royal Sauds are not the best-known Saudis. That accolade is now reserved for the Bin Ladens—a clan of nonroyals whose fate is inextricably linked to the Sauds.

My father met Mohammed bin Laden in 1965, during his first tour in Arabia. The taciturn founder of the Bin Laden Group built many of the royal family's palaces and much of the Kingdom's infrastructure, including extensive renovations of the Grand Mosque at Mecca. The patriarch of a large family from the Hadramaut* in Southern Yemen, Mohammed had a dozen wives and more than fifty children—including Osama bin Laden. My parents remember him as a reserved, no-nonsense businessman.

Born in about 1908, Mohammed bin Laden came from an impoverished clan of subsistence farmers in the little village of Gharn Bashireih, nestled

---

*"Hadramaut" translates as "Death Is Among Us," an apt name for a forbidding landscape of dry rocky desert gouged by deep wadis.

in one of the most isolated of the Hadramaut's rocky canyons. At the age of twelve, an orphaned Mohammed was sent by his family to Ethiopia, where an abusive employer reportedly once struck him so hard in the face with a bundle of keys that young Mohammed lost one eye. Thereafter, he wore a glass eye. He had little schooling and remained illiterate all his life. After making his way to Jeddah in 1931, Mohammed bin Laden first worked as a porter and dockworker. He got his first construction job renovating the home of a Jeddah merchant. But his real break occurred when Aramco hired him as a bricklayer in Dhahran. Sometime in the late 1930s Mohammed bin Laden started his own construction company; by the late 1940s, he was building private homes and palaces for the al-Sauds in Riyadh. He won contracts from the royals to build highways, airports and government ministries. By the mid-1950s, he was a very rich man.

In 1967, Mohammed bin Laden was killed when his twin-engine plane crashed. He was fifty-nine years old. His eldest son, Salem bin Laden, twenty-one years old, took charge of his father's $150 million company. Within a decade Salem would see the Bin Laden Group acquire assets worth hundreds of millions of dollars.

In the late 1970s, my parents became good friends of Salem's. They were then living in Riyadh, and Salem was one of their favorite young Saudis. A free, unpretentious spirit, Salem was very different from his quietly pious father. He was witty, well read and cosmopolitan. Like many privileged young Saudis, and in stark contrast to his father, he had been educated abroad in a British boarding school, where he was exposed to everything the Western consumer society of the sixties had to offer. He loved Western music and had learned to play folk songs on his guitar. He frequently dropped by our house in Riyadh and brought along his guitar so that he and Mother could play Joan Baez and Bob Dylan tunes.

He had an outlandish, rakish sense of humor. He loved to fly his own airplanes and thought it good fun to buzz the king's desert encampment. After he did this once too often, the king grounded him. He seemed irreverently nonreligious. He drank, though moderately. And when he was abroad, he ate pork.

Father enjoyed Salem's informality and sheer impulsiveness. Salem was not a political animal—but as his major clients were members of the royal family, he had a large repertoire of gossipy stories about the Kingdom. He and Father would remain good friends until the day in May 1988 when

Salem flew his ultralight plane into a power line outside San Antonio. But nine years before his untimely death, Salem played a key role in the Kingdom's bloodiest crisis, the 1979 Mecca uprising.

Salem bin Laden, with his wife, Sheikha, and daughter, Sara, 1975

Salem was Osama bin Laden's eldest brother, and, once he became the leader of the Bin Laden clan, his proxy father as well. One evening Salem mentioned his younger brother to my parents. "No one in the family," he remarked, "understands why Osama became so religious." The two brothers were a study in contrasts. In 1979, Osama bin Laden was a quiet, devout twenty-one-year-old, already married and father to a handful of children. He kept a stable of twenty horses and loved riding. He drew both a paycheck and dividends from the family company; Salem assigned him to supervise some of the company's renovations in Medina. In contrast to his cosmopolitan elder brother, Osama had attended an elite Arabic-language school in Jeddah, where at the age of fifteen he had experienced a religious awakening. He thought of himself as a member of the Muslim Brotherhood—the transnational Sunni Muslim political movement that represents the opposition to many of the authoritarian regimes of the Arab world. Though he attended a university in Jeddah, he never earned a degree. He refused to be photographed—all images were un-Islamic, he thought—and he watched television only for the news, making sure to turn down the volume when any music, equally illicit, was broadcast. He distrusted all things Western.

By contrast, Salem loved all things American; he and Father shared a fascination with electronic gadgetry. Salem loved to travel, usually with a ragtag group of shaggy-haired American and European groupies in his entourage. In the autumn of 1979 he bought yet another Learjet and flew it from Washington, DC, to Europe and then back to Jeddah. That autumn he flew to Cairo, Dubai, Abu Dhabi, Crete and back to Cairo. He was spending millions of dollars on real estate in America.

In late 1979 Salem bin Laden called my parents and asked if he could visit them at their Riyadh house. He had just come from Mecca. It was 11:00 p.m., but Salem—he was then about thirty-four years old—was a night person, and he needed to talk. For the next three or four hours he breathlessly related his part in the recent two-week siege of Mecca. What he had seen had astounded him. He witnessed a full-scale battle in which scores of Saudi soldiers had been shot and killed.

In the early morning hours of November 20, 1979, some 300 to 500 extremists, led by a former National Guardsman, Juhayman ibn Muhammad ibn Saif al-Uteybi, seized control of Islam's holiest shrine, the Grand Mosque of Mecca, which surrounds the Kaa'ba, the granite cuboidal structure draped with a black silk curtain, to which Muslims turn in prayer. Juhayman al-Uteybi's father had been a member of the fierce Ikhwan, the Wahhabi warriors who had helped the founder of the House of Saud, Abdul-Aziz ibn Saud, to conquer the peninsula. But the Uteybi tribe had joined the Ikhwan's rebellion in 1928–29, and Juhayman's father had fought at the March 1929 battle of Sbala where the al-Sauds finally routed the Ikhwan. Juhayman had been reared on stories about the Ikhwan. Memories of the harsh repression the Sauds used to unify the Kingdom in the 1920s had not faded. Juhayman and his followers were Salafists—a term they used to differentiate themselves from Muslims who they believed had strayed from the original teachings of the Prophet Muhammad. They were more Wahhabi than the Wahhabis.

Juhayman al-Uteybi, forty-three years old in 1979, had joined the National Guard in the 1960s, but in the early 1970s he had quit and gone to Medina, where he listened to the reactionary sermons of Sheikh Abdul Aziz bin Baz, the blind preacher who had outraged King Faisal by proclaiming that the earth was flat. He joined the sheikh's missionary organization, the Dawa Salafiya al-Muhtasiba, and became an influential aide to him. Within a couple of years, Juhayman began standing up in the mosque and preaching his own fiery sermons. He excoriated the al-Sauds for their tolerance of Western culture and their forbidden modern innovations. By the late 1970s, he had attracted a following of several hundred like-minded young men.

They dressed like the old Ikhwan; they let their beards grow and spoke of the hypocrisy of the al-Sauds. Most came of Bedouin stock, but they also included the well-educated son of a Saudi diplomat, the son of a governor, and Yusuf Bajunaid, the son of a wealthy Jeddah merchant. They called themselves the "Ikhwan Group."

Criticism of Western ways was tolerable, but denouncing the al-Sauds was not. Sheikh bin Baz had learned this lesson in the 1940s, when King Abdul-Aziz had briefly imprisoned him. But now these acolytes of the sheikh's, led by Juhayman, began to speak of how Sheikh bin Baz was himself a hypocrite, and one who was enabling the al-Sauds by providing them with a religious veil of political legitimacy. "Bin Baz may know his Sunna well enough," Juhayman wrote, "but he uses it to bolster corrupt rulers."

Juhayman wrote a series of satirical pamphlets, and in 1978 a number of these incendiary epistles were collected in a small book in Kuwait and smuggled back into Arabia. The first, provocatively entitled *Rules of Allegiance and Obedience: The Misconduct of Rulers,* mocked Sheikh bin Baz's fatwa against the display of official photographs in public buildings: "It is not permissible to hang pictures on a wall . . . a picture may lead to exalting or worshipping it, particularly if the picture is that of a king." Why then, Juhayman asked, were the royal countenances still seen in every office building in the Kingdom—and even on the Saudi currency, the riyal?

Juhayman skewered other contradictions of the Saudi state. He objected to the free availability within the Kingdom of foreign books and videos. He condemned the "worship of the riyal" and the growing numbers of foreign infidels. "How can we propagate Islam," he asked, "when our professors are Christians?" He was particularly outraged by the tolerance shown to Shi'ite Muslims. "This country calls itself the state of One God!" Juhayman wrote. "But then . . . it accepts the Shi'ites to be called Muslims . . . and opposes those who combat the heretical worshippers of Ali and Hussein."

Juhayman's critique was not confined to the al-Sauds. He described all contemporary Muslim rulers as "imposed" and therefore unworthy of allegiance. This message attracted a few non-Saudi devotees—a handful of Egyptian, Yemeni, Sudanese and other foreign dissidents living in Mecca. Two African-American Muslims joined the Ikhwan Group.

In the spring of 1978 the Saudi government launched a crackdown. Prince Nayef, the Minister of the Interior, ordered the arrest of Juhayman and scores of his followers. Juyahman eluded the dragnet and fled into the desert. But some twenty-five of his men were detained. From his desert sanctuary in the Uteybi homeland north of Riyadh, Juhayman sent messages to various *ulema* in Mecca and Medina, seeking their intercession with Sheikh bin Baz. In due course, the blind sheikh called Prince Nayef and persuaded him to release Juhayman's men. The men had been beaten in prison, and this experience only inflamed their hatred for the al-Sauds.

Late in 1978, Juhayman's followers began to talk among themselves of a dream many of them had experienced. In the dream they saw one of Juhayman's acolytes and his brother-in-law, Muhammad ibn Abdullah al-Qahtani, acclaimed by thousands of worshippers as the Mahdi in Mecca's Grand Mosque. It was Muhammad al-Qahtani's sister, also a follower of Juhayman's, who first spoke of this dream. There is no mention of the Mahdi in the Koran, but early Islamic hadiths (commentary) speak of some kind of Islamic Messiah. "The princes will corrupt the earth," the Prophet Muhammad is supposed to have said, "so one of my people will be sent to bring back justice."

Juhayman convinced his brother-in-law that he, al-Qahtani, was the Mahdi—and in the early autumn of 1979 they began to make plans for his unveiling. (Juhayman also divorced his wife and married the purported Mahdi's sister.) Juhayman raised funds from his followers to buy Soviet-manufactured AK-47s and other firearms. Using empty coffins, they smuggled these into the Grand Mosque, along with a hoard of dates and camel's milk—traditional Bedouin survival fare—and, on the morning of November 20, called their 300 to 500 followers to "prayer."

Their plan was madness. All Muslims recognize the grounds of the Kaa'ba as sacrosanct. The blood of animals, let alone human beings, is never to be shed in the premises of the Grand Mosque. Firing a gun inside the holy sanctuary is a deadly sin. Nevertheless, Juhayman and his followers pulled out their AK-47s from under their robes and began shooting in the air. When police rushed to the scene Juhayman's gunmen shot two of them dead. Juhayman seized the microphone from the attending imam and screamed, "Recognize the Mahdi who will cleanse this Kingdom of its corruptions." Juhayman broadcast his demands from loudspeakers perched atop the mosque's minarets. He accused the al-Saud princes of a long list of crimes against Islam: they imbibed alcohol; they allowed women to work in offices and appear on television; and they collaborated with "infidels" on business deals within the Kingdom. He accused the governor of Mecca, Prince Fawwaz ibn Abdul Aziz, of being a gambler and an alcoholic. Tens of thousands in Mecca heard these allegations, broadcast from the minarets of the Grand Mosque. (Prince Fawwaz had been one of the "Free Princes," associated in the 1960s with Prince Talal, and he had spent some years in exile.)

Juhayman's demands were explicitly political: he wanted the royal family to be stripped of their power and wealth. He demanded that all Western embassies be closed; that all foreign military and civilian advisers to the Kingdom be expelled; and that all oil exports to the United States cease.

Juhayman's audacity was matched by his naïveté. He had thought that the people of Mecca would rise up and join him in his revolution. They did not. But neither was the siege easily broken. The Grand Mosque was no longer just the Kaa'ba surrounded by a courtyard. Over the previous twenty years the mosque had undergone elaborate renovations—all carried out by the Bin Laden Group. Its grounds now encompassed more than forty-five acres, large enough to accommodate over 250,000 worshippers. With its layers of subterranean hermitages—normally used for pilgrims—the mosque had become a fortress. When the king's intelligence chief, Prince Turki ibn Faisal (King Faisal's youngest son, age thirty-four), arrived from Riyadh to take charge, he was shot at by a sniper stationed in one of the Grand Mosque's minarets. The bullet narrowly missed him and instead shattered a glass door. Turki soon realized that securing the Grand Mosque would be no easy task. Some of the rebels were veteran National Guardsmen and sharpshooters like Affas bin Muhaya, a son of the Uteybi tribal chief killed by King Abdul-Aziz during the Ikhwan Revolt of 1928–29.

Juhayman's men let thousands of worshippers go free, keeping twenty-five or thirty as hostages. Then they chained and locked the mosque's fifty-one heavy iron gates and stationed snipers at all the commanding heights. They had plenty of food and ammunition.

Turki called in hundreds of Saudi police and National Guard and army troops. But he could not order them to storm the mosque without first obtaining a religious fatwa permitting the soldiers to fire their weapons inside the sacred building. The chief of the *ulema* was still Sheikh Abdul Aziz bin Baz, the blind sheikh at whose feet Juhayman had studied in Medina. King Khalid met with Sheikh bin Baz and thirty other *ulema* in Riyadh, and the sheikh agreed to issue the required fatwa, but he imposed some conditions: the al-Sauds must end what the *ulema* saw as a dangerously un-Islamic trend toward social liberalization. No more women newscasters should be seen on television. The two public cinemas in Jeddah must be closed. The ban on alcohol must be strictly enforced. And the *ulema* wanted assurances that it could use millions of petrodollars for the propagation of the faith both at home and abroad. Despite King Khalid's rapid agreement, it took three days for the *ulema* to iron out a written fatwa authorizing the use of force.

Prince Turki knew he needed better intelligence before sending troops into the mosque. He called upon Salem bin Laden to provide the Bin Laden Group's architectural drawings for the renovation of the Grand Mosque. Salem arrived in Mecca shortly after the siege began, and was soon seen sitting on the hood of his car, cradling a machine gun in his arms. But he didn't have the drawings. He sheepishly explained that the Bin Laden Group was in the process of moving its offices and that it would take some time to locate the blueprints of the compound. In the meantime, Salem found a bullhorn and, standing atop an ambulance, he addressed the hostages inside the Grand Mosque, encouraging them to escape. Salem felt exhilarated when several did manage to flee the mosque.

When the blueprints for the Grand Mosque finally arrived, Salem pored over them with Prince Turki and Prince Saud (the foreign minister). All three men were disheartened to see what the blueprints showed—that deep beneath the mosque was a *qaboo,* a labyrinth of rooms and extensive hallways. Everything was solidly built of reinforced concrete lined with thick slabs of marble. The Bin Laden Group had spared no expense in the renovation. Prince Bandar bin Sultan, later Riyadh's ambassador to Washington, joked that for constructing such a fortress Salem bin Laden "ought to be given a medal—and then shot."

During the first few days of the siege, rebel snipers in the Grand Mosque's towering minarets killed dozens of Saudi soldiers. The snipers were silenced only when TOW missiles were fired into the minarets. The initial ground assault ran into a deadly ambush and was forced to retreat, with scores more killed. Four days into the siege, Saudi troops, using M-113 armored personnel carriers, fought their way inside the Marwa-Safa Gallery, a long corridor on the eastern edge of the mosque. On day five the army entered the plaza surrounding the Kaa'ba, forcing the rebels to retreat to the maze of rooms in the lower *qaboo.* Later that day Prince Turki, Prince Saud and Salem bin Laden, all in khaki army uniforms, cautiously crept inside the mosque. The bodies of dead soldiers and rebels lay scattered about the mosque's corridors. The usually crowded plaza around the Kaa'ba was empty and eerily silent.

One of the dead was later identified as Muhammad al-Qahtani, the supposed Mahdi. But despite this, Juhayman and hundreds of his followers fought on from their sanctuaries in the *qaboo*. Saudi troops found they could not enter its dark corridors without running into deadly machine-gun fire. Lobbing tear gas canisters into the *qaboo* also proved ineffective. Nearly a week into the siege, Prince Turki had failed to secure the Grand Mosque.

At this point, the al-Sauds suddenly faced another uprising on the other side of the country. Rioting broke out in the coastal towns of the oil-rich Eastern Province, home to most of the Kingdom's 350,000 Shi'ites. In February 1979 the Ayatollah Khomeini toppled the Pahlavi dynasty in Iran and turned the country into a theocracy ruled by Shi'ite clerics. Six weeks after the Shah's overthrow, I spent three weeks in Tehran and Khomeini's hometown of Qom, trying to land an interview with the Ayatollah. I failed. But the experience taught me to appreciate the fervor generated by this Shi'ite revolution. Now, young Saudi Shi'ites, acting under the misapprehension that Juhayman's rebellion in Mecca was related to Khomeini's in Iran, organized demonstrations against both the regime and Aramco. Most Shi'ites in Arabia still felt discriminated against by the Wahhabi Sunni regime, and, although more than one-third of Aramco's employees were Saudi Shi'ites, they saw Aramco—with its nearly 35,000 American employees living and working in the Eastern Province—as complicit with the regime's policies. Saudi National Guard units rushed to the scene, and in one confrontation with the crowds they fired live ammunition, killing five Shi'ites. This inflamed the Shi'ite community, and in the following days a number of Saudi soldiers were killed by youths armed with knives and iron bars. The al-Sauds imposed a news blackout, cut communications to the Eastern Province, and closed all roads surrounding the Shi'ite towns of Qatif, Safwa and Sayhat. King Khalid was forced to dispatch troops exhausted from the battles in Mecca to the Eastern Province. They used helicopter gunships and machine guns mounted in the back of pickup trucks to subdue the crowds. Some twenty Shi'ite protestors and a small number of Saudi troops were killed.

The House of Saud was now fighting a battle on two fronts. And while the Shi'ite riots were relatively easily contained, the royal family was acutely embarrassed by its continued failure to secure the Grand Mosque. Without a breakthrough, it seemed likely that Juhayman's Ikhwan rebels could remain holed up in the *qaboo* for weeks or even months. A week into the crisis, Prince Turki called on France's Service de Documentation Extérieure et de Contre-Espionnage (SDECE), the French intelligence agency, for assistance. The French sent three experienced commandos and numerous canisters of CB gas made from the highly toxic dichlorobenzylidene-malononitrile. They suggested that Saudi troops drill holes in the floor of the mosque's courtyard and drop the CB canisters into the *qaboo* below. Salem bin Laden arranged for the requisite drills and had his men bore the holes. They first dropped hand grenades and then the CB down the holes. As the rooms below were doused with this highly disabling gas, Saudi troops wearing gas masks stormed the *qaboo*, lobbing hand grenades into each room.

By the evening of December 4, 1979, two weeks after the siege began, Saudi forces finally cleared the *qaboo* and captured Juhayman and 170 of his followers. Prince Nayef announced on Saudi television that 12 Saudi officers and 115 soldiers had been killed, together with 117 rebels and 26 hostages. The official toll thus stood at some 270 killed, but the American ambassador cabled Washington that the actual number of fatalities was probably much higher. Some estimate the siege took more than 1,000 lives.

Juhayman al-Uteybi, under arrest after
the siege of Mecca, December 1979

On January 9, 1980, Juhayman al-Uteybi and sixty-two of his men were each publicly beheaded in one of eight different cities throughout the Kingdom. They included forty-one Saudi citizens, three Kuwaitis, ten Egyptians, seven Yemenis, one Sudanese, and one Iraqi. They had defiled the holy grounds of the Grand Mosque and stunned the al-Sauds with the ferocity of their armed challenge to the very existence of the monarchy. The rebels' choice, made out of messianic zeal, to seize the Grand Mosque had been in purely tactical terms a stupid one. "If he [Juhayman] had attacked my palace," King Khalid reportedly said, "he might have met with more success."

Salem bin Laden saw in the Mecca events proof that the al-Sauds were not invulnerable to the kind of revolutionary upheaval that had just toppled the Pahlavi dynasty in Iran. And he realized that, as things stood, the fortunes of the Bin Ladens were inextricably linked to those of the al-Sauds. So even before the siege was over, Salem took the precaution of setting up a secret offshore entity—Binladen International Inc.—registered in Panama City. A few months later, he moved additional Bin Laden corporate assets to Panama, telling an associate that he needed to protect his family's interests "should there be some sort of turmoil in Saudi Arabia." Like any prudent businessman, Salem was hedging his bets.

In the aftermath of the siege a visibly shaken royal family learned all the wrong lessons. "The mosque thing was such a shock," recalled Richard Murphy, who became the U.S. ambassador to Saudi Arabia in 1981. "The royal family decided then and there that no one would outflank them on the right." Like King Faisal, who had temporized with Wahhabi orthodoxy, the al-Sauds now decided that liberalization had proceeded at too quick a pace in the four years since Faisal's assassination. They now reversed course and fulfilled their bargain with Sheikh bin Baz. The conditions imposed by the *ulema,* in exchange for the fatwa authorizing the storming of the Grand Mosque, were met. Female television news announcers were taken off the air. Large cash payments were made to some of the most backward and retrograde members of the *ulema.* The Wahhabi establishment was allowed to publish and freely distribute its most xenophobic literature. To the delight of the *ulema,* Prince Fawwaz, a former "Free Prince," was fired as governor of Mecca.

But none of these steps eliminated the basic contradiction between primary Wahhabi precepts and the reality of modern life in Arabia. This contradiction lies at the heart of the Saudi state. And it has been the source of the repeated upheavals that trace their origins to the first encounters between the American oilmen and the Arabs of Arabia.

Juhayman al-Uteybi's Mecca siege ended in his beheading. But his lethal ideas survived and spread far beyond Arabia. His Kuwaiti-published pamphlets found their way to Egypt, where they influenced radical Islamic fundamentalists. As the *Wall Street Journal* reporter Yaroslav Trofimov points out in his exhaustive investigation, *The Siege of Mecca,* one of the pilgrims who witnessed Juhayman's siege was a young Egyptian student named Mohammad Shawqi Islambouli. He gave copies of Juhayman's writings to his brother Khaled Islambouli, a first lieutenant in the Egyptian army. On October 6, 1981, Lieutenant Islambouli assassinated President Anwar Sadat. His brother Mohammad is believed to be a top al-Qaeda leader who has fought in Afghanistan.

At the time of the siege, Salem bin Laden's younger brother Osama was not associated with Juhayman's Ikhwan Group. But several years later, in the mid-1980s, he expressed sympathy for the rebels. "The men who seized Mecca," he reportedly told a friend, "were true Muslims . . . innocent of any crime, and . . . they were killed ruthlessly."

Just weeks after the dénouement of the Mecca siege, Soviet troops invaded Afghanistan. This event placed further political pressures on the al-Sauds to tolerate Ikhwani ideas. Saudis, both religious and secular, rallied to the Afghan cause and contributed money to assist Afghan refugees flooding into Pakistan. Salem bin Laden himself facilitated such donations—for "humanitarian" purposes but also for arms to fight the Soviets. As Steve Coll observes in *The Bin Ladens,* his brilliant biography of the family, "organizing donations to Afghan refugees offered Salem, who was a savvy manipulator, a kind of triple play—it fulfilled his family's tithing obligations, it supported [Crown Prince] Fahd's clandestine foreign policy, and it diverted the energies of the Bin Laden family's religious wing." Osama, a member of this "religious wing," now began commuting to Peshawar, Pakistan. He was frequently invited to Saudi embassy functions in Islamabad, where he met the young head of Saudi intelligence, Prince Turki. And, naturally, Prince Turki facilitated some of Osama's own charitable activities on behalf of the Afghan refugees. As Turki's chief of staff later said, "He [Osama bin Laden] had a strong relation with Saudi intelligence and with our embassy in Pakistan."

Throughout the 1980s, Osama was a virtual agent-cum-facilitator of Saudi intelligence, funneling arms and money to the Afghan mujahideen. There is no evidence that Osama met with CIA officers—but he did work directly with Afghans who were receiving tens of thousands of dollars in cash from undercover CIA agents.

Osama returned to Saudi Arabia in 1990. Having had a hand in the liberation of Afghanistan, he was now something of a minor national hero. But then, in August of that year, Iraq's dictator, Saddam Hussein, invaded and annexed Kuwait, posing a direct military threat to Saudi Arabia. In response, the House of Saud invited hundreds of thousands of American troops to defend the Kingdom. Osama bin Laden was outraged by this reliance on infidels for defense. Echoing Juhayman's criticisms of the Wahhabi *ulema,* he accused Sheikh bin Baz—who issued a fatwa sanctioning the invitation of foreign troops—of being "weak and soft." The old sheikh, Bin Laden said, was letting his words be used by the al-Sauds "as a cane to strike . . . honest scholars."

The intellectual roots of al-Qaeda can thus be traced back to the messianic ideas of Juhayman al-Uteybi, and from him back to Sheikh bin Baz, and then further back to the Ikhwan and, ultimately, to the itinerant preacher Muhammad al-Wahhab. The fifteen Saudi hijackers on 9/11 no doubt thought of themselves as twenty-first-century Ikhwanis, reviving a powerful and deadly tradition. But, though they used the language of religion, their immediate motivations were political: they wanted to destroy the House of Saud and to end the "occupation" of Palestine. As Osama bin Laden stated in his 1996 *Declaration of War Against the Americans Occupying the Land of the Two Holy Places,* "The Zionist-Crusader alliance moves quickly to contain and abort any 'corrective movement' appearing in the Islamic countries." This made the "far enemy"—the Americans—a legitimate target.

Was the Saudi Arabia of my childhood, as the political scientist Robert Vitalis argues, "America's Kingdom"? Although the Saudis were never colonized, my childhood memories suggest a more complicated reality, a deeply troubling mutual dependency. As I have struggled in this memoir to integrate my childhood impressions with a larger historical narrative, the picture that emerges is unsettling. If postwar America became, in the words of the Harvard anthropologist Engseng Ho, "an empire without colonies," then Arabia was certainly part of that invisible empire. We Americans built Aramco, built the company towns of the Eastern Province, built the Dhahran air base, and trained the Saudi National Guard and army. It was our Army Corps of Engineers who built multibillion-dollar "military cities" throughout the Kingdom. The Saudi intelligence apparatus was modeled after our CIA—and for decades American intelligence officers, often embedded inside Aramco, were the closest of advisers to the king. Beginning in 1946, an American airline, TWA, built and managed for decades the Saudi national airline. Over the years, we trained their technocratic elites, educating more than a million Saudi citizens in American universities. In the 1960s, we opposed the Free Princes and their reformist plans for a constitutional monarchy. Both Aramco and Washington valued stability in the form of an absolute monarchy over the uncertainty of any alternative. We aligned ourselves with Wahhabi royalists and against secular Arab nationalists. And when the House of Saud was threatened by Saddam Hussein's occupation of Kuwait in 1990, we sent an army of half a million Americans to defend the Kingdom. All of this was done because of our desire to control Arabian black gold.

To be sure, Osama bin Laden was a homegrown product of Arabia's Ikhwani history. The roots of this rebellious history go back many centuries, as effectively demonstrated by Engseng Ho. Ho's observations make comprehensible in a larger historical context what is otherwise a series of incomprehensible, monstrously evil, acts of terrorism.

Bin Laden's ancestors, Ho reminds us, came from the Hadramaut, a rugged desert region of southern Yemen. Cut off from the rest of Arabia by mountain barriers and the vast emptiness of the Rub' al-Khali, the region's people made their living over the centuries as merchants and sailors, sending their sons off across the Indian Ocean in wooden dhows, both to earn their fortunes and to propagate the Muslim faith. Hadrami Arabs established their presence in far-flung outposts in India, Java, Sri Lanka and the Philippines, and also in African seaports in Kenya and Somalia. Over many generations this Hadrami diaspora built a close-knit network of mutual assistance societies; every Hadrami emigrant was equipped with the names of dozens of his compatriots in port cities across the Indian Ocean. Some became wealthy merchants, and some rose to become influential political advisers to local princely states. These Hadramis played a major role in the expansion of Islam precisely at a moment in history when the British Empire was establishing its own colonial outposts across Asia and Africa. "In the arc of coasts around the Indian Ocean," Ho writes, "the British and Hadrami Arabs were everywhere, and everywhere overlapping. A diaspora and an empire were locked in a tight embrace of intimacy and treachery, a relationship of mutual benefit, attraction, and aversion." As early as the sixteenth century, Hadrami Arabs were involved in sporadic, but often deadly, resistance against the British Empire. They led rebellions against Dutch colonization in Aceh and British rule in India. Ho points out that between 1836 and 1921 there were thirty-two uprisings along India's Malabar Coast, and most of them were instigated by Hadrami Arabs. Interestingly, the Hadramis sometimes used suicidal assaults. And, in another parallel to Bin Laden's messianic mission, they always spoke of waging jihad in the name of Islamic unity as defined by the Caliphate—the notion that all Muslims should live in a single, unified Islamic state, governed by Sharia law.

Historically speaking, Bin Laden's bloody journey has its roots in this Hadrami outlook and experience. His goals are reminiscent of the goals of his Hadrami ancestors—to expel the infidels from Arabia and unite Muslims in a resurrected Caliphate. Organizationally, al-Qaeda's profile harks back to the old Hadrami network, including its ability to transfer funds through an informal banking system known as *hawala*. Even al-Qaeda's initial targets—Aden, Tanzania, Kenya, Somalia, Indonesia, the Philippines and Pakistan—were the same venues in which Hadrami Arabs waged their rebellions against British imperialism. Consciously or not, Bin Laden is drawing on a deep historical tradition from his own culture to wage an asymmetrical war against the informal, even invisible, American empire that has replaced the British imperium confronted by his Hadrami ancestors. His ultimate goal, of course, is not America but the House of Saud—which in his eyes has become a proxy for the foreign infidels who have corrupted Arabia.

Will the Bin Laden attacks succeed in toppling the House of Saud? Does this Ikhwani history condemn Arabia to a reactionary future? I don't think so. But the contradictions within Saudi society are still deeply troubling. Soon after 9/11, two prominent Wahhabi *ulema,* sheikhs Hamud al Shu'aybi and Abdullah bin Jibrin, issued fatwas brazenly justifying the attacks. Those killed, they said, were not innocents. Many Saudis dismissed this nonsense as the usual babbling of ignorant clerics. More startling, however, was the fact that the fatwas included a blanket condemnation as apostates of any Muslims who collaborate with America. Obviously, the al-Sauds fit the definition of "collaborators." The long alliance of convenience between the al-Sauds and the Wahhabi establishment may well be unraveling.

"Though few would publicly admit it," writes Sulaiman al-Hattlan, a Saudi magazine editor, "Saudis have become hostages of the backward agenda of a small minority of bin Laden supporters who in effect have hijacked our society. . . . Because of the dominance of Wahhabism, Saudi society has been exposed to only one school of thought, one that teaches hatred of Jews, Christians, and certain Muslims, like Shiites and liberal and moderate Sunnis. But we Saudis must acknowledge that our real enemy is religious fanaticism. We have to stop talking about the need for reform and actually start it, particularly in education." Al-Hattlan wrote this in an op-ed for the *New York Times,* but similar sentiments are widely expressed in the Kingdom.

The series of attacks since launched by al-Qaeda within Saudi Arabia, killing both Americans and fellow Muslims, has strengthened the case for liberal reform. In May 2003, al-Qaeda struck an American compound in Riyadh, killing twenty-six people. In May 2004, six Westerners were killed in an attack on Yanbu and another nineteen in al-Khobar. In 2005, al-Qaeda militants attacked the U.S. consulate in Jeddah. In February 2006 two truckloads of militants wearing the uniforms of Saudi Aramco's private security force talked their way through the main gate of the Abqaiq oil complex. They were challenged by guards at the next checkpoint, and a gunfight broke out; the explosive-laden trucks blew up. All told, since 9/11 scores of foreigners have been killed inside the Kingdom, along with numerous al-Qaeda militants. In 2007, some 380 Saudi nationals were arrested in connection with these attacks.

Forty years ago the whole notion of an Islamist-Salafist insurgency carrying out assassinations and car-bomb attacks would have been absurd. Today, while unnerving, these attacks are nevertheless seen by most Saudis as acts of desperation, carried out by a handful of tiresome Ikhwani fanatics. Still, the violence has forced the growing number of Americans living in Arabia to retreat to their gated compounds. Aramcons and other expatriates now live with heavily armed guards standing at those gates.

In May 2007, I visited my childhood home in Dhahran, accompanied by my eighty-two-year-old father. The intense layers of security astonished me.

I was forced to make an appointment to gain access to the consulate compound. Driving up to the gate, we saw a squadron of Saudi army troops stationed outside the compound's wall. There was an armored personnel carrier parked on the side of the road. The four-foot rock wall that I remembered had been built up to a height of fifteen feet. Forty years ago, anyone could have driven into the consulate compound without being challenged. Back then, there had been no gate or checkpoint. This time, I was confronted by a solid iron wall. Only after a Saudi soldier bearing a machine gun inspected our credentials was the electric iron gate rolled on its tracks to the side. The first thing we then saw, right in front of us, was a sandbagged machine-gun nest in the middle of the road, manned by an armed and helmeted Gurkha—a guard recruited from Nepal. He pointed his machine gun straight at us. There were twenty-five or thirty of these Gurkhas, all over the compound. A half-dozen patrolled up and down the one paved road leading from the consulate office building to the consul general's residence at the top of the slope. They wore camouflaged uniforms, flak jackets, helmets and heavy combat boots. They carried both automatic weapons and their traditional Gurkha "kukri" knives stuck into their combat belts. I was astounded—and disheartened. My childhood home—where I had once freely wandered in and out, completely unsupervised, a child unfettered—was now an armed fortress under siege.

Aside from the security, nonetheless, the American Camp—now known as Saudi Aramco Residential Camp—was much as I remembered it. It is still a "Pleasantville"—the same suburban company town of my childhood. When we visited an American couple in their one-story ranch home, my eye was immediately drawn to a large bar—and a spacious closet reserved for the ubiquitous still.

More than 10,000 people reside within the camp, 6,000 of whom are Americans. But while numerous Saudis now live there, many Saudi employees still prefer to make their homes elsewhere. And after all these decades there are still resentments. "Some of these Americans," said one Saudi camp resident, "make it all too clear that they are here only for the money. And they don't like it when a Saudi moves in next door." On the other hand, many second-generation American Aramcons live here, employees who relished their childhood years in Dhahran and, like their fathers, have spent their careers with the company. Many speak Arabic and feel at home in Arabia. There are now more than 40,000 Americans living in the Eastern Province, and their numbers are growing. Whatever Saudi al-Qaeda does, the Americans are entrenched.

Aramco was formally nationalized in 1980, and by the end of that decade Saudis constituted more than 70 percent of the company's workforce— including its supervisory and managerial positions. By 2008, the company was worth a phenomenal $781 billion. It is the single wealthiest company in the world. Saudis control the board of directors, but the four big American oil companies still have special rights to market the oil.

Amnesty International had this to say about the Kingdom in a recent report: "Peaceful critics of the government were subjected to prolonged detention without charge or trial. There were allegations of torture, and floggings continued to be imposed by the courts. Violence against women was prevalent and migrant workers suffered discrimination and abuse. At least 39 people were executed." Other sources suggest the number of executions in 2007 was more than 120.

None of this is defensible. But it is also true that since 9/11 the pendulum has swung toward a new era of liberalization. The present ruler, King Abdullah, has opened up the press, and the Kingdom's newspapers are filled with a broad range of opinion. The Mutawwai'in—the religious police—are openly criticized for their excesses and zeal. On a recent trip to Riyadh I never saw any evidence of them in the streets. Even so, they are still there, still sanctioned by the regime.

By any measurement, Arabia has undergone momentous changes over the last fifty years. Literacy rates are now over 90 percent. Health care is universal. Most Saudi families have a modern standard of living comparable to that in any Western industrialized country. And all of this has happened without any significant social disintegration. Statistics on violent crime, drug addiction, divorce and alcoholism are still relatively low compared to the West.

The status of women remains a contentious issue. Chas Freeman, a former American ambassador to Riyadh, uses the apt phrase "sexual apartheid" to describe the segregation of women. On the other hand, conditions for them have changed dramatically in the last few decades. In Dhahran, I met Sally Al-Turki, an American woman married to an influential Saudi businessman in the Eastern Province. Sally manages a private school with more than 1,700 students, about half of whom are girls. She has lived in Dhahran for more than three and a half decades, and ardently believes that women have made enormous strides: "Saudi girls are going to school and to universities, and getting jobs in many places as teachers, doctors, nurses, social workers, etc. They are also writing in newspapers, managing their own businesses, controlling their own money, forming committees, and working to improve life generally and particularly for women and children. Many more women are opening their own businesses these days. . . ."

There are even female Saudi executives who run thriving corporations. The Arabic-language edition of *Forbes* magazine published a list some time ago of the top fifty "Most Powerful Businesswomen in the Arab World Today." A Saudi woman, Lubna S. Olayan, led the list.

Still, women are required to be accompanied by a male relative to do just about anything in the public arena. As Human Rights Watch observed in a critical report on the status of women, "Saudi women are denied the legal right to make even trivial decisions for their children—women cannot open bank accounts for children, enroll them in school, obtain school files or travel with their children without written permission from the child's father."

Yet it is hard to imagine how even such culturally entrenched attitudes can last very long in the twenty-first century. Women still wear an *abaya* over their clothes—but many can be seen shopping in modern malls with no veil to hide their faces. They are still not allowed to drive. But this too will probably change. In 2008 a petition was submitted to King Abdullah demanding that the ban on female driving be lifted. More than 1,100 people, women and men, signed the petition. One Saudi woman I met in Dhahran—she has a doctorate in chemical engineering—predicted that women would be driving within five years. An Egyptian journalist, Mona Eltahawy, argues that the Kingdom "is a country playing out its identity crises over the bodies of women." She suggests that women driving is a wedge issue that will lead to even more significant reforms: "Ultimately, that petition sent to King Abdullah is surely one not so much to end the driving ban but to push the Mutawwai'in out of the way."

But the "Magical Kingdom" of my youth faces deeper existential questions than whether women should be allowed to get behind the steering wheel. Ultimately, the critical issue is one of democracy and religious tolerance. In a Wahhabi state there is neither democracy nor tolerance for the

Shi'ites, Sufis, traditional Sunnis, and the liberal Saudi secularists educated in America. The Kingdom remains a Wahhabi state, and the al-Sauds seeking modernization will remain vulnerable to the Ikhwani charge of hypocrisy. So long as the al-Sauds base their claim to political legitimacy on the precepts of Wahhabism, they empower their Ikhwani critics. This contradictory dynamic should have been broken decades ago. Prince Talal and his "Free Princes" understood in the early 1960s that the obvious solution for this conundrum was for Arabia to become a constitutional monarchy. Only democracy can provide legitimacy independent of the Wahhabi *ulema* and their wanton fatwas. Four decades later, democracy is long overdue.

The Saudi regime has made it into the twenty-first century, where the pace of the ongoing technological revolution will inexorably force even more rapid changes on a society still impinged upon by its eighteenth-century roots. With more than 60 percent of its population under the age of twenty-five, the pressure for generational change is enormous. But precisely because the Saudis have more than ample financial resources, they are far more likely to thread the camel, so to speak, through the needle's eye than many of their fellow Arabs. They need not turn their back on tradition, but they will be compelled by the invasive power of computers, the Internet, cell phones and the coming robotic age to renounce the arbitrariness of any binding authority, whether it be clerical or monarchical. They might even discover within the Wahhabi canon itself a rationale for defending the right of each man and woman to determine how they are to live their lives. I thus find myself more hopeful today about the fate of Arabia than many other parts of the Middle East. I remember the Bedouin of my youth who seemed remarkably adaptive to technology. Arabia is now awash in modernity. The pace of economic development over the last fifty years has been astounding—suggesting that Arabia is quite capable of absorbing change. Unfortunately, the pace of political reform has not kept up with the people.

The courageous Syrian philosopher Sadik al-Azm once described the Arabs as "the Hamlet of our times, doomed to unrelieved tragedy, forever hesitating, procrastinating, and wavering between the old and the new, between *asala* and *mu'asara* (authenticity and contemporaneity), between *turath* and *tajdid* (heritage and renewal), between *huwiyya* and *hadatha* (identity and modernity), and between religion and secularity. . . ." This has been the Saudi experience in the extreme.

Book II

Defeating Arab Modernity

Life magazine, June 16, 1967

5

Cairo and Nasser's Egypt, 1965–1967

Cairo's Citadel

Nasser's greatest achievement was his funeral. The world will never again see five million people crying together.

Sherrif Hatatta

In early July 1965, we departed Dhahran aboard a Saudi Arabian Airlines jetliner bound for Washington, DC. Unlike our lonely arrival, this time the aircraft was overbooked. After boarding, the pilot announced that "Eugene Bird, American consul," had no seat and asked if anyone already seated would agree to give up their seat for him. There were no takers. After much animated negotiation, the plane took off for Amman with some passengers doubling up in first class.

Father had been assigned to serve as the commercial attaché in the American Embassy in Cairo. His job would be to assist American businessmen in Egypt and report on the country's economy. He welcomed the new posting. Cairo then was a cosmopolitan metropolis of 4 or 5 million people. It had everything that Dhahran lacked. That summer we visited the United States and then boarded a passenger ship in New York bound for Casablanca. Father had received permission to travel to his new posting rather circuitously. My parents loved long drives. They shipped our station wagon to Casablanca, where we saw it off-loaded by a crane equipped with an enormous net. We drove to Marrakech and Fez, and then spent three weeks driving across North Africa—Morocco, Algeria, Tunisia, Libya and into Egypt. We must have logged 9,000 miles that summer.

When we finally arrived in late August, we temporarily checked into a small pensione run by a middle-aged Jewish couple in the upscale, but quaint, suburban community of Maadi, located about eight miles south of Cairo on the eastern bank of the Nile River. Oddly, I thought, they spoke French at the dinner table. After a few weeks we moved into a five-bedroom villa at 14 El Nahda in Maadi. Like most of the town's villas, this lovely old house was surrounded by a large garden, filled with shrubbery and brightly colored bougainvillea. I occupied the sole bedroom on the third floor, where in the summer's heat I slept outdoors in a screened porch. I covered the floor of my bedroom with dark-red Bokhara carpets. Bedouin knives, engraved copper plates, a bright yellow Arabian cloth saddle and other Arab knick-knacks adorned the walls and bookshelves.

My sisters Nancy and Shelly had bedrooms on the second floor. Christina was finishing high school in Alexandria's Schutz School. We had shipped our gentle, beloved Saluki, Zahra, from Arabia. Mother had acquired a piano. A wide curving marble staircase dominated the first-floor living room. The interior walls were made of white plaster, and the large kitchen was lined with white, creamy granite counters. Abdu was our very slow but good-natured cook. Nearly every afternoon I returned from school to the smell of freshly baked bread. I teased Abdu relentlessly, swiping pieces of warm bread while he'd swat me away with a kitchen towel. A man named Abdullah was the "houseboy"—though he was the jolly father of five children. A teenage boy, Muhammad, served as the gardener; he was later drafted just before the outbreak of the June 1967 War—and I don't know if he survived. Abdu and Abdullah addressed my mother as "Memsahib." They called me *walid*, Arabic for "boy."

Until 1904, Maadi was the site of a few mango and guava farms. That year a railway was built from Cairo to the industrial enclave of Helwan in the south. A group of Sephardic Jewish developers took advantage of the railway to design a planned community for British expatriates and the kind of wealthy, educated Egyptians who spoke English in the office and French at home. A retired Canadian officer, Captain Alexander J. Adams, was hired to design the community. On a patch of land no larger than three square kilometers, he laid out a grid of wide boulevards, crisscrossed occasionally by equally wide streets that ran into circles called *midan*s. Some of the major boulevards and *midan*s were named after the various Jewish directors of the company that had built Maadi: Cattaui, Mosseri and Menashe. Eucalyptus and palm trees lined the streets, and wide sidewalks were built of tiny square tiles. One man-made water channel, the Khashab Canal, meandered through the town, bringing muddy brown water from the Nile to feed Maadi's lush gardens overgrown with jasmine and rosebushes. The developers insisted that all the private villas be built to high standards. Each house was surrounded by a garden of ample size. But there were a variety of architectural styles— Tudor, Arabesque, English Colonial and Italian Renaissance.

The community prided itself on its ecumenical diversity. Greeks, Copts, Jews, Italians, British, French, Byelorussians, Germans and Egyptians lived in Maadi. There were many mosques, and the daily calls to prayer were ubiquitous. But the town was also home to a half-dozen churches and one thriving synagogue, built in 1934. By the end of World War II, more than one-third of the population was Jewish. Most were Ashkenazic Jews who had come from Central Europe in the late nineteenth century. They were educated and cosmopolitan. Few kept kosher, spoke Yiddish or wore yarmulkes—except in the synagogue. They sent their children to secular schools. After several generations, they thought of themselves as an integral part of the Egyptian mosaic. They were just another minority—like the Egyptian Christian Copts or the Armenians.

Many of Cairo's expatriate diplomats and businessmen also made Maadi their home. There was a small yacht club on the Nile, adjacent to Maadi's main entrance. (Unlike Aramco's American Camp, it was not a gated community but an open town.) Social life centered on the Maadi Sports Club, founded in 1921, where expatriates mingled with upper-middle-class Egyptians—doctors, teachers, journalists, civil servants, and officers in President Gamal Abdel Nasser's army. English-style tea or iced coffee was served in the afternoon. Nubian waiters wearing freshly starched white caftan uniforms, with red sashes around their waists and topped off with white turbans, manned a well-stocked bar. The club boasted a sandy eighteen-hole golf course, from which one could see the Great Pyramids in the distance across the Nile. The second-floor veranda overlooked a large pond modeled after Claude Monet's impressionist painting *The Nympheas*. The pond contained frogs and goldfish—and attracted mosquitoes.

Many Maadi residents did all their entertaining in the club's restaurant. The bridge room, bar and library were often occupied. There were tennis courts, a cricket field and an Olympic-size swimming pool, with a ten-meter-high diving board. Each night the pool was drained and the next morning refilled with fresh water. I competed on the Maadi swim team alongside the sons of Egyptian army officers; in my memory I think we usually beat the boys from the Gezira Club, the other major sporting club in Cairo. Three nights a week one could sit outside in the garden and watch American, French and Egyptian films projected on an outdoor screen. To be sure, the Maadi Sports Club had clearly seen better days; its facilities could have used a paint job, if not a modern renovation. The club epitomized secular bourgeois values—what mattered were class and modernity, not ethnicity, and certainly not religion.

Most Egyptian members of the Maadi Sports Club sent their children to Arabic-speaking private schools, or to Maadi's elite Victoria College—which after the Suez War had been renamed "Victory College." Its alumni included King Hussein of Jordan and Michael Shalhoub—known to all on the silver screen as Omar Sharif. Maadi also had a French lycée and a British international school. I was enrolled in the Cairo American College, an American-curriculum elementary and secondary school with 400 students. About half the student body was either American or Canadian, but the remainder came from all over the world: Yugoslavian, Pakistani, Czech, Polish, Korean, Thai, Indian, Norwegian, Japanese and many other nationalities. (Edward Said, the late Palestinian-American scholar, attended this expatriate school in the late 1940s; he hated it, and so in tenth grade he transferred to the British-style Victoria College.) My history teacher was an American woman married to an Egyptian. My geometry teacher was French. And our basketball coach was a Jewish Greek Cypriot Egyptian. The school was housed in a Moorish-style palace once owned by Prince Mohammed Ali Ibrahim, a relative of the late King Farouk. The palace garage that had housed Princess Hanezadeh's Rolls-Royce was carved up into classrooms. The Turkish bath was converted into a chemistry lab. All the bathrooms were lined from floor to ceiling with pink alabaster.

I rode to school aboard a heavy black bicycle of sturdy Chinese design, manufactured locally. In those years there was not much traffic on Maadi's leafy streets—a few private cars and dilapidated buses, navigating alongside the occasional donkey carts. Sometimes I'd buy a bag of roasted peanuts or warm Arab bread covered with sesame seeds from a sidewalk vendor. I loved Egyptian *foul*—a paste of fava beans drenched in olive oil and eaten with flat, unleavened Arab bread. *Foul* could be bought for 1.5 piasters; *tamaya* (in Israel it was called falafel) sandwiches were just two piasters—roughly a nickel.

Abdu the cook did most of our grocery shopping at Gomaa's market—the tallest building in Maadi, all of three or four stories. Fresh produce, meat, fruits and alcoholic beverages were all available. Egypt produced its very own brand of beer, Stella. Coca-Cola, however, was embargoed in Egypt because the company had built a bottling plant in Israel, thus earning a place on the Arab League's economic boycott list. But Pepsi was freely available.

On Sunday mornings we attended services at the Maadi Community Church, previously known as St. John the Baptist Church. Its pastor was a boisterous German national, Reverend Otto Meinardus, who every year led a large part of the congregation on a weeklong tour of the ancient monasteries of the Sinai. Father and Mother spent ten days in the autumn of 1966 traveling to St. Catherine's, Christianity's oldest continuously functioning monastery, located in a nearly inaccessible gorge at the foot of Mount Sinai.

On weekends, I rode my bicycle to the eastern outskirts of Maadi for a view of the Muqattam Hills. I never ventured too far into the desert, where one might encounter wild dogs and herds of goats and camels. In those years a detachment of the Egyptian army's famed Camel Corps still patrolled the desert around Maadi, occasionally tracking down hashish smugglers. Sometimes I walked alone to Maadi Station and boarded a train for the twenty-minute ride to Babalouk, the commuter train-station in downtown Cairo. I always felt safe. There were crowds of people everywhere, a moving mosaic of gentle, jostling chaos. I'd wander around Midan al-Tahrir (Liberation)

Square, the city's major intersection, abutting the Nile Hilton, the American University and numerous government ministries. Sometimes I'd take a taxi with school friends to the Old City's Khan al-Khalili souk, near the medieval Citadel. Occasionally, we'd watch the latest English, American or French movies at the very grand, art deco–styled Metro cinema. After the film we might eat ice cream cones or chocolates at Groppi's Tea Room, Cairo's ritziest café, on Midan Suliman Pasha. With its mosaic floors and tiled rotunda, Groppi's exuded all the charm of a Parisian café in the heart of bustling Cairo. The largest English-language bookstore was Progress Publishers, run by the Soviet Union's propaganda publishing house. One could buy cheap, but sturdily bound, editions of Dostoyevsky, Turgenev and other Russian classics.

Cairo was the largest, most cosmopolitan city I had ever lived in. It was a city out of time—or rather a city with overlapping historical epochs, none dying cleanly or giving way to the next. It was ancient, colonial and modern all at the same time. In Arabic the city is called al-Qahirah, or "the Victorious," a reference to its glorious medieval past as a center of Islamic science and scholarship. Under Nasser in the 1960s it was rapidly becoming "Arabized," but it still had a rich diversity of vibrant multicultural pockets. There was a British Cairo, a French Cairo—with a French-language daily newspaper—a Greek Cairo, a German Cairo and a Jewish Cairo. It was a noisy city, and home to both considerable wealth and desperate poverty. Beggars roamed the streets, a few of them lepers, and tens of thousands of people lived in dusty shacks made from tin cans and scraps of discarded cardboard. Visiting Cairo's ancient cemetery, the vast City of the Dead—virtually a city unto itself with a maze of alleys and underground corridors—I was shocked to discover that thousands of homeless people were living atop the dead.

Cairo also had a burgeoning middle class and the traffic to go with it. Cairenes drove with one hand constantly pounding the horn. Transistor radios blared competing stations until five o'clock on Thursday afternoons, when it seemed as if the whole city stopped to listen to a regular program of Egypt's legendary diva, Umm Kulthum, singing an hour-long love song.* Her career predated the Nasser era—but her rise to stardom mimicked Nasser's own rise

---

*When Umm Kulthum died in 1975 at the age of seventy, some 4 million mourners filled the streets of Cairo. At one point, the mob seized her coffin and marched it to her favorite mosque. Her monthly concerts—consisting of two or three songs over a period of three to six hours—were broadcast the first Thursday of every month.

to power from humble beginnings. She was the daughter of a poor Egyptian village preacher, and Nasser himself was an ardent fan. He is reputed to have asked a colleague soon after coming to power why he could no longer hear Umm Kulthum on the radio. It turned out that the Egyptian musicians' guild had banned her because she had been known to sing for the recently deposed King Farouk. "What, are they crazy?" he exclaimed. "Do you want Egypt to turn against us?" Thereafter, Nasser made a point of frequenting her concerts, sitting prominently in the first row. Umm Kulthum's emotion-laden voice and lyrics—often evocative of nationalist themes—became closely identified with the Nasser regime. Perhaps he acquired some of his own gift for public speaking from his close attention to her rich delivery of classical Arabic poetry.

Egypt's diva Umm Kulthum, 1967

My sequestered life in an Arabian compound was no preparation for life in a crowded metropolis like Cairo. Nearly fifteen years old, I was no longer a child. I still thought of myself as an American, but during our summer in America I had ample opportunity to see that I was not like other American teenagers. They spoke a different language, filling their conversations with references to television shows and music that were foreign to me. I fell silent when the topic of baseball or football came up because I was completely unfamiliar with any of the teams. As a child abroad I had quickly come to understand that strangers in the streets of Jerusalem, Beirut or Riyadh could with one glance see that I was American. Without any effort at all, I had an instant identity. People stared at me, but I thought this was only natural. I was the foreigner. But being back in America made me feel equally out of place. I was suddenly invisible—strangers could not see at a glance who I was, and if they thought about it at all, assumed I was an American like them. This rankled. I knew I was not like them. I was different. Now, in Maadi, the curious stares of Egyptians passing on the street restored my identity. I was once again an exotic and privileged observer, living the expatriate life.

Each morning a thick sheaf of mimeographed papers was delivered to our Maadi home. This was the U.S. Embassy's daily summary of the American press. We also subscribed to the English-language *Egyptian Gazette*. About this time I started reading *Time* and *Newsweek*—which served as my window onto America. Father drove himself every morning to the embassy downtown, and in the evenings he and Mother frequently attended cocktail parties and formal dinners. Occasionally, they hosted their own dinner parties, inviting a mix of Egyptians and Americans. It was Father's job as commercial attaché to know the Egyptian business community, and he had a wider assortment of Egyptian acquaintances than anyone else in the embassy.

Most of my friends were fellow American expatriates from the Cairo American College. I often hung out with the son of a Yugoslav diplomat— yes, a Communist! He had the coolest-looking "Beatle" haircut. On weekends, I played a lot of the "conquer the world" board game Risk with Jeff Parker, the son of the political counselor in the embassy, whom I had also known when we both had lived in Beirut in 1961–62. (None of us playing Risk ever wanted to occupy the Middle East—we all knew that because it was at the crossroads of three continents, it was impossible to defend.)

I also spent a lot time with Bobby Bauer Jr., the son of the U.S. Embassy's chief public relations officer. His father, Robert Bauer Sr., was an extraordinarily funny man who always had a story or joke to tell. A native of Vienna, Bauer had studied law and was thought to have had a promising political career. But on the day that Germany occupied Austria in March 1938 Bauer, twenty-eight years old, fled his homeland and sought refuge in Prague. He was not Jewish but Roman Catholic, and a strident anti-Fascist. In Prague, he found work as a stringer for the *New York Times*. There he was invited one evening by Alex Kafka—a relative of the late Czech novelist Franz Kafka—to attend a society ball. That evening, Kafka introduced him to Maria Kahler, the twenty-year-old daughter of a wealthy German-speaking Czech businessman, Felix von Kahler. Maria's family, as she later wrote in her memoirs, were "perpetual outsiders"—of Jewish ancestry but nonpracticing Jews. They were "Old Austrians," meaning they thought of themselves as citizens of the now defunct Austro-Hungarian Empire. Maria's father had been knighted by Emperor Franz Josef. She had grown up in a Prague mansion and summered at their Svinarre castle in the Czech countryside. Her family lost everything to the Nazis and were lucky to escape to France and then Portugal, where she and Bauer were married. In 1940, a few weeks after the fall of France, Bauer, Maria and her parents all boarded a Portuguese steamer bound for New York. During the war, Bauer worked as a German-language radio announcer for the Voice of America. It was his voice that announced to the German people on June 6, 1944, that Allied troops had landed in Normandy in France. After the war, Bauer became an American diplomat—which brought him to Egypt in the 1960s.

Bauer still spoke English with a not unpleasant German accent. Like his father, Bobby was extremely bright and intensely political. I had my first real discussions about the Vietnam War with him. President Lyndon Johnson had sent the first American combat ground troops to Vietnam that summer of 1965, and the war was rapidly escalating. I was skeptical of the whole enterprise. Bobby was always much more interested in American electoral politics, shaped, he now says, "harmfully" by his reading of *Time* and *Newsweek*. He and I ran together for student council and won on a campaign promise that we would organize a snack bar on campus. Bobby became a Washington lawyer, specializing in campaign finance law. (In 2008 he became general counsel to Barack Obama's presidential campaign and is today the president's personal lawyer.)

I frequently rented a horse out in Giza and rode around the Great Pyramids and the Sphinx. Howard Blanning, a classmate who was the son of Frank Blanning, dean of students of the American University of Cairo, sometimes accompanied me on these expeditions. We went for longer rides from Giza south to the smaller but even older pyramids of Saqqara. Together with Richard Parker, the embassy's political counselor, Father bought a fifteen-foot blue wooden sailboat, docked it at the Maadi Sports Club's marina and took us out on the Nile once or twice a month. (Parker mockingly christened it in Arabic *The Blue Socialist*.) On the river, we had to avoid running into the dozens of majestic feluccas—Egypt's ancient, wooden, flat-bottomed sailing boats—often loaded down with bales of cotton. On some evenings we'd have dinner at the fancy modern Nile Hilton Hotel, overlooking the Nile and backing onto Tahrir Square, with its teeming crowds.

During school vacations, we sometimes drove to Alexandria and rented a grand colonial house on Montazah's then sparkling white beach—or we'd drive three hours east to the Red Sea, where we'd go snorkeling in the pristine turquoise waters. At the time, one could still swim by enormous schools of multicolored parrot fish, barracudas and even the occasional very dangerous stonefish.

One night Bobby Bauer and I attended a production of Verdi's *Aida* at Cairo's ornate Khedivial Opera House, built in 1869 by Pasha Ismail, the then Khedive of Egypt. We were stunned to see live camels and elephants brought onstage amid the pageantry of Verdi's music. Anything was possible in Cairo. *Aida* had in fact been commissioned by Pasha Ismail and been given its first performance in this very same opera house on December 24, 1871. A hundred years later, the famed Opera House burned down. Many Cairenes thought this an apt metaphor for what had happened to their world under the Rayyis*—the leader—Gamal Abdel Nasser. In 1965 the hero of the 1956 Suez War was extremely popular with the "street"— but after a dozen years of creeping, highly bureaucratized socialism, Nasser's Egypt had lost its bourgeois luster. Public buildings in Cairo's city center— formerly known as the European Quarter—were falling into disrepair. The city had a faded, weathered sheen.

But in 1965, Nasser remained a vibrant and charismatic figure. His televised speeches were mesmerizing. He often spoke for two or three hours at a time, without notes, carefully modulating his baritone voice, and clearly appealing to the hearts and minds of his people. He spoke a colloquial but elevated *baladi* (country) Arabic that could be understood across the Arab world. It was theatre—even poetic. Contrary to his image in the West, he was rarely bombastic. He displayed an almost impeccable dignity, which appealed to an Arab audience highly sensitive to questions of honor. For

---

*Rayyis means "president" or "leader," but in colloquial Arabic, given a slightly different intonation, it means "boss." Nasser's inner circle, including his wife, affectionately called him "boss."

a generation of Arabs, wounded by the humiliations of colonialism and the 1948 Nakba—the creation of the Israeli state in Palestine—Nasser's speeches were a rare uplifting tonic. He promised few things—except to reclaim Arab honor.

In the 1960s, Nasser was a towering figure across the Arabic-speaking world, from Morocco to Iraq, from Syria to Yemen. Even today, he remains emblematic of a lost era when hope still existed among Arabs of all classes and tribes for a modern, secular and progressive Arab nation. In America today, Nasser is chiefly remembered as an anti-American, anti-Israeli dictator. He was the butt of many political jokes. "Hitler never died," the Israeli-American historian Bernard Avishai was told as a child, "but swam to Egypt and became *nasser* ["wetter" in German]." Nasser did indeed become a dictator in the course of his eighteen years in power. His critics sarcastically called him "the Pharaoh." But initially, he had democratic aspirations. He had a deep distrust for both Communists and the Muslim Brotherhood—and an abiding admiration for things American.

Like many Arab nationalists, Nasser was educated at an American missionary school, the Wissa Charitable Secondary School in the Upper Egyptian governorate of Asyut. His father was a poorly paid postal clerk, and his mother died in 1926, when he was eight years old. When his father was transferred to Cairo, Nasser's family shared a rented house with a Jewish family. He also spent time in Alexandria, then a highly cosmopolitan city of Egyptian Arabs, Greeks and Armenians, of French, Italian and English émigrés. As a boy he loved reading, and not only in Arabic. He read a great many English books, including Dickens, Carlyle, Gandhi, Liddell Hart and biographies of famous politicians. In the late 1930s he was admitted to an officers training school. As we have seen, by then he was already a committed nationalist who fervently hoped to see the British colonial authorities expelled from Egypt.

Suave and articulate, Nasser exuded a quiet intelligence. Always well mannered and impeccably dressed, he had a commanding presence. In 1944 he married Thiya Kazem, a young upper-middle-class woman of Persian ancestry who spoke fluent English and French. They had five children. They lived in a modest house. He was in the habit of buying one suit each year—and he had a collection of several hundred bright, gaudy ties, almost all of them striped. His colleagues knew him to be incorruptible. He had no personal peccadilloes, aside from smoking three packs of cigarettes a day.

He loved American films, which he rented from MGM's Cairo office. He liked Elia Kazan's *Viva Zapata!* starring Marlon Brando. "Colonel Nasser used to watch it over and over again," said the woman who rented him the film. "[He was] fascinated with the Mexican Revolution and the peasants' uprising of 1910." His good friend the newspaper editor Mohamed Heikal claimed that Nasser's all-time favorite American film was Frank Capra's syrupy Christmas tale, *It's a Wonderful Life.* His favorite American writer was Mark Twain. He liked classical music. He spent an hour or two each evening reading American, French and Arabic magazines. His sensibilities were thoroughly bourgeois. He was a secular, modern Arab.

In religion, Nasser was a respectful but only nominal Muslim. Occasionally, he made a public show of praying in a mosque. But he had a visceral dislike for mixing politics with religion. At a time in the late 1940s when the Egyptian Muslim Brotherhood—the Islamic political movement founded in 1928—was highly popular, Nasser shunned them. In the summer of 1948, then Major Nasser fought with the Egyptian army in Palestine. He was outraged and humiliated by the experience of being sent into battle by King Farouk's regime with poorly trained troops equipped with shoddy arms. In 1949 he returned to Cairo and formed the Association of Free Officers. Initially, just fourteen officers swore allegiance to Nasser and the Egyptian people. With a revolver in one hand and the other hand placed over a Koran, they took a vow of secrecy. Over the next three years, the Free Officers distributed occasional anonymous leaflets focusing on two issues: corruption within Farouk's government and the presence of British troops in Egypt.

In July 1952, Nasser and his Free Officers carried out a nearly bloodless coup; two hapless soldiers were inadvertently shot and killed. King Farouk was forced into exile. Nasser, only thirty-four years old, was the real power behind the Free Officers, but initially he decided to take a backseat in the new regime. Instead, the Free Officers named a front man, General Mohammad Naguib, to be head of state. The new regime's opposition was the Muslim Brotherhood on the right and the Communist Party on the left. The Communists were insignificant. The Brotherhood, however, was a slumbering menace.

In the autumn of 1954, more than two years after the coup, a Muslim Brotherhood assassin fired eight shots at Nasser while he was giving a speech in Alexandria. Incredibly, all eight shots missed their target. He was reportedly wearing a bulletproof vest, supplied to him by the CIA. Nasser calmly completed his speech. But upon his return to Cairo he launched a crackdown on the Brotherhood. Seven hundred of its members were arrested. After a show trial, six men were executed. (A young Palestinian engineer named Yasir Arafat was among those arrested.) Nasser also used the assassination attempt as a pretext for consolidating his power. General Naguib was put under house arrest, and in early 1955 the Free Officers' Revolutionary Command Council formally named Nasser prime minister. A year later, he was elected president. Egypt was essentially becoming a one-party state, but the election nevertheless demonstrated that Nasser had won overwhelming support from a vast majority of Egyptians. By 1956, he wielded virtual dictatorial powers, but he did so as a populist and popular auto-democrat.

One day in 1965 as we were driving in downtown Cairo, I looked across the Nile to the Cairo Tower, which, at 613 feet, was the tallest structure in the city. I asked Father if people were allowed to go to the top of the needlelike tower. He laughed and said, "Yes, there's a revolving restaurant at the top." He added that Nasser often took his family out to dinner there. And then he told me the following story.

More than two years after the July 1952 Free Officers coup d'état that exiled King Farouk, the CIA sent one of its top operatives, Kermit Roosevelt, to Cairo. In 1953, this grandson of President Theodore Roosevelt had played a key role in the coup in Iran that unseated a democratically elected premier and restored Mohammed Reza Shah Pahlavi to power. Fortunately for Nasser, the CIA viewed *his* nascent regime with favor. One veteran CIA officer, Miles Copeland, an Arabic-speaking Alabamian, later insisted that the Agency had been apprised of the Free Officers' coup in advance and had given Nasser a "green light." Kermit Roosevelt may have had some contact with members of the Free Officers group in the spring of 1952, but he did not then meet with Nasser. In early July 1952 Roosevelt departed for Washington, where he reported that the Free Officers would make their move within the month. Copeland claims Roosevelt told him, "No one in our government must get the idea that it was our coup. It would be strictly an indigenous affair, almost totally free from our influence which we could assist only by not opposing it." This undoubtedly exaggerates his role in the coup. At most, if Washington had heard rumors of a coup, it did nothing to stop it.

By 1954, Roosevelt was on a first-name basis with Nasser. They drank scotch together in Nasser's office and enjoyed each other's company. Back in Washington, the Eisenhower Administration regarded Nasser as a reasonably pro-American, anti-Communist Arab leader. In the interests of stabilizing the regime, Washington extended Nasser some $40 million in economic and military aid. CIA's Copeland suggested that an additional $3 million—in cash—be delivered to Nasser for his own personal use. The suggestion was approved, and Copeland brought two suitcases full of American dollars to the Maadi home of Nasser's personal assistant, Hassan Touhami. When they counted the money, the two men discovered they were exactly $10 short of the $3 million.

According to Touhami, who delivered the cash to Nasser's home in Heliopolis, Nasser was astonished at this audacious attempt to bribe him. Touhami told him the money came from his friend Roosevelt. Nasser's first idea was to send the money back to Roosevelt and publicize this attempted bribery. But Touhami jokingly suggested they use the money to build a large statue of a man in profile thumbing his nose at the world. Nasser came up with a better idea. He ordered Touhami to build a conspicuously tall TV and radio tower—from which his *Voice of the Arabs* program could be broadcast. He took obvious delight in the fact that the CIA's money would be used to extend the reach of his propaganda throughout the Arab world. Nasser joked that the radio tower could be called *al-wa'ef rusfel*—"Roosevelt's erection."

Father laughed when he came to this punch line. Apparently, the American expatriate community all knew the story, and only tourists referred to the structure as the Cairo Tower. He thought the story spoke well of Nasser's integrity—not to mention his sense of humor. In retaliation, and as Nasser's relations with the American Embassy deteriorated, the Americans began referring to the Cairo Tower as "Nasser's prick."

In the early years of his regime, Nasser viewed the Israeli state with a mix of suspicion and ambivalence. His Free Officers colleague Khalid Mohieddine later told the historian Said K. Aburish, "Nasser never closed the door on peace, he left it wide open." In 1953 he sanctioned secret contacts between his representatives and Israeli officials. Among other ideas discussed by the two sides, the Egyptians said they needed 120 million British pounds to compensate Palestinian refugees. They asked for some minor territorial adjustments along the Sinai-Israeli border. And they said they needed a land link through the southern Negev to Jordan. The Israelis replied that they could talk about these points—if the Arab boycott and blockade were to be lifted.

Negotiations commenced in earnest only after Israel's Ben-Gurion resigned as prime minister in November 1953. Moshe Sharett, previously Israel's foreign minister, succeeded him. Sharett spoke fluent Arabic, and he came to office believing that peace with Israel's neighbors was not only possible but necessary. Secret talks between an Egyptian army officer and the Israeli defense attaché Chaim Herzog began in Washington and continued later in Paris. Nasser insisted that the Israelis had to take back the Palestinian refugees—as specified by United Nations resolutions. But significantly, he conceded that perhaps Israel would not have to repatriate all of them. For his part, Sharett would not budge on the issue of repatriation, but he was willing in principle to pay compensation. Though no major agreement was reached, the discussions were nevertheless carried out in an atmosphere of respect and seriousness.

The negotiations were then disrupted, however, by an Israeli intelligence operation gone awry which came to be called the Lavon Affair. Upon resigning the prime ministership, Ben-Gurion had made sure that one of his protégés, Pinhas Lavon, became defense minister. Lavon, Ben-Gurion and other hard-liners in the Israeli government were opposed to Sharett's secret talks with Egypt. They viewed Sharett as soft and liable to give the Egyptians unnecessary concessions. The Lavon Affair is still shrouded in mystery, but we do know that someone in the Israeli chain of command ordered the head of Israel's Aman (military intelligence), Colonel Binyamin Givli, to activate a sleeper cell of agents in Cairo. This was done without Prime Minister Sharett's knowledge. Colonel Givli later claimed that it was Defense Minister Lavon who issued this order, but six years later investigators uncovered evidence that Colonel Moshe Dayan, Shimon Peres and David Ben-Gurion were involved.

In any case, Givli was authorized to launch Operation Susannah—a plan to discredit Nasser's regime with a series of terrorist bombings in downtown Cairo. The bombings were carried out by Unit 131, a top-secret cell of Egyptian Jews led by an Israeli agent, Avram Dar, posing as a British citizen of Gibraltar and calling himself John Darling. Early in July 1954 a post office in Alexandria was firebombed. On July 14, the libraries of the U.S. Information Agency in both Cairo and Alexandria were bombed and severely damaged. Soon, several more post offices, a British-owned cinema, and other Western targets were firebombed. The selection of American and British targets made it look like the work of anti-Western Egyptian terrorists. Then one member of Unit 131 was arrested when his bomb exploded prematurely outside the Rivoli Cinema in Alexandria, and he was found to be carrying an eyeglass case in which police found a piece of paper with the names and addresses of all the other cell members. The cell's twelve members were arrested; nearly all were Egyptian Jews. They were such an amateurish lot that some historians have speculated that whoever authorized this caper fully expected the Israeli signature to be revealed, and thus the implementation of Susannah may have been specifically designed to scuttle Nasser's secret peace talks with Sharett.

Nasser understandably believed that Sharett had double-crossed him—ostensibly talking peace while authorizing terror attacks on American and British institutions. He put the twelve agents of Unit 131 on trial. Two were condemned to death, two were acquitted and the rest were given jail sentences. In late January, six weeks after Nasser had approved the execution of six Muslim Brotherhood members implicated in the attempt to assassinate him, the two Jews were hanged.

Prime Minister Sharett publicly denied any knowledge of an Israeli intelligence role. When the Israeli spies went on trial in December 1954, he denounced what he called a "show trial . . . against a group of Jews who have fallen victim to false accusations." But we know now from Sharett's private diaries of his horror that ranking members of his cabinet and the army had authorized such an irresponsible covert operation. He felt that Lavon, Peres, Dayan and Givli were all morally responsible, since this was exactly the kind of incendiary actions they had been urging on him for months. The point of the operation, Sharett noted in his diary, was "to set the Middle East on fire . . . to cause friction, cause bloody confrontations, sabotage targets." Sharett's friend Teddy Kollek, then a high-ranking civil servant in the prime minister's office, bluntly told him that Peres and Dayan were lying to investigators. And yet, though he knew the Lavon Affair was being used to scuttle his moderate policies, Sharett felt helpless to defend himself. "I would never have imagined," he wrote in his diary on January 10, 1955, "that we could reach such a horrible state of poisoned relations, the unleashing of the basest instincts of hate and revenge and mutual deceit at the top of our most glorious Ministry [of Defense]. . . . I walk around as a lunatic, horror-stricken and lost, completely helpless . . . what should I do? What should I do?"

He tried to continue the secret talks with Nasser. He refers in his diary to a recent meeting of Roger Baldwin, the American civil liberties advocate, with Nasser in Cairo: "Nasser talked to him about Israel, saying he was not among those who want to throw Israel into the Mediterranean. He believes in coexistence with Israel and knows that negotiations will open some day."

In late January 1955, Sharett received a cable from his ambassador in Washington, Abba Eban, reporting that "the U.S. is ready to sign an agreement with us whereby we shall make a commitment not to extend our borders by force, [and the U.S.] will commit itself to come to our aid if we were attacked." Simultaneously, the CIA told Israeli intelligence that Nasser "does not regard the initiative of the meeting canceled because of the outcome of the trial. . . . He is as willing to meet us as before and the initiative is now up to Israel." Sharett told Eban that he favored such a meeting and he supported the notion of a security commitment with the U.S.—so long as Israel retained the right "to carry out reprisal actions" for Arab acts of terror or infiltration.

These revelations from Sharett's diaries—first published in Israel in the 1970s—demonstrate that a window to a real peace settlement was still open in 1955. In Nasser, Israel had a popular Arab leader who was willing to shoulder the political risks of dealing with the Jewish state. Nasser was not an unreasonable interlocutor. He undoubtedly would have insisted, as did the Americans, that Israel should refrain from seizing more territory by force, and agree to recognize the 1949 armistice lines as its final borders. Nasser would also have pressed for the return of some Palestinian refugees and compensation for others.

But while Sharett was clearly willing to go down this road, most other figures in the Israeli political establishment were not. When rumors of possible further negotiations between the prime minister and Nasser began to circulate inside the government, enormous political pressure was brought to bear on Sharett to bring in Ben-Gurion as minister of defense. On February 17, 1955, Sharett reluctantly invited Ben-Gurion to assume the defense portfolio. On the same day he noted in his diary, "that is the end of peace and quiet." Ten days after taking office, Ben-Gurion persuaded Sharett to authorize a limited raid on an Egyptian army post in Gaza in reprisal for both the recent execution in Egypt of the two Israeli spies and for a Palestinian act of infiltration near Rehovot. Ben-Gurion assured Sharett there would be few if any casualties.

The raid killed fifty-six Egyptian soldiers. Sharett wrote in his diary that he was "shocked" by the outcome and "tormented" by the possibly dire political consequences. Nasser immediately dropped the idea of further negotiations. Sharett noted what Nasser had told the Egyptian representative to the Mixed Armistice Commission, Salah Gohar: that "he had had a personal contact with Israel's Prime Minister and that there were good chances that things would develop in a positive way, but then came the attack on Gaza, and naturally now . . . it's off."

Operation Susannah and its aftermath was an unmitigated disaster. It fueled the flames of anti-Semitism against Egypt's community of some 50,000 Jews. It led to a breakdown of the secret peace talks. And it strengthened the political hand of Israel's hawks. Nasser used the Gaza raid as the rationale for his 1955 arms deal with the Czechs—which eventually led to the Aswan Dam debacle, the 1956 nationalization of the Suez Canal Company and the Suez War of October–November 1956.

Ben-Gurion and Dayan also succeeded in scuttling the proposed U.S.-Israeli security pact—a treaty that arguably might have prevented future wars. Sharett's diary describes how Dayan rationalized this decision: "We do not need (Dayan said) a security pact with the U.S.: such a pact will only constitute an obstacle for us. . . . The security pact will only handcuff us and deny us the freedom of action which we need in the coming years. Reprisal actions which we couldn't carry out if we were tied to a security pact are our vital lymph . . . they make it possible for us to maintain a high level of tension among our population and in the army. Without these actions we have ceased to be a combative people and without the discipline of a combative people we are lost." Sharett observed of Dayan's views: "The conclusions from Dayan's words are clear: This State has no international obligations, no economic problems, the question of peace is nonexistent. . . . It must see the sword as the main, if not the only, instrument with which to keep its morale high and to retain its moral tension. Toward this end it may, no—it must—invent dangers, and to do this it must adopt the method of provocation and revenge. . . . And above all—let us hope for a new war with the Arab countries, so that we may finally get rid of our troubles and acquire our space. Such a slip of the tongue: Ben Gurion himself said that it would be worthwhile to pay an Arab a million pounds to start a war."

Sharett was an astute and honest observer, and in his diary, a pained and troubled critic of the country he led. But he lacked the political courage to go public with his views—and lacked as well the political acumen to outmaneuver Ben-Gurion and Dayan. Late in 1955, Ben-Gurion replaced him as prime minister. Sharett died in 1965, and his diaries were published in Hebrew in 1979 over the opposition of the Likud government then in power. As only a few snippets of these eight volumes and 2,400 pages have so far been published in English, his pungent observations are virtually unknown outside Israel.

In the wake of Operation Susannah, many Jewish Egyptians left the country. But tens of thousands still remained for a few more years. Maadi's Jews typically were not *haute juiverie*—the class of Egyptian Jews who circulated in Egyptian high society and sat on the boards of directors of major banks and companies. Most of those Jews lived in the downtown mansions of Zamalek or Garden City. Some of the *haute juiverie* had left in the wake of the 1948 war, but the majority had chosen to remain.

Maadi's Jews came from the professional classes—they were well-off but not rich. They were lawyers, accountants, small businessmen and teachers. They spoke fluent French, English and Arabic, and most had lived in Egyptian society for many generations. Just weeks before the Suez War, the Jews of Maadi had celebrated Rosh Hashanah and Yom Kippur in Maadi's Biton Synagogue. It was the last time Biton Synagogue would see a standing-room-only service. When Britain and France invaded Port Said in October 1956, Nasser ordered the expulsion of all "enemy nationals." Many Egyptian Jews were dual nationals of both Egypt and Britain or France. On short notice those Jews carrying British or French passports were forced to abandon their properties and depart for France or Britain, countries few of them had ever lived in or even visited. It was a personal tragedy, and in the long run an insidious blow to the secular and multicultural character of Egyptian society. Egypt, a country rich in diversity, became less so through the fifties and sixties.

In 1961, when Nasser nationalized large-capitalized companies and the private property of more than 150 wealthy Egyptian families, most of Maadi's dwindling Jewish population decided it was time to leave. Very few chose to emigrate to Israel, a place that held no particular attraction for them. Egypt had been their home; they had prospered in Cairo or Alexandria, and, as with the country's other minorities—the Armenians, Copts and Greeks—many of them had risen to high positions in the civil service and the business community. There had been no pogroms, no holocaust. Until the creation of a Jewish state, Egypt had treated its Jews well. Even then, the status of Egyptian Jews became a political issue only gradually; on a personal level, they rarely encountered blatant anti-Semitism. Nevertheless, by the time we arrived in 1965, only about 4,000 Jews remained in the country, and only two of Cairo's twenty-nine synagogues remained open.

Maadi in the mid-1960s was still a cosmopolitan place. Katy Antonius visited from Jerusalem several times a year. Her parents, Dr. Fares Nimr and Ellen Eynaud, had purchased a house in 1921 at No. 39, Road 10—very close to our place. Dr. Nimr, one of Egypt's great press barons, made his home Maadi's preeminent salon. Over the decades, most of Egypt's leading politicians and intellectuals had visited the "Villa Nimr." In the 1920s the Zionist leader Dr. Chaim Weizmann spent one afternoon trying to convince Nimr that European Jewry did not intend to displace the Arabs of Palestine. "He lied to me," Nimr later said. As a young man in Syria, the Ottoman authorities had known "Tiger Bey" Nimr as an ardent Arab nationalist. He escaped a Turkish roundup and near-certain death by swimming out to a ship in Beirut harbor and fleeing to Alexandria.

Another of our Maadi neighbors was Ali Sabri (1920–1991), the grandson of Amin Chamsi Pasha, one of Egypt's leading cotton merchants and landowners. A European governess raised Ali Sabri, and he was schooled at the French lycée. As a young man he practically lived at the Maadi Sports Club, playing soccer, tennis and cricket and competing in the diving meets. Notwithstanding this privileged upbringing, Sabri became an ardent socialist. During World War II he trained as a pilot and was one of Nasser's Free Officers. In 1962 he became Nasser's prime minister. To his Maadi neighbors' dismay, it was Sabri who announced the regime's sweeping nationalization order in July 1961. Because he was known as "Moscow's man," his Maadi friends jokingly nicknamed him "Aloushka."

Maadi was also home to American, British, French and Russian intelligence agents. In the fifties, Miles Copeland had lived in Maadi, ostensibly working as an executive for an encyclopedia company, but reporting to the CIA. So too did his successor in the 1960s, Bill Bromell, whose son

Nick was my good friend. My closest friend, Jeff Parker, also lived in a lovely old Maadi villa. His father, Richard Parker, was a brilliant Arabist and the embassy's senior political counselor.

A number of Germans with nefarious résumés lived in the neighborhood as well. One was Dr. Hannes Eisele, a general practitioner in his fifties who also was known for his landscape paintings. Rumors circulated, however, that the doctor had served the Nazis during the war at the death camps of Mauthausen and Buchenwald. Dr. Eisele (Carl de Bouche) had been both a Nazi Party member and an SS officer, and after the war he had been convicted of experimenting on inmates by injecting them with lethal chemicals. His death sentence was commuted to life imprisonment—but then in 1950 U.S. High Commissioner John J. McCloy paroled the doctor and many other Nazi war criminals as part of his effort to rehabilitate West Germany.* After a Maadi neighbor denounced Dr. Eisele's past, the doctor's practice fell apart and he died suddenly in 1967. No one knew how he had ended up in Egypt in the first place—but it was speculated that he might have been among a number of East Germans that Nasser had recruited to help him build ground-to-ground missiles for the army.

The rowdiest expatriates came from the ranks of the American oil companies. I did not run with this crowd of oil company kids. Though underage and lacking drivers' licenses, these teenage boys were increasingly regarded as a menace as they drove their Honda and Lambretta motor scooters around Maadi. On occasion they picked fights with Egyptian kids, whom they rudely disparaged as "Gyppos." One night in November 1966 five boys from the Cairo American College were badly injured when an inebriated teenage driver slammed a car into a tree. These constituted Maadi's "Ugly American" quotient.

Neither did I run with Ayman al-Zawahiri and his friends. In 1965 the future doctor and number-two leader of al-Qaeda was attending Maadi's state-run secondary school. He was exactly my age. His family never joined the Maadi Sports Club, but the club allowed nonmembers to attend their outdoor screenings of movies. Ayman's father used to take him to see the

---

*Ironically, I later wrote a biography of McCloy, *The Chairman: John J. McCloy; The Making of the American Establishment.*

same movies we saw at the club. And like our family, every year he spent part of his summers on a beach in Alexandria. Though we went to different schools, Maadi was a small place; I can easily imagine myself bicycling past the fourteen-year-old Ayman. And it makes me wonder how this place in time, this pleasant oasis along the Nile River, could ever have been home to one of the architects of 9/11.

Ayman's parents both came from distinguished Egyptian families. His father was a medical doctor and professor of pharmacology. His grandfather and great-grandfather on his father's side were scholars at Al-Azhar, Cairo's Islamic university and a center of religious studies dating back a thousand years. Ayman's maternal grandfather, Dr. Abdul Wahhab Azzam, had been president of Cairo University. He also had a career as a diplomat, serving as Egypt's ambassador to Saudi Arabia, Yemen and Pakistan.

While the Zawahiris were thus of privileged background, they lived modestly in a rented apartment in the *baladi,* the lower-middle-class section of Maadi, near the train station. Lawrence Wright's magisterial history, *The Looming Tower: Al-Qaeda and the Road to 9/11,* portrays Ayman as a serious student who at a young age came under the influence of his maternal uncle Mahfouz Azzam, a lawyer who advised the Muslim Brotherhood. According to Wright, Ayman grew up listening to his uncle's stories about Sayyid Qutb (1906–1966), the Muslim Brotherhood's leading intellectual in the 1950s and '60s. Uncle Azzam had been a student of Qutb's, and then his personal lawyer. Qutb's ideas were a mishmash of fundamentalism and Islamic anarchism. He believed that in a true Islamic society there would be no need for rulers or judges since any authentic Muslim would live by the divine law as defined by the Koran. After visiting America in the late 1940s, he came away shocked by its materialism and open sexuality. He scorned the West's secularism and its support for Israel. Qutb was a blatant anti-Semite and wrote of "the wicked opposition of the Jews to Islam." After the Brotherhood's attempted assassination of Nasser in 1954, he spent nearly ten years in prison where he was tortured—and further radicalized. He was freed in 1964, but immediately began plotting with the Muslim Brotherhood to assassinate Nasser and overthrow the regime. According to Wright, the Saudis were supplying Qutb with money and arms. Six months after his parole from prison, Qutb was rearrested. Informers within the Brotherhood implicated Qutb in the plot against Nasser. After a three-month trial Qutb was sentenced to death. He welcomed the sentence: "Thank God, I performed jihad for fifteen years until I earned this martyrdom." Though Nasser offered to commute the death sentence if he appealed, Qutb refused. Ayman's uncle Mahfouz Azzam was one of the last people to see him before he was hanged on August 29, 1966.

While I was blithely unaware of this drama, my Maadi neighbor, fifteen-year-old Ayman al-Zawahiri, was seething with anger against Nasser and his secular regime. "The Nasserite regime," he later wrote, "thought that the Islamic movement received a deadly blow with the execution of Sayyid Qutb and his comrades. But the apparent surface calm concealed an immediate interaction with Sayyid Qutb's ideas and the formation of the nucleus of the modern Islamic jihad movement in Egypt." In 1966, Ayman organized an underground cell of boyish Islamists devoted to destroying Nasserism. "We were a group of students from Maadi High School and other schools," Zawahiri later told an Egyptian court. Initially, there were only five teenage boys in the cell. It was all talk. They'd stroll along the Nile's Corniche (the riverfront promenade), watch the giant feluccas sail by and talk of the day when an Islamic caliphate would replace Nasser's secular regime. "Our means didn't match our aspirations," Zawahiri said.

By the time Zawahiri graduated from Cairo University's medical school in 1974, his secret cell had grown to some forty members. After serving his required three-year stint in the army, Dr. Zawahiri moved back to Maadi and opened a small health clinic. In 1978 he married. In the summer of 1980 he spent four months in Pakistan, providing medical treatment to Afghan refugees fleeing the war in Afghanistan. This experience further radicalized Zawahiri, and upon his return to Maadi that autumn he began plotting a coup. A number of military officers were now members of his secret cell—now formally called the Jammat al-Jihad. Unlike the Muslim Brotherhood, Zawahiri and his comrades had no intention of working through the political process to achieve an Islamic state. One of his cell members, army major Essam al-Qamari, began stealing automatic rifles and ammunition and hiding them in Zawahiri's health clinic in Maadi. Before their plans could ripen, however, yet another Islamist cell in the army moved to assassinate Nasser's successor, President Anwar Sadat. Zawahiri heard of the plot on October 6, 1981, just hours before Lieutenant Khaled Islambouli machine-gunned Sadat to death at an army parade commemorating the eighth anniversary of the October 1973 War.

While Zawahiri's Jammat al-Jihad cell had no links to Lieutenant Islambouli's assassination plot, it was not long before Egyptian authorities learned of Zawahiri's friendship with Major Qamari, who by then had fled underground. On October 23, 1981, Zawahiri was arrested on the Corniche and taken to the Maadi police station. When the police chief slapped his face, a still defiant Zawahiri reportedly slapped him back. The thirty-year-old Zawahiri was taken to a twelfth-century prison in Old Cairo's Citadel. He was stripped naked and brutally interrogated on the whereabouts of Major Qamari. Zawahiri later claimed that wild dogs were set upon him, and police used electricity to shock him and beat him with cables. The torture broke Zawahiri—and transformed him as well into an embittered fanatic, determined to inflict deadly harm on Egypt's secular authorities and its Western friends.

Zawahiri cooperated with the police and arranged a clandestine meeting with his friend and comrade Major Qamari, who was promptly arrested. Together with 300 other defendants, Zawahiri and al-Qamari were put on trial for Sadat's assassination and trafficking in arms. The trial took nearly three years, but because there was no evidence linking Zawahiri directly to

Dr. Ayman al-Zawahiri on trial for the 1981
assassination of President Anwar Sadat

Sadat's assassination, he was given a sentence of only three years for smuggling guns. Upon his release in 1984, he briefly resumed his medical practice in Maadi. But, feeling vulnerable to Egyptian surveillance, he decided to leave the country for Saudi Arabia, where he obtained employment as a surgeon in a Jeddah clinic. It was probably in Jeddah, in 1985, that he first met Osama bin Laden.

What I find astonishing about Dr. Zawahiri's trajectory is that it began in the privileged cocoon of Maadi. By Egyptian standards, he came from the upper middle class. He was an educated man, a surgeon. He knew people I later knew, men like Professor Saad Eddin Ibrahim, a sociologist at the American University of Cairo, and Abdullah Schleifer, a Jew from Long Island who converted to Sufi Islam and worked for many years as an American journalist in Cairo, Beirut and Jerusalem. In the 1970s and early 1980s Ibrahim, Schleifer and Zawahiri had intricate arguments about Islam and politics. Any of us might, in different circumstances, have had an interesting conversation with Zawahiri on a long airplane journey. But he became, in his own eyes, a committed revolutionary—and in ours, a mass murderer. If Zawahiri had not endured torture, perhaps he would have turned out differently. And yet, he had chosen the path of armed revolution against Nasser's brand of secular Arab nationalism well before he was arrested and tortured.

Nasser was always an enigma—and more so as the years passed. His regime was populist in spirit and brought real change to the lives of millions of poor *fellaheen*. Outside of Cairo, his sweeping land reform decrees transferred ownership of arable land to peasants who had toiled as serfs for centuries. The Aswan Dam gave the country electricity to power industrial plants and stopped the annual flooding of the Nile. (In retrospect, the High Dam was an ecological mistake; a series of run-of-the-river dams could have provided just as much electrical power and flood-control management.) He opened Cairo and Alexandria to common people, building public housing, public transport and free public schools for both the poor and a burgeoning middle class. Elementary education became near-universal and literacy rates climbed dramatically. An avowed secularist, Nasser closed the Muslim, Christian and Jewish religious courts that had adjudicated matters of family life for centuries. Women won the right to vote and other civil liberties.

Divorce laws were amended and coeducational schools were established. In the 1960s very few women were veiled, and many women were earning professional degrees and entering the workforce. Nasser convinced Al-Azhar, Egypt's 1,033-year-old Islamic university, to include modern science in its curriculum. Suddenly, it was acceptable for Egyptian students to study Darwinian evolution and quantum physics. In an extraordinary break with the past, Nasser persuaded Al-Azhar's clerics to issue a fatwa declaring that the Shi'ite, Alawite and Druze minorities throughout the Middle East should be recognized as legitimate members of the Islamic faith.

Yet these liberal accomplishments were slowly degraded by the gross economic inefficiencies of Nasser's lumbering bureaucracy, symbolized by the Mugammaa, an enormous building on Tahrir Square that housed the regime's notoriously inefficient civil service. Corruption was endemic—though, in fairness, hardly unique in Nasser's era. Naturally, Cairo's maze of small shopkeepers and entrepreneurs created a black-market economy, while the country's shrinking number of truly rich gave up and left for Europe or America. Thousands of university-educated men and women, not finding appropriate employment, emigrated to the West. This brain drain benefited America. Nasser's brand of Arab socialism turned out to be as stultifying as its eastern European or Russian variants.

Nasser still had the street. But for all his popularity, he was failing to measure up to his own dreams. In 1958, he was rushed into a full-scale union with Syria, creating the United Arab Republic. For a brief moment, it seemed as if Iraq, Jordan and even Lebanon might meld with Egypt to create a new "Araby"—an Arab nation. But by 1960 the winds of unity had given way to disillusionment, and Nasser himself was largely to blame. Instead of integrating Egypt with Syria, holding real elections and democratizing the new union, Nasser appointed a military governor for the Syrian "province" who ran it as a personal fiefdom. The Syrians rebelled and left the union in 1961. Nasser remained the preeminent Arab *rayyis,* but the Arab street's romance with the notion of one Araby had given way to the reality of the Arab mosaic. The Arabs of Egypt, Palestine, Syria, Jordan, Iraq, Lebanon and elsewhere still had in common one powerful language, but Arabic alone was not enough to overcome their primary loyalties, first to family and then to tribe. Nasser complained about his fellow Arabs as "tribes with flags."

In 1962 Nasser sent an initial expeditionary force of 20,000 Egyptian troops to shore up a republican regime in North Yemen. Over the next five years this army grew to some 65,000 troops. It became an albatross. Nasser frequently told the American ambassador that Yemen was "my Vietnam."

He also created a dangerous dynamic by hiring scores of East German scientists to help him build medium-range missiles. Some had Nazi résumés. The presence of the Germans inflamed Israel's worst fears, and encouraged them to redouble their efforts to build an atomic device from their supposedly peaceful nuclear reactor at Dimona. Nasser knew about Dimona—and used it in turn to justify his missile program. He told the Americans that he had no intention of going nuclear—but he refused to permit any inspections, insisting that would make it seem that Egypt was still a Western colony. Moreover, he warned that if it appeared that the Israelis were on the verge of producing a nuclear weapon, the result would be "protective war. We would have no other choice."

Internally, Nasser's Egypt was becoming an inefficient police state. In 1965 alone, the year we arrived in Cairo, the regime imprisoned some 18,000 suspected members of the Muslim Brotherhood. Many were tortured—and it is hard to believe that Nasser could have been unaware of this systematic abuse. His friend Mohamed Hassanein Heikal, the wily editor of *al-Ahram* (The Pyramids), repeatedly attacked the intelligence services for their brutality and stupidity. "Nasser was sometimes cross with me because of what I wrote in my column," Heikal later said. "But he never made any move to censor me."

Similarly, a large police bureaucracy—the Mukhabarat—was created to wiretap the phones of Nasser's friends and foes. We were quite certain that our own Maadi house phone was occasionally tapped. "Ya Habibi [My Love!]," I would yell mockingly into the phone when I thought this was happening.

Heikal railed against these abuses, both privately to Nasser and publicly in his widely read *al-Ahram* columns. In 1967, Heikal serialized a new novel by Naguib Mahfouz—later Egypt's Nobel Prize–winning laureate—that skewered the regime's corruption. When a character in one of Mahfouz's novels is asked "what's bad" about life, he replies, "Politics, news of arrests and imprisonments, and having to be alive at the same time as great men." The fact that Heikal could publish such highly critical material without being imprisoned speaks to the character of Nasser's enigmatic dictatorship. "Heikal was Nasser's alter ego," observed Dr. Louis Awad, a literary editor at *al-Ahram* who was imprisoned in 1959. "When Heikal contradicted him,

Nasser was in fact having a dialogue with himself." In 1984, I interviewed Heikal in the wood-paneled study of his apartment in downtown Cairo. He was an extremely charming and suave raconteur. Puffing on his ubiquitous Havana cigar, Heikal interrupted his own stories with incisive and even provocative questions. I could see how delightful a sounding board he must have been for Nasser.

By 1965, Nasser's relations with the Americans were deeply ambivalent. Our ambassador, Lucius Battle, plied him with books about the constraints of American politics. Because Nasser, like many Arabs, had a fascination with Jack Kennedy, Battle gave him Theodore Sorensen's biography of Kennedy, and many other books. But it was too late. The Americans had jerked Nasser around too often. He knew that only a few years earlier, the CIA had tried to organize a coup d'état to unseat him. "You know, we made a serious effort to bring down Nasser in those days," said Richard Parker, the embassy's political counselor. "We were looking for people to support. If we could have found somebody to have a coup d'état, we would have."

CIA officers outnumbered regular Foreign Service officers in our Cairo embassy. The station chief in the midsixties was Eugene Trone, an amiable and competent officer who was "declared" to the Nasser regime. This allowed him to operate in the open and meet with his counterparts in Egyptian intelligence. Nasser had the notion that the CIA, and not the State Department, was actually running U.S. foreign policy, so he always insisted on knowing who was the station chief. This attitude probably dated from his early years in power, when he regularly met with the CIA's Kermit Roosevelt. As the years passed and his relations with the Americans deteriorated, he came to fear the Agency and believe that the CIA was planning his assassination. Battle was given instructions by the State Department to see the Egyptian president and personally assure him that this was not the case.

Trone had also assured Battle that the CIA had no well-known Egyptian personalities on its payroll. This turned out not to be the case. Just as we arrived in Cairo in the summer of 1965, Battle was called to the Foreign Ministry and shown photographs of a CIA case officer, Bruce Odell, handing an envelope of cash to Mustapha Amin, a prominent newspaper editor. Odell was working under diplomatic cover, passing himself off as a Foreign Service officer. Amin had been close to Nasser in the 1950s, but their relations had cooled in recent years. News of Amin's arrest was splashed across the front pages of Cairo's dailies. In July 1965, Odell was expelled, together with Trone. The hapless Amin was convicted of treason and imprisoned.

When a covert operation like this is blown, the political ramifications are severe. The Odell-Amin case heightened Nasser's paranoia in his dealings with Americans. "Cairo was a particularly bad place for conducting intelligence activities," Battle later observed. "There were too many restraints on such activities, it was unsafe and most of the operations didn't amount to anything. For the risks we took, very little was gained through these intelligence operations."

The Agency had a long-standing relationship with Nasser's most implacable enemy—the Muslim Brotherhood. Even regular Foreign Service officers like Talcott Seelye, a veteran Arabist, considered the Brotherhood potentially a natural ally. "We thought of Islam as a counterweight to communism," Seelye said. "We saw it as a moderate force, and a positive one." Another Arabist, Hermann Eilts, had "regular meetings" in the late 1940s with Muslim Brotherhood leader Hassan al-Banna, "and found him perfectly empathetic."

When Washington's relations with Nasser soured, it was not surprising that the CIA developed its own contacts with the Brotherhood. Wilbur Crane Eveland, a covert operative of the CIA, revealed in his memoirs that the Agency had spent more than $100 million on anti-Nasser operations. Some of this money ended up in the hands of Brotherhood members who had escaped to Jordan, Saudi Arabia or Europe. And millions of dollars were reportedly deposited into a Swiss bank account controlled by Said Ramadan, the Brotherhood's supreme guide in Europe and the son-in-law of the Brotherhood's founder, Hassan al-Banna. After Nasser expelled Ramadan from Egypt, he moved to Jordan and then obtained a doctorate from the University of Cologne. By the late 1950s he was living in Geneva. In July 2005, a *Wall Street Journal* investigation by the Pulitzer Prize–winning reporter Ian Johnson concluded that Ramadan had probably been a CIA asset. In 1953, Ramadan had a meeting in the Oval Office with President Eisenhower, and in Geneva he worked closely with the American Committee for Liberation from Bolshevism, a CIA-funded propaganda outfit. German intelligence documents discovered by the *Wall Street Journal* reported that "his expenditures are financed by the American side." A 1967 Swiss government document described Ramadan as an "information agent of the

British and Americans." In 1961 Ramadan founded the Islamic Center of Geneva, which became a think tank for the Brotherhood, funded largely by the Saudis. The CIA arranged for Ramadan to travel on an official Jordanian passport. And all this Washington did in the name of anti-Nasserism.

For several decades Said Ramadan served as the Muslim Brotherhood's de facto leader in Europe, helping to build a major mosque in Munich and establishing Brotherhood chapters in other European countries.* That he did this with generous funding from the Saudis is indisputable; that he also had CIA funding in the 1950s and '60s is quite probable. During these years the Agency encouraged Saudi King Faisal's intelligence chief, Kamal Adham—the king's brother-in-law—to spend millions on the Brotherhood. And King Hussein of Jordan allowed the Brotherhood to operate freely in that country. Nasser was certainly aware at the very least of the broad outlines of the CIA's campaign against him and on behalf of the Muslim Brotherhood.

Nasser distrusted the Americans, and specifically President Lyndon Johnson, because he could see that the American president was trying to use U.S. economic assistance to pressure him into abandoning his pan-Arab nationalist agenda. By contrast, President Kennedy, who thought that Nasser could be co-opted with foreign aid, made friendly diplomatic overtures to the regime. In 1960, the last year of the Eisenhower Administration, U.S. aid to Egypt totaled only $15 million. Under the Kennedy Administration, this figure shot up to $500 million, mostly in the form of Public Law 480 (Food for Peace) food aid. Nasser quickly came to depend on these wheat shipments—only to have them suddenly cut off by a recalcitrant U.S. Congress. Angered by Nasser's Yemen misadventure, Senator Ernest Gruening of Alaska decided that Egypt had to be punished. In early November 1963, Senator Gruening persuaded his colleagues to vote, 65 to 13, to ban foreign aid to any country planning to attack any recipient of American foreign aid. The bill's obvious target was Egypt.

President Kennedy condemned the legislation: "This is the worst attack on foreign aid that we have seen since the beginning of the Marshall Plan."

---

*Said Ramadan's son, Tariq Ramadan, is today a well-known and sometimes controversial scholar of modern Islamic philosophy and jurisprudence living in Geneva.

The bill, he said, will not enhance "our flexibility in dealing with the UAR. In fact it will have the opposite result. . . . They are nationalist, they are proud, they are in many cases radical." Threatening to cut off aid, as the Eisenhower Administration did with the Aswan Dam project, could backfire. "I think it is a very dangerous, untidy world," he observed. "But we are going to have to live with it." Bypassing Congress, Kennedy asserted that the law did not apply to Egypt, and he continued the wheat shipments.

Kennedy's successor took a dim view of the Egyptian president. Under Lyndon Johnson, Washington extended the wheat shipments, but wanting to keep Nasser on a short leash, Johnson would only authorize the shipments for six months at a time. One of Johnson's goals was to force Nasser to withdraw his troops from Yemen. "It was an attempt to use aid as a political weapon," Dick Parker recalled. "And it didn't work." Nasser took this as a personal affront. His anger escalated when in the spring of 1965 Johnson wrote to inform him that Washington was going to sell additional "defensive" armaments to Israel and Saudi Arabia—but nothing to Egypt. Nasser was appalled at this one-sidedness. In a public speech, he insultingly called Johnson a "cowboy."

Johnson tried to smooth things over by telling Egyptian vice president Anwar Sadat, who was visiting Washington, "What we need is quiet diplomacy. Why does President Nasser stand up and openly attack me and the policy of the United States?" And then in his folksy manner, Johnson explained that he always solved his quarrels with his wife, Lady Bird, with whispers. "What I want to do with President Nasser is to solve our problems in a whisper." Nasser took this as an attempt to disarm him of the only weapon he had at hand—his voice. He called in the American ambassador, Lucius Battle, and said, "Please tell President Johnson that I am not convinced by what he said to Sadat about quiet diplomacy and its uses. You have got money and atom bombs, riches and power without limit. These are your means. What have I got? The main weapon of the Revolution is its masses, the conviction of the masses and mobilization of those masses. . . . quiet diplomacy would not suit us because I would be cut off from the support of my masses. . . . I must always be ready to talk to the Arab people. . . . I must put all our secrets in front of them."

Radio Cairo was Nasser's voice, his only weapon. When the Johnson Administration finally suspended wheat shipments in late 1964, Nasser lashed back with an old Arab riposte: "If they don't like our behavior, then they can go drink the sea." Nasser's way with words was both his strength and his weakness. His words would place him on the road to a war he knew to be unwinnable.

Father has always believed that the June 1967 War was not inevitable. The road to that war was lined with miscalculations and misunderstandings—mistakes that could have been avoided if Washington had been able to serve as a trusted intermediary between Cairo and Tel Aviv. But Washington was not a trusted intermediary, and neither was the June War an "inadvertent war." It was a war of choice.

Father and his colleagues in the Cairo embassy struggled hard in 1966–67 to restore lines of real communication to Nasser. Early in 1966 Nasser asked for $150 million in PL 480 wheat shipments. Washington stalled from month to month, repeatedly telling Nasser that his request was under consideration. Nasser also wanted permission to use the Egyptian pounds with which he had paid the U.S. Embassy for previous PL 480 foodstuffs to finance the building of grain silos in Alexandria. Washington said no. Nasser wanted help on refinancing his foreign debts. Among all the Western powers, only Washington said no. Nasser wanted Washington's approval for a nuclear desalinization plant to be built by Westinghouse. Washington said no. Nasser asked for Washington's help in mediations with the Saudis over the Yemeni civil war. Washington said no. And when Nasser extended an invitation to Secretary of State Dean Rusk to visit Cairo, Washington said no. "All of these things cost very little," said David G. Nes, the embassy's chargé d'affaires, "but they would have been evidence of our sympathy for Egypt and our desire to maintain reasonably cordial relations, relations, for example, as good as we had with Yugoslavia, which was a Communist country. We never were able to move forward and give them an affirmative answer on any one of these." In part, Washington was trying to pressure Nasser to get out of Yemen—and to step down from his bully pulpit. The Americans wanted a weakened Nasser, a strongman who would concentrate on Egypt's internal problems and forget about Israel. But it was also true that Lyndon Johnson didn't have time for the Middle East. He was becoming ensnared by the tar baby named Vietnam.

When, on March 5, 1967, Ambassador Lucius Battle was reassigned to Washington, Johnson left the Cairo post vacant—and it remained so for the three months leading up to the June War. Due to protocol, it would have been highly unusual for the Egyptian president to speak directly to the embassy's highest-ranking remaining officer, Chargé d'affaires Nes. As a result, Nasser had no personal contact with American officials in the three months prior to June 5. Nes repeatedly warned Washington that a crisis was brewing, but, he later claimed, his cables were ignored. Morale in the embassy that spring of 1967 was abysmal. "I have never seen him so depressed or discouraged," Mother wrote of Father in April. Despite a climate Mother described as "colder and colder," Father had a wide circle of Egyptian friends and contacts. In an atmosphere of rising tensions, he was one of the few American diplomats who still routinely received dinner invitations to the homes of Egyptian officials. He was out almost every night. "This has been no asset at the office," Mother wrote a friend, "as others have not had the same success. . . . And I guess others have commented on it. . . . Too much. The Embassy in general is a very sad place. AID [Agency for International Development] is completely disillusioned. USIS [United States Information Agency] people feel like folding up and think they wouldn't be missed, and morale is pretty bad."

Washington finally sent out a new ambassador, Richard Nolte, just two weeks before war erupted. After greeting him at the airport, Father watched as reporters asked if he had any new thoughts on the crisis. Nolte turned to them and quipped, "What crisis?"

The Six Day War—Arabs call it the Naksa, the "setback"—began with a relatively minor water dispute between the Israelis and the Syrians, who were attempting to divert the River Jordan. Whenever the Syrians sent out tractors to work on the diversion plan, the Israelis deployed aircraft to bomb them. The Israelis also attempted to take de facto control of farm plots located inside Syria's demilitarized zone along the Golan Heights. This led in the winter of 1967 to any number of "incidents," 80 percent of which, according to General Moshe Dayan, were instigated by the Israelis. Israeli armored tractors would be sent into the demilitarized zone, knowing this would probably provoke Syrian fire. "If they didn't shoot," Dayan explained, "we would tell the tractor to go farther, until finally the Syrians would lose their temper and shoot. And then we'd fire back, and later send in the Air Force." The point was to get a little more land under Israeli control.

The number of these incidents escalated in March 1967, with Israeli ground troops and aircraft attacking Syrian positions and also targeting Palestinians from the recently created guerrilla force al-Fatah. On April 7, one of these incidents erupted into a full-fledged battle. Six Syrian MIG-21s were shot down, and Israeli Mirage fighter planes brazenly flew over Damascus. The Syrians responded by shelling Israeli kibbutzim along the border. By early May, Prime Minister Levi Eshkol and General Yitzhak Rabin announced that they would use the Israeli Air Force against Damascus if the Syrian incidents continued. On May 12, United Press International reported, "A high Israeli source said today that Israel would take limited military action designed to topple the Damascus army regime if Syrian terrorists continue sabotage raids inside Israel. Military observers said such an offensive would fall short of all-out war but would deliver a telling blow against the Syrian government."

The very next day, May 13, 1967, the Soviets passed an alarming intelligence report to Anwar Sadat, then president of the Egyptian National Assembly, who happened to be visiting Moscow. The Soviets claimed to have hard intelligence that Israeli troops were massing on the Syrian border. On the following morning, U.S. Chargé d'affaires Nes met with an official at the Egyptian Foreign Office and categorically informed him that U.S. intelligence had no reports of unusual Israeli troop movements. This information was passed on to Nasser—who suspected that it was disinformation. "By this time," Nes later said, "relations between the United States and Egypt had sunk so low that Nasser seemed to believe that we were in collusion with the Israelis to destroy his regime."

Nes's intelligence was correct, and the Soviet information was wrong. But Nasser chose to believe that Israeli troops were massing for an attack on Syria. The previous year he had signed a joint defense pact with the Ba'athist military regime in Damascus, promising to come to Syria's assistance if Israel attacked. Knowing that his own military was not prepared to take on the Israelis, Nasser looked for a way to deter the Israelis from moving against Syria. He was under considerable political pressure from other Arab leaders to take a stand against Israeli incursions in the West Bank, the Golan Heights and Gaza—incursions often but not always launched by the Israelis in retaliation for Palestinian guerrilla raids.

For all these reasons, Nasser felt he had to do something to respond to the Israeli threat on the Syrian border. His choice was to increase his military forces on Israel's southern border in the Sinai. To this end, on May 16, Nasser instructed the commander of the United Nations Emergency Force to withdraw peacekeeping forces from along the Israeli-Egyptian land border in the Sinai. (With Cairo's acquiescence, these U.N. troops had been stationed on the Egyptian side of the border ever since the 1956 war. The Israelis had always refused to have peacekeepers on their side of the border.) Nasser simultaneously ordered Egyptian troops into the Sinai, on Israel's southern border, to deter the Israelis from attacking Damascus. There is no evidence that Nasser had any intention of attacking Israel. At the height of the crisis, Nasser had only 50,000 troops in the Sinai—facing an Israeli ground force of more than 160,000. This imbalance indicated that Egypt's intentions were purely defensive and symbolic. But on May 19, the U.N. secretary general, U Thant, made an inexplicable decision. Nasser had not explicitly asked for U.N troops to be removed from Gaza or their outpost at Sharm al-Sheikh, overlooking the Straits of Tiran. But instead of trying to buy time and somehow keep his troops in the Sinai, U Thant informed Nasser that if some U.N. peacekeepers were withdrawn, then all of them would have to leave the Sinai—including those stationed at Sharm al-Sheikh. As the peacekeepers withdrew from that outpost, Egyptian forces moved in to take their place. The Egyptians were now in a position to control shipping through the Straits of Tiran, which created the potential for greatly escalating the crisis.

Nasser didn't realize it, but he was creating the dynamics for a war he didn't want and couldn't win. He now compounded the crisis by announcing the closure of the Straits of Tiran. Ships flying the Israeli flag, he said, could not pass below Egyptian forces stationed at Sharm al-Sheikh. This was simple bluster, but it turned out to be a major miscalculation on his part. The straits were in Egyptian waters—and though international law suggested that ships of other sovereignties had a right to free passage in such waters, the Israelis had never negotiated these rights. After the 1956 war, Israel had unilaterally declared that closing the straits would be regarded as an act of war. Nasser immediately and publicly demurred, stating that the straits were sovereign Egyptian waters. Just the same, a tacit understanding was developed between the Egyptians and the Israelis with the help of United Nations mediators: the Egyptians would allow foreign ships through the straits so long as the ships did not fly the Israeli flag. Because the vast majority of Israeli shipping went through ports on the Mediterranean, in the ten years after the 1956 war, only 117 Israeli ships passed through the Straits of Tiran, less than one a month. None displayed an Israeli flag. No Israeli ship, in fact, had passed through the Straits of Tiran in 1966 or 1967. Nevertheless, the Israelis now loudly insisted that Nasser's closing the straits was an act of war. But whatever the legal merits of the issue, in practice the closing of the Straits of Tiran to Israeli shipping was no cause for a rush to war.

In response to Israel's protests, Nasser attempted to backpedal, telling a U.N. official that he was willing to accept a two-week moratorium on the closure of the straits and to submit the issue of Egyptian sovereignty over them to the World Court in The Hague.

U.N. Secretary General U Thant rushed to Cairo with a face-saving formula: he proposed that Israel agree not to send any ships through the straits if Egypt would agree not to inspect the cargos of non-Israeli ships headed for the Israeli port of Eilat. Nasser quickly accepted—but the Israelis rejected the deal.

On the evening of May 26, 1967, the Johnson Administration cabled Cairo that the Israelis believed the Egyptians were going to launch an attack that very evening. Nasser, awakened at 3:00 a.m., denied that he had ordered an attack. According to his confidant Mohamed Heikal, "Nasser was astonished. He could not understand where the Israelis got their story, because there was no truth in it." In an attempt to defuse the crisis, Nasser gave one of his melodious speeches later that day in which he categorically pledged not to initiate hostilities. "We are not going to fire the first shot. . . . We are not going to start an attack." But he added a provocative warning: "If Israel embarks on an aggression against Syria or Egypt, the battle against Israel will be a general one and not confined to one spot on the Syrian or Egyptian borders. The battle will be a general one and our basic objective will be to destroy Israel."

Such mixed messages did nothing to allay Israeli fears. But despite the harsh rhetoric, Nasser was clearly looking for a way out. In late May he gave the American embassy an explicit "no strike first" pledge that should have given Washington time to resolve the crisis with diplomacy. Nasser also repeated his willingness to submit the dispute over the Straits of Tiran to the World Court. On June 1, he announced that he was dispatching his vice president, Zakaria Mohieddin, to meet with President Johnson in Washington on June 6. Writing from Cairo on June 1, the *New York Times*'s James Reston reported, "Cairo does not want war and it is certainly not ready for war. But it has already accepted the possibility, even the likelihood, of war, as if it had lost control of the situation."

King Hussein and President Nasser on the eve of the June 1967 War

On May 25, the State Department decided to evacuate all embassy dependents and nonessential personnel from Egypt. Father would be staying, but the rest of us would be flown out to Athens aboard TWA flights chartered by the embassy. We packed as if we were going on a short summer vacation to the beach. I took my snorkeling gear. We were booked into a seafront hotel just outside Athens. Mother brought her guitar. She thought the whole exercise was ridiculous and assumed we would all be back in a week or two. She left her silver, jewelry and other valuables behind. I hadn't finished tenth grade. My sister Christina was set to graduate the following week from Schutz, the high school in Alexandria. She took a train down to Cairo, and Mother, Christina, Nancy, Shelly and I flew out on the last of the evacuation planes leased by the American embassy. On that day, May 26, 1967, 140 American women and children crowded into Cairo International Airport's departure lounge. Father came to the airport to see us off. He had just come back from a visit to Gaza, and on the way back he had noticed that the large Soviet-built radar complex at al-Arish was not functioning. I remember his pointing out the window to a radar unit. "See that?" he said. "It is not turning on its axis, which means it isn't even on. If there's going to be a war, the Egyptians certainly aren't ready for it."

On May 30, Father arrived at a Rotary Club luncheon, where three Egyptian friends greeted him and held their thumbs up as if to say, "The situation is better, don't you think?" Father nodded. In Israel, on June 1, General Moshe Dayan was appointed defense minister. The next day, Father attended a classified meeting in the Cairo embassy's "bubble"—the one room they considered "clean," free of bugs or wiretaps. The newly arrived ambassador, Richard Nolte, asked the attending officers for their views. "It looks to me," Father said, "that, since Moshe Dayan has been appointed [Defense Minister], Israel is going to go to war."

Nevertheless, over the next few days Father and others in the embassy thought the crisis had turned a corner. Diplomacy was gaining traction. On Sunday, June 4, the U.S. Embassy's political counselor, Richard Parker, felt relaxed enough to go sailing.

As seen from Jerusalem, however, an opportunity to remake the map of the Middle East was slipping away. By late May the Israeli army had been mobilized for nearly two weeks. The Israelis simply could not afford to keep thousands of reservists out of the civilian economy much longer. They had to either demobilize or go to war. Most members of Prime Minister Levi Eshkol's cabinet were inclined to resolve the impasse by force of arms. And, unbeknownst to Father or his colleagues in the Cairo embassy, the Israelis had received a "green light" from the Johnson Administration. On May 31 the chief of Israeli intelligence, Meir Amit, journeyed incognito to Washington and met with CIA director Richard Helms and Defense Secretary Robert McNamara, who informed President Johnson directly of their discussions. Amit told Helms and McNamara that war was inevitable unless the Americans or a multilateral naval force opened the Straits of Tiran. Helms and McNamara made it clear that with American forces bogged down in Vietnam, the Johnson Administration had no intention of being dragged into a military intervention in the Middle East. If war broke out, the Israelis would be on their own. Amit said that Israel could handle Nasser alone, and when McNamara asked how long the operation would take, Amit replied two days. The defense secretary voiced no objections when Amit said he intended to recommend to Prime Minister Eshkol that Israel go to war. "I read you loud and clear," McNamara said. Twice McNamara left the meeting to take phone calls from President Johnson, who, he assured Amit, knew of this meeting. Back in Israel on June 3, Amit told Prime Minister Eshkol that the Americans would be pleased if Israel were to "break Nasser to pieces," and that he believed the Americans would provide money, arms and political support. "The United States won't go into mourning," Amit told Eshkol, "if Israel attacks Egypt." Amit's message was decisive for Eshkol. It was the green light he needed to go to war. The next day, during a critical cabinet meeting, Eshkol confirmed his decision to launch a first strike against Egypt, explaining that there "was a movement toward a search for compromise, at Israel's expense." In other words, Israel had to go to war before diplomacy succeeded.

Even today, most Americans and Israelis retain the misapprehension that Egypt, not Israel, was the aggressor in the June War. It is certainly true that in the weeks leading up to the war, most Israelis felt an existential threat. But the archives demonstrate that Israeli leaders recognized this to be a war of choice, not a war of survival. All of Prime Minister Eshkol's generals were confident of victory, and few of them believed Nasser was in a position to launch a major invasion. Labor Minister Yigal Allon, who was directly involved in the planning for the war, later said, "The only crisis was psychological." As the Israeli historian Tom Segev writes, "Eshkol emerges as a statesman with nerves of steel who withstood pressure [from his generals] until he could achieve coordination with the United States. It is doubtful whether he believed Israel's existence was truly in danger, and equally doubtful that he was convinced Egypt would attack. He knew what the army knew: that even if Egypt attacked, Israel would win."

The Israelis were confident of their superior military capabilities, and they believed that Nasser's rhetorical brinkmanship had handed them an opportunity to reshape the map of the Middle East. The Johnson Administration saw the same opportunities. In late May the CIA told the White House that Egyptian "military dispositions in Sinai are defensive in character." The CIA estimated the total number of Egyptian, Jordanian and Syrian troops "in the vicinity of Israeli borders" at 117,000, facing an Israeli ground force of 280,000 well-equipped soldiers. In the air, Israel had 256 "operationally assigned fighter aircraft" compared to 222 Syrian, Egyptian and Jordanian aircraft ready to fly. In sum, the Israelis had a vastly superior force ready to deal Nasser a humiliating defeat. Washington knew this. On May 26, Johnson's national security adviser, Walt Rostow, told the president that "Israel is approaching a decision in favor of a preemptive attack." The same day the president was told there "were no indications that the Egyptians would attack." If war broke out, it would be a war chosen by Israel—not by Nasser.

Early on the morning of June 5, Father assured a group of American oil geologists, "We have bought ten days of time." Minutes later, Father was sitting at his desk when a friend, John Calhoun, head of American Express in Cairo, called him. In his thick Mississippi accent, Calhoun said, "I am at the airport trying to get some clients on planes to Athens, and Nasser has gone mad." Calhoun thought it was Egyptian aircraft that were bombing the runway. Father calmly told him that those were Israeli planes and that he should leave the airport. Soon afterwards, another friend called from Alexandria to report that Egyptian bombers were burning on the tarmac of the military airport.

When Father stepped outside the embassy traffic had come to a stop, and the sound of sirens was all he could hear. He asked a plainclothes policeman if this was an air raid drill. "Yes," the man responded—even as one could hear explosions coming from Cairo airport. Later that morning shrapnel fell from the sky into the embassy garden.

Though Nasser had repeatedly warned his commanders to be on their guard against an Israeli air attack, Egyptian pilots at military bases all over the country were having a leisurely breakfast when the Israelis struck. The Egyptian High Command was taken by surprise. Marshal Abd al-Hakim Amer was flying to inspect troops in the Sinai when he heard the first reports that Israeli bombers were attacking targets all over Egypt. Hastening back to Cairo, he was forced to land at its international commercial airport, as the military airport was out of commission. The Israelis flew hundreds of sorties, and by the end of the day the Egyptian air force was decimated. As Walt Rostow told President Johnson, it was a "turkey shoot" for the Israelis.

Radio Cairo reported that the surprise Israeli air attack had been repelled and that 200 enemy warplanes had been shot down. While the Egyptian people were being told lies, the rest of the world was hailing Israel's astonishing feat. Sitting in Athens, glued to the radio, Mother called it "rotten news." When she heard a report about the sacking of the American consulate in Alexandria, she noted, "I'm losing my cool." On this first day of the war, she had no information about her husband.

On that night of June 5, ten days after we'd left for Athens, Father slept in the embassy. The next day, Radio Cairo charged that American planes from the Sixth Fleet had participated in the air attack. This became known as the "Big Lie" when Israeli intelligence released a transcript of an intercepted phone conversation between Nasser and Jordan's King Hussein in which the two Arab leaders agreed to charge that American and British warplanes were aiding the Israeli offensive. (By then, both Jordan and Syria had joined the fray, thinking foolishly that Egypt would prevail.) That same day, Father witnessed twelve Egyptian policemen on horseback charging a mob of 500 protestors outside the embassy. In a letter to his family that evening, he noted that Egyptian Foreign Ministry officials were threatening to break relations with the United States. "I am betting on it," he wrote at 6:00 p.m. A few hours later, Father won his "bet": Nasser announced that he was severing diplomatic relations with Washington.

Father and his colleagues immediately began burning classified documents. They dragged mountains of paper to the embassy roof, where they stuffed them into special barrels set aside for just such a contingency. A Marine mistakenly closed the lid on one of these barrels and ignited the chemicals. A tremendous explosion followed, which blew the lid two hundred feet into the air and shot a column of fire skyward. The Egyptians thought the embassy had been hit by an Israeli bomb and dispatched fire engines to the scene.

On the evening of June 9, a haggard Nasser, his voice trembling, addressed the nation and confessed that Egyptian forces had been routed. The Sinai was gone; some 10,000 Egyptian soldiers had been killed and another 60,000 captured by the Israelis. (Eight hundred Israeli soldiers were killed.) Nasser said that he took full responsibility for the disaster and was resigning from the presidency. He said he was ready to "return to the ranks of the masses and do my duty with them like every other citizen." Within the hour, as if choreographed, millions of frenzied Cairenes poured into the streets, shouting, "Gamal, Gamal," and demanding that he remain in power. Millions more filled the streets of Beirut, Damascus, Amman and Tripoli. Their Rayyis, their twentieth-century Pharaoh, had fallen in battle, but he would not be scorned.

That same evening, Bill Bromell, the embassy's CIA station chief (and the father of my schoolmate Nick), had to go out to meet someone. At about midnight Bromell turned a corner and was confronted by a small mob. Nick later described his father's reaction in a *Harper's* magazine essay:

A young man seized him by the arms, and instead of resisting, my father took the young man's hand and guided his fingers to the skin under his own glasses. The man paused, stepped back, then turned and quieted the crowd. When he had finished, he put his arm around my father and guided him through the mass, which parted like the waters of the Red Sea. My father continued quietly on his way.

What had happened? On seeing the crowd, my father spat on his hands and rubbed them beneath his eyes. The moisture there convinced the young man that my father, like so many Egyptians, had been weeping with sorrow at the news that Nasser planned to resign. This is what the man had explained to the crowd and why they had let my father through.

Nick insisted that his father "truly was saddened" by Nasser's resignation. "He wasn't just tricking the crowd; he was feeling with them." Within hours the chanting crowds "persuaded" the Rayyis to rescind his resignation.

Earlier on June 9, the embassy began evacuating all remaining personnel. Father spent the day trying to locate various American citizens—mostly businessmen and a few longtime missionaries—to give them instructions on how to get out. He and other officers were shuttled in embassy cars to Cairo's train station in the dark early morning hours of June 10. Ignoring instructions to leave pets behind, Father brought our beautiful Saluki, Zahra, on a leash. Chargé d'affaires David Nes carried a hand grenade just in case they became entrapped. At the train station they picked their way across a floor strewn with the bodies of sleeping Egyptian soldiers. The train—with shades drawn—left about 3:30 a.m. They were headed for Alexandria, where they would board a ship bound for Piraeus. As they passed through the villages of the Nile Delta, crowds of Egyptian *fellaheen* shook the soles of their sandals at the train—the ultimate Egyptian insult. They arrived without incident in Alexandria four hours later. By then a mob had ransacked and burned the American consulate in the city. Egyptian authorities kept them waiting at dockside most of the day without food or water. That afternoon, lacking porters, they formed a human chain to pass hundreds of pieces of luggage from hand to hand and aboard the ship. Finally, at 5:00 p.m., Father and some 550 other remaining Americans—diplomats, businessmen, journalists and missionaries—boarded the 3,000-ton *Carina,* an interisland ferry that had never sailed farther from Athens than Crete. After crossing the Mediterranean, it had burst a boiler sailing into Alexandria. As the ship had berths for only 150 passengers, most of the evacuees had to sleep on the deck.

Aboard the *Carina,* the evacuees were able to pick up the BBC and learned the full dimensions of the Arab defeat: the Israelis had occupied the entire Sinai Peninsula, the West Bank, East Jerusalem and the Golan Heights. The diplomats aboard, many of them veteran Arabists, listened to the news with growing apprehension. They intuitively understood that the Israeli military victories would not translate into long-term peace. The embassy's top diplomat, David Nes, blamed his bosses back in Washington for not preventing the war, and he now decided to go public. In an interview aboard ship with a reporter from the *Baltimore Sun,* he declared that the Johnson Administration might have averted the war—but had "pooh-poohed" his warnings of a possible war. He accused the administration of stupidity and outright incompetence. When the story was published on June 13, 1967, Nes's career was finished. He retired six months later.

As most of the Arab world had cut diplomatic relations with America, there were very few jobs left for Arabists. At the age of forty-two—with four children and a wife to support—Father reluctantly accepted a posting to Bombay as economic officer. Nancy and I were sent off to a missionary boarding school in Tamil Nadu, South India.

The June War was a debacle for the Arab world. The Egyptian diva Umm Kulthum plunged into a deep depression and spent two full weeks in the isolation of her villa's basement hideaway. When she finally emerged from this self-imposed exile, she sang of loss, betrayal and disillusionment: "Why am I languishing when the world surrounds me?" Her audiences left her concerts sobbing.

To this day, most Americans don't understand what a calamity the June War was for America as well. In its aftermath 24,000 American expatriates—businessmen, diplomats and their dependents—were expelled from the Middle East. Anti-American demonstrations swept the region, and strikes in the oil fields of Arabia temporarily halted the shipping of oil. In Dhahran, a mob invaded my childhood home in the American consulate compound, and one young man broke his leg while trying, successfully, to tear down the Stars and Stripes. In the midst of the melee, Father's friend Saleh Ambah, the dean of the College of Petroleum and Minerals, showed up and persuaded a number of his students to go back to their dormitories. When afterwards police questioned him, Ambah refused to divulge any names of the student rioters. (This may well have been one of the reasons he was thrown into prison in 1970.) Some of the rioters later moved on to Aramco's American Camp, where they managed to force their way past the main gate, stoning cars and nearly ransacking the home of Tom Barger, Aramco's president.

It was also a disaster for the Arab world's remaining Jews—Jews who, if they had remained, might have been a cultural bridge between Israel and the old Middle East. Eight hundred of Egypt's 4,000 lingering Jews were detained, including the chief rabbis of Alexandria and Cairo. Much Jewish property was confiscated. Mobs in major Arab cities attacked Jewish neighborhoods. Eighteen Jews were killed in Tripoli, Libya. And across the region approximately 7,000 Arab Jews were deported. Some Egyptian Jews stubbornly remained. Edward Said's piano teacher, Ignace Tiegerman—whom Said later described as "a tiny Polish-Jewish gnome of a man"—refused to leave. "Why should I go there [Israel]?" he said. "Here I am unique; there many people are like me. Besides, I love Cairo." Tiegerman had come to Egypt from Poland in 1933. He died peacefully in Cairo a few months after the June War.

For Arabs everywhere, the June defeat was devastating. To describe it as a *naksa,* "setback," trivializes the extent of the carnage and damage. As the great Oxford-trained scholar of the Middle East Albert Hourani (1915–1993) said, "Victory is a much less profound experience than defeat." The Lebanese—now American—intellectual Fouad Ajami described how "an intense wave of self-criticism swept the Arab world, mocking the ways of an era, and beyond it, the burden of history, trying, as it were, to go to the roots of the defeat."

A Moroccan scholar, Abdallah Laroui, writing just three years after the war, summarized the self-doubt that plagued the Arab world:

> The Imam came forward repeating that we lost because we deviated from morality. . . . The opposition leader insisted that we lost because the men in power monopolized total power. . . . The engineer came forward asking for new machines and new factories . . . all found in the enemy whatever justified their argument. The theologian found justification in the theocratic orientation of our enemy; the politician in the fact that our enemy had a parliament; the engineer emphasized

the abundance of the enemy's technical schools. Only a few were able to observe that the religious faith of the enemy, his democracy, his technology, were all useful instruments but that the principal factor was the enemy's social organization, his sense of individual freedom, his lack of subjugation, despite all appearances, to any form of finalism or absolutism.

Nasser's confidant Mohamed Heikal blamed the defeat on the Egyptian army and on Egypt's entire social and political system. Only a truly democratic Egypt, he suggested, had any chance of defeating an expansionist Israel. "The Israelis don't want peace," he told the *New York Times*'s Edward R. F. Sheehan, "they want territorial expansion." Nearly a year later, Nasser expressed the enormity of the defeat by describing himself as "a man walking in a desert surrounded by moving sands not knowing whether, if he moved, he would be swallowed up by the sands or would find the right path."

Sadik al-Azm, a Yale-educated, Syrian-born philosopher, described the defeat as a "lightning bolt," a "shock" to the Arab ethos. In 1970, two years after he had published *Al-Naqd al-Dhati Ba'd al Hazima* (Self-Criticism After the Defeat), his scathing indictment of Arab society, I listened to al-Azm lecture at the American University of Beirut. Al-Azm compared the June War to the psychological blow inflicted on the Arab and Islamic worlds when Napoleon Bonaparte's 1798 French expedition invaded Egypt and defeated the Mameluke armies. "Napoleon's expedition," al-Azm later said, "inflicted severe narcissist wounds on the Islamic self-image which have yet to heal. The 1967 defeat inflicted similar wounds." Before the war Arab intellectuals like al-Azm looked upon Nasser's accomplishments—the nationalization of the Suez Canal, the building of the Aswan High Dam, the Czech arms deal, the building of Arab socialism—as tangible evidence that the cause of pan-Arabism was the wave of the future. Now all these things were shown to be "exaggerated accomplishments." Now they saw that Nasser had made too many compromises with tradition. Now they saw that he was not nearly radical enough to drag Egypt into the twentieth century.

Before the war it was possible to believe that the Arab world was on the path to modernity. "Most of these hopes," al-Azm said, "revolved around the concept of the inspired leader, and when the leader fell, everything crashed with him, leaving nothing behind but emptiness, loss and confusion."

Nasser's sonorous words had cost Arab lives, lost Arab land and created Arab refugees.

Al-Azm blamed Nasser but also suggested that the great Rayyis had failed because his people had failed him. Arab society was too attached to tradition, too ignorant of science and too tolerant of the religious establishment to enter modernity. Al-Azm compared the June defeat to Japan's defeat of Tsarist Russia in the Russo-Japanese War of 1904. Japan was like Israel—smaller, but wholly capable of embracing an alien technology—and so it was able to defeat a larger, more populous Russian empire. The Russians had learned from defeat. The Arabs, suggested al-Azm, would not.

"At the same time," he continued, "the political regimes responsible for the military defeat began utilizing religion in general and Islam in particular in a campaign designed to protect them from the aftermath of the defeat."

Perhaps it was only natural that some Arabs would turn in private to religion as a balm for national humiliation. Ayman al-Zawahiri wrote in his 2001 memoir that the Naksa—the June defeat—"added a dangerous factor that influenced the awakening of the jihadist movement." Initially, this religiosity did not manifest itself as a political movement. Thus, in 1967, the Muslim Brotherhood was still a small, sometimes ridiculed minority, and most of its leaders and organizers had been neutralized by Nasser's secret police. In the late 1960s, the political challenge came from the radical left. Young intellectuals like al-Azm turned to Marxism and the politics of national liberation. Radical groups like the Arab Nationalist Movement, al-Fatah and the Popular Front for the Liberation of Palestine attracted adherents and attention in the press. Nasser became the Arab establishment, no longer the radical nationalist. Chastened by defeat, Nasser in their view was now more pragmatic, and certainly more cautious, in his foreign policy. In late 1968 he brought the last of his troops home from Yemen. The Yemeni Republic had survived the royalist counterrevolution, but at a cost of tens of thousands of lives.

Much of this Arab leftism was theatrical. It polarized the "street" and alienated many Muslims who remained committed to tradition. Islam as a political force was like a slumbering giant, waiting to be awakened. Sadik al-Azm understood the underlying political dynamic. In 1969 he wrote another book, *Critique of Religious Thought,* in which he tackled Islam as a potentially reactionary force. "I was becoming very conscious," he said in 1997, "of the ability of this body of thought to continually reproduce the values of ignorance, myth-making, backwardness, dependency, and fatalism—and to impede the propagation of scientific values, secularism, enlightenment, democracy and humanism."

Predictably, al-Azm's book landed him in jail. Lebanese authorities arrested him in 1969 and prosecuted him for defaming Islam. Though he was found innocent and released, he lost his job at the American University of Beirut. He moved back to his native Syria and won tenure at the University of Damascus. For decades he has managed to stay out of prison and avoid exile while speaking his mind. Rare among Arab writers, al-Azm defended Salman Rushdie when the Ayatollah Khomeini issued a fatwa condemning him to death for his book *The Satanic Verses*. Most of al-Azm's own books are banned in the Arab world, where he is known as the "heretic of Damascus" or the "Voltaire of the Arab world." Such a courageous intellectual—and there are many of them living in Cairo, Beirut and Damascus—is emblematic of the Arab world's secular, enlightened future.

When I first heard al-Azm speak in Beirut in 1970, I knew official Washington considered him a pariah. A left-wing Arab intellectual was not tolerable—even if he was a Yale-trained scholar of Immanuel Kant, and even if he was a critic of both Nasserism and Islamic fundamentalism. Three years after the June War, Washington was happy to see Nasser weakened at home and abroad. By humiliating the chief living symbol of secular Arab nationalism, Israel had performed an enormous service on behalf of American oil interests. The royalists in Arabia had every reason to fear Nasser before the June War. In the wake of his defeat these existential fears disappeared.

In retrospect, it seems unfathomable that the Americans were unperturbed by the ascendancy of political Islam, funded by Wahhabi charitable organizations. But the Saudis, after all, were America's allies and business partners. If anything, Washington welcomed the "Saudi Era" as an antidote to Nasser's bombastic, messianic Arab nationalism and a great opportunity for business. Though the Arabs had kicked out all American diplomats, Washington was happy with the outcome of the June War. Nasser and Nasserism had been soundly defeated—and Washington was confident that the same fate awaited the radical, largely Palestinian leftists who had now seized the stage of Arab political theatre. Petrodollars would trump everything in the Saudi era. In the wake of the June defeat, Mohamed Heikal, the Egyptian pundit, punned that power had shifted from the Arab *thawra* (revolution) to the Arab *tharwa* (fortune).

*   *   *

If the June War was a catastrophe for Arab modernity, it also spelled the end of old-fashioned Zionism. This, of course, was not how it was seen at the time. Israelis experienced only euphoria that June. Suddenly, Israel was in possession of land three and half times its original size. The Israeli historian Tom Segev captures the triumphalist mood of the average Israeli citizen in his book *1967: Israel, the War, and the Year That Transformed the Middle East*: "The great miracle that has occurred astonishes us all," wrote an Israeli to her sister in Boston. "We were certain of destruction, and now everything has changed and we are the victors."

The war had given Israel enormous leverage to win a real peace settlement. Israel could now offer to return the occupied territories in exchange for normal relations and Arab recognition of the Jewish state within internationally sanctioned borders. On June 19, 1967, the Israeli cabinet decided by a margin of only one vote to exchange occupied land for peace. But this offer was to be addressed only to Egypt—with reference to the Sinai—and to Syria, regarding the Golan Heights—not to Jordan or the Palestinians. Gaza was specifically referred to as "fully within the territory of the state of Israel." As to the West Bank, the Israeli cabinet was undecided. A handful of cabinet ministers were inclined to return the West Bank to Jordan in exchange for a peace treaty. But most hoped that by holding on to this land, new facts would be created on the ground that would allow Israel someday to annex the region. General Dayan was famously quoted as saying, "We're waiting for the Arabs to call," suggesting that he favored an exchange of land for peace. He did not. To the contrary, he soon began lobbying for Jewish settlement of the West Bank—and he favored a program to quietly urge Palestinians to emigrate.

On June 12, Eshkol told the Knesset, "Let this be said—there should be no illusion that Israel is prepared to return to the conditions that existed a week ago." On June 28, Eshkol announced the formal annexation of East Jerusalem. Afterwards, Dayan said, "Better Sharm al-Sheikh without peace than peace without Sharm al-Sheikh."

In Jerusalem, Israeli bulldozers flattened Mandelbaum Gate; nothing was to remain of the hated symbol of the once divided city. Bulldozers also moved into the Jewish Quarter of the Old City and destroyed scores of centuries-old homes to make way for a football-size field adjoining the

Western Wall. Arab citizens of East Jerusalem were issued Israeli identity cards and Israeli license plates for their cars. The Israelis proclaimed the city unified. It was not—and it is not.

East Jerusalem's 70,000 Palestinian residents were shocked and traumatized by the war. The fiercest fighting had taken place in and around the city, with the Israelis engaging in dangerous house-to-house combat. They nicknamed Nablus Road "Death Alley." Though the Israelis denied that they had bombarded the Old City, they had in fact shelled the northeastern Muslim Quarter for ten minutes, killing approximately a hundred civilians and wounding many more. A bazooka shell tore into the door of al-Aqsa Mosque, atop the Temple Mount.

My childhood friend Dani Bahar, then fourteen years old, awakened on the first day of the war to the sound of mortar fire and explosions. "It sounded as though we were in the middle of a battle," Dani recalled. He and his parents were still living in a Sheikh Jarrah stone house. Not far away, Israeli tanks opened fire on the American consulate near Mandelbaum Gate, and Israeli paratroopers dynamited the consulate's front gate and stormed the strategically located building. Israeli soldiers ensconced in Mount Scopus—a putative demilitarized zone—lobbed mortar shells into our old neighborhood. Dani and his parents cowered in the basement of their home until a tank pulled alongside the house and suddenly they heard men speaking Hebrew in the garden. A day or two later, Dani went with his father to a local grocery store in lower Sheikh Jarrah—and along the way he saw a body lying on the sidewalk.*

Two days into the war, a squadron of Israeli aircraft dropped napalm on Jordanian positions near Augustus Victoria Hospital, setting the roof of the hospital's majestic tower ablaze. Our neighbor Dr. Vicken Kalbian was working at the hospital when an Israeli artillery shell crashed through the Kalbians' living room—it failed to detonate. It was this final trauma that persuaded Vicken and Ada to emigrate.

In Bethlehem, another Palestinian friend, Rita Giacaman, was in her

---

*After it was all over, Dani persuaded his reluctant father to visit the house he had lost in West Jerusalem's Katamon neighborhood in 1948. By then, his mother, Frieda, had no friends left in West Jerusalem, and she refused to come. So Dani and Abu Dani went alone and knocked on the door of the house. A Jewish Iraqi family had occupied the house. "We sat in the garden," Dani recalled. "I believe it was all very friendly, and I assume for my father, quite horrible."

family home on Wednesday, June 7, when the Israeli army began to bomb the town. The Giacamans were fortunate. That day a house next door took a direct hit from mortar fire, killing a sixteen-year-old child. Several other people in the neighborhood were killed. Rita's father had studied pharmacology at the American University of Beirut (AUB)—where I later met Rita—and for decades he had run Bethlehem's largest pharmacy. Like many residents of Bethlehem, the Giacamans were Roman Catholics. When it became clear that Israeli forces had swept to the River Jordan, they had debated whether they should flee to Jordan. "We were terrified," Rita later said. "We had heard the stories from 1948, and we feared the worst." They decided to stay. One day after the cease-fire was announced on June 10, the streets began to rumble with the approach of an Israeli armored column. When the Israeli-imposed curfew was lifted, her father went out to inspect his pharmacy. He returned a few hours later, accompanied by a stranger, a very tall Israeli army officer. Rita was alarmed. Her father quickly explained that this man had been his roommate at the American University of Beirut (AUB). He introduced him as his "Palestinian Jewish friend from AUB." He was clearly happy to see his old friend. The two men had not seen each other since before 1948—but the Israeli knew the Giacamans lived in Bethlehem and so he had made an effort to find them. Rita's mother says there were other Bethlehem families who received calls or visits from old Jewish friends. "The idea of occupation," Rita told me in 2009, "had not sunk in yet, friends were happy to see each other. Later, on when it became clear that the occupation would continue, things began to be very different between Palestinians and Israelis."

The Israelis came as occupiers. And in some instances, they used their power to encourage Palestinians to flee. Even in largely Christian Bethlehem Israeli vehicles equipped with loudspeakers announced in Arabic that residents should leave Bethlehem for Amman—or their homes would be shelled. Most residents of Bethlehem ignored the loudspeakers. But just a few days after the war ended, the Israelis forced the villagers of nearby Beit Nuba to evacuate their homes and bulldozed the entire village. Seven such villages in the Latrun area, with a total population of more than 20,000 Palestinians, were demolished in this manner in mid-June 1967. The Israeli writer Amos Kenan described the operation in an open letter to newspaper editors and

Knesset members. His army unit, Kenan explained, was told they had been delegated to "straighten the border at Latrun." His unit forcibly expelled the villagers and then watched the bulldozers do their work: "The chickens and doves were buried in the rubble. The fields were turned into wasteland in front of our eyes. The children who went crying on the road will be *fedayeen* in nineteen years, in the next round." Kenan was prophetic: in nineteen years these children would be throwing rocks in the first Intifada. He ended his letter on a bitter note: "Thus we have lost the victory."

Resistance to the occupation first made itself known in East Jerusalem, with the appearance of street posters calling for a student strike. In July 1967, Palestinian schools went on strike, and shops in the Old City closed their shutters. At first, the resistance was nonviolent. Petitions were circulated. Palestinian residents of East Jerusalem boycotted municipal elections. Father's old friend Anwar Nusseibeh emerged as the most prominent Palestinian leader in occupied Jerusalem. Nusseibeh publicly declared that he and other Palestinian community leaders did not recognize Israel's annexation of East Jerusalem. The Israelis responded by censoring the Arabic-language press and deporting Anwar al-Khatib, the deposed former mayor of East Jerusalem. On August 7, 1967, the first of many one-day general strikes was organized to protest the annexation of East Jerusalem. The first terrorist attacks occurred in September, with the bombing of a run-down tenement and a failed attempt to place a bomb in a cinema.

In early March 1968, Israeli soldiers arrested a Palestinian engineer named Kamal Nammari and accused him of being the Jerusalem commander of al-Fatah, the nascent Palestinian guerrilla organization. Formally charged with the murder of a Druze guard, Nammari was tried by an Israeli court and sentenced to life imprisonment. He came from a well-educated family in Wadi Joz—just down the road from our former home in Sheikh Jarrah. Days after his arrest, his home was torn apart with high explosives—one of the earliest home demolitions carried out by the Israelis against alleged terrorists. Nammari denied any links to al-Fatah or to the murder of the Druze guard, and he claimed that he had been singled out because his mother was Jewish. Nammari spent eleven years in Ramle prison in central Israel, from 1968 to 1979, and upon his release he told United Nations investigators that he had been repeatedly tortured. He named his Israeli prison guards and described being chained naked and blindfolded to a wall. His guards poured urine over him, slapped him whenever he was about to fall asleep and subjected him to electric shock therapy. He also endured a fake summary execution—and trained prison dogs were let loose on him. "Once they took me out in the Sarafand area [south of Haifa]," Nammari told U.N. investigators. "Near the cells there were two graves. One was like it was newly filled, the other was open, and they told me that my comrade was lying there and the other was for me, so that I had to talk or they would shoot me. They said, 'You have seen the Vietnamese pictures of how the Americans killed people like you, so I'll make it more like them and we'll take a picture of you so people will speak about you like that.' So they made me stand in one of the graves and they started shooting, once just in front of my legs, the second shot in the air, and then they took me back." Fellow prisoners who were also released in the wake of the 1979 Camp David Accords corroborated his story. There seems no reason to doubt his testimony. By all accounts, these tactics became routine over the next four decades.

Harsh interrogations, however, did nothing to quell Palestinian resistance. By 1969, machine-gun attacks, bombings and knifings were routine in Jerusalem. Israelis began living in a security zone. Soldiers with guns were commonplace. Another cycle had begun. In retrospect, the June War never ended.

The war also created yet another wave of Palestinian refugees; some of the 1948 refugees fled or were expelled across the River Jordan and ended up in squalid camps on the outskirts of Amman. Altogether, some 300,000 Palestinians fled the West Bank or Gaza. But many more remained in their homes, under Israeli occupation. Many Israelis were astonished to learn that nineteen years after the creation of Israel, tens of thousands of Palestinians were still living in tents and tin shacks in refugee camps scattered on the outskirts of Jerusalem and throughout the West Bank. "We have a moral obligation," Amos Elon, the acclaimed Israeli journalist, wrote in *Ha'aretz* on June 18, just a week after the war ended, "because the road to Israel's independence was paved on the backs of these people, and they paid, with their bodies, their property and their future, for the pogroms in the Ukraine and the Nazi gas chambers." But Elon's was a lonely voice. Prime Minister Eshkol told Nasser Eddin Nashashibi, the moderate leader of one of Jerusalem's oldest aristocratic clans, that the Gaza refugees should be shipped to

Iraq. "The starting point is that this is *our* only place in the world," Eshkol said. "In some place, in this place, we have to stop being a minority."

The Israeli historian Tom Segev has written that Eshkol's intransigence was a "blunder." Segev believes that Israel missed a "great opportunity [to heal] the malignant wound." The refugees could have been compensated, with some allowed to return to their homes. A demilitarized independent Palestinian state in the West Bank and Gaza could have been established in the wake of the June War. "But Eshkol, Dayan and the other partners in the blunder believed there was no reason to hurry. Lacking vision, courage and compassion, captivated by the hallucinations of victory, they never accepted Israel's role in the Palestinian tragedy, or perhaps they simply did not have the courage to admit it. . . . And perhaps they truly believed that one day they would succeed in getting rid of them."

By the end of 1967, the Israeli government was encouraging the building of Jewish settlements in the West Bank—a clear contravention of the Fourth Geneva Convention, which prohibits the colonization of conquered territory. The Labor Party government of Prime Minister Levi Eshkol announced that both the land and the settlements were necessary for state security. "A peace treaty," Deputy Prime Minister Yigal Allon said after the war, "is the weakest guarantee of the future of peace and the future of defense." He told the cabinet that, if given a choice between "the wholeness of the land with all the Arab population or giving up the West Bank, I am in favor of the wholeness of the land with all the Arabs."

This was a fair reflection of the Israeli mood. In July 1967, a poll established that 60 percent of Israelis were willing in principle to exchange the occupied territories for peace. But in the same poll 71 percent said that the West Bank should never be relinquished. Most Israelis also wanted to hold on to the Golan Heights, Gaza and the Sinai. This was evidence of a classic conflict between "head and heart." They wanted the whole land. *Yediot Aharonot,* one of the country's largest-circulation newspapers, captured the popular mood when it editorialized on June 11, 1967, that "No part of our land that has been liberated shall be returned."

But with the land came a million-plus more Palestinians. The Jewish state would no longer be so very Jewish. Counting Arab Israelis, some 2.5 million Jews would be controlling the lives of some 1.3 million Palestinians. Over the coming decades the demographics would trend toward an increasingly larger percentage of Palestinians. In 1967, such considerations were brushed aside by most Israelis. As Amos Elon wrote in 1971, the 1967 war "fused in some hearts the intransigence of aroused nationalism with the archaisms of an ancient religious faith. . . ." This attitude fit nicely with the Israeli national ethos. Theodor Herzl, the intellectual author of modern political Zionism, once said, "If you will it, it is no fairy tale." With the creation of a Greater Israel came a new Zionism that would prove to be messianic, fiercely nationalistic and increasingly theocratic. The June War was an unmitigated disaster for Israel. Indeed, one might say that the only outcome that could have been worse for Israel was losing the war.

What happened after the June War was neither preordained nor inevitable. Over the decades there were roads not taken and more than one missed opportunity for resolving the dispute over both land and national identity. In my first book, a biography of the powerful and ubiquitous Wall Street lawyer John J. McCloy, I wrote about one such missed opportunity in the spring of 1968—a heartrending story of what might have been.

President Johnson and his colleagues had done little to stop the momentum towards war in May 1967. In its aftermath, Johnson was still obsessed with Vietnam. And it did not help that as a consequence of the war the United States now lacked ambassadorial representation in most Arab capitals. Nevertheless, when all was said and done, the White House understood that America still had interests in the Middle East. Johnson and the foreign policy establishment—including men like Averell Harriman and McGeorge Bundy—encouraged prominent American businessmen to visit the Arab world as unofficial envoys, sound out various Arab leaders, and report back to Washington. Among others, they dispatched Chase Manhattan Bank's David Rockefeller and former treasury secretary Robert B. Anderson on road trips to various Middle Eastern capitals. But their most trusted envoy was Jack McCloy, a man with a long and impeccably establishmentarian résumé. McCloy had served as assistant secretary of war, high commissioner to Occupied Germany, chairman of Chase Manhattan Bank and chief of the Arms Control and Disarmament Agency. He would later become chairman of both the Council on Foreign Relations and the Ford Foundation. But his "day job" was as a name partner at the powerful Rockefeller law firm Milbank, Tweed, Hadley & McCloy, where his clients included the chief executive officers of all twenty-two American oil companies. McCloy had in fact been traveling out to the Middle East since the 1950s on business trips for Chase Manhattan, and he understood the importance of Arab oil. He had met with President Nasser, King Faisal, King Hussein, and the shah of Iran on numerous occasions. He was a discreet and credible back-channel envoy to all these leaders.

In March 1968, McCloy and George Ballou, the head of Standard Oil of California, spent three weeks visiting six countries in the Middle East. In Riyadh, McCloy had a private audience with King Faisal. In his freewheeling fashion, he pressed the monarch on the possibility of a comprehensive settlement of the Arab-Israeli dispute. After some hesitation, Faisal confided that he could accept a settlement based on U.N. Resolution 242, which called for mutual recognition and Israeli withdrawal from the occupied territories. On the difficult problem of Jerusalem, the king proposed a complicated compromise: the city could remain united so long as there was a free Islamic sanctuary in the Old City.

McCloy understood immediately that Faisal's formulation opened the door to the possibility of a real peace. Over the next ten days he saw King Hussein, the president of Lebanon and, most significantly, Nasser. McCloy's private correspondence indicates that Nasser was eager to have the United States broker a settlement based on Resolution 242.* By the time McCloy left Egypt, he felt he had a "package" peace settlement practically in his pocket. "It included," he recalled in a 1976 letter to the former Under Secretary of State George Ball, "Israeli use of the Canal, Resolution 242, supplemented by demilitarized zones, continued Israeli occupation of the [Golan] Heights with Feisal ready to work out a free Moslem sanctuary in Jerusalem, with Egypt's recognition of Israel and support by the Western European countries as well as the Soviet Union in the settlement. I really had a package in regard to which I was quite optimistic after my talks with Nasser, Hussein and Feisal."

On his return to the United States a week later, McCloy gave President Johnson, Defense Secretary Clark Clifford, Secretary of State Dean Rusk, and Assistant Secretary of State Joseph Sisco a forty-minute briefing. Every-

---

*Not only did Nasser give his unequivocal support to Resolution 242, he also later that year bluntly advised al-Fatah's chief, Yasir Arafat, to think about settling for a Palestinian state comprising solely the West Bank and Gaza. (Said K. Aburish, *Nasser,* p. 290.)

one acknowledged that he had brought back dramatic concessions from the Arabs. But Clifford bluntly argued that a broad U.S. peace initiative could not be launched in a presidential election year. McCloy thought the president—who had recently withdrawn his candidacy—was initially eager to pursue the matter, "but he simply faded away after Clifford's discouragement." Rusk sat in silence. A deflated McCloy left thinking he had "failed rather completely" in making his point. Back in New York, he drafted a long letter to Rusk. The president, he wrote, didn't seem to understand the urgency of avoiding yet another Arab-Israeli war and the need to "repair our power and influence in what is probably the most strategic area in the world." He then made a prediction:

> Nasser has had his [military] material replenished, but he is not yet ready for another gamble. He intends, I think, to undergo a long period of training with his Soviet technicians before he tries the game again. He doesn't have the pilots now, but he does think seriously in terms of renewed war as long as Arab territory is occupied by the Israelis, and, in my judgment, it will come some day if steps are not taken during this interim period to avoid it.

McCloy displayed great prescience in this analysis. Nasser began replenishing his armaments with Soviet supplies, and in July 1967 he began a limited war of attrition against Israeli troops along the blockaded Suez Canal. Both sides lobbed artillery shells at each other. Over the next three years the Israelis suffered 750 fatalities and nearly four times that number wounded. The Egyptians suffered 10,000 casualties. A little more than five years after the June 1967 War, a refurbished Egyptian army would storm across the Suez Canal, this time taking the Israelis by surprise and inflicting heavy casualties. That war would eventually lead to a separate Egyptian-Israeli peace treaty. But it would be a cold peace, not the fully comprehensive peace McCloy thought was within reach in 1968.

The lawyer in McCloy could not understand why Washington was willing to see things deteriorate further. "The simple fact," he wrote Rusk bluntly, "is our Israeli policy is not operating in favor of our national interest in the Middle East. . . . We cannot afford to have our national interest overridden by a policy which would preclude us from taking any position opposed to further Zionist ambitions." He thought Israel deserved to have firm international guarantees for her security, but she had to be confined to within her pre–June 1967 boundaries. "The issue, in short, is really one of [Israeli] expansion. Moreover, it is, I believe, entirely in the long range interests of Israel that such ambitions be curbed. . . ."

This was a succinct exposition of the views held by McCloy's oil-company clients. In their eyes, U.S. national interest in the Middle East was driven entirely by the need to guarantee American access to Arab oil. But McCloy had been to the Middle East as early as 1943, when he visited the region as President Roosevelt's assistant secretary of war. Even then, after only a few days in Jerusalem, he understood that Jewish claims to Palestine conflicted with the rights of the indigenous Palestinian population. "The whole concept," he wrote Rusk in 1968, "of the Palestinian homeland, and Israel itself, precluded expansion. It was a limited area carved for outside settlement from an already occupied area."

I learned of McCloy's aborted diplomacy in 1991, after he had died and his private papers were opened at Amherst College. Looking back as a historian, I suspect that McCloy's secret diplomacy never had a realistic chance of success because the Arab regimes—with the exception of Nasser until he lost his luster in the June War—lacked any credibility with the Israelis. From their perspective, there was nothing to talk about. They knew the Arab street hated them. They knew the Arab dictators had no legitimacy. And they could hear what Arab leaders were saying to their people in Arabic about the Jews. Israeli leaders thought time was on their side—and in the meantime, they were going to hold on to the occupied territories.

I was in Beirut when Gamal Abdel Nasser died on the evening of September 28, 1970, felled by a massive heart attack. He was only fifty-two years old. The streets quickly filled with people crying out his name, "Gamal, Gamal!" Others chanted, "Nasser is not dead, Nasser is not dead!" Men armed with Kalashnikovs fired mourning barrages into the evening heavens. Nasser's image was plastered on walls all over the city. In parts of downtown Beirut, the air was thick with the black smoke of tires set aflame. In Cairo, weeping mourners—four or five million strong by some estimates—followed the chaotic, six-mile-long funeral cortège from the Gezira Sports Club through Cairo's streets to an enormous funerary mosque. The crowds nearly caused the Qasr-el-Nil Bridge to collapse. Security forces almost lost control of the casket to the crowds. People began chanting, "What have you done to him, what have you done to him?" Others cried out hysterically, "Gamal, light of our eyes, you're leaving the Arabs and going where?" Sherrif Hatatta, an Egyptian doctor and novelist once imprisoned by Nasser, later remarked, "Nasser's greatest achievement was his funeral. The world will never again see five million people crying together."

In East Jerusalem, the Israelis lodged a formal protest when the American consulate lowered the Stars and Stripes to half-mast; Nasser would not be mourned in the Jewish state. And yet, many Arabs throughout the region still passionately venerate al-Rayyis. Despite his flaws—most notably, the bumbling police state he built—he was the last Arab leader who could plausibly claim to reflect the broad popular will. He was not a democrat, but neither was he a tyrant. Personally, he was incorruptible. He died with a modest bank account. With him died the dream of secular Arab nationalism. He was defeated by a confluence of political forces—best described, by Sadik al-Azm, as those "values of ignorance, myth-making, backwardness, dependency, and fatalism." But Americans would be remiss to deny our contributions to his defeat. Our government worked hard to ensure that Nasser would fail. The irony is that decades after his death the political vacuum is being filled by the Islam of the Muslim Brotherhood—whose theocratic, antimodernist ideas Nasser had tried to repress. The dictators who followed him, Anwar Sadat and Hosni Mubarak, marshaled all the usual tools of repression and billions in American aid to sustain themselves in power. Sadat demonstrated great personal courage in November 1977 when he flew to Jerusalem and addressed the Israeli Knesset, and the Camp David Accords he signed in March 1979 with Prime Minister Menachem Begin might have opened the door to a comprehensive Arab-Israeli peace settlement. But Israel continued to build settlements in the occupied territories and came to no peace agreement with its Palestinian, Lebanese or Syrian neighbors. Sadat was assassinated on October 6, 1981. Israel still benefits from what amounts to a hard, cold peace on its Egyptian border—but most Egyptians regard Sadat's deal with the Israelis as either a betrayal of Nasser's pan-Arabism or, if they support the Muslim Brotherhood, as a betrayal of both Islam and the Palestinians. In the long term, this can't be good for Israel.

*　*　*

Nasser's secular legacy survives as a tragic missed opportunity. The June War marked the defeat of the secular Arab project—and this defeat opened the door to a form of Islamic fundamentalism that has rebounded against both the cause of Arab modernity and the security of the Israeli state. The war itself came about because Nasser's rash miscalculations gave the Israelis the political opportunity to strike. But it was not an accidental war, and not a war of defense. It was a war of choice, and thus a calculated war of aggression. The Americans could have stopped it. And the Israeli leadership could have chosen not to take advantage of Nasser's political missteps and military weakness. Instead, they saw an opportunity to remake the map of the Middle East and they seized it. But like most wars, this one had long-term, unintended consequences. There is no good news here. Only more tragedy.

6

"A Man Without a Country," 1967–1970

Kai, Kodaikanal School, India, 1968

There have been times recently, when I thought it a pity that you should have to go through such a soul-searching period when yet so young—but I've finally decided that it is probably a very productive exercise, and one that you will not regret, though difficult at the time . . . the direction you have set for yourself is good, difficult, but not impossible. You are in good company, and need not fear being taken for a crank.

Jerine Bird, letter to Kai Bird, March 31, 1970

Our hasty expulsion from the Middle East was emotionally jarring. I had spent most of my nearly sixteen years in places where Arabic was spoken in the street. The Arab world had been my home. I had expected to finish high school in Cairo. Father had hoped to be reassigned to Cairo, but now we knew that after a summer's home-leave in the States, we would be moving to Bombay, India. For me, that was foreign territory. And so, too, was America.

What I knew of America still came from *Time* and *Newsweek*—meaning that I knew little. Mother once wrote me that she worried about the "Americanization of Kai Bird. . . . It is so easy to become a 'man without a country.'" With this in mind, my parents decided, while we were on home leave in the summer of 1967, to enroll me in a monthlong wilderness-survival-training course in Oregon, their home state. As a young man, Father had climbed many of Oregon's mountains with his high school friend Willi Unsoeld— who in 1963 was the first man to climb the difficult west ridge of Everest. His idea was that the Outward Bound mountaineering school would introduce me to my Oregon roots and simultaneously toughen me up.

I spent the month of August hiking through the Three Sisters Wilderness Area. I was the youngest of the forty teenagers enrolled in the program. One day, we scaled all three "Sisters" in fifteen hours. Each of these mountains is over 10,000 feet. We fought a major forest fire. It was hard, physical work— and every evening I had to make sure I got to the campfire before all the food was gone. In Outward Bound I realized that no one cared about my identity as an expatriate. What mattered was forming the right alliances with people I could trust—who would help me survive! At one point, we elected as patrol leader a boy who was very strong physically, but he had a mean streak. He set the pace, and he pushed it too far for the weaker boys to keep up. A group of us revolted and selected another boy to lead the patrol.

At the end of the month each boy had to "survive" four days and three nights "solo"—without a sleeping bag or food. We were given a fishing line and one hook—and three matches with which to start a fire. I survived, huddled by my fire, drinking stream water. I caught no fish and found nothing else to eat. I largely hated the experience: the blisters, the forty-pound backpack, the food and the early-morning immersions in a freezing cold mountain stream "bath." When in high school I read William Golding's *Lord of the Flies,* I thought of Outward Bound. But the experience certainly "toughened" me and I remember thinking, "After this, I can do anything."

I also learned a little more about America. In 1967 the country was beginning to come apart along generational and racial seams. That summer there were race riots in major cities. Some of my fellow trekkers were African-American teenagers who, just days before being flown out to Oregon, had been lobbing rocks at U.S. Army tanks in their Newark, New Jersey, neighborhood. Outward Bound had given a half-dozen scholarships to these boys—most of whom had never seen a forest, let alone a 10,000-foot mountain. They, too, were getting to know America.

My political education that summer also included reading Theodore Draper's 1967 book, *The Abuse of Power,* a hard-hitting critique of Lyndon Johnson's escalation of the Vietnam War. I read it on my Outward Bound three-day solo. This book radicalized me. I still have a copy. Draper made me realize that my government could lie. And, if it lied about Vietnam, perhaps lies had also been told about America's involvement in the various wars of the Middle East. Maybe, I thought, it was all of a piece. I now began reading *Time* and *Newsweek* with a far more skeptical eye than before.

In September 1967, we moved into a furnished apartment at Mayfair Gardens on Malabar Hill in Bombay, an upscale oasis in the midst of Bombay's incredibly impoverished masses. India's poverty and its wealth were on a wholly different scale from that of Egypt's. From the rooftop of our apartment building, we could peer down to a walled Zoroastrian funeral garden and watch vultures pick at the bodies of Parsis placed atop a flat-roofed "Tower of Silence." I learned that the generally quite wealthy Parsis weren't allowed to bury or cremate their dead because this would contaminate what they believe to be the sacred elements of earth and fire. India was full of such things. Gods were everywhere, hundreds of Hindu idols in all their manifestations, and Buddhists, and Jains with white masks (so as not to breathe in and thus kill an insect). India was also home to millions of Muslims.

Early in January 1968, my sister Nancy and I boarded a train in Bombay bound for Madras and then Madurai, nine hundred miles to the south, in Tamil Nadu state. From Madurai, we took a chartered bus for the ride up the Palni Hills to Kodaikanal School, an American mission school founded in 1901. The journey took three days. Kodaikanal had been a popular British hill station during the colonial era; its temperate climate provided an easy escape from the hot, humid plains 7,000 feet below. My new boarding school was perched on the shore of a lovely sixty-acre man-made lake the British had dammed in the nineteenth century. Wild bison, panthers, barking deer and the rare tiger roamed the green forests. Lush gardens were everywhere. And so were missionaries.

Virtually all of Kodai's teachers and its student body came from second-, third- and fourth-generation American missionary families. My classmates were American citizens, but most had been born and bred in India. A few were sent to Kodai from as far away as Kuwait, Muscat or other parts of the Middle East or East Asia. Once every five or six years, the mission boards would send these families back to their ancestral homes in Oklahoma, Texas, Kansas or Ohio for one year. They came from all denominations: Baptist, Methodist, Congregationalists and Episcopalian. Some were evangelicals, bent on converting Hindus or Muslims to Christianity. But most were teachers, nurses and doctors who ran schools or health clinics in isolated villages on the plains of South India. They sent their kids off to Kodaikanal School for first grade and expected them to graduate from its high school and then go to America for college. The students were expected to come back as the next generation of missionaries. Kodai was steeped in nineteenth-century Christianity. Its quaint stone church with stained-glass windows was packed on Sundays—church attendance was compulsory. On my first day on campus my "house father" confiscated all my rock-and-roll cassette tapes and returned them a week later with hymnal music taped over my beloved Rolling Stones and Beatles. I don't think Kodai facilitated my mother's desire to "Americanize" me.

Religion permeated daily life at Kodai. I ran for student body president, pledging that if elected I would work with the school administration to abolish compulsory church on Sundays. Everybody complained about church attendance. So I thought this would be a popular position. I was trounced by Ashok, the only Indian in my class—the son of a local tea plantation owner—who promised to build a snack bar! I didn't much like religion, but I liked to argue about it. One day the school chaplain observed that I might have a calling as a pastor, I fleetingly thought about it; I could see the advantages of corralling a captive audience. But when it came my turn as a senior to lead one of the Sunday services, I couldn't stop myself from playing at full blast a seventeen-minute recording of "In-A-Gadda-Da-Vida," the psychedelic rock song made famous in 1968 by the California band Iron Butterfly. I'm sure some people thought this little prank blasphemous. It certainly ended any further thoughts that Kai might someday become a pastor.

At the age of seventeen I fell in love. Joy Riggs grew up in South India. The daughter and granddaughter of American missionaries, she had spent her childhood in a tiny village in Tamil Nadu. Her soft-spoken father, Edward, was a doctor who ran a leper colony. Her mother, Frances, was a nurse. Joy had grown up speaking fluent Tamil. She had dirty blond hair and dark brown eyes and a bright, curious attitude toward life. Aside from a year back in Colorado every five years, she had spent her entire schooling at Kodai.

Dating at a missionary school came with a strict set of old-fashioned rituals. On Wednesday nights the school principal, Stephen Root, supervised a forty-five-minute "dance." He did this armed with a foot-long ruler that he used to put a distance between couples whose bodies were getting too close. He watched as we boys escorted our dates back to the girls' dormitory. We were allowed three minutes to say good night to our dates, standing on the well-lit front porch. Root used a flashlight to make sure no couples had hidden themselves in the nearby bushes. After exactly three minutes of frenzied kissing, the housemother inside the girls' dormitory flicked the porch lights to signal that time was up.

On weekends, Joy and I sometimes rented a pontoon rowboat from the boathouse and paddled to the far end of the lake, where we could make out alone. I loved taking her to the always-deserted hundred-year-old British cemetery for the same reason. The cemetery reeked of history. The gravestones dated to the mid- and late nineteenth century, and the inscriptions told something of Kodai's exotic past. Many of the gravestones spoke of young children—the sons and daughters of missionaries or British colonial officials—felled at an early age by malaria, chicken pox and measles. My favorite gravestone described a young Englishman:

> Sacred To the Memory of
> Dudley Linnel Sedgwick
> Third son of the Late
> William Fellows Sedgwick
> Of Cashio Bridge. Watford
> In the county of Hertford, England.
> Who was killed by a bison,
> whilst shooting in the Pulney Hills
> On the 29th of March, 1875
> Aged 31.

Joy and I spent a lot of time together during our senior year. But it was all very innocent. During school break I visited her home in the remote village of Ambilikai in Madurai District, Tamil Nadu. I met her parents, who lived spare, simple lives in the leper colony. I was introduced to her grandmother, Louise Whitaker, who had graduated from Oberlin College in 1908 and then returned to China, where her parents and grandparents had worked as missionaries. She and Joy's father had been forced to leave China in 1949 when the Communists came to power. That's when the family came to Tamil Nadu.

In the two years I lived in India I traveled all over the subcontinent, usually by third-class train. I visited Kerala, Madras, Pondicherry, Bangalore, New Delhi and Agra. During one school vacation Nancy and I flew in a small plane to Kathmandu. I had been studying South Asian history and was struck by some of the parallels between British rule in the Raj and the British Mandate period in Palestine. In both settings, the British had foolishly prolonged their colonial rule—and when at last they withdrew, they left behind partitioned states. The 1947 partition of the Indian Raj into a secular Indian state and a Muslim Pakistani state came at the cost of a million lives. As in Palestine, the partition of India led to major wars and an ever-festering conflict (in the Indian case, over Kashmir). Arguably, if the British had left India in the 1920s or '30s, partition never would have happened.

The Middle East was far away, but I remained obsessed with the conflicts there. At Kodai, my classmates nicknamed me the "A-rab" because I talked about it so much. In my senior year I wrote a 117-page essay on the Palestinian question. Citing, among others, George Antonius and I. F. Stone, I made a long-winded case for a binational state.

Despite our closeness, Joy and I went to different colleges. She left in the summer of 1969 for Colorado State College in Pueblo, Colorado, while I headed for Carleton College in Northfield, Minnesota.

On my way back to America, I spent nearly a week hitchhiking around Israel. In Jerusalem I looked up Dani Bahar, who was still in high school. We had tea in his home and I listened as his father complained bitterly about everything the Israelis were doing in East Jerusalem. He complained about Israeli taxes, Israeli prices, Israeli laws and Israeli soldiers. There was nothing he liked about the Israeli annexation of his city.

The day after I saw Dani, I met a young Jewish American woman named Rachel in the cafeteria of Hebrew University. She was athletically plump and had a matter-of-fact, no-nonsense attitude. As soon as she learned that I had grown up in Cairo and other Arab cities, she made it her business to educate me about the real Israel—not the caricature I seemed to have internalized. She insisted on accompanying me on my journey. We hitchhiked to Tel Aviv and then headed north along the coastal road, toward Haifa. Each time a car picked us up, Rachel would introduce us and quickly explain to the driver that I was an American who had lived for many years on the other side. I would then be interrogated in rapid-fire Hebrew, with Rachel translating. Her Hebrew was very good.

Heated arguments ensued. No one agreed with me about how this two-decade-old conflict had started or how it might end. Over the next few days Rachel and I visited a "moshav" (a collective where each family had its own cottage) and a couple of kibbutzim. Rachel patiently nudged me toward an understanding of one thing—that this was a complex, modern Western society that had already sunk deep roots into my "colonial Palestine." I could sense the vibrancy; the people I met were here to stay. And yet at times it seemed as if we might as well have been in Greece or Italy or coastal Portugal—certainly not in the heart of the Middle East. Most of the Israelis I met with Rachel were Ashkenazic Jews whose ancestors had come from Europe. They were Europeans plunked down in the Orient of my youth. Their country was a ghetto fenced in on every side but for the Mediterranean Sea. Their Arab neighbors so hated them that they could not drive their cars across any of the armistice lines that served as Israel's land borders. Yet, this did not seem to matter. I could see that life went on inside this vibrant, growing but insular society. But the Israelis did not seem to know or care about their neighbors, all those Arabs who lived a few miles away. And that was something I could not understand.

Early in September 1969 I arrived in Northfield, Minnesota, for my freshman year at Carleton. I was a stranger to America. I was eighteen years old and I still didn't know how to use a pay phone or drive a car; walking into a Safeway supermarket was intimidating. Fortunately, Carleton had a no-car policy. Northfield was a small town of 10,000 people with two private colleges—Carleton and St. Olaf College. There were a couple of gas stations, one movie theatre and a single street of small shops. I was completely unprepared for the snowstorms that hit Minnesota in late October, and all winter I walked around freezing in a lightweight corduroy jacket. For much of that winter I felt a heavy sense of dislocation. No one understood that I was a foreigner. When asked where I came from, I just said, "Oregon." I wrote Joy love letters two or three times a week, and always felt lonely.

I was determined to go back to the Middle East. Carleton encouraged foreign study, and I learned that I might be able to spend my sophomore year in Beirut or Cairo. Although Carleton was a highly regarded liberal arts college, at the time it offered no courses at all in Middle Eastern history, languages or culture. In the spring of 1970 I applied for a program to attend the American University of Beirut for the 1970–71 academic year. I would study Arabic and history. I would escape America.

Most of my social life revolved around the antiwar movement. That first autumn I attended an antiwar demonstration in Minneapolis. Every evening a group of us met in one of the dormitory lounges and watched Walter Cronkite's CBS news reports on the war. The news was always grim.

Having turned eighteen in September 1969, I had to walk down to the Northfield post office and register for the draft. I had already decided that I was not going to Vietnam. In India, I had studied the writings of Mahatma Gandhi, and I thought of myself as a "situational" pacifist. Gandhi had convinced me that most wars could not be justified. A war against the Nazis was one thing—but as far as Vietnam was concerned, I was a pacifist. And yet, I was not religious. Missionary school had cured me of that. I never went to church. If I was not yet a full-blown atheist, I was certainly drifting there. Nevertheless, I applied to the Selective Service Board for conscientious objector status. I had come to America prepared to do this, having written the previous spring a typed sixteen-page double-spaced essay explaining why I should be exempt from military service. I never mentioned Jesus, but I argued, "Pacifism is a way of life, not simply a moral or religious principle invoked on one particular occasion." Citing my childhood in the Middle East, I described my passages through Mandelbaum Gate, the Israeli soldiers with their machine guns and the Arab Legionnaires with their rifles fitted with bayonets. "I have always known of war and violence. It is not foreign to me." In lurid, overwrought terms, I described Nasser's Egypt, and Cairo as "a city where the army personnel carriers are like locusts." I recounted how, together with my mother and sisters, I had been evacuated from Cairo on May 26, 1967: "One week later, Cairo was bombed and the people among whom I lived were being drafted and sent to the front. I have often wondered what it was all for. How foolish are the Arabs? How foolish are the Jews who won that war? How many more people hate? How many more refugees? How many more young men cut down in the bloom of existence? For what principle were they shot?" I concluded, "I am not capable of taking military orders or of living under military regulations."

I was very earnest about all this and tried to explain my thoughts in long, rambling letters to my parents. They were surprisingly supportive. "There have been times recently," Mother wrote, "when I thought it a pity that you should have to go through such a soul-searching period when yet so young—but I've finally decided that it is probably a very productive exercise, and one that you will not regret, though difficult at the time . . . the direction you have set for yourself is good, difficult, but not impossible. You are in good company, and need not fear being taken for a crank."

Father was ironical about it. "I went gladly to the Navy," he wrote me. But he did not try to talk me out of what I had coined my "aggressive pacifism." Still, he warned me that even nonviolence could provoke violence.

Most of my classmates thought my CO application an exercise in futility; very few such applications were granted, and most of those went to Quakers, Mennonites and others with a long-standing pacifist religious upbringing. I had only a letter of support from Kodaikanal School's Methodist pastor. Astonishingly, it worked. Draft Board Number 10 (Washington, DC) accepted my argument, and in the summer of 1970 I was classified I-O, a "conscientious objector available for civilian work contributing to the maintenance of the national health, safety or interest." Only later did I learn that Draft Board Number 10 was for the sons of expatriates, and, not surprisingly, few of these privileged boys were ever sent to Vietnam. By then, however, I had turned in my draft card in a public meeting on campus.

That winter my course work was eclectic. I was taking Judaic Thought, A History of Czarist Russia, an independent study of Mahatma Gandhi, a seminar called On Civil Disobedience, Israeli folk dancing and ice hockey. Clearly, I was being primed for something. (I failed the ice hockey because I couldn't stand the 10-degree Fahrenheit temperatures.)

My extracurricular activities were all political. Another classmate, Fred Rogers, and I helped organize a bus to take Carleton students up to Minneapolis for a teach-in on the Palestinian question. Fred had also spent some time in Dhahran, where his father had taught at the College of Petroleum and Minerals. He was one of the only people on campus who were sympathetic to the Palestinian cause. (He later became treasurer of Carleton.)

I remember getting into a heated argument with an Israeli student. Ludicrously, I was trying to convince him to come to our teach-in. A crowd gathered and watched in stunned silence as we went at it. I think people were amazed to see that there was an issue that could generate as much political passion and heat as Vietnam. I persuaded no one.

On April 28, 1970, dozens of Carleton students headed up to Minneapolis again, this time for an antiwar demonstration at the corporate headquarters of Honeywell Inc. This Minnesota company was then a leading manufacturer of antipersonnel cluster bomblets—a deadly weapon that sprays shrapnel across a wide territory and is designed to kill and maim indiscriminately. Honeywell sold cluster bombs to the U.S. Army for use in Vietnam, where they were killing thousands of civilians. I also knew that Honeywell had sold these weapons to Israel. The CEO of Honeywell, Edson W. Spencer, was chairman of the board of trustees at Carleton College. (As a "senator" recently elected to the student government, I had been lobbying the college to dump $500,000 worth of Honeywell stock—or at least vote its shares against management. The college refused to do either.) So Carleton students had a special motive to participate.

The demonstration was organized by Marv Davidov, then thirty-eight, a now legendary social activist who had become radicalized by his experience in the army in the mid-1950s. In 1969 Davidov founded the Honeywell Project, a nonprofit organization devoted to getting Honeywell out of the death business. (A Honeywell subsidiary still manufactures cluster bombs, and Israel used them against Lebanon in 2006.) On this occasion, Davidov, wearing a black beret and sporting a bushy mustache, managed to organize some 3,000 people to demonstrate at the corporation's annual shareholders' meeting. Molly Ivins, a young reporter for the *Minneapolis Tribune,* wrote a story about Davidov's Project Honeywell and reported that Jerry Rubin, the "Yippie" anarchist soon-to-be Wall Street venture capitalist, had spoken for an hour the previous night to gathering protestors.

I think Davidov actually owned a symbolic Honeywell share and so was allowed inside the shareholders' meeting. The rest of us gathered in front of the Honeywell building and shouted antiwar slogans. Suddenly, from around the corner we were astonished to see a phalanx of police officers marching in our direction. Ominously, they wore gas masks and carried nightsticks. When they got within a hundred yards, they stopped in a military line formation, shoulder-to-shoulder, and waited. Two of them rolled out what appeared to be a miniature cannon. Naturally, some of us started to back away. Others, clearly veterans of tear gas attacks, drew out handkerchiefs and tied them around their faces. One young man ran toward the building's main glass door and threw a beer bottle. The door shattered. And at that moment, the police cannon fired a tear gas shell at us. Everyone ran, and that was pretty much the end of our "action."

I felt very "turned off" by what had happened. We seemed so ineffectual, so juvenile. The shattering of Honeywell's front glass door marred our message. I hated what Honeywell was doing, and I saw no reason why Carleton College should be associated with Trustee Ed Spencer and his cluster bombs. But now we protestors were the ones who had used violence.

Just two days later, on April 30, President Nixon announced the invasion of Cambodia with 32,000 soldiers. And on May 4, 1970, National Guardsmen at Kent State University in Ohio opened fire on unarmed students protesting the invasion. Four students were shot dead and nine others were wounded. We called it the Kent State massacre, and by the next day eight million students at more than 400 universities went on strike. The Carleton student body voted overwhelmingly to join the strike. The country seemed to be coming apart. Some of my fellow students set up impromptu classes on how to make a "Molotov cocktail." Violence was in the air. I was an angry, self-righteous eighteen-year-old who knew for a certainty that the world was on the cusp of radical change. But I was trying hard to be a pacifist, and I abhorred the idea of burning something down. Having imbibed Gandhi and Thoreau, I talked about Satyagraha and civil disobedience. Oh Lord, was I earnest! The day after the Kent State killings, one of my roommates, Ed Pultz, and I decided to organize a nonviolent act of civil disobedience. We posted sign-up sheets on several bulletin boards around campus, inviting people to join us in blocking the doors of St. Paul's major draft induction center. We thought a dozen people might join us. Within a day we had eighty-six signatures. We hastily formed an organizing committee, reserved several buses to take us up to the Twin Cities—and called a lawyer with the American Civil Liberties Union and asked if he would represent us. Bearing in mind what had happened at the Honeywell demonstration just a week earlier, we gave everyone a quick briefing on nonviolence and civil disobedience.

At 5:00 on the morning of Thursday, May 7, we boarded our buses and headed for St. Paul's Old Federal Building, the site of the induction center. Eighty-six Carleton students (and two faculty members) blocked all five doors to the building. Earlier I had issued a press release in the name of "The Carleton College Ad Hoc Strike Committee," stating, "This responsible act of civil disobedience is our alternative to the tragedy at Kent State." I was listed as the committee's designated spokesman. As we approached the Old Federal Building, guards inside locked the doors. We locked arms and sat down, blocking all five entrances. Throngs of civil servants waited to get inside. A busload of draftees—mainly rural boys from small towns in Minnesota—parked around the corner. After about an hour the press arrived. So did the police, and they started making arrests. We were disturbed to see that the police had either taped over the numbers on their badges or taken them off altogether. I saw a federal marshal kick some students and pull the hair of some girls as he marched them to the police vans. There was no other violence or resistance. I got about halfway through reading my prepared statement for the television cameras when several policemen grabbed me by each arm and walked me into a police van. As they pulled me away, I handed my unfinished statement to a twenty-six-year-old assistant professor of government, Paul Wellstone, who was able to finish reading the statement

THE NORTHFIELD AS STAGED QUIET BUT EFFECTIVE SIT-IN AT THE OLD FEDERAL BUILDING
In court May 13, all but one of the group pleaded not guilty

Carleton-St. Olaf Sit-In Cases Boggle Minnesota Federal Court

Kai, blocking the doors of a draft induction center, St. Paul, May 7, 1970

before he too was arrested. Wellstone and the college chaplain were the only faculty members to join us. Paul was then an untenured professor—and he was obviously risking his job by participating in this action.

At the municipal building we were fingerprinted, photographed and searched. The police labeled me the "ringleader." We spent six hours in the city jail's "drunk tank" before being released on personal recognizance. "The jail was really crappy," I wrote my parents the next day. "Very depressing. We made it homier—sang songs, whistled and made a general nuisance of ourselves." I felt only exhilaration. We had made a statement, and it had been aired on the evening news. The next morning's papers put us on the front page. Carleton being a liberal place, we were greeted that night on campus with a torchlight parade and a midnight rally. One thousand students—out of a total of some 1,350—voted for a campuswide strike. "People are going to turn this country around," I confidently predicted in a letter to my parents.

Several weeks later, we returned to the Twin Cities for a two-and-a-half-day jury trial; lawyers from the American Civil Liberties Union argued that because President Richard Nixon had announced that he would ignore student protests against the Cambodian invasion, we had been compelled to exercise our First Amendment rights by this act of peaceful civil disobedience. Professor Wellstone took the witness stand to explain why he had joined the protest. Our lawyers persuaded Congressman Donald Fraser (D-MN) to testify on our behalf. The jury convicted us of a federal misdemeanor, and Judge Philip Neville gave us the choice of five days in jail or a $45 fine.

I paid the fine. I thought briefly about doing the jailtime. A year or two earlier, my mother had given me a copy of Henry David Thoreau's essay *On Civil Disobedience,* and I remembered Thoreau's retort to Ralph Waldo Emerson when his friend came to bail him out of prison for refusing to pay a poll tax in protest of both slavery and the Mexican War of 1846–48. Emerson asked, "Henry, what are you doing in there?" Thoreau replied, "Waldo, the question is what are *you* doing out there?" But I felt I had made my point. Two or three students did jailtime.

This was my first and last arrest. It was Wellstone's first, to be followed by many more. The son of Ukrainian Jewish immigrants, Paul went to college on a wrestling scholarship. Warmhearted and funny, he was an optimist, an openhearted idealist who always thought the best of people—even his

Assistant professor Paul Wellstone, Carleton College, 1969

political opponents. In 1970 he knew the war was wrong and that it had to be opposed. But unlike the fringe leftists whom the media loved to put on television, he didn't blame the country for the war. Carleton was his first teaching job. He had two children at the time and no job security. Being arrested was not a good career move, and indeed, four years later, Carleton would deny Paul tenure. But the campus rallied behind him, and eventually he won an extraordinarily rare reversal of that decision. In 1990, he won a U.S. Senate seat in an upset victory over a Republican incumbent. He was running for a third term when he died in a plane crash in October 2002.

In 1970, I was an angry young man, self-righteous to a fault, and naïve. But these were black-and-white times, when it was easy to believe that momentous things were about to happen. The antiwar movement was on the evening television news every night.

Back in Eugene, Oregon, Grandfather Newhouse, a veteran of both world wars, was horrified by what I had done. Grandma wrote me that he was so upset that I had best not visit Oregon that summer. My own open-minded parents took the news of my arrest as a grim inevitability. Sitting in Bombay, they had read a news report in the *International Herald Tribune* about Carleton students at a sit-in in Minnesota and suspected right away that I had been involved. They wondered whether they should just cable me bail money. "But wait," Mother wrote worriedly, "he is level-headed. Then [Kai's] letter arrived. Just as we expected: jail, bail, protest. All we can understand. But the rest. . . ."

I had produced a seven-page handwritten letter trying to explain myself. My words were, to say the least, alarming. "Nixon's action," I wrote, "has finally shown conclusively that he is after not peace but a military victory that would support a corrupt, dictatorial and militaristic regime in Vietnam. Priorities at home are being ignored." I then called for the abolition of the National Guard that had killed four students at Kent State. I ranted against the army, the police, the prison system, corporate America, conspicuous consumption and advertising. "All over the country," I confidently wrote to my parents, "things are happening." The movement was going to "bring this administration down and turn the country around." I then informed my parents that 177 Carleton students had turned in their draft cards—and "I am one of them." The plan was to collect 100,000 draft cards from all over the country and then deliver them in a truck to Attorney General John Mitchell. (I don't know if that ever happened.)

My parents worried that revolutionary fervor had made me lose my head. They did not object to nonviolent civil disobedience: "We would probably have done the same ourselves under the same circumstances." But they took issue with my youthful arrogance. Mother promptly reprimanded me. "Whom are you expecting to persuade with that rhetoric?" she asked. "You haven't said a word about what you will create. . . . Where is your humility?" Yes, there were inequalities the world over, but "utopia isn't around the corner. . . . Who are you, or any other eighteen year old to say that you have all the answers?" Mother urged me to take some courses on economics. Her letter demolished my radical conceit. In my defense, I can see now there were clues in my correspondence that I still had a head. The same letter containing my rant against Nixon and the "system" also contained the admission that perhaps I was "taking myself too seriously. I don't want to be a fanatic. Yet, I do want to be something, to stand for something." And within days I was reassuring my parents that "I still have a head, and it thinks much along your lines."

I had been back in America for only eight months, and already I had been teargassed, imprisoned for a day and convicted of a federal misdemeanor. I had registered for the draft and then turned in the card in a protest demonstration. I hadn't had a haircut all year. It was the sixties, so some might say these experiences were essential steps in my re-Americanization. But I felt deeply alienated from a country I was just getting to know after so many years of distant allegiance. I looked at cops with mild suspicion. I was not

a Weatherman; I didn't believe in robbing banks or bombing federal buildings. But I knew there was something horribly wrong about a country that
could tolerate five long years of ground combat in Vietnam. My teenage
idealism was quickly giving way to cynicism. To my mind, Washington's
cynical alliances in the Middle East—with Arab kings and Israeli "colonial-
ists"—came through the same Cold War, anti-Communist prism. America
could not see the world except through the distortion of this prism, and so, it
seemed to me at the time, Washington acted without seeing or understanding the people on the ground. The angry young expatriate in me saw that
most Americans knew nothing of Vietnamese history, let alone Palestinian.
In both Southeast Asia and the Middle East, my country's foreign policy—
which my father labored to represent as a diplomat—seemed wholly mis-
guided, if not criminally negligent.

For all my disaffection, I had not given up on the electoral process. I was
a Democrat. That summer I spent two weeks as a volunteer for a thirty-nine-
year-old Democratic congressional candidate, James Abourezk—who happened to be of Lebanese ancestry. I didn't know this until I arrived in South
Dakota. Jimmy Kolker,* the Carleton senior who recruited me, had told
me only that he was an antiwar candidate. Abourezk's parents ran a small
grocery store on one of South Dakota's Indian reservations. He'd never been
to the Middle East. I remember him quizzing me about Lebanon during a
long drive across South Dakota. He gave me a budget of $75 to get out the
vote on the Pine Ridge Indian Reservation in South Dakota. He won the
primary race by some 600 votes out of 20,000, and that November he won
South Dakota's sole congressional seat. Two years later he became a U.S.
Senator. He proved to be a cantankerous, outspokenly populist senator. I
was disappointed when he decided in 1978 not to run for a second term.

Soon after being arrested that spring, I dropped in on Professor Eleanor Zel-
liot, who was supervising my independent study on Gandhi. Eleanor was
a soft-spoken Quaker and a scholar of modern Indian history. Every few
weeks she invited her students to her cottage in groups or singly to sip dry
sherry and discuss whatever was on their minds. Carleton was like that—
professors were very accessible. On this occasion, Eleanor took me aside and

---

*Kolker later joined the U.S. Foreign Service and rose to ambassadorial rank.

cautioned me: "You know, Kai, you must be careful. The government can do things." I shrugged this off. I was eighteen.

There were certainly excesses in the sixties. The year I came to Carleton a faction of the Students for a Democratic Society split away to form the Weathermen, an underground group that planted a series of bombs, targeting empty buildings. They inflicted millions of dollars' worth of property damage and managed to kill three of their own activists when a bomb they were assembling accidentally went off in Greenwich Village. (In August 1970 a massive bomb exploded in the middle of the night at the University of Wisconsin's Army Mathematics Research Center, killing a physics researcher, but this was not the work of the Weathermen.) But most of the excesses of the antiwar movement were rhetorical. The true excesses of those years all had the signature of the Nixon-Kissinger administration. Eleanor was not being paranoid. We now know from archival documents released on Nixon's COINTELPRO surveillance program that the FBI had informants on Carleton's campus. It also placed agents in Marv Davidov's Honeywell Project. When this was revealed later in the 1970s, Davidov sued and won a settlement from the government.

I left America that summer believing that momentous changes were occurring, and I almost regretted leaving—but the pull of the Middle East was too strong. I was looking forward to spending nearly a year at the American University of Beirut. I did not know it, but the antiwar movement had hit its peak that spring of 1970. Thereafter, the movement's energy moved from the street to electoral politics. Whereas, arriving in Beirut late that summer, I was entering a region of the world sitting on the precipice of truly dangerous political upheavals.

7

Black September, 1970

The BOAC plane explodes at Dawson's Field, Jordan, September 12, 1970

The PLO is dead, wiped out, and finished as an effective fighting force. But I have to remind Washington that this part of the world has been the scene of at least one resurrection.

American diplomat in Amman, Jordan, September 1970

On Sunday, September 6, 1970, just a few days after arriving in Lebanon, I was sitting in a rose garden in the quaint mountain village of Shemlan, a sleepy enclave of two dozen solid stone houses. It was a clear, beautiful day. The view was spectacular. Off in the distance below was the seaside metropolis of Beirut, perched beside the sparkling blue waters of the Mediterranean. The city was just eighteen miles to the northwest, but it was still a good hour's drive due to the narrow, winding mountain roads. The one restaurant in the village, the Cliff House, served savory herb-encrusted grilled chicken, *shwarma* (grilled lamb sandwiches with yogurt), cheap Lebanese red wine, *arrack* and a full *mezze* course of hummus, baba ghanoush, black olives and fresh, flat Arab bread.

I had just turned nineteen and I was where I wanted to be—back in the Middle East. Along with twenty other American college students, I had signed up to spend nine months in Beirut. Our university program in Shemlan included intensive Arabic-language tutoring for two weeks before regular coursework began at the American University of Beirut (AUB).

Shemlan was then home to the British-run Middle East Centre for Arabic Studies (MECAS), where since 1947 legions of British and a few American diplomats and intelligence officers had polished their Arabic. The legendary Soviet spy Kim Philby visited the school in the early 1960s, and another KGB spy, George Blake, had been a full-time student in 1960–61 when he was unmasked and arrested by British authorities. Blake later escaped from prison and joined Philby in his Moscow exile. The local Maronite Christian villagers called MECAS the "School for Spies." Shemlan had a splendid bird's-eye view of Beirut's International Airport—which is why, a few years later, the village was much fought over during the 1975–1990 Lebanese civil war.

Later that September afternoon, my lackadaisical study of Arabic was suddenly interrupted when word came over a fellow student's shortwave radio that four commercial airliners had just been simultaneously hijacked in the skies over Western Europe. All told, some 600 passengers had been kidnapped in the air. The hijackers were young Arab men. But then, some three decades before 9/11, they were secular Marxists and Palestinian nationalists, not fundamentalist Islamists. They all belonged to the Popular Front for the Liberation of Palestine (PFLP), a Marxist guerrilla group that was a component of the Palestine Liberation Organization (PLO). One of the hijacked planes, a Pan American jumbo jet, had been refueled in Beirut. It then took off to Cairo with a PFLP explosives expert aboard. A hundred feet above the Cairo runway, a commando lit a fuse and told a stewardess that they had eight minutes to get the passengers off the plane. As the plane screeched to a halt in the early morning darkness, the cabin crew blew the emergency chutes open and yelled at the 173 passengers to evacuate. Three minutes later, as some crew members were still just feet away from the aircraft's wingtips, the $25 million jumbo jet blew apart on the tarmac. Miraculously, no one was injured.

The hijackers had also seized control of a Trans World Airways (TWA) 707 jet and a Swissair DC-8 airliner and diverted them both to Dawson's Field, an abandoned British military landing strip in the northeastern desert of Jordan. The hijacking of a fourth plane, an El Al passenger jet bound for New York from Amsterdam, was foiled by Israeli security guards aboard the plane. Early news accounts reported that an unidentified male hijacker had been killed, while his accomplice, a twenty-six-year-old Palestinian woman, Leila Khaled, had been subdued and then detained by British authorities after the plane made an emergency landing in London.

Three days after this initial spate of hijackings, my fellow students and I sat on the rough-hewn stone terrace in the garden, listening to another British Broadcasting Corporation (BBC) newscast. A reporter was saying that a fifth plane had just been hijacked and had landed at Beirut International Airport. We looked down, and off in the distant valley below us we could see a gleaming airliner, a British Overseas Airways Corporation VC-10, the very plane the BBC reporter was at that moment describing on the radio. Curiously, it was parked at the end of the runway.

BOAC Flight 755 from Bombay had been commandeered shortly after nine thirty that morning just as it was approaching Beirut at an altitude of 30,000 feet. It had circled the city for an hour and then as it came in for a landing the hijackers radioed authorities on the ground to "steer clear of the plane or we'll blow it up." It now sat on the runway being refueled. PFLP guerrillas soon drove up to the control tower and began negotiations with Lebanon's minister of transport, Pierre Gemayel. There were 11 crew members and 105 passengers aboard—including 24 British schoolchildren, unaccompanied by their parents, who were returning to boarding schools in Britain. When Gemayel appealed to the hijackers to allow the women and the 24 children to disembark, the hijackers on the plane radioed, "We are leaving with everybody or we are blowing up the airplane with everybody."

The sleek, blue-tailed VC-10 took off and flew east—and, though I didn't know it until two days later, my lovely blond, brown-eyed Kodaikanal high school sweetheart went with it. Joy and I had spent much of the summer together. She had campaigned with me for Jim Abourezk in South Dakota, and then we had spent much of July and August traveling around her native South India. We had kissed each other good-bye in New Delhi—and I had flown off to begin my studies at the American University of Beirut (AUB). Joy, however, secretly planned to pay me a surprise visit in Beirut on her own way back to her college in Colorado. I was unaware that she was on the hijacked BOAC flight.

Joy Riggs, August 1970

Joy's ordeal had begun on Wednesday, September 9. Sitting in Shemlan, I read numerous newspaper articles about the spectacular hijackings. It was front-page news around the world. Many of the press stories focused on the fate of the female hijacker, Leila Khaled, sitting in a London police station. A spokesman for the PFLP told foreign reporters that they were demanding Khaled's release. At first, I read accounts of the hijackings with the detached interest of a spectator. This was not happening to me. And then two days later I received a phone call from the American Embassy informing me that Joy Riggs was a passenger on the hijacked BOAC flight. Suddenly, I found myself having to reconcile my childhood sympathies for the Palestinian refugees with the supreme irony that these people had just taken my girlfriend hostage. I took the news with foolish equanimity. I was young and optimistic, and this was three decades before 9/11. Joy was an innocent, so I was somehow sure that she would survive.

From press accounts it was clear that Joy's BOAC flight had been hijacked in retaliation for the failed attempt to hijack the El Al flight. With Leila Khaled sitting in a British police station, the PFLP thought they needed more British hostages with which to secure her release. So a British plane had been targeted. Thus, I realized that Joy's ordeal was intertwined with the fate of Leila Khaled and her accomplice, who was now reported to be a twenty-seven-year-old American, Patrick Joseph Arguello.

Arguello and Khaled made an odd pair. Arguello was born in the United States in 1943, but when he was three years old, his Nicaraguan father and American mother took him to Managua. When he was thirteen, he and his family fled Nicaragua, fearing arrest by the Anastasio Somoza dictatorship. In Los Angeles, Patrick went to Belmont High School and graduated magna cum laude from UCLA in December 1966. His brother Robert was a Los Angeles policeman.

"Patricio"—as his friends called him—was a quiet, soft-spoken young man, handsome and book-smart. In 1967 he was awarded a prestigious Fulbright Fellowship, which he used for graduate study in medicine in Chile. A year later he returned to Nicaragua, where he fell in with the Sandinista guerrilla movement. There he was traumatized by the murders of several Nicaraguan Sandinista friends. In 1969, Somoza's police arrested him for his political activities, but because he had an American passport they bundled him aboard the next plane, a flight that happened to be bound for Geneva. "He was a gentle, nice man," recalled Janet Shenk, a Smith College student who briefly dated him in Geneva. "We spoke only Spanish to each other. I didn't even know he was an American citizen. We didn't talk much politics, but he was the first person to show me the journal of the North American Congress on Latin America (NACLA).* It opened my eyes to see that there were Americans who cared enough about Latin America to do serious research on the region. Later, I went to work for NACLA, so Patricio was important to me. I saw a lot of him for a few months and then suddenly he disappeared. He came back several months later wearing a full beard. I hadn't realized it, but he had gone to Jordan."

In the spring of 1970, a Sandinista operative in Geneva persuaded Arguello and at least two other Nicaraguans to go to Amman, Jordan, where he was given weapons training in a camp run by the Democratic Front for the Liberation of Palestine, a small Marxist guerrilla group. Arguello came back to Geneva in June—which was when Janet saw him sporting a beard. But late that summer he disappeared again, this time to a camp near the ancient ruins of Jerash in northern Jordan run by the PFLP, George Habash's

---

*NACLA was an activist left-wing research group, founded in 1966.

Popular Front for the Liberation of Palestine. Arguello agreed to participate in a spectacular action: the simultaneous hijacking of four airplanes on one day. Perhaps this American Sandinista thought he could become another Che Guevara.

His comrade, Leila Khaled, was born into a middle-class Palestinian family in Haifa in April 1944; one of twelve children, she once joked that her family could "either form a soccer team or take on the 'twelve tribes' of Israel." Her father was a shopkeeper and owned their home on Stanton Street, not far from Hadar, the city's Jewish quarter. When she was a child of four, Leila's best friend was Tamara, a little Jewish girl. "I knew that there was no distinction between us," Khaled later wrote in her 1973 memoir, *My People Shall Live*. "I was conscious of being neither Arab nor Jew."

Leila Khaled in Beirut, 1970

But in 1948, Haifa was engulfed in sectarian violence. "Arabs killed Jews, Jews killed Arabs," Khaled wrote. "But Jewish violence was organized and disciplined. They were thoroughly mobilized and they knew what they were fighting for. Arab violence was ill planned, random activity carried on by individuals. The Zionists had camaraderie as well as gunpowder; they had well-organized armed forces and they excelled in psychological warfare. Their leaders were at the head of their columns; ours were securely ensconced in Mount Lebanon or Cairo."

One of Khaled's earliest memories, at the age of four, was seeing a man killed by a bomb that exploded in the street outside her home in 1948. She watched as blood spurted from the dying man's stomach: "I hid under the staircase and stared at the corpse in the street outside." On April 13, 1948, Khaled's family left for Sour (Tyre) in southern Lebanon, where they had relatives. Her father stayed behind, intending to ride out the fighting and guard his property.

"My instinctive reaction was that I must remain at home. Nobody explained to me why we were leaving and I didn't understand. Mother packed the children into the little rented car with a few of our personal belongings, and was ready to set off until she counted the children and found that one was missing. All knew instantly that I was the one. Two of my sisters found me hiding behind the date box and hauled me out like a sack of potatoes. Nawal screamed, 'The Jews will kill you if you don't come!' as she pulled me by the hair."

Nine days later, Haifa fell to the Haganah, and Khaled's father stood by helplessly as his home was looted and his business confiscated. He was deported penniless to Egypt. It took him three months to make his way to Tyre. Relying on the generosity of an uncle, the Khaleds did not have to live in a tent, like most of the 1948 refugees. Her father found sporadic work and her mother sold off the jewelry she had brought with her from Haifa. For many years they supplemented their meager income with food rations and clothing from the United Nations Relief and Works Agency (UNRWA). Eventually, they found a modest top-floor apartment on al-Salammad Street, overlooking the blue-green bay of Tyre. In the distance they could see one of Lebanon's largest and poorest Palestinian refugee camps. The Khaleds were fortunate compared to most of their compatriots; but their children still attended a school housed in a tent. Leila was a bright student, and in 1960, when she was sixteen, she won a scholarship to attend the American Girls School, a high school run by American missionaries. She became fluent in English as well as Arabic.

She and her siblings were all politically active. When she was only thirteen, Leila started attending meetings of the Arab Nationalist Movement (ANM), a clandestine group founded by Dr. George Habash (1926–2008), a charismatic medical doctor and Greek Orthodox Palestinian. By the late 1950s, pro-Nasserite ANM cells were proliferating across the Middle East. For a time the ANM controlled large portions of Tyre, and when American

Marines invaded Lebanon in 1958 in an attempt to shore up the conservative regime of President Camille Chamoun, fourteen-year-old Leila Khaled joined demonstrations protesting the intervention. One day the Lebanese gendarmes opened fire on the crowd. She saw two men shot and killed—an experience that further radicalized her.

In her teenage years, some of Leila's teachers were Americans, including an African-American woman, Miss McNight. She told Leila about Martin Luther King and his nonviolent struggle to overturn segregation. Leila soon grew to think of the vivacious, quick-witted black woman as her big sister. "But our politics differed," Khaled wrote. "She was surprised when I expressed deep hatred of the Jews and taught me not to make sweeping declarations. She pointed out that not all Jews were Zionists; some were, in fact, anti-Zionist. I reflected on her distinctions and tried to adopt them into my thinking."

Khaled spent the academic year 1962–63 enrolled at the American University of Beirut, where she had further encounters with Americans. She arrived at AUB with fifty Lebanese pounds to her name, roughly $100. She lived in Jewett Hall, the women's dormitory, and her roommate was an American, Judy Sinninger. "Her social life never ceased to amaze me," wrote Khaled in her 1973 memoirs. "One week she had three different dates, with three different men and she kissed each one of them with the same passion in the grand room at Jewett in front of a lot of other girls. I asked Judy how she could do it. She passed it off: 'It was all nice, clean American fun with no strings attached.' I laughed and admired her for her amorality."

Judy became a good friend, and the two roommates had long, heated debates about current events. Judy defended President Kennedy's handling of the Cuban missile crisis that October, while Leila thought it was "criminal and barbarous on the part of the United States to threaten atomic holocaust unless it got its own way." Judy criticized President Nasser's "invasion" of North Yemen that autumn and argued that the Egyptian leader's real agenda was to control Arabian oil. Nasser, she said, was in the pocket of the Soviets. Leila defended Nasser's support for a republican regime against the corrupt, medieval Yemeni imam. And she argued that Arabian oil should be used for the benefit of all the Arab people. "Judy was an imperial citizen," Khaled later wrote, "however liberal and idealistic she may have been. I was a Palestinian Arab woman without a homeland, living in exile in an American colony in Ras Beirut. She had everything to lose; I had everything to gain. One's social consciousness is indeed determined by one's social conditions."

When the academic year ended, Khaled knew she lacked the funds to return the following autumn. AUB had broadened her horizons, but she left with a decidedly jaundiced view of the university. "Only one of my four professors was of Arabic origin, and I couldn't tell the difference between him and his three other fellow professors. They were all American in outlook, behavior and manners. They were pseudo-ivy leaguers in a provincial school that only excelled in producing CIA spies and ministers. I don't know which was the lesser evil of the two."

Khaled had a brother in Kuwait and after a few months she found work as an elementary school teacher. Predictably, she was turned off by Kuwaiti society, and bored. When President Kennedy was assassinated that autumn, she cried, much to her own surprise. "I suspect that my tears were a natural human reaction," Khaled observed. "My prejudices couldn't stop them until it was too late. I am not sorry I cried."

Sometime that year, Khaled accompanied her mother to East Jerusalem. Fifteen years had passed since they had fled Haifa, and during this entire period they had not seen Leila's grandparents, who had remained in Israel. Occasionally, separated families were allowed to greet each other across Mandelbaum Gate. After arranging a meeting time, Leila and her mother showed up at Mandelbaum Gate. "The meeting was a nightmare of barbed wire," Khaled recalled. "My aunts, my cousins, and mother carried on a teary dialogue for about an hour. Little or nothing was said beyond conveying greetings and fleeting reminiscences. We were all drenched with tears." As they parted, Leila's grandmother reached across the barbed wire and placed her necklace around Leila's mother's neck and kissed her. This was apparently against regulations, because an Israeli guard immediately snatched the necklace. "Mother fought back," Leila wrote, "but the man with the gun prevailed." That was the last time she saw her grandmother.

Khaled returned to Kuwait and for the next four years she struggled to make a living teaching. Then came the disastrous June 1967 War. "Expecting victory," Khaled wrote, "I refused to believe the outcome." Nasser's great edifice, the promise of Arab nationalism, was dead. "I smashed my radio and went into a prolonged period of silence. My whole world collapsed."

Ironically, it was another American woman who goaded Khaled into action. Leila was back in Tyre, visiting her mother (her father had died in

1966), when a young American volunteer for the YWCA stayed in the Khaled home for a week. Jane Marlowe had come to work with children in one of the Palestinian refugee camps. A sensible Catholic girl from the Bronx, Marlowe disapproved of violence; she called Fatah a terrorist organization because it had planted road mines in northern Israel that had harmed Israeli children. She suggested that the Palestinians should live in peace among their Arab brothers. Leila was incensed: "Jane had read her *New York Times* well and pontificated 'objectively' on the need for 'peace and stability' in the area."

The two women argued heatedly until Jane suddenly paused and, surveying Khaled's middle-class apartment, she turned and asked, "Are you a refugee, Leila? . . . Do you expect to live in Palestine more luxuriously than you are living here, if and when you get there?" "Perhaps not, but that is not important," I answered. "It is very important," she insisted, "because you wouldn't give up what you have here and you're not doing anything personally to reach your goals."

Leila was stunned. And then she admitted that Jane was right, and that so far in her life she had only talked about injustice. She had not done anything to change things. From that moment, Khaled later wrote, she was determined to act, "not just talk, and memorize the arguments against Zionism."

Soon afterwards, back in Kuwait, she walked into a bookstore where the shopkeeper was selling PFLP Christmas cards. Leila brazenly asked him if he knew how to contact the PFLP; she wanted to join. It was a natural step. As a young teenager, she had been a camp follower of the Arab Nationalist Movement, founded by Drs. George Habash and Wadi Haddad in 1951. Both men were products of AUB's medical school (Habash graduated first in his class). After the June 1967 War, Habash and Haddad morphed the ANM into the Popular Front for the Liberation of Palestine, urging a new generation of Palestinians to take up arms. Disillusioned with Nasser, Habash embraced the politics of the gun. The Front's inaugural statement declared, "The only language which the enemy understands is that of revolutionary violence." Habash represented the intellectual side of the burgeoning Palestinian nationalist movement. By comparison, his rival, al-Fatah's dour Yasir Arafat, seemed coarse and inarticulate. Habash believed that if the Palestinians were going to redress their grievances against the Israelis, it would have to be done on a world stage. Leila Khaled and the PFLP were a perfect match.

Late in 1968 she joined the PFLP's Special Operations Squad, and soon afterwards she was sent to a military training camp near Amman. She was given weapons training—but she was also taught to read the instruments on a Boeing 707 flight deck. On August 29, 1969, Khaled boarded TWA Flight 840 in Rome bound for Tel Aviv. The 127 passengers and crew included many Americans, a young U.S. Foreign Service officer named Thomas D. Boyatt, two Israeli men and four Israeli women. (The PFLP had intelligence that General Yitzhak Rabin was booked aboard the flight, but this proved to be incorrect.) Together with Salim Issawi, another Palestinian from Haifa, Khaled managed to hijack the plane—and, after a short diversion over Tel Aviv and Haifa so that she could get a glimpse of her birthplace—they landed the Boeing 707 in Damascus. There, Khaled and Issawi blew up the plane's cockpit after allowing all the passengers to leave. Afterwards, she went around to the shaken passengers, offering them candy and her apologies. One woman turned to her and said, "I don't understand. Who are the Palestinians?" Khaled thought her hijacking would soon change that.

The Syrian authorities placed her and Issawi under house arrest for forty-five days—and then let them go back to Beirut. The four Israeli women were detained for a day and then allowed to depart. The two Israeli men were held by the Syrians until December, when they were exchanged for a number of Syrian and Egyptian prisoners held in Israel.

Khaled was not the first female hijacker; an Argentine woman had hijacked a plane to the Falklands three years earlier. But Khaled's successful hijacking of the TWA plane turned her into a household name in the refugee camps of Lebanon, Jordan and Gaza. Celebrating students at AUB mobbed her. Her photo was published in newspapers around the world, and the underlying caption often identified her as the female "Che Guevara." The PFLP sent her on a tour to the Gulf states, where a British businessman was introduced to her at a party hosted by an Arab embassy in Qatar. "She was feted like a visiting astronaut," he said.

The hijacking was also making a name for the PFLP. A year earlier, in July 1968, PFLP commandos had taken control of an El Al airliner outside of Rome and diverted it to Algiers. They released most of the passengers but held hostage a dozen Jewish men for five weeks, until Israel agreed to release sixteen Palestinians convicted of various acts of violence. In February 1970 an explosion in the cargo hold of Swissair Flight 330 bound for Tel

Aviv resulted in a crash that killed all forty-seven people aboard. (A break-away faction of the PFLP, the PFLP–General Command, initially claimed responsibility but then retracted its claim.)

The idea for hijackings came from Habash's colleague, Dr. Wadi Haddad (1927–1978). Like Habash, Haddad was born into a Greek Orthodox family in Safed, in present-day Israel, and he obtained his medical degree from AUB in 1952. In the early 1950s he and Habash ran a clinic for the poor in Amman. But they were early and ardent advocates of both Arab nationalism and armed struggle. At AUB they had been members of a group calling itself "Youth of Vengeance." In 1957, Habash, Haddad and their ANM cadres were accused of plotting with Palestinian elements in the Jordanian army to overthrow King Hussein. When Hussein dismissed the recently elected assembly and imposed martial law, Haddad was arrested and imprisoned for three years. Habash fled to Syria, but he was tried in absentia and sentenced to thirty-three years in prison.

Upon Haddad's release, he too fled to Syria, where in 1963 he began organizing commando raids into Israel. He soon learned that guerrilla warfare against Israel was extremely difficult, if not futile. Palestine's dry, rocky plains were not the jungles of Vietnam. And the Israeli enemy was highly motivated to defend the new Jewish state. Soon after forming the PFLP at the end of 1967, Haddad began arguing for a new strategy. "Trying to get men and weapons across the River Jordan is a waste of time and effort," Haddad told a small gathering of the PFLP's top officers in 1968. "Armed struggle of that type will never achieve the liberation of Palestine. . . . We have to hit the Israelis at the weak joints. What do I mean by the weak joints? I mean spectacular, one-off operations. These spectacular operations will focus the world's attention on the problem of Palestine. The world will ask, 'What the hell is the problem in Palestine? Who are these Palestinians? . . . In the end the world will get fed up with its [Israel's] problem; it will decide it has to do something about Palestine. It will have to give us justice." Haddad's argument persuaded his colleagues, and they allowed him to train young *fedayeen*—literally "self-sacrificers"—on how to take control of a commercial airliner. In some instances, his commandos were given flight training so that if necessary they could land the aircraft. Inside the PFLP, Haddad became known as the "Master."

Leila Khaled was the "Master's" most celebrated foot soldier. Though the

Syrians obligingly released her after her 1969 hijacking, Khaled was by now a high-profile wanted woman, at least by the Israelis. Incredibly, on March 13, 1970, she submitted to painful plastic surgery in Beirut so that she could do it all over again. It took her two months to recover from the procedure. Late one evening that summer Khaled was sitting in Dr. Haddad's Beirut apartment when several rockets struck the bedroom. Haddad and Khaled were unscathed, but Haddad's eight-year-old son, Hani, had a chest wound. Khaled rushed him to AUB's hospital, where an American doctor asked her if she had any money for the boy's treatment. "Are you a doctor or a carpet salesman?" Khaled shrieked. Dr. Haddad rushed in looking for his son—and the American doctor, recognizing Haddad as a medical colleague, apologized. "Yankee doctor, the revolution will make AUB's hospital a hospital for the poor and your kind of doctor will have to be disbarred or sent back to America," Khaled told him.

Mossad's attempt to assassinate the "Master" only strengthened Khaled's resolve. So late that summer she volunteered for a particularly dangerous assault on an Israeli commercial airliner. On September 6, 1970, she boarded an El Al Boeing 707 in Amsterdam. Flight 219 was bound for New York with 148 passengers and 10 crew members—including two plainclothes El Al air marshals. Khaled had first met her accomplice, Patrick Arguello, in Stuttgart only a few days earlier. Arguello was wearing a business suit and Khaled was provocatively dressed in a miniskirt and shapely bolero waistcoat—and a Mexican sombrero. Posing as the newly married "Maria Sanchez" and "Mr. Diaz" of Honduras, Khaled and Arguello calmly walked through security. They were closely questioned by an Israeli officer and their hand luggage was carefully inspected. "Do you have anything sharp or dangerous?" asked the Israeli.

"Such as?" replied Khaled.

"Such as a pistol, a knife or anything sharp?"

"No sir," replied Khaled, "what would a girl like me ever do with a pistol or knife, officer?"

The Israeli smiled and was about to dismiss them, when he asked in English if she spoke Spanish. Khaled brazenly replied, "Sí, señor." At this, she and Arguello were waved through to the plane. They took their seats in the second row of the economy section. The plan had called for four PFLP hijackers—this was, after all, an El Al flight, and they knew that armed

Israeli guards were very likely on board. But as it happened, the two other comrades that should have joined them were turned back by El Al security. (Unfazed, these two agents went to the Pan Am counter, paid cash for two first-class tickets and boarded a Pan Am Boeing 747 jumbo jet. This was the plane that was later destroyed that day on the tarmac in Cairo.)

Though now there were only two of them, Khaled and Arguello decided to go ahead with the operation. Arguello knew his comrade only by the alias "Shadiah." In the minutes before they rushed the cockpit, Khaled whispered to him that she thought the flight crew had no idea who they were. Arguello replied, "Are you Queen Elizabeth?" To which Khaled said, "No, I have had an experience before. I'm Leila Khaled." He seemed duly impressed and gave her a little victory salute. Perhaps the knowledge that she had done this before steeled him for what he was about to do.

Arguello had stuffed in his pocket an all-plastic Italian starting pistol, specially modified to fire .22 caliber revolver cartridges. He also had a plastic hand grenade. Khaled had two such hand grenades stuffed down her brassiere. About twenty-five minutes after takeoff, as the plane approached British airspace, they rose from their seats and stormed the cockpit. A passenger later described Patrick as he ran forward: "He let out a bellow and he had this little tiny pistol in his hand." As they ran through the first-class lounge, an El Al steward, Shlomo Vider, rose from his seat and tried to grab Arguello. "The man with the gun," recalled a first-class passenger, Harry Hamel, "gave the steward a conk in the back of the head, and the steward started to gush blood immediately on his clothes." Arguello pointed his plastic gun at the other stewards—and then told Khaled, "Go ahead, I'll protect your back." She turned back to the cockpit and banged on the door. It was locked—and locked inside the cockpit were not only the pilot and copilot but also one of two El Al air marshals aboard the flight that day. In violation of El Al's regulations, this air marshal had entered the cockpit to chat with the pilots on takeoff from Amsterdam.

As Khaled banged on the door, demanding to be let in, she suddenly heard a gunshot. Arguello had fired a bullet through the floor. At this point, the bleeding steward, Vider, made another attempt to rush Arguello. "I saw the man hijacker point his gun at the steward and fire," said a passenger. "The steward fell back holding his stomach." A gun battle now erupted between Arguello and the second armed air marshal, who came running up from his seat at the back of the plane. Fourteen shots were fired, seven each by Arguello and the air marshal.

As the bullets flew, the Israeli pilot, Captain Uri Bar-Lev, decided to put the plane into a "zero-g" deep nosedive. Khaled and Arguello were thrown off balance. As the plane leveled out, a nearby passenger then managed to knock Arguello over the head with a whisky bottle, and Khaled was beaten to the floor by passengers.

What happened next is in dispute. The Israeli air marshals report that Arguello threw a hand grenade down the aisle that failed to explode. Khaled insists that they had instructions not to detonate their grenades. In fact, one source suggests that when authorities later examined the grenades, it was discovered that they had no detonating mechanisms. They were intended to threaten the passengers but not harm them. Khaled claims she had pulled the pins from both of her grenades, and they were then squeezed out of her hands in the ensuing melee.

Khaled told police investigators in London that it was only after she and Arguello were beaten and bound that an Israeli security guard murdered her American comrade. "I saw everything," she later said, speaking in English at a Beirut press conference. "They shot four bullets in Pat's back while he was lying tied up and armless [disarmed]." In her memoirs she wrote, "Suddenly an Israeli guard emerged from the cockpit area. Patrick was lying on his side. The man turned him over on his stomach and started tying him up with wires and a necktie. Someone asked, 'How are they?' A voice replied, 'We don't know. He is . . . we're not sure. She's three-quarters dead.' The man stepped on Patrick's hips and Patrick looked at me in agony, his hands tied behind his back. Then the Zionist guard fired four shots into Patrick's back. Someone screamed from the back of the plane, 'Please stop the bloodshed. Please, Please, Please!' "

The Israelis sharply denied her account and later insisted that Arguello was hit by an undisclosed number of bullets in the course of the gun battle. One lodged in his thigh and shattered a bone. Another passed through his right arm and lungs. And the third entered his stomach and came to rest in his pelvis. When the plane made an emergency landing at Heathrow, Arguello was alive but bleeding to death.

British police boarded the plane as soon as it landed, but when they moved to take custody of Khaled, an Israeli officer intervened. A shoving match ensued as the British tried to drag Khaled out of the plane and the Israelis screamed that she was their prisoner. The British prevailed, and Khaled was hustled into an ambulance with Arguello lying on a stretcher. He died in the ambulance en route to Hillingdon hospital, with Khaled by his side. She later told police, "I didn't intend to hurt or kill anybody on the flight. I was going to hijack the plane and get it flown to Amman." And yet, her accomplice had fired the first shot. The plane's severely wounded steward, Shlomo Vider, had taken five bullets; he barely survived and spent the next two weeks in the hospital.

Ten days later, at a British inquest into Arguello's death, the coroner's seven-man jury determined that he had been shot at point-blank range—but that the fatal shot to his abdomen could not have been fired when his arms were tied behind his back. The unnamed Israeli air marshal's gun muzzle had literally been touching Arguello's clothes when it was fired. The jury's most unusual verdict was "lawful homicide." The inquest jury never called for Khaled's testimony, nor did they hear from the El Al air marshals. The two El Al security guards demanded to be put on another plane for Tel Aviv immediately; the British managed to delay their departure for two hours and briefly interviewed them aboard an El Al plane.

Khaled was detained under heavy guard in the West London Ealing police station. But not for long. By then the PFLP had 310 hostages parked in two planes on the desert floor at Dawson's Field, twenty miles northwest of Amman, and their spokesmen in Beirut were telling reporters that they would not release the hostages until Leila Khaled and six other guerrillas held in German and Swiss jails were released. They were also demanding that Israel release an unspecified number of the roughly 3,400 Palestinians imprisoned in Israel. Whatever happened now, the PFLP had certainly caught the attention of the world. As Walter Cronkite intoned on the *CBS Evening News,* "Palestinian guerrillas, in a bold coordinated action, created this newest crisis Sunday, and in so doing they accomplished what they set out to do: they thrust back into the world's attention a problem diplomats have tended to shunt aside in hesitant steps towards Middle East peace." *Time* magazine observed, "If the world has become a global village, as Marshall McLuhan would have it, the Palestinians have become its most troubled ghetto minority."

In the minds of most Americans, the Palestinians did not exist. A year earlier, Israel's Golda Meir had famously said: "It was not as though there was a Palestinian people and in Palestine, considering itself as a Palestinian people, and we came and threw them out and took their country away. They did not exist." For men like Bassam Abu-Sharif, the PFLP's spokesman, the hijackings were a defiant retort. Abu-Sharif was standing on the desert floor when the TWA aircraft approached Dawson's Field in the darkness. The pilot had to land the plane on that hard-packed desert ground, guided only by the headlights of jeeps and a line of flaming oil drums. Upon landing, the hijackers opened the escape chutes and allowed the passengers to exit. Abu-Sharif was amused to see some of them running off into the desert—only to realize sheepishly that they had no place to run to. Abu-Sharif later wrote in his memoirs, "I asked one American who had done this where he thought he was. 'Somewhere in Africa?' he asked dazedly. 'No,' I told him. 'You are in Jordan, and we are Palestinian guerrillas.' 'In Pakistan?' he asked, completely bewildered. 'No,' I said patiently. 'We are Palestinian. From Palestine. You know, the country that is occupied by Israel.' But he didn't know. He had obviously never heard of Palestine."

About forty minutes later, the Swissair DC-8 began its own approach to Dawson's Field. Touching down, Swissair Captain Fritz Schreiber suddenly floored the brakes and slammed his four engines into full reverse thrust, blowing up clouds of sand and dust. The plane's ventilation system was soon sucking this dust inside the aircraft. "The cabin was filling up with cloudy stuff that smelled like smoke," recalled one passenger, Cecily Simmon. "You could hardly breathe." When the dust had settled, everyone could see why Captain Schreiber had hit the brakes: the DC-8 had come to rest only fifty yards from the TWA airliner.

On September 9, Joy Riggs and her older brother Louis, twenty-one, boarded BOAC Flight 775 in Bombay—a plane the PFLP decided to hijack in response to Arguello's and Khaled's aborted hijacking of the El Al flight out of Amsterdam. The BOAC plane flew first to Dubai for a short layover. "When we reboarded the flight," Joy later told me, "I saw these young men and I remember thinking, 'My, those guys are pretty good looking.'" It was one of these young men who initiated the hijacking. The plane had one more layover in Bahrain and then flew on to Beirut. "Just half an hour before landing at Beirut," Joy wrote me later, "a man stood up between the first and second class compartments holding a gun. I could not believe it. Louis was dozing peacefully and I woke him as quietly as I could with the 'delightful' news." Pretty soon the intercom crackled with broken English: "Sit in your seats and buckle your seat belts." There were three hijackers, "all extremely nervous and wild-eyed." During those first few minutes they repeatedly threatened to blow the plane up if anyone moved. No one did. But then one of the young men announced, "Now we will blow up the plane," and after a fearful pause, "if you move."

One hijacker entered the flight deck and ordered the pilot, Captain Cyril Goulborn, to continue on to Beirut. "He had rather large staring eyes," Goulborn recalled, "was obviously very agitated and pointing a gun at me." Goulborn calmly invited his unexpected visitor to sit down and "discuss the matter. . . . Tell us what you want us to do." Approaching Beirut, the hijacker suddenly told Captain Goulborn to turn the plane around and fly to Tel Aviv. This was an ominous development. When some members of the crew tried to suggest that landing at Tel Aviv might lead to a dangerous confrontation, the lead hijacker replied, "No, we go to Tel Aviv." Upon flying into Israeli airspace, the hijacker attempted to communicate in Arabic with Israeli air controllers. When they did not respond, he became increasingly agitated, until he finally ordered the plane back to Beirut, where it landed at about 12:30 p.m. By then, Captain Goulborn estimated he had fuel for less than twenty minutes of flying time.

Lebanese authorities quickly acceded to the hijackers' demand that the plane be refueled. But that was not all. Three PFLP representatives soon arrived at the control tower with further demands. One of them spoke English with an upper-class British accent; this Oxford-educated guerrilla explained that he had instructions to insert two more of his people onto the BOAC plane, together with some unspecified baggage. Once more, the authorities agreed, and within an hour Joy and her fellow passengers saw two additional hijackers board the plane, one of them a woman, Mona Saud, lugging what turned out to be bags of explosives. In a bit of theatre, Mona walked down the aisles, passing out passenger landing cards where the destination had already been filled in as "Revolutionary Airport." The plane took off about 2:30 p.m., and soon afterwards one of the hijackers gave the pilot coordinates for landing at Dawson's Field in northern Jordan.

"Things relaxed a little," Joy recalled, "and we were permitted to go to the toilet one at a time." Around 4:00 p.m. the pilot started searching for Dawson's Field. As the plane approached Amman, Captain Goulborn invited all of the hijackers into the cockpit and asked them to help him identify the former British landing strip. Fearing that the pilot was playing games with them, the hijackers became agitated and started to argue amongst themselves—all the time waving their guns around in the air. Flying over Amman, Captain Goulborn backtracked north. By now, the plane was again running low on fuel. Suddenly, Goulborn saw two large commercial airliners parked on the desert floor. The strip looked long enough—but unfortunately, one of the planes, a Swissair jet, was smack in the middle of the desert runway. Captain Goulborn circled the area once more and then made his final approach. "The visibility was very poor, a lot of sand blowing about," recalled First Officer Trevor Cooper. "We landed slap-bang on top of the Swissair. It was an extremely good landing, very, very good indeed." Cooper meant that it had been a very risky landing, and his captain had skillfully evaded plowing into the Swissair plane.

Peering through their porthole, Joy and Louis could see scores of jeeps filled with young men carrying Kalashnikov AK-47 machine guns. Ominously, off in the distance sat a line of tanks and armored personnel carriers manned by King Hussein's Bedouin soldiers. A herd of camels wandered past the aircraft. The BOAC plane bumped slowly across the desert floor and came to a stop a short distance away from the TWA and Swissair planes hijacked three days earlier. The hijackers hustled the crew out of the cockpit and wired it with explosives. As soon as the forward hatch was opened, some 150 PFLP commandos greeted the passengers with whoops, and waving their guns in the air. It was an eerie, and very one-sided, celebration. Joy thought to herself it was "like a lousy war movie."

"A woman dressed in that funny camouflage khaki uniform addressed us," Joy recalled, "and told us that we were to be held as hostages until certain prisoners from the PFLP were released in London—Leila Khaled—and other countries." The guerrillas also announced that the VC-10 had been renamed "Leila." Back at London's Ealing police station, upon hearing the news, Leila Khaled told her interrogators, "A plane has been hijacked just for me." As night fell and the BOAC passengers tried to make themselves comfortable, one of the hijackers passed through the aisle, collecting every passenger's passport. That night they nibbled on leftovers from the plane's kitchen galley: some peaches, cut-up frankfurters and rolls.

The next day, Thursday, all twenty-one Arab passengers and one Indian citizen aboard the BOAC plane were released. Their departure gave the remaining passengers substantially more room to spread out and make do in their cramped quarters. Left aboard were five Americans, one Canadian, a scattering of other Europeans and fifty-two British citizens, including the twenty-four schoolchildren all under the age of fifteen—bound for their boarding school in England, and accompanied by one adult escort.

"The commandos, for the most part, were friendly and kind," Joy wrote to me. "We were fed irregularly and had sufficient water most of the time. We were lectured on the Revolution frequently. The children thought it was a fun camp-out. They were really marvelous; they never lost their cheerfulness." Some sang songs. "The singing saved us from chronic depression." When a particularly dogmatic female guerrilla—nicknamed "Bombshell Bessie" by the hostages—serenaded them with "revolutionary" songs, the children in the back of the plane suddenly responded with a rendition of a Beatles tune: "We all live on a blue and white plane . . ." sung to the tune of "Yellow Submarine."

One British boy, eleven-year-old Michael Hatcher, revealed to everyone's amusement that he had smuggled aboard his pet lizard and a turtle. On two occasions the passengers were allowed off the plane for short stretches, and some of the children delighted in sliding down the emergency chutes. Once, the hijackers piled some children in a jeep and took them on a whirlwind tour of the "Revolutionary Airport." By day two, the Palestinians were bringing in fresh tomatoes, grapes, tinned meat, flat Arab bread, olives and, on one occasion, some cold roasted chicken. They even distributed bottles of whisky.

Beneath the veneer of this "hospitality," however, lurked obvious dangers. These were men (and women) with guns and explosives. Joy was not a witness to some things. On Thursday afternoon the plane's first officer, Trevor Cooper, was getting off the plane, with the permission of the hijackers, to take a short walk. He turned to Suzy Potts, a young British girl with whom he had been playing cards, and pointed out a "Lexicon set"—a card game—and remarked that perhaps they could play that upon their return. One of the lead PFLP hijackers happened to overhear the comment—and misunderstood. Shortly afterwards, Cooper was asked to accompany one of the hijackers to a tent fifty yards away. Cooper walked inside the tent and saw two PFLP *fedayeen* armed with machine guns—and their commander. This man now pulled a pistol and, aiming it at Cooper's head, said that he wanted to see the "sonograph." Cooper said, "What is a sonograph?" The PFLP man insisted that he had heard Cooper tell the young girl about a "sonograph." Suddenly becoming agitated, the PFLP commander warned Cooper that he had ten minutes to hand over the "sonograph." Bewildered, Cooper insisted he didn't know what a sonograph was—at which point the three men shoved him into a van and drove off into the desert for about a mile. They then forced Cooper out. "As soon as I got out, I saw that there was this grave that had been dug—at which stage I really thought I had had it. They forced me to get into the grave, kneel down, the three of them stood on top, on the bank—they all had machine guns at this stage—all pointing at me and they gave me sixty seconds to tell them where this bloody sonograph was or else I had had it. And I broke down . . . I just thought I had had it. . . . I was just curled up with my head down waiting for them to shoot. . . ."

Finally, after what seemed like an eternity, the hijackers dragged Cooper back to the van, and as the sun was setting they put him back aboard the BOAC plane. Cooper was a wreck. He broke down and never slept that night.

Joy was unaware of this awful incident. But she nevertheless knew that a deadline had been declared. She and Louis were listening to news from the BBC report on a small shortwave radio. "The commandos were usually friendly," she later wrote her parents. "But they were fiercely dedicated to their cause and made us understand that they would blow us all up if our nations forced them to. The DEAD line was 72 hours away." On the second morning, the Palestinians told everyone to stay in their seats and then they went through the plane picking up all hand luggage and alcohol. For the first time, their demeanor was one of cold fury. "I was convinced," she wrote to me, "they were preparing to blow us up. Evidently, that's what they intended us to think because soon after we settled down they asked us to write telegram messages to our Embassies. I wrote one for us Americans to be sent to the U.S. Embassy with a copy for the press. No one in the outside world would believe these people were serious! Kai, they were fanatical about their cause. They *would* [have] killed us all for a good reason. We listened to BBC newscasts when they allowed us to but it was depressing."

Joy's handwritten plea on a scrap of BOAC stationery was soon published in Western newspapers, addressed to the U.S. Embassy:

Conditions getting worse. Commandos
serious in their threat. Please
do not gamble with our lives.
Release their prisoners immediately.
Help us now.
Joy Riggs, Louis Riggs (& three other illegible names)

Tensions had risen on that Friday, the third day of captivity, because the *fedayeen* had listened to news broadcasts that suggested the Americans or the Israelis were preparing to intervene. The U.S. Sixth Fleet was steaming toward the eastern Mediterranean, and President Richard Nixon had dispatched twenty-five Phantom jet fighters and four C-130 transport planes to a U.S. air force base in Turkey. One of the lead hijackers on the BOAC plane, Abu Fadil, warned the passengers, "We don't want to kill you, but if we have to, I'm afraid we shall."

"We all got to know each other fairly well," Joy wrote me later. "I spent a good deal of time thinking about how I would rather die. Decided being blown up would be less painful." And yet, she also "felt very unready to die and didn't really expect to. . . . I just felt it would be a damn shame to become a mess of black carbon so young in life."

During the day, it was hot and muggy inside the plane. Friday there was such a severe sandstorm that the guerrillas had to close all the hatches, making things even more stuffy. And while they had sufficient drinking water, there was not enough water for the hostages to wash their faces or brush their teeth. At night the temperature in the desert plunged, and Joy came down with a heavy chest cold and a fever. "Nights were the worst," she wrote. "I'd wake up with bad dreams, freezing cold." She and Louis took turns sleeping on the floor. On only two occasions were they allowed off the plane to stretch their legs.

"As bad as it sounds, I never could get over how really kind they [the hijackers] were. They loved the children and when one guerrilla tried to maul one of the teenage girls one night, he was punished."

Four days after they landed at Dawson's Field, early on Saturday morning, September 12, the hijackers gave everyone five minutes' notice that all the women and children were to be taken to Amman. "The only time I argued with them," Joy later said, "was when they announced that they were taking off the women and children. I told one of the hijackers that Louis [twenty-one years of age] was practically a kid and I wanted to take him with me. The hijackers just bundled me off with the other women." They were driven to Amman's Intercontinental Hotel. There, they spent an agonizing afternoon waiting for the men to be released. At one point, a stewardess came rushing into the room and said, "They've blown up the planes." Another stewardess broke down crying. "It was terrible," Joy recalled, "we could see off in the distance these huge black plumes of smoke, and I thought, 'Oh my God, what has happened to Louis.' "

When Louis finally walked into the Intercontinental late that evening, he was so shaken he could hardly speak. He had been one of the last passengers to leave the BOAC plane. He and the last remaining hostages were hurried into a minivan parked just 250 yards from the aircraft. Louis glanced back in time to see an explosion rip apart the BOAC cockpit, followed by two more explosions in the center and rear of the plane. They were close enough that the shock wave of the explosions rocked the minivan. Moments later the two other planes went up. All told, $50 million worth of commercial aircraft were destroyed.*

Afterwards, a tension-laden standoff ensued between Jordanian army troops and the guerrillas. "They [the passengers] were almost killed," Joy wrote. "The commandos took them off the planes and then blew up all three aircraft. The Jordanian army thought they had liquidated us, so they moved in rapidly with tanks and guns. Of course, the commandos shoved their machine guns right into the hostages' faces and waited. The Jordanians finally retreated. . . ."

Joy knew that nine of her fellow passengers and crew were still being held hostage somewhere in Amman—"but Britain has released Leila [Khaled] so they should be all right." In fact, the guerrillas still controlled some fifty-seven passengers from the three planes. And although, as secular Marxists, the PFLP insisted that "Zionism is our enemy, not Jews," this, ominously, did not stop them from identifying nearly a dozen passengers of Jewish background, regardless of nationality, and whisking them off to PFLP safe houses in Amman. "I was four years in a concentration camp in Hungary," said Alexander Herman of Brooklyn, the father of seventeen-year-old Mir-

---

*The *fedayeen* apparently used about three-quarters of a kilo of plastic explosive for each of the cockpits. They reportedly off-loaded a stash of 2,400,000 British pounds from the Swissair plane before it was destroyed. (David Raab, *Terror in Black September*.)

iam, one of the Jewish hostages selected for continued detention. "I lost four children by Hitler, and now I am going through the same thing again."

The PFLP had hoped that the few dual-national Israeli-American hostages might be held in exchange for an unspecified number of Palestinians held in Israeli prisons. In the midst of the crisis, the Israeli government let it be known that they had picked up for detention an additional 400 Palestinians in the West Bank—and some of them just happened to be relatives of George Habash. The 57 hostages were kept hidden in various Amman refugee camps for another two weeks—and that in the midst of an escalating Jordanian-Palestinian civil war. Their ordeal was prolonged, but eventually they were all released, unharmed. Clearly, in this instance the PFLP leadership never intended to kill anyone. And though the Israelis refused to release any of their prisoners, the PFLP did obtain the release of Leila Khaled and six other PFLP agents held in Swiss and German prisons.

The hijackings had been staged to garner worldwide attention for the cause of Palestinian self-determination. As the PFLP's Habash explained it to a German magazine on September 16, "When we hijack a plane it has more effect than if we killed a hundred Israelis in battle. For decades world public opinion has been neither for nor against the Palestinians. It simply ignored us. At least the world is talking about us now." On this point, Habash was right: the hijacking had put the Palestinian cause front and center in the media. What he didn't understand was that this very success was likely to foster more violence.

The Israeli prime minister, Golda Meir, protested Khaled's release, telling a television reporter, "She will do it again, kill Israelis. She'll kill men, women and children. This is what her organization stands for." The fact that the Europeans had surrendered to the PFLP's demands so readily was an ominous sign. The Israeli security establishment thought that this would encourage the Palestinians to hijack more aircraft—or do worse—in the years to come. And, of course, they were right. But at the time, sitting in Beirut listening to the news reports of the hijackings, I was relieved that Khaled had been released. In 1970, at the age of nineteen, I didn't think the Palestinians would ever have killed hostages. I'm not so sure now. If Khaled had remained a British prisoner—or if she had been sent to Israel—I think it quite likely the PFLP would have escalated their threats. And then, to make them credible, they might actually have killed someone. I only learned about what the *fedayeen* had done to First Officer Trevor Cooper—a mock execution in the desert—in recent years from a former hostage, David Raab, who wrote a detailed book about his experience, *Terror in Black September*. As Joy herself wrote, the hijackers were "serious in their threat." In any event, the hijackings had all sorts of unintended, but decidedly bloody, consequences.

When it was over, reporters mobbed the hostages. A press conference was held inside the Intercontinental Hotel on the evening of September 12. Joy was the first American to step forward to speak into the bank of microphones. Imagining this scene now, nearly four decades later, I am astonished by her fortitude. After a four-day ordeal, this nineteen-year-old woman had something to say—and it wasn't to condemn the Palestinians. "At the press conference," she later wrote me, "I expressed sympathy for the plight of the Palestinians. On the way from the planes to the hotel they drove us through one of the refugee camps and you could see how these people were living. And I suppose I had heard a lot about them from you."

Joy had heard me talk fervently about the Palestinian cause. "I said in Amman to a reporter," she wrote, "that I could understand why the refugees are unhappy and frustrated. (Very, very naughty of me!*) . . . Kai, the coverage we got was incredible. An army of reporters descended on us at Amman. Flattering only for a few minutes and then a pain in the A—. . . . Hot lights and stupid questions till I thought we'd die."

As she spoke, gunfire and artillery could be heard in the streets of Amman, a city that was erupting into an outright civil war between the Palestinians and King Hussein's Bedouin troops. Her hotel room was riddled with bullet holes from recent skirmishes. "But it didn't bother me a bit. It was such a relief to be able to wash, and brush my teeth, and move around."

The next morning, Joy, Louis and most of the other hostages were flown out of Jordan to Cyprus and then onward to London—where she met with the U.S. ambassador and dined out with the American consul general. No one was harmed, and no one was killed—except Leila's comrade, the American Sandinista Patrick Arguello. (When the Sandinistas toppled the Somoza

---

*A missionary child, Joy was taught to see things through the eyes of others. Shortly after her ordeal, Joy's mother, Frances, wrote from India, "How cruel and careless can we become? And what made these Arabs like that? I'm sure somewhere we have failed them." (September 15, 1970.)

regime in 1979, they would build a memorial to Arguello—and then when the Sandinistas lost an election, the memorial was taken down.)

Joy had survived what later became known in the media as the Black September hijackings. She wrote, "We're all fine now and have been pampered a great deal. All of us are still suffering from minor psychological discomforts. I get very nervous when there are loud noises or particularly when a loudspeaker addresses us. I almost passed out once when a photographer swung around with a black shiny camera pointed right at me. Everyone else is that way too. Write and please stay away from the Arabs (?). I love you. [signed] Joy."

I did not take her advice. That autumn my roommate in Beirut was Nawfal Younis, a Palestinian who had grown up in Ein-al-Halweh (Sweet Spring), an overcrowded refugee camp near the southern port town of Sidon. Like Leila Khaled, Nawfal had studied at a mission school and was lucky enough to get a scholarship to attend the American University of Beirut. He was a shy and seriously intense young man, determined to become a doctor. (He would succeed.) That autumn he took me to his cinder-block and tin-roof home in Ein-al-Halweh, and I met his family. Open sewers poured through the narrow streets. I took a photograph of one of the numerous graffiti slogans painted on the sides of the walled-off houses: "We fight Israel because it occupies our land—Fatah." Posters of a demure Leila Khaled, eyes shyly downcast, were pasted on the walls everywhere. (Leila herself was now back in Beirut, a revolutionary hero.) This widely disseminated propaganda photo remains an iconic image of Palestinian resistance and female power. It was obviously staged to bestow on her the romantic revolutionary aura of a female Che Guevara: Khaled holds a Kalashnikov in her delicate, feminine hands, her shiny black hair is wrapped in a kaffiyeh, and she's wearing a distinctive ring on her wedding finger. "I made it from the pin of a hand grenade—from the first grenade I ever used in training," she once explained to a reporter. "I just wrapped it around a bullet."

One evening a few weeks after the hijackings, I was sitting in Uncle Sam's, the garish West Beirut hamburger joint and now a popular hangout for university students. Sitting in the next booth was a large, immaculately dressed Palestinian. He wore a freshly pressed white shirt with cuff links, and a handkerchief was stuffed neatly in the front pocket of his tweed jacket. By his appearance he might have been a graduate student or a postdoctoral teaching fellow at AUB. A fellow student—I don't recall who—introduced us. Educated at Oxford, he spoke with a very affected, polished British accent. And soon he began speaking of the hijackings. He was, it turned out, a member of the PFLP and had been in the control tower as the Front's negotiator on the day the BOAC plane landed at Beirut.

I was stunned. What should I say to this man? Perhaps I should have shared with him a letter I had just received from Joy, dated September 22, in which she confessed, "I've got a hangover from the hijacking. . . . The past few nights I've had nightmares about being confined in a small space. I wake up agitated and frustrated." I turned to this unlikely revolutionary and explained quietly that "my girl" was on that plane. What would they have done, I asked, if the British had not released Leila and the other PFLP cadres in European prisons? Would they have killed the hostages? "Oh no," replied the PFLP man, "at the very worst we might have marched them off into the desert and kept them as ransom for a while longer. You know, there is a rich history of hostage-taking among the Arab tribesmen. We have no other way to get the world's attention. But we would not have killed anyone." We finished our burgers, and I went back to my dorm room, feeling depressed and confused.

Jordan was falling apart. The hijacking crisis had underscored for everyone that King Hussein was losing control over the country's internal security. The various *fedayeen* militias had long since taken complete control of the refugee camps. They ran welfare services, schools and clinics inside the camps. But they now also controlled whole neighborhoods of Amman; Palestinian men armed with Kalashnikovs manned roadblocks throughout the city and refused passage to the Jordanian army. The PLO collected taxes and owned property and a variety of businesses. King Hussein's government had also lost control of the northern city of Irbid, the country's second-largest city, with a population of 150,000. Early in September 1970, the king's Bedouin troops in Irbid ambushed and massacred twenty-three *fedayeen* and then desecrated their bodies. "They were completely mutilated," a shopkeeper told *Newsweek*'s Loren Jenkins. "Some had their hands with their intestines, others their eyes gouged out or had been dismembered." An outraged citizenry turned the city's administration over to the PLO. "People's committees" were organized street by street, barricades were erected to keep out King Hussein's police and soldiers, and trenches were dug on the outskirts of the city.

Three years after the June 1967 War, the PLO—more precisely, perhaps, the PLO's dominant faction, al-Fatah—had truly become a state within a state. While the PFLP's spectacular hijackings had momentarily grabbed the world's attention, Yasir Arafat's al-Fatah *fedayeen* were quickly becoming the real power in Jordan. The PFLP, with its estimated membership of 2,500, was the PLO's second-largest member group, but Fatah was by far the more numerous. Over the previous two years Fatah had launched a number of guerrilla raids across the River Jordan. But, as the PFLP's Wadi Haddad had observed, this kind of pinprick attack on isolated Israeli military posts or settlements could never be expected to defeat Israel's vastly superior conventional forces. On the other hand, by 1970 Fatah's militia was beginning to look like a real army. They had jeeps, trucks, armored personnel carriers and tanks. And without a doubt, the PLO—which included Fatah, the PFLP and a number of smaller political organizations—had the majority of the Palestinian population behind it. King Hussein and his Hashemite, Bedouin-based constituency were a distinct political and demographic minority, even without the West Bank Palestinians now under Israeli occupation. Jordan's nomadic Bedouin tribes, many of whom had accompanied Hussein's grandfather during the Hashemite exile from the Hejaz, lived largely in the desert and historically viewed the sedentary Palestinians of the cities and small towns with suspicion.

Humiliated by his loss of the West Bank, King Hussein thought he had no choice after 1967 but to allow the PLO to fill the political void. In the aftermath of the 1968 battle of Karameh—where the *fedayeen* and the Jordanian army had bloodied an Israeli armored column—Hussein had conceded, "I think we have come to the point now where we are all *fedayeen*." But he was in a delicate position. He tried reaching out to some of the old aristocratic Palestinian families, giving them positions in the government. And, to be sure, there were some wealthy Palestinian businessmen for whom the prospect of a state headed by Yasir Arafat was extremely distasteful. But the street was not with them. If it hadn't been for the army and the Mukabarat—the secret police—the Hashemites would have long since been gone. Even some members of the royal family believed their days were numbered. In June the king's nephew, Sharif Nasser, suggested it was time for them to consider an orderly exile, leaving Jordan to the PLO. But Hussein stubbornly declined to even consider abdication. He was going to fight.

"The PLO factions were the darling of Arab intellectuals and the Arab street," recalled Hume Horan, the U.S. Embassy's chief political officer and one of the Foreign Service's most gifted Arabists. "King Hussein was extraordinarily isolated. Washington wondered how Hussein could last, with half of Jordan's population being Palestinian, a hostile Syria was to the north, an Iraqi tank division was encamped at the Jordanian oasis of Zarqa, and every Arab under twenty thought Hussein a stooge for Zionism and Western imperialism." Many observers thought Jordan seemed ready to slip from King Hussein's hands into Arafat's. Nevertheless, Horan and his boss, the newly arrived U.S. ambassador, L. Dean Brown, would do everything they could to keep Hussein in power.

Early in 1970 the previous American ambassador to Jordan, Harry Symmes, had made it clear to President Richard Nixon and his national security adviser, Henry Kissinger, that he believed the Hashemites' days were numbered. After a mob ransacked and burned the American cultural center in Amman, Symmes saw power slipping from King Hussein's hands: "I didn't think the King was effectively in charge of the situation—and even if he tried to be in charge that he would succeed." Symmes agreed with many of his fellow Arabists in the State Department who were arguing that Washington should prepare for the emergence of a Palestinian state in Jordan, and he therefore thought it prudent to have discreet contacts with various Palestinian figures. But then, in the spring of that year, King Hussein's secret police, the Mukabarat, bugged the ambassador's phone and intercepted conversations between him and a *fedayeen* official. King Hussein promptly declared Symmes persona non grata. This was fine with the Nixon White House. Kissinger regarded Symmes as a liberal—and infected with "clientalism," an "excessive" concern for the interests of a client state, as opposed to U.S. interests. In September Nixon, on Kissinger's recommendation, replaced Symmes with Dean Brown, a gruff ex-Marine who shared the national security adviser's conservative geopolitical worldview.

"By the summer of 1970," Kissinger later wrote in his memoirs, "the young, able and courageous King was in grave peril. The guerrillas, resentful of his efforts to promote a political settlement with Israel, increasingly challenged his army. . . . His collapse would radicalize the entire Middle East. Israel would not acquiesce in the establishment of guerrilla bases all along its Jordanian frontier. Another Middle East war would be extremely likely. Thus, Jordan, in my view, was a test of our capacity to control events in the region."

That summer, the mutual suspicion, distrust and fear that had long characterized relations between the Hashemite establishment and the Palestinian *fedayeen* grew especially intense. Lawlessness was commonplace. Both the *fedayeen* and the army committed atrocities. In June 1970, armed gunmen attacked King Hussein's convoy and he personally participated in a street battle. On September 1, he barely survived an assassination attempt by *fedayeen*. The CIA's station chief in Amman, Jack O'Connell, now rushed to the palace and bluntly told Hussein that the time had come to mount a crackdown on the PLO. Hussein knew the outcome of such a showdown would not be at all certain, but he was well aware that his Bedouin troops were eager to take on the *fedayeen*. During an inspection of an armored column, just weeks earlier, Hussein had spotted a brassiere flying atop a tank's radio antenna. Laughing, he asked the tank's commander, "Women aboard?" "No, sir," replied the officer. "It's we who are the women now." Hussein spent three hours that afternoon talking to these soldiers, trying to explain why they must patiently await the right moment to confront the *fedayeen.*

Hussein's regular army had some 60,000 troops, including 2,000 in the air force. But more than half of these men—and even many of the officers—were Palestinians. Hussein felt that he could count on the loyalty of only about 25,000 men. It was Bedouin officers, however, who manned the armored units, a fact which in the event would prove decisive. And he could also rely on the loyalty of those elite officers and troops of Circassian ancestry. Refugees themselves, most Circassians had fled their homeland in the Caucusus in the wake of a disastrous war with Russia in the 1860s. The Ottomans welcomed these often blond-haired, blue-eyed Muslims into the empire, and some 3,500 settled in the ancient ruins of Amman. After World War I, when the British placed King Abdullah on the throne, the Circassians aligned themselves with the Hashemites. When King Abdullah first arrived in Amman on March 2, 1921, he stayed in the home of Said al-Mufti, the emir of Amman's Circassians—and later one of his prime ministers. The Circassians grew rich from their ownership of large tracts of Amman's real estate;

by 1970, Jordan's Circassians numbered some 50,000—but they represented the cream of Jordanian society. Many of King Hussein's ranking officers, ambassadors and high government officials were Circassians. The Palestinians resented the favoritism shown the Circassians—who in turn regarded the downtrodden Palestinians as a threat to the status quo. About this time, the patriarch of a prominent Circassian family said of the Palestinians: "Savages! Mere savages who wanted to seize power."

Poised against King Hussein's Bedouin and Circassian troops was the Palestine Liberation Army, the PLO's regular force of some 10,000 men. Al-Fatah had an additional 15,000 men under arms, and Habash's PFLP had another 2,000 *fedayeen*. As civil war loomed, the PLO distributed guns to thousands more young men in the refugee camps. All told, the Palestinians had something on the order of 40,000 armed *fedayeen*. The PLA had 30 old Russian tanks, while King Hussein's Bedouin troops possessed 150 tanks. And then there was a wild card in the form of a division of 12,000 Iraqi troops stationed in northeastern Jordan. King Hussein had invited this Iraqi force into his kingdom just prior to the June 1967 War, and they had remained ever since. In an outright civil war, Hussein feared the Ba'athist regime in Baghdad might deploy these troops in support of the Palestinians.

Many analysts thought the Hashemite regime was outgunned both militarily and politically. If things had been allowed to take their natural course, the PLO and its majority Palestinian constituency would likely have prevailed over the Hashemite minority. On September 21, when the fighting was well under way, the British prime minister, Edward Heath, told his advisers that he doubted whether there were "any advantages to be derived from prolonging, possibly only for a short time, the increasingly precarious regime of King Hussein." It seemed to the prime minister that the "plucky little king's" days were numbered, and if so, the pragmatic thing to do was to prepare to deal with a transition to a Palestinian regime. Heath's foreign secretary, Sir Alec Douglas-Home, warned, "The Palestinian revolt strikes a very deep chord in Arab hearts. Any Western country, therefore, which intervenes to try to save Jordan will be involving itself in a deep quarrel in Arabia as a whole, the consequences and end of which none could foretell."

London's pragmatism, however, was not shared in Washington or in Jerusalem. Neither the Nixon Administration nor the Israelis could stomach the notion of a Palestinian state on the East Bank of the River Jordan. "It was pretty clear that if the King looked to be going under," recalled the American embassy's Hume Horan, "the Israelis would not allow a radical Iraqi-cum-Syrian-cum-Palestinian state to pop up on the East Bank. There was a lot of very sensitive traffic back and forth between us and the Israelis and the Jordanians as to who might do what if certain things happened." President Nixon called the Palestinians terrorists and privately urged Hussein to stand firm and confront the *fedayeen*. As Henry Kissinger noted on September 9, "The President's instincts are to crush the *Fedayeen* now."

On Wednesday, September 16, 1970, four days after Joy and all but fifty-seven of the plane hostages had been released, King Hussein dismissed his civilian government and appointed a martial-law cabinet. He was about to wage war on the majority of his own citizenry. That evening fifty tanks moved into positions above the main refugee camps of Amman. King Hussein told L. Dean Brown, the new American ambassador, that he was "betting all his chips." It was going to be an "all or nothing showdown." Brown addressed his staff: "We have just gotten word from the Palace that the army is going to move against the *fedayeen* early tomorrow morning." The CIA's O'Connell sat in the palace, plotting strategy and stiffening the king's spine for the fight ahead. Electricity and water supplies to the refugee camps were cut.

At dawn the next morning, the Arab Legion began their assault, lobbing artillery shells at guerrilla positions on Jebel Hussein and into the large camps of Wahdat and al-Husseini. The bombardment was indiscriminate, hitting residential quarters in the tightly packed camps. One young guerrilla wrote in his diary of his astonishment at the brutality of the attack: "Then something totally unexpected happened. The cannons of the tanks shelled the houses in a totally unnecessary way. Savagely, without even differentiating between homes and commando offices. It was really frightening. We were paralyzed, seeing the houses collapse in suddenly and seeing in the unexpected rubble many of the small private things of people. . . ."

King Hussein announced a twenty-four-hour curfew and ordered his men to shoot to kill any violators. They nevertheless encountered stiff resistance from *fedayeen* firing their AK-47s and grenade rocket-launchers from trenches and fortified positions all around Amman. Instead of sending in troops to engage in deadly house-to-house combat, Hussein ordered artillery shells fired at any house from which small-arms fire was detected. "It was very messy," recalled the embassy's Hume Horan. "The Jordanians didn't want to send their good infantry against the guerrillas in the slums of Amman. They felt the urban geography would negate the Army's edge in discipline and weaponry. So they led their assaults with armor, the infantry following close behind. Through field glasses you could see the tanks roll up toward some buildings. Lurch to a stop. Then the main battle guns would go, 'BOOM!' and part of the buildings would collapse. Out would swarm some Palestinians. The tanks would chase them, firing machine guns, with the infantry also in pursuit." The result was devastating carnage. The Royal Jordanian Air Force dropped phosphorus and napalm bombs on the refugee camps. The International Red Cross reported seeing scores of bodies bloating in the sun. Radio Damascus charged, "This is the work of Jordan's Nero, King Hussein." From his bunker in one of the refugee camps, Arafat vowed, "The fight goes on until the fascist military regime in Jordan is toppled."*

Over the next ten days, the *fedayeen* held their own in Amman and even turned down a cease-fire offer. They managed to knock out many Jordanian army vehicles with bazookas. Many were able to survive the Jordanian shelling by hunkering down in some 360 subterranean bunkers carved out beneath the refugee camps of Amman. Most of northern Jordan now was also under their control—which prompted speculation in Washington that the Syrians, with the backing of the Soviet Union, might intervene on behalf of the guerrillas. In anticipation of such a development, President Nixon told the *Chicago Sun-Times* that he was prepared to send U.S. troops "should Syria and Iraq enter the conflict and tip the military balance against the government forces loyal to King Hussein."

On Saturday, September 19, Syrian tank columns—hastily repainted in the colors of the Palestine Liberation Army—rolled across the border and began pounding Jordanian army units around Ramtha. By the next day more than 200 Syrian tanks were on the move. Later that day some 100 Syrian tanks engaged a Jordanian armored column that included just 30 tanks. In the ensuing battle, the Jordanians managed to knock out 30 Syrian tanks—but they lost 10 of their own. At this point, King Hussein was informed that they could not hold out much longer.

Hussein immediately called London and Washington. According to British cabinet minutes declassified more than thirty years later, Hussein sent a "series of messages . . . reflecting the extreme anxiety with which he

---

*The future dictator of Pakistan, Brigadier General Muhammad Zia-ul-Haq, was then stationed in Jordan as head of the Pakistani military training mission; oddly, Zia was given command of the Jordanian Army's 2nd Division.

now regarded the situation." He asked his benefactors to threaten "international action." Most astoundingly, he "also asked for an air strike by Israel against the Syrian troops." At 3:00 a.m. on September 21, a panicked King Hussein called U.S. Ambassador Brown and requested "immediate physical intervention, both air and land. . . ." An Arab monarch was asking Israel to bomb other Arabs.

The British quickly forwarded Hussein's appeal to Washington, and we now know that the Nixon Administration immediately conveyed the request to Israel's prime minister, Golda Meir, who was visiting New York at the time. Henry Kissinger summoned Israel's ambassador, Yitzhak Rabin, who confirmed that his country was more than willing to save the "plucky little King." Israel, he said, would launch air attacks or send in ground troops—whatever was necessary. Nixon was delighted. On September 22, the Israeli air force launched reconnaissance flights over northern Jordan, using U.S.-supplied Phantom jets to swoop low over the Syrian tank columns and sending a message that the next time they might be coming with bombs. The Israelis also moved two armored brigades to the River Jordan, signaling that they were ready to intervene. Nixon dispatched two more aircraft carriers, a helicopter carrier and twelve additional destroyers to the eastern Mediterranean. The American president had 20,000 combat troops poised to intervene from either bases in Turkey or the Sixth Fleet. Incredibly, Kissinger and Nixon even rattled their nuclear sabers, warning the Kremlin that if they didn't force their "client state" Syria to pull back, American forces would intervene. "We could not allow Hussein to be overthrown," Nixon later wrote in his memoirs, "by a Soviet-inspired insurrection. . . . It was like a ghastly game of dominoes, with a nuclear war waiting at the end." We now know from Egyptian foreign minister Mahmoud Riad's memoirs that, far from inciting the Syrian intervention, the Soviets asked Nasser to persuade the Syrians to pull back. Kissinger and Nixon, in fact, had misread Soviet intentions.

Syrian forces began to withdraw back across the border on September 22—not only because of diplomatic pressure from the Russians, but because their own defense minister, Hafez Assad, refused to provide air cover for the armored columns. (Assad was soon to overthrow the Syrian president who ordered the intervention.) Inexplicably, the Iraqi forces at Mafraq also withdrew, prompting the Palestinians to complain bitterly about the "Iraqi stab in the back."

King Hussein's Arab Legion exploited this opportune moment. They launched a successful counterattack against the *fedayeen* lines in the north, driving hundreds of guerrillas across the Syrian border. The king also redoubled his bombardment of the camps around Amman. Portions of the overcrowded Wahdat refugee camp became a charnel house. Over the next ten days, some 3,400 *fedayeen* and civilians were killed. (King Hussein later insisted that no more than 1,000 Palestinians were killed.) The Nixon White House knew many Palestinians were dying. The CIA's Richard Helms told Henry Kissinger, "You can't fire into those refugee camps without killing a lot of people." Some estimates of those killed on both sides range as high as 4,000, with thousands more wounded in the ten days between September 17 and September 26. The army showed no mercy to wounded *fedayeen*. "I had no idea the army would behave like this," said Dr. Sa'ad Ma'asher, a surgeon at one hospital. Soldiers raided his hospital one day and seized any wounded men they could find and carried them off in jeeps. "There were atrocities," admitted the American embassy's Horan. "One night Palestinians raided a military hospital and killed many wounded Jordanian soldiers. There were situations where groups of Palestinian rebels were not read their Geneva Convention rights and just vanished from the scene. But these were bad days. . . . It was a time when no quarter was asked by or given to some of these combatants." When it was all over, soldiers prevented reporters from taking photographs as bulldozers filled in mass graves in the Wahdat refugee camp. And yet, in the end, Horan believed, "The good guys won."

By the end of September, King Hussein's forces had indeed "won" the civil war—but at a terrible cost in terms of human lives and public opinion. Hussein's prime minister, Brigadier General Muhammed Daoud, announced his defection to Libya. Daoud, the highest-ranking Palestinian in Hussein's army, couldn't stomach what his monarch was doing. His sixteen-year-old daughter, ashamed of his association with the regime, had slapped his face. There were signs all around that Hussein had lost the trust of his own people. "I was indignant," he told *Le Monde* soon afterwards, "when I learned that my own chauffeur to whom I entrusted my children was a terrorist. He was arrested firing a mortar at my palace. I have also discovered that my cook had important guerrilla connections too." He was nevertheless determined to impose his will.

Before Hussein's Bedouin troops could expel the *fedayeen* altogether and take control of the refugee camps, the Hashemite regime came under enormous political pressure from Egypt's Nasser to halt the carnage. Radio Cairo was calling the assault on the camps "genocide." Nasser cabled Hussein that the "ghastly massacre" in Amman must end. Finally, on September 25, Arafat was smuggled out of Jordan on a flight to Cairo. The next day Hussein flew into Cairo for a tension-filled summit meeting with Nasser, Libya's leader Muammar Qaddafi, King Faisal and other Arab leaders—including Arafat. Both Arafat and Hussein wore sidearms, and sat glowering at each other. Nasser pressed the two men to reach a cease-fire, telling them, "There are men, women and children dying. We are in a race with death." After hours of bitter recriminations, the two parties finally did agree to a cease-fire. Under the terms of the Cairo Agreement, the *fedayeen* would leave the refugee camps in Amman and retreat to positions facing Israel along the River Jordan. As chairman of the PLO, Arafat pledged to persuade the PFLP to release the remaining fifty-seven hostages in Amman. In return, the Hashemite regime would recognize the PLO's right to wage guerrilla warfare against Israel: "Full support for the Palestine revolution is ensured to enable it to carry out its sacred duty, the liberation of its land." Hussein may have won the battle, but he had lost the public relations war. He had saved his throne, but he would remain for many years to come a pariah in the Arab world.

On the evening of September 28, 1970, Nasser suffered a massive heart attack. He died that evening. Just a few hours earlier, the remaining fifty-seven hostages in Amman had been released and in exchange the British freed Leila Khaled. Ironically, she arrived in Cairo just in time to attend Nasser's chaotic funeral. Some days later she was photographed laying a wreath at the gravesite. When asked by Michael Brunson, a British television reporter, how she felt about Nasser's death, she replied curtly, "I'm very sad."

"Do you feel in any way responsible," pressed Brunson, "for all that has happened—that perhaps you started in train the whole great crisis throughout the Middle East?"

"Not at all," replied Khaled.

Within weeks, the Cairo Agreement began to unravel. Intermittent clashes between the battered *fedayeen* and Hussein's army continued for months. That autumn Hussein appointed Wasfi al-Tal as his new prime minister. A half-Kurdish businessman from a well-known Irbid family, al-Tal was known to be a staunch opponent of the *fedayeen,* and he took a hard line, urging Hussein to liquidate the PLO once and for all. By the spring of 1971 the PLO was once again publicly demanding Hussein's removal, calling his regime a "puppet separatist authority." In response, Hussein told al-Tal to "deal conclusively and without hesitation with the plotters who want to establish a separate Palestinian state and destroy the unity of the Jordanian and Palestinian people."

On July 13, 1971, Jordanian army troops reopened their offensive against the *fedayeen,* attacking their last remaining large outpost in the Ajlun area of northwestern Jordan. Prime Minister al-Tal announced that the Cairo accords were a dead letter. After ninety-six hours of artillery and napalm strikes, the *fedayeen*'s defenses collapsed. At least 1,000 *fedayeen* were killed or wounded, and some 2,300 were arrested. The PLO later claimed that Jordanian troops tortured al-Fatah's charismatic one-eyed commander Abu Ali Iyad. Tortured or not, his body was tied to a tank and dragged through the streets of Palestinian villages.

Hussein's secret police picked up and detained 20,000 Palestinians, many of whom were eventually expelled across the Syrian border. Arafat and the PLO's leadership moved to refugee camps like Sabra and Shatila in West Beirut. This too had unforeseen consequences. Within a few years, the PLO's burgeoning presence in Lebanon—another "state within a state"—would become a major factor in igniting the Lebanese civil war in 1975. And this in turn led to the Israeli invasions of Lebanon in 1978 and 1982—when Arafat and the PLO were pushed out of Lebanon and forced into exile in Tunis. (At least 130,000 Lebanese and Palestinians died in the years 1975–1990, when the civil war finally sputtered out.) The Black September hijackings had brought the Palestinian cause to the attention of the world community in 1970. But the ensuing Black September Jordanian-Palestinian civil war proved to be an unmitigated disaster for the Palestinians. They had now been serially defeated: in the 1936 Arab revolt, the 1948 Nakba, the June 1967 War and now the Jordanian civil war of 1970–71.

King Hussein never acknowledged the ruthlessness of his bombardment of the refugee camps. He told the British ambassador that what he had done was "a cancer operation that had to be performed to save Jordan's life." Even today, discussion of Black September is taboo in Jordanian society. It is not spoken of, and Jordanian schoolchildren don't read about it in their textbooks. To this day, we really don't know how many people died in the Jordanian civil war.

Most people outside the Middle East didn't care. They were told that the bad guys had lost. This became the message of a public relations campaign launched by King Hussein's close friend John Fistere (1908–1992). A former OSS officer, Fistere worked for *Fortune* magazine until 1958, when he quit and formed a public relations agency in Beirut. His major client was Hussein—and his real employer was the CIA. In the wake of Black September, Fistere worked hard to burnish Hussein's reputation. Inside Jordan itself, this was a hard sell for many years. But in the Western media, King Hussein burnished his reputation as the "plucky little King."

After the PLO was finally expelled from Jordan, an American diplomat in Amman reportedly cabled Washington, "The PLO is dead, wiped out, and finished as an effective fighting force. But I have to remind Washington that this part of the world has been the scene of at least one resurrection."

The Nixon Administration, however, had no doubts. Nixon and Kissinger were ecstatic about the outcome. Nasser was dead, Arafat was on the run and the Palestinian resistance seemed to be decisively defeated. They now also saw Israel—a country of a few million people surrounded by embittered, hostile neighbors—as a valuable strategic asset in the Cold War. "The President will never forget Israel's role in preventing the deterioration in Jordan and in blocking the attempt to overturn the regime there," Kissinger told Israel's ambassador in Washington, Yitzhak Rabin. "He said that the United States is fortunate in having an ally like Israel in the Middle East." Nixon rewarded the Israelis with a stunning increase in military aid, from $149 million in 1968–70 to $1.15 billion in 1971–73.

Within weeks a number of Lockheed C-141s, each carrying thirty tons of military supplies, landed at Dawson's Field beside the blackened debris of the three commercial airliners. The Americans were making sure that King Hussein would always have enough arms to keep the Hashemites in power. And, of course, the king continued to receive his CIA stipend.*

* * *

---

*Later, he used part of it to hire a private security company, owned by the son of ex-president Gerald Ford, to protect his children at their American boarding school. See Nigel Ashton, *King Hussein of Jordan: A Political Life.* New Haven, CT: Yale University Press (2008), p. 190.

The Palestinian uprising of 1970 had nearly turned the Hashemite kingdom into a Palestinian-controlled state. From the point of view of most Palestinians, external forces had denied them this victory. Palestinian leaders from Yasir Arafat to George Habash felt betrayed by their Arab brothers. Syria's defense minister and soon-to-become dictator, Hafez Assad, had refused the air support for the Syrian tanks that might have defeated King Hussein's armor. The Iraqi division stationed in Jordan had stood by passively while the *fedayeen* were routed. But ultimately, it had been the threat of Israeli and American intervention that had sealed the PLO's defeat in Jordan. That defeat created an atmosphere of desperation in Palestinian circles. To my horror and dismay, some Palestinians now embraced a politics of blood vengeance. Their first victim was King Hussein's prime minister, Wasfi al-Tal, the man who had carried out the final July 1971 assault. That autumn, on November 28, al-Tal was walking into Cairo's Sheraton Hotel, accompanied by Egyptian bodyguards, when four young Palestinians attacked him. One of them, Izzat Ahmad Rabah, stepped forward and fired several shots. Al-Tal reached for his own gun, but he hadn't the strength left to fire. As bystanders and al-Tal's wife watched in horror, one of the assassins, Monsa Khalifa, crouched by the dying prime minister and licked some of his blood off the floor. As they were arrested, the men shouted, "We are Black September. . . . We have taken our revenge on a traitor."*

Wadi Haddad had a falling-out with George Habash after the Black September hijackings. In terms of public awareness of the Palestinian cause, many in the PFLP believed the hijacking spree had ultimately backfired. But Haddad persisted and formed his own breakaway faction, the PFLP–External Operations. And though Habash may have become disillusioned with hijackings, the PFLP found other deadly means to hit the "Zionist entity." On May 30, 1972, three members of the nascent Japanese Red Army gunned down twenty-six people, mostly Puerto Rican tourists, inside Israel's international airport at Lod. According to Christopher Dobson, a British reporter for the *Sunday Telegraph*, Habash had chaired a meeting in Tripoli,

---

*The four assassins were never brought to trial, and four months later President Anwar Sadat quietly let them board a flight to Damascus. A fifth accomplice, a female university student, had been standing by, ready to toss a grenade if the pistol shots had not felled Wasfi al-Tal. She disappeared.

Lebanon, in which the Red Army agreed to carry out terror attacks on Israeli targets on behalf of the PFLP. But other sources make it clear that Wadi Haddad planned this particular operation. In September 1972, two years after the Jordanian civil war, Palestinian commandos from a new clandestine group calling itself the Black September Organization took the Israeli Olympics team hostage in Munich—and then killed them all in the midst of a gun battle with German police. The Black September Organization was composed of radicalized Fatah and PFLP recruits determined to carry out revenge attacks on both the Israelis and King Hussein's regime. Though to some degree autonomous, it was controlled by Fatah.

In the mid-to-late 1970s, both Fatah and the PFLP began to move away from the tactic of striking foreign targets. Arafat slowly came to embrace diplomacy and a two-state solution. But Habash and the mainstream PFLP led a "rejectionist front" within the PLO, insisting that the only viable and just solution was one state: a secular democratic state for Jews and Arabs in all of historical Palestine. This remains the PFLP's position today.

Wadi Haddad and other extremists continued for a time to launch spectacular foreign operations. In June 1976, Haddad engineered the hijacking of an Air France Airbus to Entebbe, Uganda—and a week later the Israelis launched their own commando raid on Entebbe, mistakenly shooting three of the remaining 105 hostages, but killing all six of the hijackers, along with forty-five Ugandan soldiers. Another hostage, Dora Bloch, aged seventy-three, had been removed to a hospital, where she was shot dead by Ugandan troops. The rescue operation's commander, Lieutenant Colonel Yonatan Netanyahu, was killed by a Ugandan army sniper. (Netanyahu was the brother of Israel's future prime minister, Binyamin Netanyahu.) After this disastrous episode, Wadi Haddad was formally expelled from the PFLP. He died of leukemia in East Germany two years later.

Throughout the 1970s, the Israelis retaliated against each and every Palestinian attack. It was an old cycle, but a much more bloody one than in the decades before the Jordanian civil war. In Beirut on July 8, 1972, Mossad planted a bomb in the car of the PFLP's chief spokesman, Ghassan Kanafani. When Kanafani turned on the ignition, the car exploded, killing him and his twenty-one-year-old niece. Seventeen days later, a small package was delivered in the mail to Kanafani's deputy, Bassam Abu-Sharif, the PFLP spokesman at Dawson's Field during the hijackings. Abu-Sharif opened the package, and seeing that it was a biography of Che Guevara, he cracked the binding to inspect the book—which promptly exploded. The book bomb nearly killed him. He lost two fingers and a thumb on his right hand, two fingers from his left hand, part of his ear, and pieces of his thigh and stomach. When he finally left the hospital two months later, he'd lost nearly ninety-five pounds. "By the end of my stay in hospital I did not feel the desire for revenge on my attackers. I felt something strangely like pity for them. . . . I would still fight, with all I had, for a Palestinian state. But now, having suffered it at first hand, I knew violence would never work."

In the spring of 2007 I met Bassam Abu-Sharif in his Amman home. When Joy had seen him at Dawson's Field conducting press interviews with a bullhorn in hand, he had been a dashing, handsome young man. Now, he had weathered with age—and the marks of his 1972 wounds. Abu-Sharif left the PFLP decades ago, and today he favors a two-state solution.

His neighbor and former comrade, Leila Khaled, disagrees. Khaled married a doctor in 1982 and is now a middle-class housewife with two grown sons. But she is still a member of the PFLP and sits on its executive committee as well as on the Palestine National Council. Sometime in the early 1970s the Israelis planted a bomb under her bed in her Beirut apartment. Leila spotted it when she looked for her slippers beneath the bed. It would have exploded if she had sat on the bed. Mossad agents tried to assassinate her again on Christmas Day 1976. Upon entering her residence that day, Leila stumbled across the bodies of her younger sister and her sister's fiancé. "I found their bodies," Khaled told the British journalist Eileen MacDonald. "They had been shot." The Israeli assassins had mistaken her for Leila.

Khaled is unrepentant about what she did in 1969–70, and she remains committed to the creation of a single binational, secular democratic state in the whole of Palestine. When asked recently by an American reporter what kind of resistance tactics she favors today, Khaled answered, "All kinds of resistance, resistance means everything. Beginning with the word 'no' and ending with holding arms. And in between there are many ways, [including] a political struggle, a popular struggle. They want us to accept them as they are: racist, discriminating, an apartheid regime in Israel. This is what we don't want. We cannot coexist with such people. . . . But the key or the solution is the return of the Palestinians—without that this conflict will continue." And she means that the conflict will continue, if necessary, beyond her lifetime: "If I am unable to return and live in freedom in Palestine, my children will return."

After 9/11, she told reporters that she condemned those hijackers for taking the lives of innocents. She did not think her hijackings helped in any way to inspire the 9/11 suicide hijackings. "That was an act of terror and did not serve a humanitarian cause," she says. "What we did was a means of struggle. We said why we were doing the operation. Those who killed themselves and others in New York had no cause. . . . We do not glorify death, we are the victims of those who want to prevent us from living. We do not ask for miracles. We are not fighting for death; we are struggling for our dignity. We want to live."

Black September is partly a story about another road not taken. I find myself asking what might have happened if the Hashemites had lost and a Palestinian state had emerged from the Jordanian civil war. We now know that the Israeli political and military establishment was itself divided on whether saving King Hussein's throne was good for Israel. Golda Meir, Yigal Allon, Abba Eban and Yitzhak Rabin surmised that since Hussein was the most moderate of the Arab leaders, he might someday conclude a separate peace deal with Israel. "The opposing opinion," wrote Mordechai Gur, the Israeli general in charge of the Syrian-Lebanese front in 1970, "supported the transformation of Jordan into a Palestinian state. . . . They suggested allowing the guerrillas to achieve their aims and to take control over all of Jordan. In this they saw the ideal solution to the issue of the Palestinians." Ezer Weizmann, Moshe Dayan, and Shimon Peres made this argument—and so too did General Ariel Sharon. But the views of Prime Minister Meir and her allies prevailed.

This was almost certainly a serious missed opportunity. In retrospect, Sharon was probably right and Meir wrong. A Palestinian state in place of Hashemite Jordan might well have been in Israel's long-term interest. Numerous mainstream Israeli politicians had long spoken of the "Jordanian solution" as the answer for Palestinian self-determination. But when confronted with the best opportunity to create a Palestinian state on the East Bank, the Israeli leadership chose to support the status quo. This has had tragic consequences. The Israeli historian Avi Shlaim concludes, "Right-wing Israelis not only expected but wanted actively to support the PLO in its drive to transform the Hashemite Kingdom of Jordan into the Republic of Palestine. . . . Hussein's victory also persuaded some, though by no means all, right-wing Israelis that they could not solve the Palestinian problem at Jordan's expense."

Kissinger claims that he knew nothing of this internal Israeli debate. But in the midst of the crisis, on September 20, 1970, he told his aides, "I'm not really sure the Israelis would mind it if Hussein should topple. They would have no more West Bank problem." And just a few days later he read an official memorandum of a conversation in which Israel's foreign minister, Abba Eban, speculated that Israel might indeed be better off without the Hashemite regime:

> Foreign Minister Eban told [U.S.] Ambassador [Charles] Yost at the UN on September 23 that while Israel, on balance, favored Husayn as of this time, "the world would not come to an end if he departed the scene." Eban said the Palestinians would become more responsible when saddled with the day-to-day burdens of government, and the long-term trend in Jordan was toward greater recognition of the fact that Jordan was 70 percent Palestinian. Yost added that Eban seemed to imply that, sooner or later, Israel has to find an accommodation with the Palestinians and that it might in the long run be easier if they dominated the state of Jordan.

Kissinger read and initialed this memorandum—but evidently he dismissed Eban's views and later claimed to have forgotten about the memo. Years later he insisted to the British scholar Nigel Ashton that "any move to undermine Hussein would have provoked a crisis in their [the Israelis'] relations with Washington." As usual, America's Cold War imperatives—and so blind support for a pro-American, anti-Communist, anti-Nasserite monarch—made more sense to Kissinger than actually addressing the root cause of the region's unrest.

The real victors were those hard-line Likudite Israelis who were determined to colonize and take over the West Bank. The Palestinian defeat in Jordan gave them many more decades to create new facts on the ground in the form of Israeli settlements in the occupied territories. If a Palestinian state had emerged in September 1970, the Israelis and the Palestinians would have been compelled to deal with each other on a pragmatic basis. Some may object that thirty years later Yasir Arafat proved himself incapable of making the transition from outlawed guerrilla fighter to a supple politician. But a lot happened in those thirty years. A younger Arafat—and one surrounded by his most astute aides—might well have made the same transition that a younger Menachem Begin made from terrorist to politician. Recently declassified documents from the CIA show that Arafat was telling the Agency in the early 1970s that the creation of a Palestinian state in Jordan was probably the most he could achieve for his people. The CIA's ranking Arabist, Robert C. Ames—our former next-door neighbor in Dhahran—held numerous secret conversations with Arafat's security chief, Ali Hassan Salameh, who, incidentally, led the Black September Organization and planned the 1972 Munich massacre. Salameh came from a wealthy Palestinian background and was known in Beirut as the "Red Prince." In one such meeting, on July 9–10, 1973, Salameh told Ames—as Ames subsequently reported to his boss, Richard Helms—that "A basic change in Fatah ideology has finally been accepted by the Fatah leadership. Israel is here to stay and to have as one's basic tenet the establishment of a democratic state of Jews, Muslims and Christians in what is now Israel, is just not realistic. But the Palestinians must have a home and that home will be Jordan. . . . Jordan, therefore, will be the prime target of the *fedayeen,* with acts of terrorism against Israel maintained to sustain the movement's credibility. . . . Arafat wants a real state or nothing."

But neither the Israeli government nor the Nixon Administration wanted a Palestinian state in place of Jordan. In the 1970s and '80s Arafat's PLO was dealt one defeat after another—and the most pragmatic of his aides were assassinated, either by the Israelis or by hired killers like Abu Nidal. On January 22, 1979, Salameh himself was assassinated by Israeli commandos in Beirut. In the early morning hours of April 10, 1983, the future prime minister of Israel, Ehud Barak, then an Israeli commando, gunned down Arafat's chief spokesman, the poet Kamal Nasser, in his West Beirut apartment. Two other leading PLO officials were assassinated during the same operation, code-named "Spring of Youth." The Israelis also assassinated Abu Jihad in Tunis in 1988, and in 1991 the Abu Nidal group (supported by Iraq's Saddam Hussein) murdered Abu Iyyad. Another leading PLO intellectual, Dr. Issam Sartawi, was assassinated in 1983, probably by the Abu Nidal group. All of these men had in one way or another encouraged Arafat to abandon "armed struggle"—a position which the PLO finally adopted in 1988. And all of them would have favored a Palestinian state in Jordan.

In 1972, King Hussein offered Israel another version of the "Jordanian solution." He proposed to create a "United Arab Kingdom" composed of a Palestinian state/region in the West Bank and a Hashemite state/region on the East Bank. Each region would have autonomy within a federal structure, with its own regional parliament and an elected "governor." East Jerusalem would become the "capital" of the Palestinian region. West and East Bank would be united under Hussein's monarchy. Israeli foreign minister Abba Eban dismissed Hussein's idea as "fanciful." Once again, the Israelis could have had a good shot at a two-state solution—but presumably the idea of returning the occupied territories and East Jerusalem to any Arab control was unthinkable. Yasir Arafat was relieved. He didn't want to share power with Hussein. He later told a biographer that if Israel had accepted Hussein's plan, "the PLO would have been finished."

In retrospect, it seems the best chance for a two-state solution evaporated when the Hashemites, supported by the Israelis and Americans, defeated the Palestinian revolution in Jordan in 1970–71. But clearly, the fact that a Palestinian state did not emerge from the civil war does not preclude it as a theoretically possible outcome. Such a scenario is what historians call a "counter-factual." A good counter-factual narrative compels us to imagine what might have been—and so provides us with a deeper understanding of what did happen. And just about anything would have been better than what did happen after Black September.

Here is yet another counter-factual: The PFLP spokesman Bassam Abu-Sharif reports in his 1995 memoir, *Best of Enemies,* that Wadi Haddad recruited a young man who went by the name of Abu Harb (Father of War) to take flight training. This was not for hijacking purposes. Haddad had procured a small twin-engine plane that he planned to stuff with explosives. When Abu Harb had completed his training, Haddad would have had him take off from the Beka'a Valley in Lebanon and fly south at a very low altitude to evade Israeli radar. He thought such a plane could probably make it all the way to Tel Aviv, giving the Israelis only a few minutes to detect the plane and scramble their fighter aircraft. Abu Harb's ultimate mission was to pilot his flying bomb into Tel Aviv's tallest building, the Shalom Tower. Haddad thought the small plane might even bring down the tower. However, Abu-Sharif writes, on his very last practice run Abu Harb crashed the plane. He survived but was severely injured. After this, Haddad gave up and went back to the "conventional" business of hijacking. But for an accident, Israel might have had its own 9/11 four decades ago.

Beirut confronted me with a personal quandary. All my life I had been taught that the Palestinians had genuine grievances. And yet, I could never have done what the American Nicaraguan hijacker Patrick Arguello did on September 6. I could never have brandished a gun. I believed in nonviolence. In Beirut, surrounded by people with guns, I was constantly trying to explain why I sympathized with their cause but not their tactics.

In those years even the most highly educated Palestinians supported the notion of armed struggle. Soon after the September hijackings I walked into the Fifth of June Society, a nonprofit organization in Beirut dedicated to educating Westerners about the Palestinian cause. Soraya "Tutu" Antonius, the daughter of George and Katy Antonius, was the society's director. Tutu was as feisty and sharp-tongued as her late mother. The daughter of the author of *The Arab Awakening* was a privileged intellectual—later she became a novelist. But in the early 1970s she sounded like Leila Khaled. "I think things will get worse," Antonius said. "The struggle has to be resolved by violence because in twenty-five formative years of the so-called state of Israel nonviolence has only bred violence. Until it started, nobody could have accused the Palestinians of having even a stick in their hands. Now they know that resistance has to be fought for. I have never heard of a country being given its independence without a struggle." These sentiments were spoken thirty-five years ago. The conflict has only gotten worse.

I've always thought that nonviolent resistance was both a moral and an effective strategy. I argued with my friends in Beirut that if Arafat and his *fedayeen* had laid down their guns in 1970 and marched on Amman, the Hashemite regime would have collapsed. I was a child of the sixties—the decade in which nonviolent resistance against Jim Crow segregation laws had ushered in a revolution in civil rights. I asked why the same tactics here in Beirut, Cairo and Amman could not achieve self-determination for the Palestinians. No one really listened. No one thought Yasir Arafat was Mahatma Gandhi.

One evening in the winter of 1970–71, I was sitting in my dorm room in Beirut trying to explain these ideas to an Iranian theology student, Assurbanipal Babilla. Banipal was an Assyrian Christian, highly educated and a wonderfully provocative raconteur. On this occasion Banipal was baiting me, challenging my sincerity, and so I drew my draft card from my wallet— this must have been a second card, because I had turned in one draft card at a rally the previous spring. Brandishing it before Banipal, I lit a match to it. When it had burned to one edge I threw what was left, and the ashes, into a beautiful hand-carved teak box I had bought in Kashmir. It remains there to this day. Burning the card was a bit of theatre, but it had no consequences. On December 1, 1969, the U.S. Selective Service System had held a tele-vised lottery to determine who was to be drafted to serve in the military. The lottery randomly assigned the birth dates of draft-age males a number corresponding to the day of the year (1–366—including Leap Year Day). I remember watching the event on television; I was relieved to hear my birth date assigned the draft number of 161, just above the cusp of those being drafted with a lower number. As far as the Selective Service System was con-cerned, I had both a conscientious objector (CO) status and a student defer-ment—and with a lottery number of 161 I was unlikely to be called even for CO service.

That autumn, just weeks after Joy's release, I participated in a massive demonstration in the streets of Beirut, protesting King Hussein's atrocities in Amman. We were also protesting against U.S. Secretary of State Wil-liam Rogers and his "Rogers Peace Plan" for the Middle East. My Pales-tinian friends told me that the Rogers Plan was hopelessly one-sided and pro-Israeli. That was simplistic. The plan was really a reformulation of the 1967 U.N. Resolution 242. It called for Israel to withdraw from the territo-ries it had occupied in 1967, and in exchange Egypt and Jordan would sign peace treaties with Israel and recognize its right to exist as a sovereign nation. Jerusalem would be shared as an open city, perhaps under some interna-tional façade. The Palestinian refugees would be given compensation, and presumably resettled outside of Israel. This last point, of course, was objec-tionable to the PLO, which insisted on the right of return. My Palestinian friends argued that the Rogers Plan was a cynical attempt to lure Egypt and Jordan into betraying the Palestinian cause. It seems even clearer now that the Rogers Plan was wholly reasonable, at least as a first step. If all the parties had accepted it, the Palestinians would have been a lot better off than they are today. In June 1970, to everyone's astonishment, Nasser embraced the Rogers Plan unconditionally. Not so the Israelis. They rejected it out of hand

and launched a vigorous lobbying campaign against it in the United States. A peace treaty and formal recognition, they claimed, did not meet Israel's security needs.

Despite all this, I marched in solidarity with the Palestinians through the streets of Beirut, protesting the fact that the Rogers Plan had no provision for Palestinian refugees to return to their homes. They had hijacked my girlfriend and held her hostage for three days and four nights in the Jordanian desert, but I still thought of them as the victims in this long conflict. I was still very much a partisan.

I decided not to attend one demonstration on the Corniche, in front of the American embassy, where a group of American and Palestinian students burned the American flag. I avoided the embassy that day out of sentimental attachment to what had once been my home. We had lived in a third-floor apartment of the embassy building in 1961–62, when I was just ten years old, and I had fond memories of running down its long hallways and cavorting with the embassy Marines. I used to hang out in their dorm rooms, watching them polish their brass buckles and shine their black patent leather shoes. And yes, I'd watch them march out to the flagpole in their dress uni-

My Beirut home in 1962, the American embassy was destroyed
by a truck bomb on April 18, 1983

forms as they lowered the flag each evening and carefully folded it into a three-cornered bundle of red, white and blue. So perhaps this comforting childhood memory made me avoid the embassy that day in the autumn of 1970.

Some thirteen years later, in the midst of the Lebanese civil war brought on in large part by the PLO's expulsion from Jordan, a Chevrolet van packed with explosives drove slowly down the seaside Corniche, and then turned sharply into the embassy's semicircled driveway and crashed into the front door. A moment later the suicide bomber at the wheel triggered a massive explosion, and the central portion of the seven-storied embassy crumbled to its foundation, killing seventeen Americans and forty-six Lebanese employees. Among those killed that day were every member of the CIA station, including the Agency's director of Near East operations, Robert C. Ames, who had been our next-door neighbor two decades earlier when he was stationed in Saudi Arabia. My childhood home in Beirut was gone.

Book III

Jews, Israelis and the Shoah

Hitler is greeted by the citizens of Graz, Austria, April 1938

8

The Night of Broken Glass

Susan Goldmark, Kathmandu, Nepal, 1973

Every morning, I had to greet everyone with a "Heil Hitler."

Helma Blühweis, aged eighteen

After Black September, Joy Riggs and I drifted apart. Due to the hijacking—and then her precipitous evacuation from Amman to Cyprus, London and back to Colorado—I didn't see her again until the summer of 1971. We continued to correspond, but the separation took its toll. Looking back, I was too young, too innocent. Somehow I could not transform my high school romance into a mature adult relationship. In my mind, Joy would forever remain that first, innocent love.

I had planned to spend the summer of 1971 with Joy in Colorado, but my visit was cut short when my grandfather fell seriously ill. My parents asked me to help manage his transition to a nursing home in Eugene, Oregon. He was dying from both a weak heart and cancer. I spent a depressing summer watching him fade away. Afterwards, I resumed my studies at Carleton College in Minnesota. And there, in the spring of 1972, I met another woman.

When Susan and I were first introduced by my sister Nancy in a college cafeteria, her ancestral heritage didn't even register with me. She was working that night in the cafeteria, waiting on tables, so she was adorned in a white cook's coat, splattered with spaghetti sauce. She was stunning. And the red sauce made her seem adorable.

Susan was breathtakingly beautiful. And yet she seemed oblivious to her own special beauty—or perhaps she didn't care. She was a quietly serious nineteen-year-old woman. She had long dark brunette hair that formed a perfect widow's peak on her forehead. Her Slavic olive-toned skin contrasted sharply with knowing blue eyes. She moved with the long-legged grace of a ballerina—which she had been for some years as a child, dancing in George Balanchine's production of *The Nutcracker*. She played the piano every day when I met her, and, though I preferred rock music, she insisted on taking me to the college music rooms, where I put on a headset and dutifully listened to Beethoven and Bach and Mozart. She was sharp-tongued and sharp-witted, and her papers for Professor Alfred Soman's class on intellectual history—one of the toughest courses on campus—earned A's, while I could muster only a gentleman's B.

That she was Jewish was inconsequential to me, or so I thought.

We were both active that spring in the 1972 presidential campaign of Senator George McGovern. One day in San Francisco, after many hours canvassing door to door, a group of us is watching the evening news on television. A news flash announced that a squad of terrorists from the Japanese Red Army had just gunned down twenty-six people, mostly Puerto Rican tourists, inside Israel's international airport at Lod. The television broadcaster speculated about whether Black September—the shadowy terrorist group formed in the wake of the 1970 Jordanian civil war—might have coordinated the Lod attack with the Popular Front for the Liberation of Palestine (PFLP). I thought I knew better. I'd only left Beirut a year earlier, and I knew this new group was not a part of the PFLP. Naïvely, I thought the PFLP would have had nothing to do with such an act of mass murder. I had picked up some souvenirs in Beirut, including a PFLP button, and that day I happened to have it pinned on the underside of my lapel. Susan was sitting there—and, Lord help me, I flashed the button at her.

She was impressed—negatively. I remember taking the button off and passing it around the group, using it to talk about my experiences the previous year in Beirut. I was disheartened that the Palestinian cause was now becoming so closely linked in the minds of most Americans to bloody terrorism. And yet I also knew that many Americans were unaware of the history behind the headlines in the Middle East, and most simply didn't care. I was resentful and angry that I couldn't engage people, even my fellow students, on the issue. So, yes, I was wearing a PFLP button that day as a deliberate provocation. At the same time, my passion for the plight of the Palestinians was already tiring. My year in Beirut had underscored for me how difficult, how intractable, the conflict was. Two peoples, one land. I was not going to spend a lifetime on a hopeless cause. And yet, I could not abandon it altogether.

When I next saw Susan the following autumn, I somehow managed to get past the PFLP button incident. She later told me she thought I had been an idiot. Quite so. Still, she allowed me to hang around, courting her. I now think her Jewish background gave us something in common. As a Jew living in America, she was thoroughly American in all the little ways that perhaps I was not. But she was not like other Americans. There were little hints to suggest she was not even like other Jewish Americans. She had a certain edge, a brittle intelligence. She was watchful, and never, ever complacent. At first, I didn't understand the full import of this body armor. I just knew that she was somehow different and that she could tolerate this expatriate who often felt like a foreigner in his own country.

Historically, Jews in the Diaspora had always been the "other." They were the exceptions, the tiny minority in a sea of gentiles. They were distinct for what they were not. But early in the last century the Jewish Diaspora was confronted by what the Berkeley historian Yuri Slezkine characterizes as three choices: European Jews could become Zionists intent on creating a new nationality by emigrating to Palestine, or they could throw their lot in with the Bolshevik Revolution in Russia—or they could emigrate to America, a country where Jews would be just one more ethnic or religious group among a sea of "others," all considered to be Americans. The latter option has quite clearly proven to be the most successful. Going to America was quintessentially "good for the Jews." It has been a phenomenal success story. But why? As Slezkine explains it:

> The Modern Age is the Jewish Age, and the twentieth century, in particular, is the Jewish Century. Modernization is about everyone becoming urban, mobile, literate, articulate, intellectually intricate, physically fastidious, and occupationally flexible. It is about learning how to cultivate people and symbols, not fields or herds. It is about pursuing wealth for the sake of learning, learning for the sake of wealth, and both wealth and learning for their own sake. It is about transforming peasants and princes into merchants and priests, replacing inherited privilege with acquired prestige, and dismantling social estates for the benefit of individuals, nuclear families, and book-reading tribes (nations). Modernization, in other words, is about everyone becoming Jewish.

Susan was very much a beneficiary of this Jewish Age in America. She was thoroughly modern. But her family was nevertheless new enough to America to make me feel that we were both strangers in this country. We both belonged here, but she and I were different from the norm. I could talk with her about what it was like growing up among the Arabs. She listened—and sometimes she argued with me. She had never been to Israel or anywhere else in the Middle East, but she was never dismissive of my experience.

I graduated from Carleton in 1973, and that summer Susan went on a Carleton-sponsored junior-year-abroad program to live in Kathmandu, Nepal. My sister Nancy attended the same program that year. Nancy, of course, had traveled all over India and Nepal. But this was Susan's first experience in a developing country. At the same time, I had won an extraordinarily generous travel grant of $7,500—a lot of money for a twenty-one-year-old—from the Thomas J. Watson Foundation. I was supposed to use the money for a photojournalism project in North Yemen. I arrived in Sana'a, Yemen's ancient capital, in July 1973. I bought a motorcycle, rode all over the country and snapped thousands of photographs with a professional-looking Nikon. Having learned that it was easier to sell photographs to Western publications if they were accompanied by some text, I started to write magazine essays. Sana'a was a wonderfully exotic place—but my heart was in Kathmandu.

I couldn't tolerate the separation from Susan. So, after barely three months on this Yemeni adventure, I caught a plane for Nepal. I left Yemen just a few days prior to the outbreak of yet another war in the Middle East on October 6, 1973. (This time it was clearly a war initiated by Egypt in a surprise assault across the Suez Canal.) I heard about it just as I landed in Kathmandu. But not even a war would tear me away from Susan. We lived together that winter of 1973–74 in Kirtipur, a village near the university, on the outskirts of Kathmandu. It was a magical time. A couple of weeks after my arrival, we had dinner with Boris Lissanevitch, a former Russian ballet star who had fled the Bolshevik Revolution and eventually ended up in Kathmandu in the 1950s. He ran what was then the best hotel in town, the Royal Hotel, and his bar and restaurant, the Yak & Yeti, was the most expensive place to eat in Kathmandu. His specialty was borscht—what else! I remember that evening sitting around a fireplace as tall as myself, sipping a Bloody Mary and listening to Boris tell Susan and some of her fellow students stories about his itinerant life. Later, I noted in a diary, "Susan wore a maroon colored Tibetan dress down to the floor and a matching dark red blouse that came up high on her neck. The dress was wrapped tightly and in front was draped a multi-colored apron, worn usually only by married Tibetan women. Her hair was loose and very dark and the whole effect was striking. She was too beautiful, too striking in front of everyone else. I could feel almost everyone watching her, resenting her advantage."

I was in love. But then gradually, as Susan ever so cautiously allowed me inside her world, I learned that this strong-willed and capable young woman also harbored inchoate, but decidedly dark, fears about life. She was not only Jewish; she was also the only child of two Holocaust survivors from Austria. And, as I would learn over the coming years, Susan's parents had inevitably saddled her with weighty psychological baggage.

As she was growing up, her mother, Helma, cryptically told her that due to the war she had never gone to high school in her native Austria, let alone college. Likewise, her father, Willy, had never gone to university. So naturally, they felt Susan absolutely had to excel in school. She was reminded every day that material things in life could always be taken away—but that a good education could travel anywhere. As a child, she remembers with consternation her mother repeatedly throwing out old toys or mementos on the grounds that it wasn't wise to have too many possessions. Strangely, Helma always kept a packed suitcase in an otherwise empty hallway closet. (I later saw it!) She was always prepared to flee. Susan remembers that for a time her mother would drag her to Catholic Mass and sit in the back pews—as if contemplating that life might be safer if she raised her child as a Christian in a Christian world. As I was later to learn, none of this behavior was uncommon among Holocaust survivors.

Helma eventually got a job as a legal secretary. She was quick to learn shorthand. Willy joined his brother as a partner in his father's small business, a factory that did the dyeing for manufacturers of women's hosiery. His parents—the Goldmarks—had arrived in America on one of the last boats out of Portugal before the war broke out. Willy was a tall, athletic man who spent his entire life in manual labor, working in a factory and on weekends as a bartender and maître d'. He spoke English with a thick German accent.

Most of Susan's elementary school friends were children of refugees. Susan grew up on Wadsworth Avenue in an Upper Manhattan neighborhood dominated by Jews from Germany, Austria and other European countries. Her aunt Frieda and uncle Freddie—also refugees from Austria—lived in the same apartment building, together with their young children. All of these children could see that their parents were different from "normal" Americans. For one thing, they spoke English with a German accent. They were clearly European in their demeanor and dress. Susan herself spoke only German until she was five years old. But when she started going to school, she promptly refused to speak that foreign tongue anymore, even in the Wadsworth apartment. She knew she was different from the other kids in school, and like all children she wanted to conform, to be a part of the fabric of American life.

At a young age, Susan had been told very little about the war or why her parents were refugees—they had not wanted to explain too much, too early, of this sad story—and so, inevitably, she learned what had happened to her parents in little pieces, here and there. (She only learned the whole story when she had to read the manuscript of this book.) She was, to paraphrase Helen Epstein, the author of *Children of the Holocaust,* a woman "possessed by a history she had never lived." She knew there were horrible things harbored in this family history, and part of her really didn't want to go there, and of course that made her feel guilty merely for wanting to live her own life. The history was what Epstein called "an iron box buried so deep inside me that I was never sure just what it was."

Eventually, it dawned on me that I could not understand Susan without at least an empathetic knowledge of the Shoah. Conversely, I now realize that no one can comprehend the Middle East's Nakba without an understanding of Europe's Shoah. The two events occurred in different places and times, but they are intimately connected and continue to reverberate against each other through the generations.

On March 12, 1938, when Susan's mother, Helma, was barely twelve years old, Adolf Hitler drove to Braunau, the border town in Austria where he had been born. To his delight, a wildly cheering citizenry greeted him. "I have in the course of my political struggle won much love from my people," he later remarked, "but when I crossed the former frontier (into Austria) there met me such a stream of love as I have never experienced. Not as tyrants have we come, but as liberators." German troops occupied Austria without having to fire a single shot. Within days, however, the Nazis had rounded up more than 70,000 Austrians and thrown them into concentration camps.

For Helma, the Anschluss—the German annexation of Austria—marked the final end of her childhood. The previous year her mother had died of cancer, leaving her alone with her father, Alois Blühweis, the owner of a prosperous tannery, leather factory and upscale leather-goods store in downtown Graz. Alois had been born on May 29, 1876, in the small Croatian town of Križovljan (near Varaždin), when it was still part of the Austro-Hungarian Empire. His parents had sent him to Graz as a teenager to apprentice in the tannery trade. A hardworking young man, Alois was eventually able to buy the tannery from his boss, Eduard Hofmann, and by the turn of the century he was a wealthy and well-established member of Graz society. He kept the old name of the business, Eduard Hofmann & Company. Alois was a congenial, easygoing man who got along with everyone. He boasted a finely groomed, curled mustache and dressed in the finest conservative suits. He was the kind of largely secular Jew who attended Graz's sole synagogue only once or twice a year, on Rosh Hashanah and Yom Kippur, the High Holy Days.

On July 1, 1906, he married Hermine Victoria Esther Jassniger, a Catholic by birth, who agreed to convert to Judaism. At twenty-five years of age,

Alois Blühweis in Graz, 1906

Hermine was a gifted pianist who played Viennese and classical music for her friends and family. They were married in the Graz synagogue by Rabbi Muhsan, and a year later their first daughter, Gertrude, was born. Their second daughter, Helma, didn't come along until nineteen years later. By then, the Blühweis household was ensconced in a luxurious ten-room villa at 35 Elisabeth Strasse in an elegant residential part of Graz. When Helma was four or five years old, they moved into a lovely four-bedroom apartment just above the leather-goods store at Number 22 Griesgasse in downtown Graz. The Blühweises had a cook, a maid and a nanny, and a chauffeur for the family's Daimler-Benz sedan. A copy of a well-known painting—*Die Toteninsel* (Island of the Dead) by Arnold Boecklin—dominated the living room, together with a grand piano. Until she died of cancer at the age of fifty-seven, Hermine insisted that her younger daughter practice the piano every day.

But soon after the Anschluss, Helma's piano lessons abruptly ended. Just a month after Hitler's troops marched into Austria, Helma arrived at school and heard her teacher announce that henceforth every day she, the teacher, was to be greeted with a Nazi salute and a "Heil Hitler!" The teacher then turned to Helma, the only Jew in the class, and said, "But you, Helma, you will not be required to do this because you will no longer be coming to school." Helma went home and cried.

In October 1938 a stranger appeared at their door. Georg Margutsch was a squat, entirely unremarkable-looking man. But he was armed and wore the insignia of a Nazi Party member. Without ceremony, Margutsch demanded that Alois hand over all his keys, explaining that he was authorized to confiscate the Blühweis residence and leather factory. (Austrian archival documents reveal that Margutsch had been delegated to take over the Blühweis property by Richard Gibiser, a secret Nazi Party member since 1932, with the SS rank of Obersturmführer—Senior Storm Leader. Gibiser was in the leather business himself—and therefore one of Alois Blühweis's competitors. He also happened to be a next-door neighbor and a friend of the family. Thus, the betrayal was particularly personal.) Oddly, Margutsch informed Alois that he would allow him and his daughter to sleep in the windowless kitchen pantry. Helma remembers that Margutsch routinely referred to her father as *Saujud*—"Jewish swine."

Widowed and now penniless, the sixty-two-year-old Alois hardly knew where to turn. He had never thought it could come to this. Some years earlier, after his late wife had seen a gang of Graz university students smashing the windows of a bookstore selling the works of Jewish authors, Hermine had told him that maybe they should consider emigrating. Alois had scoffed at the idea.

Now he realized that he would soon have to leave Graz. His first thought was to move to Zagreb, where his younger brother was the publisher of a local newspaper. And in the meantime he wrote a letter to his elder daughter, "Trude," who in 1934 had married an Italian civil servant, Leone Endrizzi. The couple now lived in the German-speaking town of Bressanone in the Southern Tyrol district of northern Italy. Endrizzi had married well; his wife came to him with a generous dowry. After earning a college degree in agricultural science, he had found employment as an agricultural inspector with the district government. He was addressed as "Dr. Endrizzi." He was Catholic, and when he married Gertrude, her family did not object when she agreed to convert. Like most civil servants in Mussolini's Italy, Endrizzi had at some point found it practical to join the Fascist party. Naturally, he did not advertise his wife's Jewish heritage.

Despite all this, Alois assumed his son-in-law would help him in his present circumstances. Sometime that summer Gertrude managed to visit from

Italy; she gave her father some provisions, and he slipped her some of her mother's jewelry. Alois told her that he hoped to join her in Italy, but in the meantime he and Helma would soon move to Zagreb. He did not leave soon enough.

On the night of November 9, 1938—a date known to history as Kristallnacht, the "Night of Broken Glass"—mobs directed by German SS officers rampaged through the streets of Graz, ransacking Jewish-owned businesses and homes. Graz's only synagogue, a beautiful structure built in 1892, was pillaged, dynamited and then burned to the ground. The synagogue's seventy-year-old rabbi, David Herzog, was dragged from his home, beaten and thrown into the River Mur. Many of Graz's 10,000 Jewish residents suffered similar brutalities.

That night two SS officers came to the Blühweis apartment, looking for a young Jewish employee. They first came to the door of one of Alois's tenants and asked for the young man by name. Awakened by the commotion, Helma heard the voice of a woman saying, "No, that young man has emigrated, but the owner of this building is Jewish. Why don't you take him?" Thus betrayed, Alois was quickly roused from his bed in the pantry, and Helma watched with horror as he was roughly thrown down the steps. The SS took him away, beating him mercilessly—and like Rabbi Herzog, he was thrown into the river. He barely survived. Early the next morning a milkman riding by in a horse-drawn cart heard moaning from the river embankment. He stopped and discovered Alois lying there. The milkman managed to get him into the cart, and Alois was just conscious enough to tell him where he lived. Helma remembers seeing her father come home a broken man. He had lost all his teeth, and the two SS men had stomped on his legs, breaking both, together with several ribs.

Twelve-year-old Helma somehow alerted Sidy Wolf, the daughter of her mother's only sister. That side of the family was Christian, and Sidy was married to a Joseph Wolf, a dentist who agreed to come surreptitiously in the middle of the night and fashion a set of false teeth for Alois. Dr. Wolf did this at some risk to himself, since non-Jewish doctors were now forbidden to treat Jews under penalty of death. Dr. Wolf also managed to find a doctor willing to set Alois's broken legs in a cast. Over the next few weeks Helma and these few family friends nursed her father to the point where he could walk with crutches. Determined now to leave, Alois approached the man who had seized his estate and explained that he could not cross into Yugoslavia without paying an exit fee to the Nazi regime. Margutsch obligingly offered Alois the small sum necessary—but there was a condition. With a gun pointed to his head, Alois Blühweis signed a document relinquishing ownership of all his property.

In early January 1939 Alois and Helma left by train for a small town on the Austro-Yugoslavian border. His brother in Zagreb had hired a guide to smuggle them across the border. With Alois walking painfully on crutches through snowy fields, they quietly crossed "no-man's-land" into Yugoslav territory, where they caught a train to Zagreb. They arrived in that Croatian city in mid-January, penniless and with only the clothes on their backs. Alois's sister, Adele Horvath, gave them shelter, and his younger brother Rudolf, a wealthy man who published Zagreb's daily morning newspaper, gave him a small monthly stipend. Rudolf was astonished at his brother's sudden misfortune—and he insisted that such a thing could never happen in Yugoslavia. For the following three years Alois and Helma relied on Rudolf's charity. Helma was not able to go to school, but she took weekly lessons in Serbo-Croatian from a cousin, Erika, and her father arranged for her to take dressmaking lessons so she might have a trade.

And then, in April 1941, the Germans and their Italian allies invaded and occupied Yugoslavia. The Italian Fascists occupied most of the Dalmatian coast. The Nazis set up a puppet government in the nominally independent country of Croatia, encompassing parts of Serbia and Bosnia-Herzegovina. Zagreb became its capital. The Germans installed as the local Führer Ante Pavelić, the brutal chief of the Ustasha, the Croatian Fascist Party. Pavelić immediately launched a series of pogroms against Serbs, Roma (Gypsies) and Jews. He proclaimed his intention to purify Croatia of its Christian Orthodox, Jewish and Roma populations. In fact, he planned to annihilate the relatively small Jewish and Roma populations and either kill or convert to the Roman Catholic faith the two million Orthodox Serbs. Soon after Pavelić's elevation to power, Pope Pius XII honored him with a private audience in Rome.

Like all Jews in Croatia, Alois and Helma were now required to wear a yellow star pinned, front and back, to their coats when they left their aunt's apartment near the train station. Signs were posted in public parks reading "No Dogs or Jews." Jews were not allowed to shop for food until 4:00 p.m.—by which time there was little to buy. But because Helma was a pretty, blond, blue-eyed, "Aryan-looking" teenager, she found she could "pass." So she refused to wear the yellow star and would go out earlier in the day to forage for food in the markets, though with at best limited success. Most nights her aunt cooked only a scanty "goulash" made from potatoes, a bit of onion and a tablespoon of oil. Sometimes they ate black noodles, and on very rare occasions Alois would buy a sausage for Helma. She remembers "the black bread we bought was so hard you had to place it in some warm water before you could chew it. I was always hungry."

Soon people began disappearing, often picked up off the streets by Ustasha trucks, never to be seen again by their neighbors. Just a month after the Ustasha came to power, Helma learned that Erika Blis, the cousin who had given her weekly lessons in Serbo-Croatian, had been picked up with her husband and together with about fifty other Zagreb Jews, trucked to the Dalmatian coast. Denied food or water for two days, the group was finally allowed to get down from the truck, and then they were fed bread and butter. The butter, however, was laced with strychnine and they all died a painful death. The Ustasha apparently murdered them just as a brazen demonstration of their ruthlessness—and to intimidate not only the Jewish community but all Croatians. Erika's brother, Mirko Blis, was devastated. A prominent lawyer and journalist, Mirko soon went underground and then his Christian girlfriend smuggled him into Italy, where he survived the war years in Nepi, an Italian village just north of Rome, under loose house arrest. (It was literally called *confino libero* under Italian law—"free confinement.")

His mother, Alice Blis, was not so fortunate. She chose to flee to Budapest, where she had a sister. And in the spring and summer of 1944 she and some 400,000 other Hungarian Jews were shipped to Auschwitz. (I later wrote about the fate of the Budapest Jews in my biography of John J. McCloy, who in 1944 was the assistant secretary of war and the man responsible for deciding not to bomb the railroad tracks leading to Auschwitz or the death camp's gas chambers. McCloy always maintained that bombing Auschwitz would have been a diversion of military resources from winning the war—even though American bombers were dropping tons of munitions that summer on an I. G. Farben factory just a few kilometers from Auschwitz.)

Sometime in the summer of 1942, Uncle Rudolf Blis's properties were confiscated. He cleverly used his remaining money and influence to check himself and his wife into a sanatorium, virtually disappearing from society. Almost alone among the Blühweises, he and his beautiful wife survived the war. But Alois, once again alone and in desperate circumstances, now wrote repeatedly to his daughter Gertrude in Bressanone, begging her to send a letter of invitation so he could legally enter Italy. Months went by and no letter was forthcoming. At the end of 1941 Gertrude finally wrote that she could not produce such a letter, explaining that to do so might endanger her Italian husband's position as a civil servant. Alois was devastated.

His next step was to approach a fellow Jew who was known to be selling forged exit documents. In late January 1942, he paid the man for one set of documents for himself. He told Helma that he would try crossing the Italian border with the false documents and if all went well, he would send for her. He had intended to leave Zagreb on February 8; but as that was Helma's sixteenth birthday, he delayed his departure until the next day.

That day, February 9, Alois was supposed to catch a train at 10:00 a.m.—but at 8:00 a.m. the Ustasha came and arrested him. Once again Helma saw her father being dragged away. Also arrested were all the other men who had bought false papers from the Jewish forger, who turned out to be working for the Ustasha—perhaps, who knows, to save his own life. Initially, Helma learned that Alois had been taken to Zagreb's Zbor, the municipal convention center, where detainees were being held. She was never allowed to see her father, but the guards would permit relatives to exchange clean clothes each day for dirty laundry. If the guards handed over dirty laundry, you knew your relative was still there. Helma brought clean clothes to her father for four or five days—but one day the guards had no dirty laundry for her, and she knew her father was no longer in Zagreb.

Alois was taken to Jasenovac, a large concentration camp established in August 1941 on the bank of the Sava River, just sixty-two miles south of Zagreb. Jasenovac may not today evoke the powerful symbolism of an Auschwitz or a Bergen-Belsen, but it was in fact the third-largest killing field during the European Holocaust. We know from the International Red Cross that Alois was indeed an inmate of Jasenovac, but we're not entirely sure when or how he died. Historians believe that some 600,000 people perished in Jasenovac, including some 20,000 to 25,000 Jews—not nearly as many as at Auschwitz, but nevertheless an astonishing number. And these men, women and children died not in gas chambers but one by one, felled by Ustasha guards wielding curved knives strapped to their wrists. On the night of August 29, 1942, an Ustasha guard named Petar Brzica allegedly set the record by cutting the throats of 1,360 inmates. He was rewarded with a gold watch, a silver tea service and a dinner of roasted suckling pig with red wine.

After that bloody August night the Germans began shipping Croatian Jews to Auschwitz for extermination in the gas chambers. In April 1945 the thousand Serbs and Jews then remaining in Jasenovac rose in revolt, but the Ustasha guards shot 525 of them. Only 80 prisoners escaped that day, including 20 Jews. One of these escapees, a man named Cabiglio, provided Helma with an affidavit in 1947 stating that he had known Alois in Jasenovac, and it was his recollection that Alois had been bludgeoned to death by Ustasha guards, probably in the early autumn of 1942. Alois was then sixty-six years old, only one man among the more than six million victims of the Shoah. In Croatia less than 10 percent of the estimated 30,000 Jews survived the war.

At the time, Helma was told that her father had been shipped out of Zagreb—to where, she really was not sure—but everyone had heard of Jasenovac. There was little she could do. Alois had told her that if he disappeared she should go to an old friend, a Mrs. Andrakovich, and sell two pieces of jade he had managed to squirrel away. She was then supposed to use the money to smuggle herself into Italy. On the day she sold the jade, she met Greta Bernfest, a tall, freckled redhead, and a Jewish native of Zagreb. Mrs. Andrakovich gave both Helma and Greta refuge in her home for several weeks. And then Helma spent some time with Cousin Mirko's girlfriend, Vera Kochanek, a non-Jew, who hid her in her apartment. Helma must have felt that time was running out for her. But in late March she received a note instructing her to go to the offices of the Italian military attaché in Zagreb; her sister, Gertrude, had finally found a way to help her. Gertrude had been giving piano lessons to the two daughters of an Italian army general in Bolzano. This man, a General Bologna, was persuaded to issue a "repatriation document" permitting one Helma Blühweis to "return" to Italy. The document was good for thirty days.

So it was that on April 16, 1942, Helma found herself aboard a train bound for Trieste and then on to the small town of Bressanone, just 28 miles south of the Austro-Italian border. She had a raincoat, a little suitcase and nothing else. "I had no money for food," Helma recalled. "I was hungry, but I was afraid to draw any attention to myself." After two or three days she finally arrived in Bressanone and moved in with her sister's family, the Endrizzis.

Nestled in a valley between the Rienza and Isarco rivers, Bressanone was a quaint Tyrolean resort town dotted with gabled roofs, narrow cobblestone streets and pastel-colored houses. It could have been an idyllic wartime sanctuary. From the beginning, however, Helma found herself in an awkward situation. The Endrizzis sent her to school for a short time, until some local official decided that Helma, as a foreign national, wasn't entitled to enroll in an Italian school—or to receive a ration card. Each week she had to register herself at the municipal police station. She slept on an old couch, and though she was his wife's sister, Dr. Leone Endrizzi made her eat with the servants. He gave her menial household tasks and treated her like a maid. He made it obvious that Helma's presence was a burden. One day that winter of 1942–43, Helma was sitting in the kitchen eating a boiled potato with a little butter when Leone walked in. Seeing the butter, he grabbed it out of her hand and said, "In my house you eat the potato with no butter; you're lucky you have even a potato." To be sure, Leone was not singling out Helma. Butter in wartime Italy was a luxury, and Leone rationed such "luxuries" even for his own children.

It is easy to see why Dr. Endrizzi felt threatened by Helma's presence. He was an Italian district government official, and thus an obligatory member of the Fascist party. Photographs of him dressed in the black Fascist uniform hung on the walls of their Bressanone apartment. He must have felt that his job would be in jeopardy if it became widely known that he was harboring a Jew—let alone that his wife was Jewish.

Dr. Endrizzi was not an anti-Semite. And in any case, Italian anti-Semitism was something quite apart from the German strain. When Benito Mussolini seized power in 1922, Italy had a minuscule population of some 47,000 Jews in a sea of 47 million Catholics. Initially Il Duce's brand of Fascism scorned German racial theories, and Mussolini even welcomed Jewish German refugees. Astonishingly, not a few Italian Jews joined the Fascist party. As my friend Alexander Stille observes in his penetrating history of the Jewish Italian holocaust, *Benevolence and Betrayal,* "more than 10,000 Jews—about one out of every three Jewish adults—were members of the Fascist Party."

But then on July 14, 1938, Mussolini's official organs published a "Manifesto" announcing that scientists had established that there was indeed "an

Italian race" of Aryan origin, and that "Jews do not belong to the Italian race." That summer it was announced that Jewish children could not attend public schools, and subsequently the regime restricted the legal rights of Jewish Italians in many other ways. It had taken nearly sixteen years for state-sponsored anti-Semitism to become an integral part of Italian Fascism. But even so, when Helma arrived in Italy in 1942, the regime was implementing its racist laws in a somewhat haphazard and uneven fashion. Not a single Jew had yet been deported to Germany—though after Mussolini declared war on the Allies in June 1940, hundreds and then several thousand foreign Jews were rounded up and placed in one of fifteen internment camps in southern Italy. By late 1942 about 1,000 Italian Jews had been arrested, and some were sentenced to "enforced residence" in remote villages. In Trieste, Fascist gangs frequently vandalized Jewish shops and beat up Jews they found on the street. On the other hand, while Rome's 12,000 Jews were discriminated against and found life under Mussolini difficult, they were not yet being hunted. Still, in such an atmosphere, Dr. Endrizzi had every reason to believe that Helma's presence in his household jeopardized his livelihood and the safety of his wife and their three children. Under the circumstances, it is remarkable that he allowed Helma to remain in Bressanone as long as he did.

One day in early August 1943, Gertrude came to Helma and said she would have to leave. She explained that a *carabiniere,* a policeman, had tipped them off that Helma would be picked up the next day and deported to Poland. Instead of money, Gertrude slipped her a gold pendant embedded with small diamonds—and told her not to mention it to her husband. Fortuitously, Gertrude knew that an elderly patient in Bressanone's famous Kneipp tuberculosis sanatorium was driving south, so Gertrude arranged for Helma to accompany her. This woman, a wealthy Italian marchesa, was glad to have the company, especially as she thought Helma's fluent German would be helpful in negotiating their way past German army checkpoints. They drove for three or four days before arriving back in the marchesa's villa in the town of Macerata, just south of Ancona on the Adriatic Sea, nearly halfway down the Italian "boot."

The marchesa allowed Helma to live in her attic for a couple of weeks—until one day she decided that her presence was too dangerous. Once again, Helma was asked to move on. The old woman bought her a train ticket for Rome, and had her driven to the train station in Ancona. Helma boarded the train, but she hadn't traveled very far before she saw German soldiers boarding her train. Frightened that they might demand to see her papers, she quickly disembarked. For weeks she got on and off one train after another, and sometimes she walked for days through the Umbria countryside, sleeping outdoors in the summer heat. She used the little money she had to buy bread, and she picked apples from passing orchards.

She finally arrived in Rome in the first week of September 1943—a time when Italians were celebrating the end of Fascism. She had every reason to believe that Allied troops would soon be seen in downtown Rome. American and British troops had landed in Sicily on July 10, 1943, but their rapid advance through southern Italy had ground to a halt that summer in the trenches of Cassino. On July 25, Mussolini's government collapsed, to be replaced for only forty-five days by a weak and ineffectual anti-Fascist regime led by Marshal Pietro Badoglio. On September 8, just days after Helma's arrival in the "open city," Marshal Badoglio signed an armistice with the Allies, officially ending Italy's participation in the war. Two days later, however, Rome was flooded by thousands of German occupation troops. Suddenly, Rome was a very dangerous place to be. "The Germans are all over the town," wrote one resident in her diary on September 13, 1943, "and they have begun looting in earnest. They stop people in the street and take their jewels, rings, chains, watches and money from them at the muzzle of a revolver."

In short order, SS commandos freed Mussolini from an Italian prison and reinstalled him as the nominal head of state. But in practice the Germans were in full control, and they were now determined to do what Mussolini had always refused to do—deport the Italian Jews. On September 25, SS Chief Heinrich Himmler informed his subordinates in Rome that "All Jews, regardless of nationality, age, sex and personal conditions must be transferred to Germany and liquidated. . . ." Helma was very much in the wrong place at the wrong time.

She, of course, was unaware of these developments—except for the ominous signs that the Germans were in full control. Not knowing where else to go, she reluctantly pawned the gold pendant her sister had given her and used the few lire she received to check into a simple rooming house. She stayed only a couple of nights, in part because she sensed that the landlady was pro-Fascist—and seemed to suspect that Helma was a Jewish refugee.

Helma's sister had told her that when she arrived in Rome, she should seek shelter at a Catholic convent. "I slept in a variety of convents," Helma recalled. "They'd let you stay only at night—you'd have to get out after 7:00 a.m. and then come back in the evening. There was usually a bed with clean linen, and a white curtain pulled around each bed, like in a hospital ward. They fed us breakfast and dinner. In good weather, I'd spend my days wandering the parks, or if it was raining, I'd go to a museum. I spent a lot of time at the Vatican and its nearby museums, because it seemed to be the safest place to be. . . . No one thought the Germans or Allies would bomb St Peter's Square."

Her circumstances were still highly precarious. German soldiers were not yet raiding Rome's many convents and monasteries, but they watched who came and went. Usually, after a week or so the nuns would tell Helma that it was time for her to try another convent. "When I ran out of convents, my sister had given me the address of General Bologna, the same Italian officer who had helped arrange my 'repatriation' papers out of Zagreb. He was by then stationed in Rome. He and his family had a gorgeous apartment on Via San Marino. They let me stay there, provided I did housework. I did this for about two weeks, and then they told me one morning that it was too dangerous and I had to leave by the evening."

As she left that night, wearing her raincoat and carrying a small satchel of all her belongings, Helma began to cry. She had no idea where to go. She hadn't walked more than a hundred feet when two young women asked her why she was crying. When Helma explained she had no place to sleep, the women—two sisters—offered her a sofa in their one-bedroom apartment just across the street, at 51 Via San Marino. Rachel and Amelia Fernandez-Diaz lived with their elderly mother. They were Greek-speaking Sephardic Jews, refugees from Turkey who had ended up in Rome. Rachel worked for a construction company. None of these women had ration cards, so they had to buy their food on the black market. "We had very little money, so we ate black pasta with a couple of drops of oil and roasted garlic. That was a feast." Helma found a part-time job of sorts: "I don't know how it happened, but to make a little money I began teaching German twice a week to two Italian prostitutes. They needed a little German in order to do business with the German soldiers. So I taught them to say things like 'I love you' in German. They had everything. I got paid. They were very generous. Most prostitutes are."

Rome was now a city rife with fear for both Catholic and Jewish Italians. Earlier that autumn the Germans had declared a curfew that began at

9:30 p.m. An Italian journalist, Paolo Monelli, described the growing list of restrictions that made life's daily routines fraught with peril: "It was forbidden to ride a bicycle, forbidden to walk along certain sidewalks, forbidden to cross certain streets, forbidden to stock up on food, forbidden to telegraph or phone outside Rome, forbidden to enter or leave the city, forbidden to spend the night at friends' houses. It was dangerous to carry a package under your arm, to walk with a rapid gait, to have a beard grown too recently or to wear dark glasses. It was a mortal danger to hide a fugitive . . . or to listen to the [Allied] radio broadcasts from Bari or Palermo."

Helma's shared apartment on Via San Marino didn't have any running water, so each day she had to walk down the street to a public water pump situated not far from Mussolini's villa. "One day I went to the well with my bucket when a bomb suddenly struck the street. The man in front of me was beheaded. And I got hit with a piece of shrapnel within millimeters of my eye. But the shock of seeing this person in front of me instantly killed distracted me. I didn't realize that I had been hit until the blood started to pour . . . someone took me to a hospital and I got it stitched." Many Allied bombs fell on Rome that autumn—and Helma only narrowly escaped this one. For the rest of her life, she bore a small scar over her left eye.

Oddly enough, under German occupation Helma's status as an unregistered refugee now made her a more elusive target than Italian Jews. On the rainy morning of October 16, 1943, German SS security police surrounded the Jewish ghetto near one of Rome's ancient theatres. At 5:30 a.m. the SS forced many of the ghetto's 4,000 residents into the streets and herded them into waiting trucks. Later in the day the SS targeted individual Jews outside the ghetto. Armed with copies of the 1938 census of Rome, which listed the names and addresses of Rome's Jewish residents, the SS men methodically rounded up 1,015 Jews that day. They might easily have captured many more, but a few days earlier Pope Pius XII had quietly allowed more than 4,000 Jews to seek sanctuary either in the Vatican itself or in Rome's many monasteries and convents. Those who were detained spent two days in detention in the Collegio Militare—just six hundred feet from Vatican City. The Pope knew of their plight, but he made no public protest to the Germans. Two days later these Jews were put on trains bound for Auschwitz. Only 16 of the 1,015 deported from Rome survived the war. Over the next several months, similar SS sweeps in other cities of northern Italy picked up another 7,345 Jews; 6,746 of them were gassed at Auschwitz.

Helma eluded the deadly dragnet. Sometime that autumn she learned that the International Red Cross was giving refugees small monthly subsidies; she signed up and thenceforth went to a villa in downtown Rome to collect her stipend. One day in early January 1944 she was emerging from the Red Cross villa when a tall man in his midthirties approached her and introduced himself as "Giuseppe" (Joseph). Giuseppe Levi, a Sephardic Jew from Yugoslavia, had observed Helma picking up her stipend, and he surmised that if she was a refugee, she might well be Jewish. And yet, she was very young, blond and blue-eyed—and could obviously pass for the Austrian that she was in fact by birth. Acting on his instincts, Giuseppe candidly explained that he needed someone like her for a delicate task. He said he worked for an underground cell consisting largely of Yugoslavs who needed to smuggle people across German lines. Helma soon learned that a remarkable Capuchin friar, Father Benedetti, led this underground organization.

Father "Benedetti" was a Frenchman born in 1895 as Pierre Péteul. Wounded at Verdun during World War I, he later earned a doctorate in theology in Rome and entered the Franciscan Capuchin order as Father Marie-Benoît. He was a serious scholar and one of the Vatican's experts on Judaism. At the outbreak of the war he was stationed at a Capuchin monastery in Marseilles. Thousands of French Jews were then trying to escape Vichy France, so Father Marie-Benoît quickly equipped the monastery's basement with printing and photographic facilities with which to forge identity papers, passports and fake baptismal certificates. Working through the French Resistance and various Jewish organizations, Father Marie-Benoît created a network of guides who took groups of Jews twice a week across the mountains to either Spain or Switzerland. He thus rescued as many as 4,000 Jews. When the Nazis occupied Marseilles and the rest of Free France in November 1942, he persuaded Italian authorities to allow thousands of Jews in Nice to cross into Italian-controlled territory.

In the summer of 1943, with the Gestapo hot on his trail, Father Marie-Benoît moved to Rome, where he assumed the alias of Father Benedetti. When he briefed Pope Pius XII on the plight of French Jewry, the Pope reportedly responded, "Who could ever expect this from noble France?" Father Benedetti may well have been instrumental in persuading the pope to open Rome's convents and monasteries as sanctuary for thousands of Jews that autumn. Father Benedetti also reproduced his Marseilles forgery factory in the Capuchin monastery at 159 Via Siciliano in downtown Rome.

(Just across the street was the Pensione Jaccarino, a prison where the Gestapo regularly tortured and executed Italian partisans.)

Throughout the nine-month German occupation of Rome, Father Benedetti provided thousands of Jews with forged identity papers and forged food ration cards. He rented rooms in boardinghouses for refugees and sent priests to provide them with forged papers, food and clothing. In September 1943 his network was aiding just over 100 foreign Jews; nine months later he was assisting some 4,000—of which 1,500 were foreign Jews. At one point, he became the acting president of the major Jewish relief organization, the Delegazione Assistenza Emigranti Ebrei (the Committee to Assist Jewish Emigrants, or Delasem), which handed out small stipends to thousands of refugees. The Delasem board members met in secret in Father Benedetti's office in the Capuchin monastery.

Pope Pius XII was essentially turning a blind eye to the rescue operations of Father Benedetti and other individual priests and nuns. But the Church's official policy regarding Nazi Germany, the war—and in the end, quite shockingly, even the Holocaust—was one of silence, neutrality and sometimes a bit of quiet diplomacy. Numerous individual Jews were being protected through the Vatican's network of churches, monasteries and nunneries. But this pope would not take a confrontational stand against the Nazis. He refused to excommunicate Hitler, and he did not speak out against Hitler's assault on European Jewry.

So Father Benedetti raised money for his rescue operations from the local Jewish community and various foreign embassies. He routinely sent couriers to Switzerland who brought back large sums of cash to finance all these illegal and quite risky operations. At one point, the American Joint Distribution Committee deposited $15,000 a month in a London bank account, against which Father Benedetti persuaded local suppliers to extend him credit. Later, the Vatican funneled several million dollars to fund his various operations. By 1943, Father Benedetti had become an astute money launderer, a smuggler of human beings and a consummate runner of a large network of agents.

Helma was recruited into Father Benedetti's network in early 1944, just as the Germans began a concerted campaign to round up and deport all the Jews they could find to the death camps in Germany and Poland. While Father Benedetti's forgery factory produced high-quality travel documents, he knew they could look even more authentic if produced on genuine German letterheads. As they sat on a park bench near the villa of the International Red Cross, Giuseppe Levi explained to Helma that they needed someone to infiltrate the German army command and steal German letterheads, seals and rubber stamps with which they could forge authentic-looking travel documents. It was an audacious request.

"He asked me if I would do this," Helma recalled, "and I was stupid enough to say yes. I just thought it was an adventure." Over the next two weeks Giuseppe and several other men from his cell briefed Helma on her new identity. "They gave me a false Italian identity card, stating that my name was Elena Bianchi and that my birthplace was Benevento—which was south of Naples and therefore already in Allied hands. They briefed me day and night on what my story was: My parents had died, but I had a grandmother in Austria who had raised me and taught me German. I had then been caught in Italy when the war broke out." As part of her training she would be allowed to sleep, and then abruptly awakened and asked to explain who she was.

"Eventually they told me to go to the Hotel Quirinale on Via Nazionale, three blocks from the Piazza Esedra. The hotel had been taken over as a German command post, and I was to apply for a job there." Helma did as she was told. The German officers she met bought her story—but only after they plied her with questions about her supposed birthplace, Benevento. They asked her to name prominent landmarks, streets and cathedrals. But Helma had been well briefed by her handlers and was able to answer all the questions without hesitation. Finally, after testing whether she could indeed read and write German, they assigned her to the offices of the Luftwaffe Staffel Süd (Air Command South), housed in a lovely villa in the Parioli area of Rome. She was to work as a typist-secretary taking dictation. Her immediate boss was a German army lieutenant in his early thirties named Zerres. Prior to the war Zerres had worked as a journalist in Prussia, and now his job was to put out a newsletter that circulated among the German troops in Rome. He used a Dictaphone with waxed tubes, and Helma typed his dictation onto blue stencil sheets. "Every morning, I had to greet everyone with a 'Heil Hitler.'" It was a job.

For the first time in five years Helma was eating three meals a day, including a hearty breakfast served at the office. The Germans paid her salary in deutschmarks. Helma liked Lieutenant Zerres. "He was very nice," she recalled. "All the other officers used to come into the office in the morning and cry out 'Heil Hitler!' But Lieutenant Zerres said it in a perfunctory, subdued manner. You got the sense that he wasn't as enthusiastic as all the others. His best friend was a Lieutenant Gephardt, a chubby fellow."

Initially, Helma found no opportunity to filch identity papers or anything else of use to her comrades in the underground. She just came to work each day and did her job. She was surviving, and that was quite enough. Once a week she went to a church, sat discreetly in a back pew and briefly met a member of her underground cell. Usually her contact was Giuseppe Levi. After exchanging a few whispered words, she would leave and return to her job. There were risks. No one told her, but the Gestapo raided Father Benedetti's office several times, searching for evidence to implicate him in illegal activities. Helma herself had one close call. One day she was typing at her desk when a woman walked into the office; Helma immediately recognized her as the proprietress of the small rooming house where she had spent two nights. She knew that not only was this woman pro-German but that she knew her, Helma, as Helma Blühweis—not Elena Bianchi—and she probably had Helma pegged as well as a Jewish refugee. On blind impulse, Helma grabbed her raincoat and, carrying it in such a fashion as to discreetly shield her face, she hurriedly walked out. She did not think the woman had spotted her, but she could not be sure. Nevertheless, she took another risk and showed up at her job the next day.

All around her, terrible things were happening. In February 1944 Rome's newly installed puppet police chief, Pietro Caruso, ordered his officers to "proceed urgently with the arrest of pure Italian and foreign Jews." Informants were awarded 5,000 lire for turning in a male Jew, and half that amount for a woman or a child. Helma heard repeated rumors about various atrocities that spring. One of the worst concerned a gruesome massacre in the Ardeatine Caves outside Rome. On March 23, Italian Communist party partisans planted forty pounds of TNT in a metal trash cart on the Via Rasella, a narrow street near the Barberini Palace. At half-past three in the afternoon they detonated the bomb just as a detachment of 156 German SS troops passed nearby. The explosion could be heard throughout central Rome. The blast decimated the German column: 42 Germans lay dead while another 44 were seriously wounded. In retaliation, the SS rounded up 335 anti-Fascists (including 77 Jews) who had been languishing in prison, and drove them to man-made caves, part of the ancient Christian catacombs carved along the Appian Way. There the victims were forced to kneel in groups of three or five with their hands tied behind their backs. And then they were all shot in the back of the head. It took the Germans three hours to kill everyone. When they were finished, they dynamited the entrance to the caves. A day later the Fascist press broke the news to a shocked city.

After Helma had been working under an alias with the Nazis for about three months, Lieutenant Zerres discreetly asked her out on a date—but he said no one in the office should know. Helma agreed to meet him the following Sunday in a public park overlooking the Roman Coliseum. They sat on a park bench, and Zerres explained that he needed her help. He confessed that if and when the German army retreated from Rome, he and his friend Gephardt intended to desert. He wanted to know if Helma knew anyone who could provide them with civilian clothes and a safe apartment in which they could hide. Helma expressed no surprise and merely replied that she would ask around. Soon afterwards, she met with her recruiter, Giuseppe Levi, and told him about this encounter. Giuseppe told her to make Zerres an offer: Giuseppe could procure the civvies and an apartment—but Zerres would have to produce in turn a sheaf of German army letterheads, rubber stamps and some blank identity cards with all the appropriate signatures. When Helma conveyed this offer to Lieutenant Zerres, he immediately accepted.

Soon afterwards, Zerres took Helma aside in the office and handed her the letterheads, blank identity cards, stamps and seals. Helma hastily took the package and stuffed it into her handbag. She then handed him the key to an apartment containing two civilian suits hanging in a wardrobe. The exchange took place in late March or so, just as the German military defenses south of Rome began to weaken that spring. Giuseppe Levi was delighted.

One day in early May 1944, Helma came to work and was told that everyone in her office would be moving north to Florence. There were to be no exceptions; all civilian personnel were ordered to be prepared to board a German army truck in a matter of days. Fearing that if she stopped coming to work the Germans would search for her, Helma went to an Italian doctor the next day and asked him to put her leg in a plaster cast. The next day she hobbled into the office on crutches and announced that she had broken her leg. Predictably, the Germans gave her permission to stay in Rome. Two or three days later, the Germans were gone and Helma had the cast cut off. It would be three years before she learned the fate of Lieutenants Zerres and Gephardt.

Her ordeal was not yet done. The Germans had not abandoned the city; and even as they fought a last-ditch defense against the advancing Allied forces, the SS mounted more nighttime raids, seeking to arrest, and often kill on the spot, any anti-Fascists or Jews. Helma was still living at 51 Via San Marino with the two Sephardic Greek sisters and their mother, Mrs. Fernandez-Diaz. The janitor who lived downstairs was a staunch Communist. Upstairs lived a young Italian woman, Liù Gazzaniga, and her boyfriend, who served in the Italian army. The boyfriend was an ardent, even recklessly outspoken anti-Fascist. One day his words attracted the attention of the SS, who came to the apartment building and arrested Gazzaniga. During three days of harsh interrogation, she revealed nothing about her neighbors. But after this incident, Mrs. Fernandez-Diaz feared that the SS might come back and detain everyone during one of their nocturnal raids. So she asked the janitor, who happened to be a bricklayer, to construct a sleeping nook in the basement where everyone could hide during the night. He built a wall with one small gap at the bottom through which Helma and the other women crawled each night. On the other side were a couple of mattresses. The janitor would cover the gap in the wall by pushing a piece of furniture up against it. "Every night we slept there," Helma recalled. "This went on for about a month." In the distance the women could hear the rumble of artillery. They had no radio and no newspapers, so they had no idea that the final stage of the hard-fought Battle of Montecassino was raging just seventy-five miles south of the city. Every morning they emerged from their crawl space hoping to see some sign of Allied troops.

Finally, on June 4, Rome fell. Helma had survived 268 days of Nazi occupation. She and her neighbors stood on the sidewalk and watched as Allied tanks rolled by. "We couldn't believe that this was the end. That evening was the first and last time that I got drunk. We feasted on a bottle of wine." She was eighteen years old—and miraculously, she had survived the war and the Holocaust.

Father Benedetti also survived. Some months after his network recruited Helma, the Gestapo tried to arrest him. Father Benedetti was persuaded to go underground, and to the amazement of many of his friends he escaped. When Rome was liberated, the remaining Jewish community showered him with praises at an official ceremony in one of the city's synagogues. He became known as the "Father of the Jews." More than two decades later, on April 16, 1966, Father Marie-Benoît (aka Father Benedetti) was officially anointed as a "Righteous Among the Nations"—a distinction Israel reserves for non-Jews who risked their lives to save Jews during the Holocaust. At the dedication ceremony, where a tree was planted in his honor, Father Marie-Benoît made a point of thanking a number of Jews who had risked their lives by working with him, including Helma's recruiter, Giuseppe Levi.

Just two days after Rome's liberation, Giuseppe Levi contacted Helma and told her that Allied intelligence officers wanted to debrief her. British and, later, American intelligence officers carefully questioned her about her activities. "They took away my German army identity card," Helma recalled. "And they asked me a lot of questions. They wanted to know everything I had seen and done with the Germans. But Giuseppe knew what I had done, and he vouched for me. They found my real identity documents stored in the Swiss legation in Rome. And then the American Military Government of Occupied Territories (AMGOT) offered me a job as a translator for their officers who were interrogating German prisoners of war. I worked there for four months."

In 1947 Helma received a letter from Lieutenant Zerres. He had taken the trouble to track her down, using the name and address of Helma's aunt in Graz. (When Helma had applied for the secretarial job with the Germans, she had been asked to list a relative.) Zerres wanted to know if "Elena Bianchi" had survived the war. Now he related that he and his friend Gephardt had gone to the apartment, stripped off their uniforms and fled in the civilian clothes Helma had delivered. They had then split up, going in different directions, hoping to be picked up by Allied troops. Zerres was indeed interned in an Allied POW camp—but he later learned that Gephardt had been caught by German troops and shot as a deserter. In postwar Germany, Zerres was once again working as a reporter. He must have had some affection for Helma, because the two of them corresponded well into the 1950s.

In 1946 Giuseppe Levi got Helma a job with the American Joint Distribution Committee, where he was personnel director. By then she had taught herself English by going to the cinema and watching Hollywood films. One day they sent her to interview Jewish survivors of the death camps, many of whom would end up emigrating to Palestine. "They had nowhere else to go.

The Americans were not giving visas to these poor emaciated people from Auschwitz. Palestine was the only possibility. The Joint Distribution Committee hired these rusty old boats and we would go at night . . . very clandestine, and load these people on the boats bound for Palestine. But then we heard that most of these people were intercepted by the British and ended up in detention camps in Cyprus."

In February 1947 Helma went back to Graz to see Aunt Berta Sándor, her mother's only sister. She stayed about a week. "I went by our old house with my aunt and we knocked on the door." Georg Margutsch—the same Nazi who had seized the Blühweis property in 1938—answered the door. Aunt Berta politely explained that the twenty-one-year-old woman standing next to her was Helma Blühweis, who had lived in this apartment until she was twelve years old. "Needless to say," Helma recalled, "he seemed shocked to see that I was alive." They asked if they could see Helma's childhood home. After an awkward hesitation, he briefly allowed her to walk around the apartment. Margutsch was using part of the building as his office and was renting out the rest of it. He had also built a large villa outside Graz. "My aunt took me to see it from the outside; she pointed it out and said, 'This was built with your father's money.'" Aunt Berta encouraged Helma to stay in Graz and institute proceedings to get her father's property back. But Helma thought a life in Graz was impossible. "I wanted to get out of Europe as fast as I could. Why would I want to live among the Austrians who had tortured us? I wanted to go someplace where I would not be plagued by memories." Her aunt gave her a few mementos from her prewar life in Graz: a silver sugar bowl, an oil painting of her father and a few pieces of jewelry.

By then she had applied for immigration visas to four countries: Venezuela, Argentina, South Africa and the United States. "I figured I'd go to the first country that accepted me." She didn't bother with Palestine because she knew that the British Mandate authorities were blocking Jewish immigration. She didn't think of herself as a Zionist pioneer. Even if Israel had existed, her ambition was to go to a place that was free, where she knew she would be safe from the dreaded knock on the door. "Israel or Palestine never, ever entered into my thoughts. None of my friends went there either."

Many Holocaust survivors ended up in Palestine, either because they aspired to the promised Jewish homeland or because they couldn't obtain visas for anywhere else. But Helma's attitude was by no means rare among the survivors. For some Jews, their experience had taught them that the promise of the European Enlightenment had turned out to be a cruel fraud. For them, the Jewish Diaspora would always be a trap waiting to snap shut with the next pogrom, and the only safe place to be was in a Jewish homeland. But even after the Holocaust, many Jews instinctively disagreed.

Sara Roy, a Harvard scholar and herself the daughter of a Holocaust survivor, relates how her mother decided she did not want to live in a Jewish state:

> After the war ended, my aunt Frania desperately wanted to go to Palestine to join their sister, who had been there for ten years. The creation of a Jewish state was imminent, and Frania felt it was the only safe place for Jews after the Holocaust. My mother disagreed and adamantly refused to go. She told me many times during my life that her decision not to live in Israel was based on a belief, learned and reinforced by her experiences during the war, that tolerance, compassion, and justice cannot be practiced or extended when one lives only among one's own. "I could not live as a Jew among Jews alone," she said. "For me, it wasn't possible and it wasn't what I wanted. I wanted to live as a Jew in a pluralist society, where my group remained important to me but where others were important to me, too."

Helma's aspirations in 1947 were not colored by any such political or intellectual ideas at all. She still thought of herself as Jewish, but if asked, she wouldn't have had an opinion about Zionism. Her intention was just to go to the first country that gave her a visa. She also knew that each year the U.S. government issued only 400 visas for citizens of Austria. So she counted herself fortunate when in the summer of 1947 she received an American visa as a displaced person. Because America was accepting so few survivors of the Holocaust, most of Helma's friends in Rome's refugee community eventually emigrated to such Latin American countries as Brazil, Venezuela, Paraguay, Argentina and Cuba.

Before leaving, she took a train to Bolzano to visit her sister, Gertrude—who was dying of cancer. She spent one day and then left to board the SS *Saturnia* bound for New York. Earlier in the war this rusty vessel had served as a floating hospital for the American military. Instead of cabins, the passengers had to sleep in dormitories. On July 17, 1947, she caught sight of the Statue of Liberty as her ship came into New York. Twenty-one years old, and almost alone in the New World, she disembarked with one little cardboard suitcase—and $40.

Helma had met her future husband in Rome—and he had arrived in New York just two months earlier. Viktor "Willy" Goldmark was then a thirty-year-old refugee from Vienna. Willy was also a survivor—and a robust, gregarious man with a healthy appetite for whatever life offered him. When Susan first introduced me to her father in late 1972, he was sitting at a Formica table in Katz's Delicatessen at 205 East Houston Street, sipping a celery soda. I'd never heard of celery soda. But I tried one and liked it—and I savored as well the extra-lean corned beef sandwich he ordered for me. I'd never been in a place as Jewish as Katz's, probably the best deli in New York. Salami logs hung from the ceiling, and every table was stocked with huge bowls of fat kosher dill pickles, horseradish and yellow mustard. I think Willy and I took to each other right away because within minutes we were arguing loudly but good-naturedly about everything from Richard Nixon to the Arab-Israeli conflict. The Israeli flag and various pro-Israel bumper stickers adorned Katz's walls—along with photos of celebrities and politicians eating kosher hot dogs. Though a Democrat, Willy had voted for Nixon that November. And, of course, he blamed the Arabs for everything—from the price of gasoline to trying to "drive the Jews into the sea." But Willy was fun. He was boisterous, opinionated and quick-witted. He was full of laughter—and his stories about surviving the Holocaust were lighthearted and always told with a smile. In this, and in many other ways, he was quite different from Helma.

Susan had grown up hearing her mother complain about her life, hinting at the terrible ordeals she had endured. She conveyed to her daughter all her pent-up fears and the lingering dread of her life story—but she told her nothing of the actual facts. Helma quite unconsciously taught her daughter not to inquire too closely; the Holocaust was alluded to all the time, but it was not something you taught your child about. Susan thus grew up without knowing a narrative of her mother's survival. She knew only that her mother kept a packed suitcase in her closet—an ominous message that the world was a dangerous place. The result was that she absorbed her mother's fears, but knew nothing about her mother's courage or fortitude—or of the many people who went out of their way to help her to survive. She knew nothing of the dangers her mother had endured—and nothing of her immense good fortune in the face of these evils. She only knew, in that vague guilt-ridden manner that only a mother can impart to a daughter, that her mother had lost everything as a teenager—and that by contrast her own life in New York was supposed to be that fairy tale known as the American Dream.

By contrast, Willy was effusive and naturally fulsome when it came to talking about the war years. But from his telling of it to Susan, his Holocaust experience was an adventure, and at times almost a lark, as he bribed the lazy Italian internment camp guards with smuggled cigarettes and booze. His stories sounded like rosy obfuscations—just as much so as Helma's silent angst. And both left their mark on Susan.

Some aspects of Willy's narrative were in fact as dark as Helma's. Willy had grown up in Vienna, and on the eve of the Anschluss it seemed just possible that this son of a grocer might have a career as a concert pianist: he was that good with his beefy workman's hands. But within days of Hitler's occupation of Austria, their grocery was robbed and methodically vandalized; a truck pulled up and Austrian Fascists carried away all the merchandise. Willy's neighbors—many of them daily customers of the store—stood around approvingly, shouting "Heil Hitler!" Shortly afterwards, one of their employees appeared in an SA uniform with a "requisition" document in hand stating that the grocery now belonged to him. The Goldmarks knew this employee had been arrested in 1936 for being a Nazi Party member; when he was released after three months, he returned to the grocery and begged Willy's father to rehire him. He got his job back—and now, two years later, he was here to seize the Goldmark grocery as his own. Willy's father, Samuel, told his employee, "If you want to requisition a grocery, why don't you take that one down the street? You know it is six times larger than this one." Samuel had never been much of a businessman. He spent most of his time in the synagogue, studying the Torah, leaving the grocery to his wife. But he had temporarily saved his grocery—at the expense of another Jew's business. Such were the choices in Hitler's Vienna.

Samuel and Lea Laufer Goldmark remained in Vienna until that November's Kristallnacht—after which it was Lea who took the initiative to get out. Samuel happened to be in the hospital for a minor ailment. So Lea and her daughter, Frieda, packed a small trunk and told the neighbors that they were going to visit Samuel in the hospital. They walked out of their apartment, leaving behind everything but a few family photographs. It was Christmas Day, 1938. After checking Samuel out of the hospital, they went straight to the train station and caught a train for Brussels. If they had stayed even a year longer, they probably would have ended up in Auschwitz. But in 1938 Germany was still allowing its Jewish citizens to leave legally, so long as they didn't take any property. When war broke out in September 1939, they made their way to Paris, and when Hitler took Paris in June 1940, they fled to neutral Portugal. In Lisbon they were fortunate enough to obtain an American visa, and boarded one of the last boats to New York before Pearl Harbor. By then they had lost contact with their two sons, Willy and Bunio.

Astonishingly, Willy had decided in December 1938 to stay behind in Vienna, ostensibly to take care of the grocery store, or sell it. He later intimated that the real reason was a *shiksa*—a non-Jewish woman. For Willy, affairs of the heart always, always took precedence over practicalities, however compelling, however fraught with urgency or danger. So he passed over his chance to escape Europe with his family in order to pursue a woman. For an incorrigible optimist, there was no other choice but to follow his heart. So Willy stayed, and to earn a little money he repaired motorcycles for the Nazi military. And why not?

But, perhaps inevitably, Willy's amorous adventure ended precipitously; he broke off the affair—and the scorned *shiksa* then threatened to betray him to the Nazis. Willy decided it was time to make his exit. He pawned everything of any value, including his ski boots and a beautiful pair of skis, and set out to join his brother in Milan. Bunio had moved to Italy right after the Anschluss—or maybe even before it—and gone to work for a Goldmark uncle who had a small tailoring business. Surreally, when Willy applied for a German passport, he was told that he first had to obtain a letter exempting him from military service. They laughed at him when he appeared at German army headquarters. "You're Jewish?" they exclaimed. It was a joke to them—but then they took him out into the street and forced him to get down on his hands and knees and clean the cobblestones with a toothbrush. Finally, on February 22, 1939, he got his exemption letter and passport from the Central Office for Jewish Emigration, then headed by a thirty-two-year-old SS officer, Adolf Eichmann. (Susan and I still have the passport, adorned with a black swastika, framed on our bedroom wall.) He managed to take a train across the border to Milan without incident.

In Milan the brothers worked as salesmen for their uncle. Willy had the personality of a hustler, so it was surprising when he couldn't sell a single suit. Instead, he soon took to exchanging lire for dollars on the black market. "I made very good money every day."

He found Italy a true haven from anti-Semitism: "The Jews did very good under Mussolini. There was no Jewish politics, because the Jews looked like the Italians, they behaved like the Italians, they worked with their hands like the Italians, so there was no problem. There were only 47,000 Jews out of 47 million, so it was nothing. And when you don't know a people you cannot hate them. Can you hate an Eskimo? You can't hate an Eskimo. You can hate someone in your neighborhood, but not an Eskimo."

Still, Willy understood that his status in Fascist Italy was precarious. In Vienna he had written the American consulate, requesting an immigration visa. In Milan he tried again, even though he knew that America's doors were largely slammed shut. With their limited quota system the Americans were taking in very few immigrants. And they were not making any emergency provisions for the plight of European Jews desperate to get out of Fascist Europe. Years later Willy complained that the problem German Jews faced in the late 1930s wasn't getting exit visas out of Germany, it was obtaining immigration visas to America—or any other safe haven.

In June 1940—just after Mussolini declared war on the Allies—foreign Jews all over Italy were suddenly subject to arrest. Eventually, some 3,500 foreign Jews were sent south to various concentration camps—and another 5,000 were sentenced to enforced internal exile in isolated villages. Sometime that summer the two Goldmark brothers were detained by Italian *cara-binieri*. Initially, they were taken to Milan's overcrowded city prison, San Vittore. Conditions in the prison were filthy. But after five days, they were separated and sent to different internment camps. Wearing manacles on both his legs and wrists, Willy was shipped by train to a small, newly opened detention camp south of Rome. There the detainees—Jews and Italian political dissidents—lived in tents for several months. "I was always hungry," Willy remembered. "There was so little food, even the guards were hungry." Eventually, he was shipped to the small town of Isernia, about 110 miles southeast of Rome. There were no more than a hundred other detainees. He languished there for nearly fifteen months until January 9, 1942, when he and all the other Jews of Isernia were shipped to Ferramonti in the southern province of Calabria.

Built on a swamp near the Crati River, this desolate and remote camp was Italy's only real concentration camp. It would be Willy's home for nearly two years. Everyone lived behind barbed-wire fences in crudely built white wooden barracks. Thirty beds were crammed into each hut. Armed "Black Shirt" fascist militiamen (Camicie Nere) patrolled the perimeters of the camp and manned the guard towers. Officers from the Italian police security forces administered the camp. There was no electricity, and little running water. During the hot, muggy summers—when temperatures routinely soared over 100 degrees Fahrenheit—many of the detainees suffered from typhus, scabies and dysentery. Thirty-seven internees died from these diseases and were buried in the local Tarsia community cemetery. During the camp's existence 820 cases of malaria were recorded. Bedbugs were rampant. Daily life was miserable and monotonous.

But if conditions at Ferramonti were initially extremely spartan, it was also true, as Willy intimated to his daughter, that the inmates gradually took control of their surroundings and made living conditions tolerable. They were allowed to elect a camp spokesman. They dug water wells and built a canteen and baths. Eventually, they had a library with several hundred books and a theatre as well. A charitable organization in Milan shipped a concert grand piano—which must have delighted Willy.

Over time, the Italian police began detaining women as well, and so whole families began to populate Ferramonti. Over three years, twenty-five children were born. A school and nursery were built, and a rabbi organized a small synagogue. By 1943 the camp was home to more than 2,000 people, mostly German Jews but also a variety of Jews from all over Europe. The chief rabbi of Genoa, Riccardo Pacifici, was so distressed by the plight of these Jews that he made three trips to Ferramonti, where he led services and tried to comfort the internees. Ironically, Rabbi Pacifici would be deported to Auschwitz in November 1943, while most of the internees in Ferramonti would survive the war.

Ferramonti grew into a small village where the residents coped with the vicissitudes of daily life while living beneath guard towers. Still, food in the camp was poor and always scarce. Internees were given a daily allowance of only 6.5 lire, which barely sufficed for basic staples, let alone clothing and other needs. The Italian guards were not abusive, just indifferent. And if the inmates had something to bribe them with—cigarettes, liquor or bits of jewelry—well then, they could be quite accommodating. They were integral to the camp's black-market economy, allowing the inmates to smuggle in goods so long as they got their cut. Willy regularly persuaded an Italian *carabiniere*—in this case, a member of the elite police security forces—to buy fifty-kilo bags of sugar; after paying the guard a hefty markup, Willy sold the sugar inside the camp for a small profit. "I had him in my hip pocket," Willy boasted. For a time he had a monopoly on such camp necessities as cigarettes, salt, flour and sugar. "Did I make money?" Willy exclaimed. "I owned the camp!" One day he told the *carabiniere* that the camp was short on cigarettes; the next day the *carabiniere* appeared with two suitcases full of cigarettes. "The local village had not a single cigarette," Willy recalled with laughter, "while inside the camp the smoke was going like crazy!"

He also worked in the camp post office, where his job was to forward any letters in a foreign (other than Italian) language to a military censor outside the camp. But when the guards were not looking, Willy would call over the mail's intended recipients and let them read their letters. Only then were the letters sent to the censor—and invariably they came back heavily blacked out.

As the months rolled by, life in Ferramonti became both more normal and more surreal. The Vatican assigned a French- and German-speaking Alsatian Capuchin priest to the camp, ostensibly to minister to the spiritual needs of eighty-five Jewish internees who had long before converted to Catholicism. Friar Calliste Lopinot built a chapel and held daily Mass. In addition, however, the good friar clearly had missionary ambitions for his audience of captive Jews. A Catholic publication at the time observed of the Ferramonti inmates, "numerous also are the non-Christians whose unhappiness and personal reflections help them to understand the message of the Saviour." Friar Lopinot later claimed to have baptized seventy-nine Jews.

Willy probably laughed at the Capuchin friar's spiritual ambitions. He was comfortable in his Jewish skin—and he knew what was important in life. A woman. He had fallen in love with Fanny "Faye" Diamantstein, a slim twenty-year-old brunette with fetching dark eyes. Faye was already married to a Dr. Deutsch, an Austrian she had met in Milan and whom she had followed to Ferramonti. But this did not stop Faye from having an affair with the brash, handsome Willy. A family story has it that Willy had a showdown with Faye's doctor husband—and that he won both the fistfight and Faye.

To his credit, Father Lopinot also made strenuous efforts to minister to the material needs of the inmates, Jews and non-Jews equally. He funneled charitable donations from individual monsignors within the Vatican to supplement the camp's food budget. And he arranged to forward mail from the inmates to their relatives abroad through the Vatican's Information Service. Willy had no idea where his parents or siblings were. But in the spring of 1942 other internees began receiving mail from relatives—and so learned of the deportations to Poland from countries all over Europe. That summer they listened to BBC broadcasts that confirmed rumors of widespread roundups of Jews in Vichy France. Naturally, they began to worry whether they too would be deported north.

"For some days morale in the camp has been very bad," Father Lopinot reported to the Vatican on September 10, 1942. "News has arrived of the deportations of German Jews from free France to Poland. . . . This news has hit the internees like a thunderbolt. They are terrified. . . ."

That autumn they heard eyewitness testimony about what was happening in Poland. In early December 1942 three Polish Jews who had miraculously escaped Nazi-occupied Europe were picked up by Italian authorities and shipped to Ferramonti. Their firsthand stories about German atrocities in Poland confirmed everyone's worst fears. So the camp's elected spokesman, Israel Kalk, sat down in January 1943 and wrote a letter addressed to Myron Taylor, America's official representative to the Vatican, begging him to persuade Washington to admit foreign Jews in Italy threatened with deportation. "A dreadful awe," Kalk wrote in his imperfect but quite plain English, "keeps the minds of the Jewish prisoners because almost everybody among them has near relatives who had been deported to Poland some months ago and they know that there is no hope to see them any more because there is no way back from that Hell of despair." There was no response from either Taylor or the Roosevelt Administration.*

_____

*The plight of European Jewry—including the existence of deadly concentration camps in Poland—was widely known by early 1943. On December 13, 1942, Edward R. Murrow told his listeners on a CBS broadcast from London, "What is happening is this: millions of human beings, most of them Jews, are being gathered up with ruthless efficiency and

*   *   *

Willy was unaware of it, but in the summer of 1943 he and other Ferramonti inmates were almost shipped north. Throughout 1943 the Germans constantly exerted pressure on the Italians to close Ferramonti. Finally, early in July the Italian Ministry of the Interior ordered the transfer of all Ferramonti internees to the province of Bolzano, in German-controlled Italy. If this had happened, Willy would almost certainly have been shipped to one of the extermination camps. But history intervened, and on July 25 Mussolini's government collapsed and the order was never carried out.

Finally, just as Allied troops were landing in Sicily, German troops threatened to enter the camp—either to kill the inmates or to deport them to the north. They were only dissuaded when some of the Italian guards falsely reported that a typhus epidemic was sweeping through the camp.

One morning in early September Willy awoke and suddenly noticed that all the black shirts and the elite police security forces had disappeared. "The first day I walked out of the camp," Willy later told me, "and every fifteen or twenty steps I stopped and looked around—I was surprised that I had no guards behind me. I walked a mile or two. I was a free man!" Fearing their guards might come back, many fled to the nearby mountains and hid out for several days. Soon they could look down from the mountain refuge and see German troops retreating, their trucks filled with furniture and the occasional piano they had looted from Italian villages. For a few days, Willy survived on fresh figs; he ate so many figs he got sick to his stomach. (Years later, he so often retold this story to his young daughter that Susan still associates figs with freedom.) Finally, on September 14, 1943, British troops officially liberated Ferramonti.

Not having anywhere else to go, Willy and Faye remained in Ferramonti until Naples was liberated. By then, Faye was six months pregnant, and Willy married her in Naples. Their twin boys, David and Frederick, were born in Naples on October 9, 1944. The marriage would not last.

---

murdered. . . . The phrase 'concentration camp' is obsolete." The basic, incredible facts were being reported in such august newspapers as the *New York Times*. But Washington's officialdom still treated this information as just that—incredible. A special agency empowered to rescue Jews from Europe, the War Refugee Board, would not be established in Washington until January 1944.

*   *   *

By the autumn of 1943, Samuel and Lea Goldmark—Willy's parents—had not heard any news of their son for nearly three years. They owned a small hosiery repair shop at Second Avenue and Third Street in lower Manhattan. It wasn't much of a living, but it was something, and they were safe. One day in early October, a friend and fellow refugee from Vienna, Joseph Horowitz, was sitting in a movie theatre when a newsreel aired a clip about a recently liberated concentration camp in southern Italy. Suddenly, Horowitz saw splashed on the big screen a row of camp survivors standing in a food line—and for a brief moment he thought he saw Willy's face. Horowitz stayed to watch the movie all over again just so he could see the newsreel. This time he was sure it was Willy. Horowitz ran to the Goldmarks and announced, "I saw Willy in the movies!" They were incredulous, but coincidentally the *New York Times* had published a photo of Willy and other men from Ferramonti being fed by troops from the British Eighth Army. When Lea was shown the photo, she fainted with shock. Her boy had survived the war. The *Times* headline read, "Son Safe, Photo Shows: Refugee Mother Sees Picture of Man Rescued from Italians."

Viktor "Willy" Goldmark, fourth from left, on liberation day
at Camp Ferramonti, Italy

* * *

As soon as the war ended, Willy's new wife emigrated to New York with the twins. Willy's own visa—under the Austrian quota—didn't come through until the spring of 1947. He paid $233 for a ticket aboard an American Export Lines passenger ship, the SS *Saturnia,* which sailed to New York on May 8, 1947. By then, he was already in love with Helma. They had met in Rome when both of them were working for the American Joint Distribution Committee—Helma as a secretary and translator, Willy as a stockroom attendant. "I left Faye for Helma," Willy confessed.

Helma Blühweis, New York, 1948

Things were complicated. Willy and Faye had to obtain a divorce—and later, Helma chipped in so that Faye could return to Italy and "look for another husband." But finally, on March 17, 1950, Helma and Willy were married in a civil ceremony in New York. They had very little money. Willy was working in his father's hosiery business in lower Manhattan, and bartending on the weekends. Helma found a job as a secretary with an import-export company at 120 Wall Street. As a pretty blonde, she was chosen by a New York tabloid to be their "Office Orchid" of the week. Underneath a glamorous black-and-white photo, she was quoted as saying, "Only in America is there complete freedom. It is my career, my hobby, my future. I'll never go back to Europe. My parents [*sic*] died in a concentration camp."

In April 1953 their daughter, Susan, was born. But within a few short years the marriage was already in trouble. "I wasn't made for marriage," Willy told me years later.

When he died suddenly of an embolism in June 1987, we rushed up to New York for the funeral. He had just turned seventy years of age. Standing in the receiving line, Susan was greeting the mourners when one elegant blond woman introduced herself and whispered, "I was your father's companion." And then a few moments later, a second woman whispered the same words. And when later that week we were cleaning out Willy's apartment, yet another woman knocked on the door and shyly explained that she had come for her "things." She was an African-American woman, much younger than Willy. They had met while on jury service. She said he was a wonderful man.

Susan just laughed. We were not surprised. Willy was incorrigible. A few years before his death I had learned from Susan's half brother Dave that Willy had a "secret" daughter. Leslie was just thirteen. Her mother was a Puerto Rican immigrant who worked in Willy's Brooklyn hosiery factory. He had never married Leslie's mother, but each Saturday he would come by and take Leslie out to museums or the park and buy things for her. He had done the same for Susan when his marriage with Helma ended in divorce in 1963. Some people make their lives complicated. But whatever his failings as a husband, Willy had tried to be a good father.

In the summer of 1959 Helma took Susan to Europe. They went to Graz and knocked on the door of Number 22 Griesgasse. Georg Margutsch once again opened the door, and once again Helma asked if she could walk around her childhood home—and show it to her young daughter. Margutsch waved them in and stood by nervously as Helma showed Susan—then aged six—where she had spent her childhood in the years before the Anschluss. She was home, but her home was no longer hers.

Over the years, as I learned pieces of Helma's story, I began to ask her why she had never taken any legal steps to retrieve her property from Margutsch. She always dismissed the notion, saying it was not possible. In fact, Austrian archival records prove that she had indeed filed a property claim with an Austrian court in 1946. "Please note," she wrote the Austrian District Court, "that restitution of my one-half share of the property is my only means of survival and I beg you not to delay my request for restitution." She received an acknowledgment of the claim—but nothing else. And so she had given up and moved on with her life.

Unlike the Germans, the Austrians never established any legal mechanisms to compensate Jews and other victims of the Nazi era. (Helma and her late sister's family, the Endrizzis, could have brought a civil suit in an Austrian court against Georg Margutsch—but for some reason this never happened.) Though Austrians were often the most enthusiastic Fascists, after the war they proclaimed themselves victims of Hitler's annexation; any crimes committed after the Anschluss were exclusively the fault of the Germans. This hypocritical position was reversed in the late 1990s, when the Clinton Administration's special envoy, Stuart Eizenstat, negotiated a restitution settlement in Vienna. The Austrians agreed to set aside $210 million to compensate victims of the Holocaust. Nineteen thousand survivors registered their claims, and the Austrians established a General Settlement Fund for Victims of National Socialism. This commission was authorized to investigate the historical and legal validity of each individual claim.

Helma registered her claim, and to my surprise she was able to submit a substantial number of papers documenting her claim to the property at Number 22 Griesgasse. And then she waited. Five years later she finally received an answer from the Austrians. They confirmed her father's ownership of the property—but they nevertheless rejected her claim. Their investigators had found court records dated November and December 1948 indicating that Georg Margutsch had negotiated a deal with Helma's brother-in-law, Leone Endrizzi. Margutsch had allegedly paid Endrizzi, as the representative of his wife, the recently deceased Gertrude Blühweis Endrizzi, an undisclosed sum of money. In return, Endrizzi had relinquished all rights to the property. Austrian court records also included a document dated February 5, 1949, which stated that Helma Blühweis had by power of attorney formally "relinquished all of her right and title" to the property in return for 20,000 schillings "to be paid to Dr. Fritz Strassmann on her behalf."

Helma was astounded and outraged. The mere thought of negotiating with the man who had stolen her father's property was repellent. In 1949 she was living in New York City, and she had never ceded any power of attorney to anyone. Neither had she ever seen the alleged 20,000 schillings, and the attorney mentioned in the court files, Dr. Fritz Strassmann, was a stranger to her. All of it was a forgery, she thinks, concocted by Margutsch with Leone

Endrizzi as his accomplice. The Austrians admitted that they could not find in the files her signed affidavit conveying a power of attorney. But they did find a record that the document had been pulled from the file several years later by Dr. Strassmann—who turned out to be an attorney in the employ of Margutsch. The whole legal deceit thus appears to have been cleverly contrived by Margutsch and Strassmann. The sons and daughter of Dr. Leone Endrizzi believe their late father was not a party to the deal. They correctly point out that their father's signature does not appear anywhere in the court records. His alleged power of attorney—like Helma's—was withdrawn from the court records in August 1951. So this leaves the door open to the possibility that Dr. Endrizzi was also a victim of the fraud. Helma believes otherwise because of at least two clues. First, the court documents submitted by Margutsch contained her address in New York City—slightly modified, it seems, so she could not be contacted—and Helma does not understand how Margutsch could have obtained this address other than from her brother-in-law. And secondly, the court records also contain a reference to a January 21, 1947, affidavit Helma had notarized in Rome attesting to the death of her father. Helma believes she sent this private "death certificate" to her sister and brother-in-law prior to her departure for New York, and she can't account for Margutsch knowing of it unless Dr. Endrizzi had given it to him. Still, it remains a mystery.

Whatever happened, in the end we know Helma was defrauded. And she only learned of the fraud fifty-nine years after the fact. It is probably too late to seek justice in the Austrian courts. Margutsch died in the early 1970s; his son inherited the property in 1971. The Margutsch heirs sold the property in the early 1990s. Helma has no recourse. There would be no justice and no compensation. The Nazi had won everything.

Helma's and Willy's Holocaust survival stories are both extraordinary—and entirely unexceptional. They are extraordinary on a personal level. These things happened to them, and they managed to survive in the most precarious of circumstances. And yet their stories are unexceptional in that such things happened in these awful years to many thousands of people. All of these survivors have their stories. And collectively these stories resonate. They are both a gift and a terrible burden.

Helma survived as a low-level spy in the employ of a resistance cell run by a Capuchin priest. There is considerable irony in this because the Vatican under Pope Pius XII was essentially silent throughout the destruction of European Jewry over a period of six years. And despite this controversial historical legacy, Vatican officials seem ready sometime in the near future to honor this wartime pope with beatification.

Helma and Willy survived and eventually made a new life in America. (Recently, the Austrian government offered to restore Helma's citizenship. She accepted.) But their ordeal might have been considerably shorter—and many more Jews might have avoided the gas chambers—had America opened its doors to Jewish refugees in the 1930s. But in those years American politicians pandered to native anti-Semitism and feared to do anything that might make it seem that the fight against Fascism was a fight to save Jews.

Helma and Willy lost everything in Austria. Like the Kalbians in Jerusalem, Helma went back and knocked on the door of her father's house and was allowed to see what she had lost. She never forgot, and like the Kalbians, she still wants her home back—not because of its value, but as a matter of simple justice.

Holocaust survivors like Helma and Willy have stories that we can comprehend. As extraordinary as they are, these are experiences that we can imagine ourselves enduring. But the larger historical narrative of the six million Jews who did not survive is ultimately beyond any understanding. The great Italian writer Primo Levi (1919–1987) wrote in his deeply moving book *Survival in Auschwitz,* "Perhaps one cannot, what is more one must not, understand what happened, because to understand is almost to justify." In this sense Levi argues that the Holocaust—and what men like Hitler, Himmler, Goebbels and Eichmann did—is forever inexplicable and incomprehensible.

Levi was an Italian Jew from Turin who in 1943 fled into the mountains of northern Italy and joined a partisan resistance group called Justice and Liberty. But on December 13, 1943, Fascist militia captured him. A month later he was deported to Auschwitz. He was twenty-four years old. At Auschwitz he was selected for a labor unit and thus spared from the gas chambers. The Germans branded him with the number 174517. Against all odds, he survived until January 27, 1945, when Russian troops entered the death camp. His survival story might have been Helma's or Willy's if they had lingered in northern Italy beyond the summer of 1943.

I briefly met Levi at the home of his American editor, Arthur Samuelson, in 1986. At the time, I knew only that this diminutive man had survived Auschwitz to write about it. He was an extremely shy man whose large eyes stared at me with an intensity I will never forget. He was almost birdlike, tiny-boned, fragile—but also impervious. He possessed a certain graceful patience, as if willing to be infinitely observant. He spoke very little English, and he seemed overwhelmed by the attention he was receiving on his brief visit to America.

Levi's account of his experiences explains better than any historian why the Holocaust is an absolutely singular event in human history. The sheer inexplicability of an event like the Shoah is a difficult concept to convey to an audience of Europeans or Americans. It is even more difficult to explain to Middle Easterners, a people who had virtually nothing to do with the events in Nazi Europe. In 1978, I traveled as a journalist to Lebanon— which had just been invaded by Israel. We were part of a "fact-finding" delegation of journalists and various "activists." One day we were escorted into a PLO-controlled office building where we were introduced to a member of the Palestine National Council. Father Ibrahim Ayyad (1910–2005) was a kindly-looking old gentleman, dressed in the black robes of a Benedictine priest. As we sat around a large rectangular table, this priest-politician proceeded to lecture us about the plight of the Palestinian people and the cruelty of their enemy to the south. At one point, he bluntly compared the Israelis to the Nazis and said that the Palestinians had endured crimes worse than the Jewish Holocaust.

I interrupted him, and gently queried whether he actually meant to use this particular analogy. Did he know what had happened in the gas chambers of Poland? Father Ayyad responded with renewed vehemence that the true Holocaust was what was happening today to the Palestinian people. At this point, my friend Henry Schwarzschild, who was part of our delegation, rose and walked out in protest. Henry had been born in Germany and raised in Berlin to a fully "assimilated" family of modern German Jews. In 1939, when Henry was fourteen years old, they had all escaped to America. In 1961, he had been arrested in Mississippi as a Freedom Rider. By 1978, Henry was working for the American Civil Liberties Union as their chief lobbyist against the death penalty. He was a sweet man. So I too rose from my chair and told Father Ayyad that this was a ridiculous comparison—and then I walked out in protest. I had not yet read Primo Levi, but I knew enough to understand that the Jews, so far, have a monopoly on that particular word.

Levi wrote:

> The German camps constitute something unique in the history of humanity, bloody as it is. To the ancient aim of eliminating or terrifying political adversaries, they set a modern and monstrous goal, that of erasing entire peoples and cultures from the world. Starting roughly in 1941, they became gigantic death machines. Gas chambers and crematories were deliberately planned to destroy lives and human bodies on a scale of millions. The appalling record belongs to Auschwitz, with its 24,000 dead in a single day, in August 1944.

Nothing like this has happened before or since. To be sure, we have been witnesses to genocidal plagues in places like Rwanda and Cambodia. But there has been nothing like the organized industrial killing apparatus of the German death camps. The Palestinians have suffered decades of injustice and occupation, but they have fortunately not had to endure a Holocaust. And yet, it has also been their misfortune to have as an adversary a people who did.

The 350,000 survivors who came to Israel in the late 1940s were often brittle, emotionally wounded people. Many suffered from mercurial bouts of depression, anger and anxiety. Some had an intense desire to tell their stories but found it hard to find anyone who would really listen. Most survivors tried very hard to assume their new identity as Israelis, adopting Hebrew names and learning the language. Many Sabra Israelis—those born in Palestine—derided them as "block-headed Jews" and publicly labeled them "yekkes," a derogative, clownish term. The underlying question was always, "Why had these people allowed themselves to be rounded up and shipped like cattle to death camps? Why hadn't they resisted?" In the eyes of many Sabras, these refugees from Europe were the soft and weak remnants of the Diaspora. If they were to be redeemed and integrated as Israelis, they would have to be "reeducated." "They must learn love of the homeland, a work ethic, and human morals," said one Israeli politician—as if these survivors were somehow defective human beings. Ben-Gurion had an even darker view: "Among the survivors of the German concentration camps there were people who would not have survived if they had not been what they were— hard, evil, and selfish people—and what they underwent there served to destroy what good qualities they had left."

Not surprisingly, many Holocaust survivors left Israel in the 1950s; by 1952 some 40,000 early immigrants had left Israel, many of them survivors. It was tough to make your way as a pioneer in the new Jewish state. (By the year 2000 an estimated 800,000 Israelis had emigrated elsewhere.) Ironically, the new immigrants often occupied the homes of Palestinians who had fled or were expelled during the war. The Israeli historian Tom Segev observed: "Entire cities and hundreds of villages left empty were repopulated in short order with new immigrants. . . . Free people—Arabs—had gone into exile and become destitute refugees; destitute refugees—Jews— took the exiles' places as a first step in their new lives as free people. One group had lost all they had, while the other found everything they needed— tables, chairs, closets, pots, pans, plates, sometimes clothes, family albums, books, radios and pets. Most of the immigrants broke into the abandoned Arab houses without direction, without order, without permission."

But here is another important irony pointed out by Segev: if in 1948 the new state of Israel disparaged the Holocaust survivors as "weak Jews," today the Holocaust has become a core narrative for the state's existence. Rather than receding into history, the legacy of the Holocaust has become a central motif in Israeli national life. Every schoolchild studies it. The Yad Vashem museum is a major national institution, and Israeli politicians constantly exhort their people to never forget the six million.

After decades of war and terrorism, the Holocaust is seen as justifying anything the Israeli state does to defend itself. "Never Again" is not just a slogan but national policy. Avraham Burg, speaker of the Knesset from 1999 to 2003, has written, "Israel's security policy, the fears and paranoia, feelings of guilt and belonging are products of the Shoah. . . . Sixty years after his suicide in Berlin, Hitler's hand still touches us." The destruction of European Jewry is seen as the clearest evidence that Jews cannot safely live anywhere but in their own state. And yet contradictions abound.

Over the decades of conflict the Zionist dream of creating a new national identity has given way to something else. Gone is the goal of creating a "new man" in place of the "weak" Diaspora Jew, confined to the ghettos. Instead of creating a state like any other state where its citizens can live a normal life like the citizens of France or England or any other nation-state, Israel has become its own ghetto, where its Jews are in fact less safe than Diaspora Jews. Far from convincing Diaspora Jews to come to Israel, the Jews of Israel see across the seas the world's largest Jewish community residing quite happily in America. Far from distancing themselves from Diaspora Jewry, the Jews of Israel increasingly identify with traditional Jewish life as practiced for nearly two millennia in the Diaspora. Israel is becoming less "Israeli" and more "Jewish" with each passing war. And as it becomes more Jewish and less "Israeli," the Jewish state finds it steadily more difficult to forge a peace with its neighbors.

The Palestinians seem never to have understood this essential fact about their enemy: that Israel is a society still deeply traumatized by the Shoah. Hitler shot himself in 1945. But when Palestinians maim and kill in the name of resistance to the occupation, Israeli society resurrects Hitler. It's not fair, it's not even remotely comparable historically, but this is the psychological demon at work. "In our eyes," Avraham Burg wrote in 2007, "we are still partisan fighters, ghetto rebels, shadows in the camps, no matter the nation, state, armed forces, gross domestic product, or international standing. The Shoah is our life, and we will not forget it, and we will not let anyone forget us." Despite all the wars won, despite the modern state they have built, Israelis believe in the marrow of their bones that they are alone in the world, and that any attack must be met with overwhelming force because—*never again*. Armed struggle was the worst tactic the Palestinians could have used against a whole society marked by trauma and paranoia. But there has never been a high-profile, politically viable Palestinian Gandhi, and then over the decades it is the Palestinians who have become drenched in victimhood. For the Israelis, however, the Shoah always trumps the Nakba.

In June 1975, Susan and I were married by Carleton College's chaplain, but in a nod to Jewish tradition, we drank from a wineglass and wrapped it in a cloth napkin, and then I stomped on it with gusto. The simple ceremony was held on the "Hill of Three Oaks" in the college arboretum. Our parents attended, as did a score of college friends and several faculty members, including my former cellmate, Paul Wellstone. Afterwards, Willy put his arm around his daughter and whispered—out of my earshot—"Well, he's a nice guy, but you could have done better."

That summer we left America for what turned out to be a fifteen-month honeymoon around the world, financed again by a travel fellowship from the Thomas J. Watson Foundation—this time awarded to Susan. We land-traveled through Europe, the Middle East and much of Asia. We worked as freelance journalists, selling articles to magazines and periodicals like *The Nation* and the *Far Eastern Economic Review*. In Cairo, Susan scored an interview with Jehan Sadat, the president's wife. The interview was pub-lished in the *Chicago Daily News*.

Jehan Sadat and Susan Goldmark, Cairo, October 1975

As freelance journalists we attended the military parade in Cairo celebrat-ing the second anniversary of the war launched on October 6, 1973. (Six years later, members of Islamic Jihad assassinated President Anwar Sadat at this same parade ground.) After a month in Egypt, we flew to Amman and crossed over the Allenby Bridge into the West Bank. In Jerusalem, I intro-duced Susan to Dani Bahar, who graciously took us around the city. We interviewed the newly elected mayors of Hebron and Nablus, and in Jeru-salem and Tel Aviv we spoke with Israeli officials, scholars and journalists. We spent three or four days at Kerem Shalom, a left-wing kibbutz near the Gaza Strip, just inside the Green Line. A few weeks prior to our visit these kibbutzniks had demonstrated their disgust and loathing for the forever truculent General Ariel Sharon by dumping a truckload of manure on the front lawn of his nearby ranch. Most of the Israelis we met seemed irreverent, smart and upbeat. Eight years after the June 1967 War, many Israelis did not hesitate to go shopping in West Bank vegetable markets. Thousands of Palestinians from the West Bank and Gaza worked regularly inside Israel. Palestinians chafed under the arbitrariness of Israeli military rule, but the occupation was not yet an *occupation*. And there were relatively few Israeli settlers living in the West Bank or Gaza.

Kai and Susan in Rawalpindi, Pakistan, January 1976

Anwar Sadat would not make his dramatic visit to Jerusalem for another two years, but Susan and I felt certain from our many conversations with Israelis and Palestinians that a peace settlement was within reach. The two sides still disputed each other's historical narratives, but the future seemed inevitable: Israel would exchange land for peace, and a demilitarized Palestinian state would be created in the West Bank and Gaza, with East Jerusalem as its capital. We were very hopeful. And, of course, we were mistaken.

9

The Hebrew Republic

Hillel Kook, third from left, with Menachem Begin, fourth from left

What am I? Well, you say, "He is a Jew." What do you mean? . . . Being a Jew, what is my position in the world? What is my relationship to human society? In simple terms, what nation do I belong to? I say I am a Hebrew. My allegiance is to the Hebrew nation. My country is Palestine.

Hillel Kook, aka Peter Bergson, 1946

Late in the summer of 1976, Susan and I finally returned to America. We'd had many adventures. We had land-traveled from Jerusalem to Tehran to Kabul and finally ended up in Islamabad, where we filed weekly news stories for the Hong Kong–based *Far Eastern Economic Review*. After only three months, Pakistan's prime minister Zulfikar Bhutto expelled us for a story I had written on press censorship. Things were no better in India, where we were forced to write under pseudonyms due to Prime Minister

Indira Gandhi's Emergency Rule. We were among the first journalists to report on Gandhi's infamous program of enforced sterilizations of young men. (Police were literally cruising India's towns and villages, randomly picking up young men and trucking them off to sterilization clinics.) Working in Bangladesh for a month, we encountered some of the worst poverty we'd ever seen. Susan proved herself to be a tough interviewer and a quick wordsmith. But journalism left her unsatisfied. It was insecure and sometimes dangerous—we were teargassed one day in Dacca while covering a political rally by the opposition. So in the autumn of 1976 Susan enrolled in a graduate program at Princeton University to study economic development. I followed her and spent much of 1976–77 either freelancing or working as an associate editor at *Newsweek International.* That gig lasted six months, and then I was fired. Apparently, I was too opinionated in my reporting.

By early 1978, I had secured a tenuous, part-time, three-day-a-week position as the assistant editor of *The Nation.* Three months later, Victor S. Navasky suddenly became my new boss. Victor had just abandoned a promising career at the *New York Times* to become the editor and effective owner of America's oldest weekly magazine, dating back to 1865. Founded by Boston and New York abolitionists, *The Nation* had an illustrious muckraking reputation. It first turned a small profit for two years in the 1940s, but in the wake of the McCarthyite scourge, the magazine fell on hard times. Under Carey McWilliams, it continued to publish great journalism, but its readership gradually declined to perilous levels. By 1978, paid circulation had fallen to somewhat less than 20,000, consisting largely of libraries, along with a bickering collection of aging New Dealers, Adlai Stevenson liberals, elderly lapsed Communists and the occasional survivor of the sixties cultural wars. These demographics—and hefty deficits—didn't augur well for the magazine's future survival.

Happily, the magazine's survival was Navasky's responsibility, not mine. (Today, Navasky is editor and publisher emeritus, and *The Nation* has a healthy circulation of nearly 200,000—and, miraculously, it even makes a small profit.) I had first started writing for the magazine in 1976 from India and Bangladesh. But my job in its New York office was to solicit and edit contributions from great investigative reporters like Fred Cook, Robert Sherrill and a slew of younger and often completely inexperienced writers— such as the then very young Eric Alterman, who published in *The Nation* his first piece of journalism, on the MX missile, a topic of which, of course, he knew very little. (He now knows a great deal more about many more subjects, but I still wouldn't rely on him for his knowledge of throw weights of nuclear missiles.) My interns included Nick Goldberg, now an editor at the *Los Angeles Times*; Amy Wilentz—who eventually married Nick and went on to become a novelist and essayist for places like *The New Yorker*; David Corn, who became the magazine's Washington editor; Tim Noah, now a *Slate* columnist; and Katrina vanden Heuvel—who much later succeeded Navasky. In other words, at the tender age of twenty-six, I had a terrific job, surrounded by quite interesting talent. Soon, I was working ten or twelve hours a day, and often seven days a week.

Victor Navasky was also working hard, not only editing the magazine and helping its young publisher, Hamilton Fish III, to scrounge for cash to cover the annual deficit, but also completing his second book, *Naming Names,* a history of the McCarthy era and an investigation of the Hollywood writers who "named names" and those who refused. Simultaneously, that year Victor devoted an entire issue of *The Nation* to a critical review of Allen Weinstein's new book, *Perjury: The Hiss-Chambers Case.* This, of course, got him into a lot of trouble. Expressing any doubt that Alger Hiss might not be exactly the spy everyone assumed him to be was grounds for banishment from the Establishment.

Victor Navasky, sketched by Edward Sorel

For all these reasons, I deeply admired Navasky. He quickly became my journalistic mentor, teaching me the craft of writing editorials and how to inspire young freelancers to rewrite their wooden prose for the third or fourth time—all for a payment in the "high two figures." I called Victor my "rabbi"—a term Wall Street lawyers still use to describe the wizened name partners who take under their wings a young associate.

That spring Israel invaded Lebanon, determined to put a stop to PLO-sponsored attacks launched from Lebanon. PLO *fedayeen* had virtually taken over South Lebanon and were routinely shelling civilians in North Israel. On March 11, 1978, an eleven-member Fatah commando team led by an eighteen-year-old woman, Dalal Mughrabi, landed on a beach near Haifa. After killing an American tourist, they hijacked several vehicles and drove south towards Tel Aviv, shooting at other cars along the way. All told, thirty-seven Israelis died that day. It became known as the Coastal Road Massacre. Two days later, Israel launched Operation Litani, sending in 25,000 Israeli troops to occupy southern Lebanon. The invasion led to a temporary lull in Lebanon's ghastly civil war.

That summer, I received an invitation to participate in a "fact-finding" tour of Lebanon by the Association of Arab-American University Graduates. The association offered to pick up all expenses, which was a problem, since we suspected they had an agenda. Still, I wanted to go on this junket, and while Victor thought the trip would likely result in some original reporting for the magazine, he didn't have the budget to pay for it. But as usual, Victor had a perfect solution for a lawyer educated at Yale Law School: I would take an unpaid leave from the magazine, and if I wrote anything, the association's funding would be acknowledged. This would protect the magazine's good name—and save it some money to boot.

The junket turned out to be a wholly operated franchise of the PLO. We were met at the airport by a PLO bus, guarded by *fedayeen* armed with Kalashnikovs and escorted to a hotel in Ras Beirut owned by the PLO. After a week of touring the refugee camps, I got off the propaganda bus and headed for Israel.

Navasky had made me promise to look up an Israeli businessman in Tel Aviv named Hillel Kook. This seemed to be Navasky's sole contact in the whole of the Middle East. But it proved to be a good one. I soon learned that Kook was a former agent of the Irgun Zvai Leumi, an underground organization that had launched terrorist attacks against the British in the 1930s

Expires December 31, 1980

Kai BIRD
Name
The Nation
Affiliation
New York, NY
Location

Kai's *Nation* magazine press pass, 1980

and '40s. (The Irgun was the group responsible for the Deir Yassin massacre in 1948.) By all accounts, Kook himself had not participated in any terrorist attacks. But he had been the Irgun's undercover "ambassador" in America.

And what was Navasky's association with this "terrorist" organization called the Irgun? As he explains it in his memoir, *A Matter of Opinion,* he secured his first real job (at $2.50 an hour) in September 1946, when the brilliant, Oscar Award–winning New York playwright and screenwriter Ben Hecht hired him to pass the contribution basket after each performance of Hecht's new play, *A Flag Is Born,* at the Alvin Theatre on Broadway. Navasky was just fourteen; a year earlier he had celebrated his bar mitzvah. *A Flag Is Born,* a one-act play starring Marlon Brando, was a dramatic tribute to the European Jews killed in the Holocaust—but also a tribute to the Jewish freedom fighters who were then trying to expel the British from Palestine and create a Jewish national homeland. At one point in the play, an Irgun fighter exhorts Brando to join them, saying they fight "in the streets of Jerusalem . . . in the hills of Lebanon, in the deserts of Judea. . . . We battle the English, the sly and powerful English. We speak to them in a new Jewish language, the language of guns. . . . We promise to wrest our homeland out of British claws." (Arabs were completely absent from Hecht's drama.) The British government lodged a protest against the play, and Judah Magnes, the president of the Hebrew University in Jerusalem, wrote a letter to Eleanor Roosevelt, protesting her attendance: "Are you in favor of supplying money and arms for the terrorists . . . ?"

Young Navasky was under the impression that the contents of the collection basket he circulated were going to the Haganah to encourage Jewish immigration to Palestine. (Hecht told reporters that the play raised a million dollars.) But, as Navasky soon learned, "in fact the money would really go to the Irgun Zvai Leumi, which was in the business of engaging in acts of terrorism against the British." Indeed, the following year, in May 1947, Hecht used his own proceeds from the play to pay for an ad in the *New York Herald Tribune* congratulating the Irgun on "[blowing up] British trains, robbing British banks, killing British tommies."

Navasky reports that this experience was one of two events that stimulated his "political awakening." (The other was cheering for Jackie Robinson when the Brooklyn Dodgers hired the first African-American to play baseball in the major leagues.) The irony of Navasky's early brush with the Irgun was not lost on either of us. I am not sure who told him that Hillel Kook would be an interesting man to look up in Israel, but I am very glad that I had a chance to interview Kook.

When Kook was working in America as an undercover agent for the Irgun, he used the alias "Peter H. Bergson." In 1978, I found Bergson/Kook in a café in the old Arab city of Jaffa, just south of Tel Aviv. At the time, Israeli entrepreneurs were busy renovating Jaffa's ancient stone houses with the intention of turning the old seaport into a quaint artists' colony. Kook was then a sixty-three-year-old businessman who had made a considerable fortune on Wall Street in the 1950s and '60s. He had come back to Israel in 1968 and retired to Kfar Shmaryahu, a wealthy enclave north of Tel Aviv. He dressed as a man of means, wearing a finely tailored dress shirt and light wool pants. A strikingly handsome man with blue-gray eyes and a full salt-and-pepper beard, Kook even then exuded charisma. He was debonair and articulate—and what he had to say captivated me.

Over numerous cups of Turkish coffee, Kook told me his life story. He spoke not with bitterness but with irony—rather like a man who knew he

Hillel Kook, aka Peter Bergson, 1998

had lived through some extraordinary history. His political journey was a revelation. At the age of twenty-seven, I thought I knew some Israeli history. But Kook taught me otherwise. At one point in our long conversation, he pulled out his Israeli identity card and exclaimed, "Look, Israel is the only state in the world that legally defines 'Arab' as a nationality. Here on my identity card I must claim to be either 'Arab' or 'Jewish.' In fact, I fought for the establishment of Israel precisely to become an Israeli Palestinian. Yes, yes, I am a Palestinian, a Hebrew in a political state called Israel located in historical Palestine."

Three decades later, I remain convinced that Kook's ideas about Israeli identity are essential to any lasting resolution of the conflict. As a biographer, I have always believed that one man's life story can shed light on a larger historical epoch. So it is with Kook. His story is an emblematic story of Israel.

*   *   *

Kook was born in 1915 in Lithuania. His father was a rabbi and his uncle was Rabbi Abraham Isaac Kook, who later became Israel's first Ashkenazic chief rabbi. Hillel Kook was just nine years old when his family fled a pogrom and emigrated to Palestine in 1924. The Kooks settled in Afula, and Hillel received a religious education as a teenager. With rising Jewish-Arab tensions, he soon gravitated towards the Revisionist Zionist movement. In 1931, at the tender age of sixteen, he helped to found the Irgun Zvai Leumi, a militant paramilitary organization dedicated to creating a Jewish national homeland by force. Kook saw some combat at the start of the Arab uprising in 1936; he was the Irgun's post commander in the Jewish settlement of Motza, near Jerusalem, when it came under fire from the Arab village of Kalandia. But his true talents lay in the realm of propaganda. The following year, at the age of twenty-two, he was dispatched to Poland, where for the next four years he served as a personal aide to Ze'ev Jabotinsky, the founder and guiding ideologue of the Revisionist Zionist movement. Jabotinsky and his band of "Revisionists" broke away from David Ben-Gurion and other mainstream Zionists in 1935, forming their own separate party, the New Zionist Organization.

Jabotinsky (1880–1940) had developed a complicated political pedigree. He was fiercely nationalistic, and right-wing in his economic views. He viewed the British Mandate authorities as Zionism's foremost enemy—and yet he dreamed of establishing a haven for European Jewry modeled after Britain's liberal democratic polity. As a Zionist, he was emphatically nonreligious. He envisioned a secular democratic state on both sides of the River Jordan, and he believed that this could be accomplished by force of arms and the mobilization of world opinion. But while he envisioned a Jewish majority, he also insisted that the Arab minority should be accorded full political rights. In 1940 he wrote that "in every cabinet where the prime minister is a Jew, the vice-premiership shall be offered to an Arab, and vice versa." Arabic and Hebrew would have equal footing in the new state. What was important to him was the creation of a state where Jews would no longer be singled out as Jews. "We are a people as all other peoples," he wrote in 1911. "We do not have any intentions to be better than the rest. As one of the first conditions for equality we demand the right to have our own villains, exactly as other people have them." He railed against "those Jews who do not remove the rust of the exile from themselves and refuse to shave their beard and sidelocks. . . ." But he also ridiculed his Jewish socialist rivals like Ben-Gurion. And as a principled secularist, he would have been horrified by the privileges and special political status Ben-Gurion accorded the Orthodox rabbinate in the new state of Israel.

Jabotinsky was exiled from Palestine by the British Mandate authorities in 1930, so he spent the last ten years of his life in Europe, observing the rise of Fascism. By 1936, he was so worried about the safety of the Jewish community in Poland that he formulated a controversial plan for the orderly evacuation of all Jews to Palestine over a period of ten years. Extraordinarily, he persuaded the governments of Poland, Hungary and Romania to endorse the plan. His critics charged that he was inadvertently fanning the flames of anti-Semitism. But Jabotinsky publicly insisted that the Jews of Poland "were living on the edge of the volcano" and that they should leave for Palestine.

Jabotinsky was right, of course, but like all prophets in the wilderness, he had few listeners. He died of a heart attack while visiting New York in August 1940. But before he died he persuaded his twenty-five-year-old aide, Kook, to move to New York, where he was to serve as the Irgun's clandestine fund-raiser, propagandist and de facto ambassador. With Jabotinsky's death, Kook became the Irgun's ranking leader outside of Palestine. Adopting the alias Peter Bergson, Kook quickly formed an underground cell of ten Irgun activists, including screenwriter and author Ben Hecht and the Polish-American cartoonist Arthur Szyk. Initially, they promoted the creation of a Jewish Brigade within the British army and lobbied for Jewish immigration to Palestine. They probably also illegally laundered money in America bound for the Irgun's underground militia.

But then on November 25, 1942, Bergson read a short news report on page 10 of the *New York Times* that left him horrified. The news story dryly reported that the State Department had confirmed that two million Jews had been killed in Nazi Europe. That very day, after meeting with a State Department official who authenticated the reports, Bergson gathered his Irgun cell members and announced that the situation called for an "emergency committee to rescue European Jews." Thereafter, he abandoned his Irgun activities and turned his energies to various rescue schemes. Bergson's decision seemed straightforward to him at the time. "We responded as a human and as a Jew should," he later said. "Why did we respond the way we did? The question should be, why didn't the others?"

As he was soon to learn, the idea of rescuing Jews turned out to be more controversial than laundering money to buy weapons for the Irgun in British-occupied Palestine.

The Holocaust was not a secret. Reports of the mass killings began leaking from Europe soon after Reinhard Heydrich, chief of the Reich's Main Security Office, communicated Adolf Hitler's "Final Solution of the European Jewish Question" to an assembly of Nazi officials at Wannsee on January 20, 1942. As early as December 1941, the *New York Herald Tribune,* a paper noted for its skeptical treatment of Nazi atrocity stories, had concluded that what was happening in Europe was nothing short of "systematic extermination." In June 1942, Polish officials in exile in London released a report through the Warsaw Jewish socialist organization, the Bund, which calculated that 700,000 Jews had been killed in Poland alone by mobile killing squads. The substance of this report was broadcast by the BBC and carried by a few American newspapers. The *New York Times* ran the story on page 19. But by the end of 1942, some of America's most prominent journalists were leaving no doubt as to the credibility of such reports.

Millions of Americans—and ranking officials in the Roosevelt Administration—were exposed to such reports. In early December 1942, President Franklin Roosevelt told a delegation of visiting Jewish leaders, "Representatives of the United States government in Switzerland and other neutral countries have given us proof that confirms the horrors discussed by you." There was confirmation, and yet there was disbelief. There was still no fundamental comprehension of either the enormity of the evil or the possibility that something could be done to slow or stop the killing machine. President Roosevelt did nothing in 1942–43 to publicize the plight of European Jewry, to rescue Jews on the periphery of the Nazi empire—or, indeed, to expedite the immigration to America of those Jewish refugees who had managed to escape Nazi Europe. Such paralysis extended even into the Jewish American community. The *New York Times* editorialized about the "world's helplessness to stop the horror while the war was going on. . . ." The consensus among the leadership of mainstream Jewish organizations was that the best way to aid European Jewry was to bring about an early defeat of Hitler.

Bergson disagreed. At the very least, he thought, he could publicize the massacres—and this alone might persuade America to open its borders to

Jewish refugees, and perhaps mount diplomatic or military operations to rescue Jews. In early 1943, he raised money to publish a full-page ad in the *Times,* brazenly announcing:

> FOR SALE To Humanity
> 70,000 Jews
> Guaranteed Human Beings at $50 a Piece

In smaller print, the ad explained that Nazi officials in Romania were willing to cancel the deportation of 70,000 Jews to the death camps in exchange for payments of $50 per head. The ad went on to call for the establishment of an Allied intergovernmental committee to "formulate ways and means of stopping this wholesale slaughter of human beings." Written by Ben Hecht, the ad copy was designed to provoke—and it did not fail. Mainstream Jewish American organizations charged Bergson and his friends with "fraud." Rabbi Stephen S. Wise, chairman of the American Jewish Congress, refused to join in Bergson's campaign. Rabbi Wise had himself announced in November 1942 that two million Jews had been killed in Europe. But he thought the "Bergsonites'" aggressive publicity campaign was bad publicity. Wise preferred to exercise quiet diplomacy in Washington.

Undeterred by controversy, Bergson persuaded Ben Hecht to write and produce a ninety-minute "pageant" entitled *We Will Never Die,* which memorialized the murdered Jews of Europe. With music composed by Kurt Weill, and starring Paul Muni, Stella Adler and Edward G. Robinson, the pageant's March 9, 1943, double premiere drew 20,000 people to each performance in Madison Square Garden. All told, over 120,000 people in Boston, Philadelphia, Chicago, Washington and Hollywood were exposed to its searing political message. Bergson proved to be an adept publicist, persuading such media moguls as William Randolph Hearst to endorse the notion that the government should do more to rescue European Jewry. "Remember . . . This is not a Jewish problem," Hearst editorialized. "It is a human problem." Bergson met with Eleanor Roosevelt and persuaded her to devote one of her *My Day* newspaper columns to praising the pageant.

On March 3, 1943, the *New York Times* finally editorialized that the plight of European Jewry called for a radical reform of restrictive U.S. immigration regulations. A *Times* columnist, Anne O'Hare McCormick, urged the Christian community in America "to do the utmost to rescue the Jews remaining in Europe." Major newspapers around the country echoed these sentiments.

And yet, the Roosevelt Administration's policy towards Jewish refugees or the ongoing Holocaust changed not a whit. America's borders were not opened. During the three and half years America was at war with Germany, only 21,000 Jewish refugees were admitted to the United States—just 10 percent of the number who might have legally been admitted, even under the restrictive country quota system of those years. (The 1924 Immigration Act permitted a total of 153,774 immigrants per year—but of the 150,000 slots reserved for European countries, fully 83,574 slots were allocated for immigrants from Great Britain and Ireland. In practice, less than half of this quota was used. And during the twelve years of the Third Reich, only 35 percent of the German-Austrian quota was used.) Nor was anything done to "rescue" Jews still surviving on the fringes of the Nazi empire, in places like Romania, Greece and Spain, until Bergson forced the issue.

By the end of 1943, Bergson was obsessed with the idea of "rescue." In July of that year he formed the Emergency Committee to Save the Jewish People of Europe. Members included Arthur Szyk, Ben Hecht, Samuel Merlin, Esther Untermeyer, Max Lerner, Stella Adler and Congressman Will Rogers Jr. To the horror of mainstream Jewish American leaders, the Emergency Committee publicly accused the Allies of "cowardice" for their failure to do anything to save European Jewry. The committee took out full-page ads in the *New York Times,* the *Los Angeles Times,* the *Washington Post,* the *New Republic* and *The Nation* in which readers were brazenly asked, "HOW WELL ARE YOU SLEEPING? Is there something you could have done to save millions of innocent people—men, women, and children—from torture and death?" Simultaneously, Bergson lobbied Congress to pass a "rescue" resolution urging the Roosevelt Administration to create a new government agency whose sole mission would be to rescue Jews in Europe.

Instead of joining Bergson's campaign, American Zionist organizations attempted to discredit those they now called the "Bergsonites." The American Jewish Conference released a blistering statement, calling Bergson's Emergency Committee "sensationalist" and ineffectual. (Note, however, that by 1945 the Emergency Committee boasted more than 125,000 members, making it one of the largest Jewish organizations in the country.) Such prominent Jewish American leaders as Rabbi Stephen Wise, Nahum Goldmann and Congressman Sol Bloom attacked the Bergsonites as irresponsible and unrepresentative of the American Jewish community. They tried to persuade the Roosevelt Administration to deport Bergson. The IRS opened up an investigation of the Emergency Committee's finances—they found no irregularities.

Criticism of the Bergsonites was more or less uniform among elite Jewish opinion. Eugene Meyer, the publisher of the *Washington Post,* privately wrote a friend that he thought calls for rescue of European Jews amounted to "harassment" of President Roosevelt. The president, after all, was trying to win a war, and Meyer rejected the idea that "it is necessary for any pressure group, however well meaning, to devote its time and money to the business of 'molding American opinion' on this subject."

Most Jewish Americans—and most Zionists—either saw what was happening inside Nazi Europe as another pogrom or, if they wholly understood that Jews were being systematically exterminated, nevertheless bought the argument that the only way to rescue them was to "win the war." One prominent American Zionist, Rabbi Abba Hillel Silver, argued that the slaughter of European Jewry was merely evidence of a "persistent emergency in Jewish life." The endless cycle of pogroms would not end, Rabbi Silver, insisted, until the Diaspora disappeared into its own national homeland. Jewish homelessness, he declared, was "the principal source of our millennial tragedy." In short, these Jewish Americans argued, nothing could be done for European Jewry until the war was won and a Jewish state was created in Palestine. And in the meantime, Rabbi Silver's priority was to mobilize the Diaspora to emigrate to Palestine.

Rabbi Silver was no doubt sincere in these views. He was an idealist, and by no means a cynic. But in retrospect, he and other mainstream Jewish leaders quite clearly demonstrated a lack of imagination—perhaps they simply could not comprehend the incomprehensible news from Nazi-occupied Europe. Bergson could, and he and his followers pragmatically set out to do what they could to rescue Europe's remaining Jews. That the Jewish American establishment opposed them only made their task that much harder—and cost lives in Europe.

In January 1944, the Roosevelt Administration finally acceded to the demand for a new government agency devoted to rescue. Bergson can claim overwhelming credit for the establishment of the War Refugee Board. It would not have happened without his publicity campaign. In my 1992 biography of John J. McCloy, *The Chairman*, I gave credit to Bergson, but I also argued that the tipping point came with the intervention of Roosevelt's treasury secretary, Henry Morgenthau Jr. Only now do I realize Morgenthau would never have done anything had not Peter Bergson educated the public with his audacious campaigns. Until December 1943, Morgenthau had been content to let the State Department handle the question of Jewish refugee rescue. But then Morgenthau learned that the State Department had been blocking for more than six months a scheme to rescue 70,000 Romanian Jews in exchange for $170,000. (These were the "Jews For Sale" described in one of the early Bergson-Hecht newspaper ads.) Worse, Morgenthau also learned that the State Department had hidden from him a cable from the U.S. legation in Switzerland that confirmed the existence of Hitler's plan to exterminate the Jewish people. For Morgenthau, this was the last straw. In early January 1944, his staff wrote a devastating critique of the State Department entitled "Report to the Secretary [of State] on the Acquiescence of This Government in the Murder of the Jews." The report charged that the State Department was "guilty not only of gross procrastination and willful failure to act, but even of willful attempts to prevent action from being taken to rescue Jews from Hitler."

Within days of receiving this report, Roosevelt agreed to establish the War Refugee Board. And within weeks the WRB was able to take any number of concrete measures to rescue Jews. A license was issued to the World Jewish Congress to allow that organization to transfer funds abroad in order to finance the evacuation of refugees from France and Romania into Spain, Switzerland and North Africa. A similar operation was authorized to evacuate more than 5,000 abandoned children in France at a cost of $600,000. Yet another program was arranged with the Union of Orthodox Rabbis of the United States and Canada to finance an underground operation whereby Jewish refugees in Poland could be encouraged to seek refuge in Hungary. In order to fund this operation the WRB approved the direct transfer of hard currency into enemy-occupied territory. The Swedish diplomat Raoul Wallenberg was persuaded by the WRB to go to Hungary, where from July through December 1944 he handed out thousands of "protective passports." His activities were entirely funded by the WRB. Wallenberg alone is conservatively credited with having saved some 15,000 lives. Finally, the WRB negotiated with Romania to transfer some 6,400

Jewish internees from concentration camps to Bucharest. The WRB was in effect buying Jews—exactly what Bergson's controversial ads had proposed. And they might easily have saved many more lives. In the summer of 1944 the WRB lobbied the Roosevelt Administration's War Department to bomb the railroad tracks leading to Auschwitz—and the gas chambers inside the death camps. If they had done so, perhaps 100,000 Hungarian Jews would never have been transported to Auschwitz. Tragically, Assistant Secretary of War John J. McCloy rejected the idea, on the grounds that such bombing missions would constitute a diversion of military resources away from winning the war.

Bergson's Jewish American critics had been wrong to think that nothing could be done. Bergson believed many more lives could have been saved had the War Refugee Board been founded a year earlier, and he blamed Jewish American leaders for this delay. He was outraged to learn that Nahum Goldmann had told the State Department that he, Bergson, was inciting anti-Semitism in America. Bergson was astonished that the fear of instigating anti-Semitism could so blind men like Goldmann and Rabbi Wise to the urgency of saving Jewish lives. He was also stunned when these leaders opposed a 1943 congressional resolution that called upon the president to establish a special commission to save the remnants of European Jewry. And just why did they oppose the resolution? They objected to the language "save the Jewish people" and insisted that the resolution should specify saving the "Jewish people by opening the gates of Palestine." Once again, some Jewish American leaders feared that without specifying that the rescued Jews would go to Palestine, and not to America, the resolution would inflame American anti-Semitism. And the ardent Zionists among them insisted that opening the "gates" of Palestine was politically paramount. To Bergson's mind, this had the effect of "dooming" people who should have been rescued unconditionally. Rescuing any and all Jews and placing them in whatever safe havens were available anywhere was obviously a priority over the Zionist aim of bringing Jews to Palestine.

Bergson also bluntly argued in his speeches that saving Jewish lives should have become a proclaimed war goal. He pointed out that the Allies had publicly warned the Nazis that if they used poison gas against Allied troops the Allies would do the same against them. Why, he asked in a radio broadcast that attracted considerable controversy, hadn't the Allies issued a similar warning about the continued gassing of Jews in the death camps? The Roosevelt Administration knew by then that the Nazis were using poison gas to kill Jews on an industrial scale. "Why was it so outrageous," Bergson later asked, "to say that you should use poison gas [on the Germans] if you kill Jews? I say it was a crime that they didn't do it. . . ."

That many more European Jews were not rescued is a black mark on the escutcheon of America. "Jews could have been saved," Bergson argued in a 1978 interview. "The proof is very simple. As the whole horror was over, hundreds of thousands of Jews survived. . . . If the Jewish leadership had acted, if the Jews would have acted, the number of survivors would have been double, triple, fourfold. . . . And if I were a Jewish leader—dead—I would be turning in my grave. And if I were alive, I would have a very guilty conscience."

Bergson/Kook's activities were criticized by his Irgun comrades back in Palestine. They had not been happy when he had changed his agenda from raising funds for guns and illegal immigrants into Palestine to rescuing Jews from Europe. As the war wound down, Menachem Begin, who had become the Irgun's chief commander in late 1943, began to criticize Kook for diverting resources away from the fight to establish a Jewish state. Begin, sitting in British-occupied Palestine, was focusing entirely on the coming "revolt." He adamantly believed that the Jewish state would have to be created by force, and the primary enemy would be the British. On February 1, 1944, Begin's Irgun proclaimed a "revolt" against the British mandatory government. The Irgun began attacking British installations in Palestine, assassinating British officials and carrying out terror attacks on British soldiers.

Kook had not given up on his dreams for a "Free Palestine," free from British rule. Back in New York, Kook told Ben Hecht, "The British must be driven out, and Palestine must become a Hebrew republic." He was still an Irgunist—but by 1944 his definition of Revisionist Zionism was very far afield from Begin's. Unlike Begin, he believed a political campaign was necessary to win over international public opinion. And, again unlike Begin, he was acutely aware that winning the hearts and minds of the Palestinian Arab population would be a critical factor in the viability of the new state. To this end, it was essential not to define the new state in religious terms:

Israel should be a "Hebrew" state, not a "Jewish" one. In May 1944 he wrote a "Manifesto of the Hebrew Nation," in which he drew a hard distinction between being "Jewish" and a political identity he labeled "Hebrew." His manifesto proclaimed:

> We, the Hebrews, descendants of the ancient Hebrew nation, who remained alive on God's earth despite that great calamity that our people have experienced, have come together in the Hebrew Committee of National Liberation. The Jews today who live in the European hell together with the Jews in the Land of Israel constitute the Hebrew nation. We must state it clearly: the Jews of the United States do not belong to the Hebrew nation. These Jews are Americans of Hebrew descent.

The manifesto made clear the new direction in which Kook's thinking had evolved. Once the most radical of all the Zionist groups in America or Palestine, he and his "Bergsonites" were well on the road to what Kook was even then calling a "post-Zionist" worldview. His Hebrew Committee of National Liberation opened what they called an "embassy" in downtown Washington, claiming to represent the Jews of Palestine and the "captive" Jews of Nazi-occupied Europe. Treasury Secretary Henry Morgenthau Jr., the highest-ranking Jewish American in the Roosevelt Administration, wondered aloud to one of his aides how Bergson could claim to represent "the Hebrews of Europe and Palestine." His assistant suggested that Bergson was just doing what General Charles de Gaulle was doing on behalf of the Free French. To which Morgenthau replied, "Yes, but I don't happen to think the Jews are a race. I think it is a religion. . . . I happen to think of myself as an American citizen of the Jewish faith." His aide responded, "Bergson agrees with you a hundred percent."

In April 1945 Bergson wrote a long letter to Chaim Weizmann, the president of the World Zionist Organization, challenging the old Zionist to define his terms. "The Jews must decide," Bergson wrote, "*what* they are." He pointed to the uncomfortable fact—uncomfortable, at least, to an orthodox Zionist like Weizmann—that most American Jews "wish to remain Americans." Bergson himself was not put out by this fact. American Jews, he thought, should not be considered "Hebrews" or potential "Israelis" but simply Americans of Hebrew extraction. "Like all Americans, they have a national extraction (Hebrew) quite apart from and in addition to their religious affiliation, which is Jewish. . . . Rabbi [Stephen] Wise is an American who practices the Jewish religion."

This must have sounded like blasphemy to Weizmann, who like most mainstream Zionists believed that the Jewish mission was a long-term ingathering of all Jews everywhere back to the Promised Land. Weizmann believed that all Jews in the Diaspora lived with a fundamental identity problem. "They are a people," he testified in 1947, "and they lack the props of a people. They are a disembodied ghost. . . . We ask today: 'What are the Poles? What are the French? What are the Swiss?' When that is asked, everyone points to a country, to certain institutions, to parliamentary institutions, and the man in the street will know exactly what it is. He has a passport. If you ask what a Jew is—well, he is a man who has to offer a long explanation for his existence, and any person who has to offer an explanation as to what he is, is always suspect. . . ." For Weizmann, there was no such thing as a Jewish Frenchman or a Jewish American. To his thinking, all these people were "disembodied ghosts" whose identity could only be resolved by becoming citizens of a Jewish state.

To Bergson's way of thinking, this was "messianic Zionism." Such a formulation of Zionism flouted the desires of the vast majority of Diaspora Jews, who genuinely thought of themselves as both Jews and full citizens of France or America or Brazil. They were not "ghosts" at all. For Bergson, Weizmann's messianic Zionism was a canard. Not only was it impractical, but such thinking was going to obstruct the task at hand—rescuing the remnants of European Jewry and bringing them to a new, free state with its own national identity. Bergson—like his mentor, Jabotinsky—had a one-word definition for his brand of Zionism: normalcy. He envisioned the proposed new free Hebrew state as a place where Jews could practice their Jewish religion if they so desired, but their national identity would in any case be "Hebrews." To his mind, it would be a mark of extremism for Zionists to insist that all Jews must migrate to Palestine—just as it is a sign of intolerance for non-Jews around the world to insist that all Jews must assimilate. To the contrary, Kook believed that Jews, like anyone of any religious faith, have the right to choose their national allegiance. And with the coming creation of a Hebrew state, they could either choose to be Israelis or choose to remain Jewish Americans, or Jewish Englishmen or Jewish South Africans.

Implicitly, this meant that once the new "Hebrew" state was created, Zionism as a movement would have no further purpose.

Kook had a very clear set of ideas about how the new state would function—exactly like any other modern, secular democracy. It would have a constitution guaranteeing equal political rights and civil liberties for all its citizens, including its non-Jewish citizens. Kook assumed in 1945 that within a couple of years some one and a half million Jewish refugees would arrive in Palestine. These new "Hebrews" would constitute a majority of the population, but Muslim and Christian Palestinians would compose a sizable minority. Yet they would certainly be full-fledged citizens of the new state, which would have no state-sanctioned religion.

Weizmann did not reply to Kook's letter. To a doctrinaire Zionist, someone like Kook was best ignored. Weizmann dismissed him as a thirty-year-old pest, a troublemaker with a knack for self-aggrandizement.

But in America, despite the disdain of Rabbi Stephen Wise and other "mainstream" Zionists—few of whom would ever actually emigrate to Palestine—the Bergsonites and their Hebrew Committee of National Liberation were successfully gaining adherents and raising substantial sums of money. By 1945, Kook was operating in virtual independence of the Palestine-based Irgun. Brash and articulate, he had hundreds of contacts on Capitol Hill, in Hollywood and in the New York intellectual community. He had his own sources of funding and his own ideas. Bergson used these monies to fund his lobbying and publicity campaigns—and to smuggle European refugees past the British blockade into Palestine. None of his funds at this point were going to buy arms for the Irgun—a fact ascertained by J. Edgar Hoover's gumshoes.

In April 1945, Bergson led a delegation of the Hebrew Committee of National Liberation to San Francisco, where they lobbied official delegates to the founding session of the United Nations. Bergson was very clear about whom he claimed to represent: he said his Hebrew Committee spoke on behalf of "Hebrew" Palestinians and all stateless European Jews. The Jewish Agency also sent its people to San Francisco, claiming to represent all Jews everywhere in the Diaspora. Bergson challenged this claim. "There were Jewish delegates in twenty of the fifty delegations there," he later observed. "On behalf of which Jewish nation was the Agency speaking? This is not a quibble!"

Bergson didn't win official recognition, but he made further contacts and won new followers to his vision of a free "Hebrew" state. His rivals in the Jewish Agency were appalled. Eliahu Epstein, who three years later would become Israel's first ambassador to the United States, reported back to his Agency colleagues: "There is little doubt that dissident groups in the United States have apparently gained some hold on Jewish opinion. . . . I have been told that Bergson and his associates have succeeded in attracting to their cause groups of people who have previously been indifferent to Zionism and non-Jews of high social and political position."

Bergson had several meetings with Arthur Hays Sulzberger, the publisher of the *New York Times,* in 1945–46. Though Sulzberger was a Jewish American—some of his ancestors had come to America in the seventeenth century—his newspaper often editorialized against the Zionist cause. Like Henry Morgenthau, Sulzberger thought of himself as an American of Jewish ancestry. And he was sensitive to the prospect that Zionist advocacy might allow some Americans to charge him and other Jewish Americans with dual loyalties. In their very first meeting, Bergson bluntly told the publisher that he, Sulzberger, was an American of Hebrew descent who practiced Judaism as a religion. By contrast, Bergson was a "Hebrew" fighting for the freedom of his homeland, Palestine. And then he pointed out that so long as there wasn't a "Hebrew" state the distinction between Bergson's identity and Sulzberger's would be blurred. Many Americans would simply label both men as Jews. It was important, therefore, that people understand the distinction between those who are "Jewish" by the criterion of religion—and those "Palestinians" who were Jews as defined by their nationality. "I am a Hebrew," Bergson/Kook once said in 1946, "a person who has no other national allegiance except that of the Hebrew nation." Sulzberger liked this argument.

In early 1946, Bergson was voicing fundamental questions no one else wanted to ask, let alone answer. "Here I am, an individual, standing before you," he told a joint American-British commission investigating the Palestine question. "What am I? Well, you say, 'He is a Jew.' What do you mean? . . . Being a Jew, what is my position in the world? What is my relationship to human society? In simple terms, what nation do I belong to? I say I am a Hebrew. My allegiance is to the Hebrew nation. My country is Palestine." This was meant to provoke, to be sure, but Bergson's purpose in asking such questions was to make sure that the proposed "Free Palestine" would emerge as a viable and modern state.

Not surprisingly, Bergson's activities and his ideas earned him many enemies. The British Mandate authorities in Palestine considered him a leader of a terrorist organization and placed a bounty on his head. Mainstream American Zionists like Nahum Goldmann were still trying to have him deported. And back in Palestine, the Irgun's military commander, Menachem Begin, wrote Bergson a long letter in 1946, admonishing him to focus on his "primary" assignment, supplying the Irgun with arms. Begin also criticized Bergson for using the term the "Palestine Free State" in his speeches and literature. Begin thought this left the door open to a binational state—and that was not his goal. Begin insisted that henceforward Bergson refer to the "Free State of Eretz Yisrael." This was the first of many disagreements between the two Irgunists.

Hillel Kook flew to Palestine on May 15, 1948, the very day on which David Ben-Gurion proclaimed the independence of Israel. He arrived with impeccable Zionist credentials. One might have thought that a man who had done so much to publicize the plight of European Jewry—and embarrassed the Roosevelt Administration into rescuing thousands of trapped Jewish refugees—might have been greeted in the new state as a hero. But Kook soon discovered he was a pariah. Though regarded as one of the Irgun's five or six senior commanders, he had profound ideological disagreements with Begin. His best friend at the time was Ze'ev Jabotinsky's son, Ari, and both men disliked Begin's religiosity and sentimentality. "The whole Jabotinsky family hated Begin," recalled a mutual friend. Begin, they thought, simply didn't understand Revisionism as Jabotinsky had defined it. Kook still believed in a "Hebrew republic"—not a Jewish state. Both his Irgun credentials and his advocacy of a secular Hebrew republic marked him as a dangerous dissident in the eyes of Ben-Gurion's Zionist establishment. Even before Kook's return to Palestine, Ben-Gurion had called the Bergsonites and their Hebrew Committee "a group of self-appointed people who represent nobody but themselves."

That summer—in the midst of the war of independence—Ben-Gurion forced a showdown with the Irgun. In late June he ordered Palmach fighters under the command of Yitzhak Rabin to fire on an Irgun ship, the *Altalena,* as it attempted to land refugees, Irgun fighters and armaments on Tel Aviv's beaches. While the Palmach was in need of weaponry, Begin had insisted that these arms be specifically allocated to Irgun troops then being integrated into the newly established Israeli army. Ben-Gurion saw this as a challenge to his authority, and an attempt by Begin to create an "army within an army." Kook reportedly disagreed with Begin, but had no control over the Irgun commander. In the event, the *Altalena* affair ended with a bloody confrontation. And some say it almost precipitated a civil war among the Jews of Palestine. Thirty-two Irgun fighters were killed, some of them machinegunned by the Palmach as they attempted to swim ashore from the sinking ship. Begin escaped. But Ben-Gurion ordered "Peter Bergson-Kook's" arrest on trumped-up charges of draft evasion. Kook was detained for two months and finally released on August 27, 1948.

The Irgun's munitions ship *Altalena,* burning near a Tel Aviv beach,
June 1948

Nevertheless, five months later, on January 25, 1949, Kook was elected to the new state's 120-member Constituent Assembly, winning a seat on Menachem Begin's Herut party list. Herut secured only fourteen seats in the Assembly—and of those, three were taken by Kook and two other Bergsonites, Shmuel Merlin and Ari Jabotinsky ("Bergsonites" being the term generally used by now for those who accepted Bergson's concept of a secular Hebrew Republic). Their voice in the Constituent Assembly, however, was pathetically weak. Ben-Gurion's party, the center-left Mapai, won a plurality of forty-six seats—but the lack of a clear-cut majority meant that Ben-Gurion was forced to form a coalition government. He shunned the support of either the left-wing Mapam (nineteen seats) or Begin's right-wing Herut. Neither would he have anything to do with the small Maki (Communist) party (four seats). Instead he formed a coalition with the United Religious Front, a collection of Orthodox religious parties which had won sixteen seats in the Constituent Assembly.

This was a decision weighted with heavy consequences. By casting his lot with the Orthodox, Ben-Gurion created a political dynamic that led to the rabbinate gaining inordinate influence over the daily lives of the secular Israeli majority. The Orthodox rabbis opposed any division between synagogue and state, and had no use for secular norms. And they demanded and soon received the right to determine in rabbinical courts who was a Jew and who was not. Furthermore, having taken the Orthodox as his coalition partner, Ben-Gurion found it politically expedient to postpone a host of fundamental decisions about the new state.

According to Israel's Declaration of Independence, the Constituent Assembly was elected with the sole mandate to write a constitution. As it happened, there was already in existence a draft constitution, written by Dr. Leo Kohn, a legal adviser to the Jewish Agency. Kohn's document attempted to address some, but only some, of the hard questions raised by the Bergsonites. It embraced "the principle of the complete equality of all citizens." It incorporated a host of civil liberties, including freedom of speech and "the free exercise of all forms of religious worship. . . ." But left unresolved was the fundamental question of national identity. Was the new state to be defined as "Jewish" or simply "Israeli"? Moreover, was Judaism to be accorded special legal privileges and protections? Was there to be a clear division between synagogue and state? How was citizenship to be defined in the new state? And what was the legal relationship, if any, between Israeli citizens and the Jewish Diaspora? Kook and his Bergsonites had concrete answers to all of these existential questions. But Ben-Gurion and his allies had no desire to raise these questions, let alone answer them.

A fight between secular-minded Jews and the Orthodox rabbinate was the last thing Ben-Gurion wanted to deal with in 1949. So on the very first day of the Constituent Assembly's deliberations, February 14, 1949, he rose from his seat and unilaterally proposed that the Assembly reconstitute itself as the state's first duly elected Knesset, or parliament. Alone among the 120

Assembly delegates, Kook cried out, "Putsch!" But, joining his Mapai party to the votes of the Orthodox, Ben-Gurion mustered enough support to ram his proposal through, and the Assembly became the Knesset.

Amos Elon, the well-known Israeli writer, later observed: "So Ben-Gurion did the deal with the Orthodox, whose world didn't touch him and therefore didn't threaten him. He himself was a complete nonbeliever. His son had married a non-Jewish woman in London, and he thought nothing of it. It just never occurred to him that these Orthodox rabbis could eventually constitute a danger."

In 1953, the Knesset approved the Rabbinical Courts Jurisdiction Law, which granted Orthodox rabbinical courts jurisdiction over a wide range of social and political matters. Henceforth, only Orthodox rabbis were licensed to preside over marriages or grant divorces for Israel's Jewish citizens. And only Orthodox rabbis would determine who was a Jew. This was no small matter, since only Jews were eligible to buy state-owned land, and only Jews were eligible for welfare subsidies and interest-free mortgages controlled by the Jewish Agency. Various Israeli laws and Supreme Court decisions define "Jews" as a nationality. The government routinely funds various Orthodox Jewish religious institutions. Those citizens of the new state who were labeled "Jewish" by the Orthodox rabbis soon had privileges denied to non-Jewish citizens.

After only two years in the Knesset, Hillel Kook became sorely disillusioned with the new state. He thought Ben-Gurion was allowing himself to be blackmailed by the rabbis and that he was legitimizing a "messianic Zionism" just at the moment when the Zionist movement should have closed up shop in deference to the new state. He understood that his "Hebrew" formulation was probably a lost cause. And yet, he thought it was a serious mistake not to make it clear to the world—and, most importantly, to the Arabs—that the new state of Israel defined itself in secular, not religious, terms. If Israel was a secular state, that opened the door to its Arab inhabitants becoming full citizens. If Israel was to be defined as a "Jewish state"— well, that of course closed the door to non-Jews. But he knew he had lost this political debate. And ultimately, he blamed Menachem Begin, who he thought had hijacked Ze'ev Jabotinsky's vision of a secular Hebrew republic. Despairing of any change in his political fortunes, Kook resigned his seat in the Knesset in 1950 and abandoned politics. In 1951 he left Israel with his wife and daughter and moved to New York City, where he worked for the next seventeen years as a highly successful stockbroker on Wall Street. He became a wealthy man—and told himself that it would take a "new generation" of Israelis to reject the "ghetto" Zionism of Begin and Ben-Gurion. In 1968, he returned to Israel and once again began speaking out against the Zionist establishment. Occasionally, journalists would interview him—but he came to regret that he had left Israel for so many years. After the June 1967 War, he realized that the "new generation" of Israelis was even more in thrall to "messianic Zionism." Few Israelis were willing to discuss the fundamental questions of Israeli identity. And, while conventional Zionist politicians claimed for Israel all the rights and privileges of a sovereign state, they were unwilling to define that state's geographic borders. Neither were they willing to answer the question "Who is an Israeli?" And they continued to claim that Israel was a "Jewish nation" and the home of all Jews everywhere.

Few listened to Kook. He died, a lonely voice in Israel's political wilderness, in 2001.

In December 1981, three years after I met Hillel Kook in Jaffa, Victor Navasky and I edited a special issue of *The Nation* titled "Myths of the Middle East." Nearly three decades later, I would be guilty of inappropriate modesty if I did not claim a certain prescience for what we wrote. The editorial introducing this special issue could be published today without the change of a single word. We argued that the "greater threat" to Israel's security was not Palestinian terrorists but the danger from within: "Israel's democratic character—and its legitimacy and distinctiveness as a Middle Eastern state—is placed in increasing jeopardy with the passage of each day of the military subjugation of 1.2 million Palestinians in the West Bank and Gaza. The more 'successful' Israel is in introducing a large settler population into the occupied territories, the closer it is to becoming a total garrison state."

We then observed, "Among the misconceptions obscuring the road out of the present impasse are those having to do with the nature of contemporary Zionism." And then we asked some of the questions Hillel Kook might have asked: "Did Zionism mean a homeland for all Jews? Was this homeland for Jews and no other people?" We answered these questions as Kook would have answered them: ". . . after the establishment of the state of Israel in 1948, it gradually became clear that messianic Zionism—with its assertion that all Jews are one nation, that the ingathering of the Diaspora is the raison d'être of Israel—was an outmoded or unrealizable idea." Obviously, most Jews around the world, and most specifically, most Jewish Americans were not coming. Our editorial argued that Israel should define its citizens as Israelis—not Jews—and that therefore it made no sense to offer automatic citizenship to any Jew anywhere. (We suggested, however, that perhaps the Law of Return should remain applicable until the Holocaust generation had died out.)

In conclusion, we pointed out, "political Zionism succeeded in creating a state called Israel, a Hebrew nation in a part of historical Palestine." Quoting Uri Avnery, the Israeli writer and peace activist, we proclaimed that "Zionism is dead." In this "post-Zionist era" the conflict was not one between Arab and Jew but between Arab Palestinians and Hebrew Palestinians. This important distinction paves the way for a two-state solution, based on territorial compromise between the Hebrew-speaking and Arabic-speaking Palestinians.

The problem—then and now—with this formulation is that messianic Zionism did not die with the establishment of the state of Israel. Unfortunately, messianic Zionism continues to thrive in the hearts of a sizable minority of Israelis. And even the majority of Israelis still find it unthinkable to repudiate the notion that Israel is a "Jewish" state rather than a Hebrew-speaking state in which Jewish culture and religion are merely components of Israel's national identity.

"Messianic Zionism's claim of a Jewish right to Eretz Israel," we wrote in *The Nation* in 1981, "the biblical Holy Land, impels modern Israelis to conclude, as did an early Zionist, Dr. Arthur Ruppin, in 1936, 'It is our destiny to be in a state of continual warfare with the Arabs.'" Messianic Zionism cannot afford to compromise, precisely because it claims to speak for all Jews, everywhere, and not just the Hebrews of Israel. As Golda Meir told a group of battle-hardened soldiers on the Golan Heights in the midst of the 1973 October War, "If all the blood that is being shed in keeping Israel alive is only for the three million [Israelis] of today, it is not worthwhile."

Such a sentiment is an obfuscation of reality. Meir's messianic Zionism would have Hebrew-speaking Israelis fight and die on behalf of a non-Hebrew-speaking Jewish Diaspora that has no intention of ever making *aliyah*—emigrating (literally, "ascending") to Israel. This makes no sense, and furthermore, it belittles the interests of those Hebrew-speaking Israelis who are trying to make a life for themselves and their families in a country constantly at war.*

If Israel had been at peace these last six decades, perhaps messianic Zionism would have naturally withered away. But there is no peace, and the ongoing conflict continually reinforces tribalism, religiosity and messianic sentiments. Paradoxically, Israel is being torn in two radically different directions at once. As the Israeli-American historian Bernard Avishai observes, "We are now in a society that is more democratic, more liberal, more secular, more Israeli—but yet, ironically, more Israeli Jewish." What he means by "Israeli Jewish" is "a Jewish culture that is more overtly halakhic"—that is, a society governed by rabbinical courts and religious ritual. About 76 percent of Israel's population—or 5.4 million people—define themselves as Jewish. But most Israelis are still culturally secular, some 1.5 million Israelis are either staunch nationalist Orthodox or ultra-Orthodox Jews. And due to their high birthrates, the Orthodox community as a whole is growing rapidly. By definition, the Orthodox are antisecular, and over the years they have succeeded in imposing their archaic rules on the secular majority. They determine who is a Jew and who is not, and sometimes what is culturally forbidden. They have the political muscle to persuade the state to fund their religious schools. The ultra-Orthodox get their young men and women exempted from military service. The nationalist Orthodox form the backbone of the settlers' movement to colonize the occupied territories. They ardently believe in their right to live in an exclusively "Jewish state"—which helps to explain why 40 percent of all Israelis would like to see their government "support the emigration of Arab citizens." A small majority openly opposes equal rights for Israeli Palestinians. This is, to say the least, a highly undemocratic sentiment. But it has become quite clear that the Orthodox cherish "state Judaism" over democracy. Even the Hebrew spoken by the Orthodox, saturated as it is with archaic religious concepts and overtones, seems to reinforce tribalism. All politics comes down to one question: Is it good for the Jews? As Avishai observes in his deeply incisive book *The Hebrew Republic*: "You cannot live in Hebrew and expect no repercussions from its archaic power. You cannot live in a state

---

*Rabbi Judah Magnes, the president of the Hebrew University, said in 1947, "If I do not want a Jewish state, it is because I do not want perpetual war with the Arabs."

with an official Judaism, in addition to this Hebrew, and expect no erosion of citizenship. You can, as most Israelis do, speak the language, ignore the archaism, and tolerate Judaism. But then you should not expect your children to understand what democracy is."

I am under no illusion that Avishai's argument for a "Hebrew Republic" will soon persuade the American public—let alone most Israelis. The time is not right. No one is ready to listen, just as few listened to Bergson when he tried in 1948 to make the case for a Hebrew—not a Jewish—state in Palestine. But this is what should happen—and in time, I dare say, it will happen.

I would like to think that within the lifetime of my son, Joshua, Israel will become a Hebrew-speaking republic with a constitution that guarantees equal political rights for both its Hebrew-speaking and its Arabic-speaking citizens. Perhaps someday its language rather than its religion will define Israel's national identity. Israel could gradually shed its theocratic aspects and erect a different "iron wall," but this one will be a twenty-first-century "iron wall" between synagogue and state. A constitution will strip the rabbinical courts of any political powers or privileges. The physical "iron wall" that today divides Israelis from Palestinians living in the West Bank will be torn down. There will be no Mandelbaum Gates—but instead, open borders, free trade and a healthy, multicultural and economic interchange between all the peoples of ancient Palestine. There will probably be an Arabic-speaking Palestinian republic, quite likely composed of the former Hashemite Kingdom and the West Bank and Gaza. All of this will be possible, even necessary, because a hundred years in the future "sovereignty" won't mean what it does today. No doubt, many thousands of "Hebrews" of Jewish ancestry will be living in the Palestinian state—just as there will be a sizable number of Arabic-speaking Palestinians living in the Israeli republic. Perhaps the two republics will be federated. But in some way, somehow, these two peoples will be living together and sharing a land once periodically drenched in blood. That's my vision. I think it quite inevitable. But I am also certain that a hundred years from now people will look back to the early twenty-first century and wonder at the fools who delayed peace with their messianic notions.

Epilogue

⟨❧⟩

As the years rolled by, Susan laid claim to little pieces of her Jewish identity. When we were in our early thirties, she embraced more of the tradition and annual rituals. She took me to Rosh Hashanah and Yom Kippur services every year. And, of course, when Joshua was born, it was her idea to employ a *mohel*. And when Joshua turned ten, she cast around for a synagogue to join so that he could begin to study for a proper bar mitzvah. We joined Temple Micah, a Reform temple on Wisconsin Avenue in Washington, DC, and, much to Joshua's annoyance, he was compelled to attend both weekly Sabbath services and Hebrew classes. His resistance to this whole regimen was often formidable. But we slyly told him that this, too, was part of the tradition. On the appointed day, soon after his thirteenth birthday, he rose to the occasion and read in Hebrew a long passage from the Torah about Abraham. Standing on the *bimah,* I was moved to tears.

So my son will be Jewish. I will forever celebrate this fact. But as for his mother, this is only one aspect of his identity. Having lived in the same town house in downtown Washington for the first fifteen years of his life, he is also thoroughly American. He is well aware of his Jewish grandmother's survival story, and as a boy he spent many Passover Seders at the table of Aunt Frieda, who escaped Nazi Europe for America in 1940. He knows, too, that his other grandparents attend Episcopal services at St. Margaret's Church in downtown Washington. So he is Jewish, but his *goyish* grandparents, not to mention his *goyish* father, are also part of the mosaic of his identity.

My wife and son are thus part of a rich Jewish tradition, living as both

Americans and Jews in the Diaspora. They are not about to make *aliyah*—
to become Israeli citizens just because of their Jewish heritage. Theirs is a
choice made by millions of other Jewish Americans. There are, of course,
more people in America who identify themselves as culturally or religiously
Jewish (about 7.0 million) than in Israel (5.4 million). Over the last sixty
years a mere 75,000 Americans of Jewish ancestry have made *aliyah* to Israel.
There is nothing surprising about this fact. Jewish Americans have not only
thrived in America but greatly enriched American culture. It would have
been a national tragedy for America if Jewish Americans had collectively
decided in 1948 to emigrate to Israel. This would also have virtually ended
the two-thousand-year-old heritage of the Jewish Diaspora throughout the
world. And, quite apart from whether this would have been "good for the
Jews," it would have been a terrible thing for the *goyim*. America would have
been a less secular and less multicultural country.

As I write these words, I am once again an expatriate, this time living in Kathmandu, Nepal. Like the Jews of the Diaspora, I am a wanderer. In the spring
of 2007 Susan was offered a job with the World Bank in Nepal. Moving to
this Asian city seemed like a natural step in my life. I told myself that I could
write about Jerusalem, Dhahran, Cairo and Beirut sitting in Kathmandu just
as easily as from Washington. It is, of course, a strange place, filled with the
exotic sights and fragrances—and the filthy air—of a large Hindu-Buddhist
Asian city. Nearly every morning, I awake with the late Edward Said's sensa-
tion of being "out of place." Like him, I seem to be in perennial exile. I live
in a country where things are happening all around me for which I am not
accountable. I am once again just the privileged observer, the foreign "other"
who floats through a society not his own. And yet, over the years I have come
to understand that this expatriate's invisibility does not absolve me of some
responsibility. With regard to the Middle East, I know too much. But I also
know that I am powerless to change anything in any concrete sense. I have
only some words, some history, that might explain why the American experience in the Middle East is so troubled, and why the Arab-Israeli conflict
persists more than six decades after the founding of Israel.

Though I spent virtually my entire childhood in the Middle East, and
though it is not home, I worry about it as if it were my home. I mourn for
it, I fear for it—and I also greatly fear it. Modernity, if not ever completely

defeated, seems to have been put on hold throughout much of the Middle East. A tired old pharaoh still reigns in Egypt. Royalty still rules in Jordan and Arabia. Islamists still seem to be winning hearts and minds in a political vacuum. After 9/11, Adonis, the much-admired Lebanese poet, wondered, "could the fire that we lit to resist the invaders devour us?"

On the other hand, surely the pendulum will swing once more. The Syrian philosopher Sadik al-Azm thinks the Jihadists have already lost: "Despite current predictions of a protracted global war between the West and the Islamic world, I believe that war is over. There may be intermittent battles in the decades to come, with many innocent victims. But the number of supporters of armed Islamism is unlikely to grow, its support throughout the Arab Muslim world will likely decline, and the opposition by other Muslim groups will surely grow. September 11 signaled the last gasp of Islamism rather than the beginnings of its global challenge."

I hope so. But now that I have gone back and embedded my childhood memories of this troubled landscape inside a complicated historical narrative, I find it difficult to muster any optimism for the future. This is particularly true for the Palestinians and Israelis. For more than sixty years both peoples have been ill served by uncompromising, chauvinistic leaders who could not be bothered to see into the hearts and minds of their adversaries. Both sides have invariably found it possible to pass on an opportunity to make peace. Both sides have preferred to rely on guns. Indeed, as the American-Israeli historian and journalist Gershom Gorenberg suggests, both sides seem to have a psychological need to pick up the gun: "Neither Palestinians nor Israelis are unusual for using deadly weapons to achieve political goals, or for making warriors into heroes. What may make Palestinians and Israelis stand out is the overwhelming place of victimhood in their national memories. In very different ways, the experience of powerlessness made picking up the gun a goal for both—an end, not just a means."

Israel today is Janus-faced. There is the Jerusalem of my childhood— which has become increasingly Orthodox and socially conservative, a cultural battleground of epic proportions. It remains a sharply segregated city where few Jewish Israelis wander the streets of East Jerusalem and few Palestinians cross to the other side. And then there is Tel Aviv, a veritable living symbol of modernity, vitality and renaissance. Lovely beaches, Bauhaus architecture, cafés, bookstores, boutiques, wine bars and modern art galleries. Hebrew literature flourishes, and dozens of magazines and newspapers conduct vigorous daily debates; in Tel Aviv one can think or say anything. As Bernard Avishai observes, "nearly everybody in Israel—Ashkenazim, Mizrahim, Russians, and Arabs—is marinated in a popular Hebrew culture whose center is Tel Aviv." Oddly enough, this exquisite Mediterranean city reminds me of Beirut. And like Beirut, Tel Aviv is a Promised Land for anyone who wishes to live in a twenty-first-century globalized culture. It is the future and the humane face of the coming Hebrew Republic.

I know Hillel Kook's vision of a Hebrew Republic sounds today impossibly naïve. But like all modern states, Israel is already becoming "multicultural" in the Americanized sense. It is, after all, a place populated by Jewish Russians (and many not-so-Jewish Russians), Jewish Ethiopians, Jewish Iraqis, Jewish Americans, Jewish Egyptians, Jewish Italians, Jewish Austrians and, of course, Christian and Muslim Palestinians. In early 2007 prominent Palestinian citizens of Israel signed a petition in the form of a "Vision Statement" suggesting that it was time to stop defining Israel as a Jewish state and instead to create a "consensual democracy for both Arabs and Jews." I know this is anathema to most Israelis today. My friend and colleague Eric Alterman bluntly insists, "To call this view 'marginal' among Jewish Israelis would greatly overstate its popularity." But reality is a stubborn thing. The demographics can't be ignored: 25 percent of all Israeli first-graders today come from ultra-Orthodox Jewish families—and another quarter are Palestinian Israelis. Can Israel's democracy long survive as a "Jewish state" alongside a rapidly growing Palestinian minority?

In recent years, many Israelis on both the right and the left have sought refuge in the notion that if real peace is not possible in the short term, then at least they can fence themselves off from the Palestinians. They argue that the physical separation of the two peoples by a concrete wall and fence will allow Israel's citizens some sense of normalcy. This policy of separation is called *hafradah* in Hebrew. But few Israelis think that *hafradah* can work in the long term. The land is too small and the peoples too near.

On my last trip to Israel I had lunch in the home of Benny Morris, perhaps Israel's most prominent modern historian. It was the spring of 2007, and Benny had once again stirred controversy. All his books are controversial. Writing about the 1948 war, Morris has basically ratified an essential aspect of the Palestinian historical narrative. Drawing on Israeli archival documents, he wrote: "hundreds of thousands of Palestinians were driven from or fled their homes." It was not a systematic ethnic cleansing, but he concludes that in some instances, Israeli leaders consciously decided to expel Palestinians from whole villages, neighborhoods and towns. Morris stands by his history. But after the second Intifada, he changed his mind about the possibility of any peaceful coexistence. The hatred of the Palestinians for the Jewish state, he concluded, is too deep for any real peace. So now he has openly suggested that it was unfortunate that the 1948 war left so many Palestinians inside Israel. Perhaps, he says provocatively, there would be peace today if there had been at that time a sweeping transfer of virtually all Palestinians to Arab lands outside of Israel. Practically speaking, Morris has become an advocate of *hafradah*—separation—and he sees the "separation wall" as an ugly necessity. (Curiously, in his most recent book, *One State, Two States: Resolving the Israel/Palestine Conflict,* he argues that even a Palestinian state in the West Bank and Gaza is probably not sustainable, and so he reluctantly concludes that the only viable solution is for the Palestinians to create a confederation with Jordan. In the near term, this idea seems both stale and unlikely, since the Hashemite regime in Amman seems no more willing to relinquish power today than it did in September 1970.)

Morris is an intellectual curmudgeon. If his judgments sometimes seem mercurial, he at least asks tough questions. He does not shy away from controversy. In December 2008, he wrote an op-ed in the *New York Times* in which he observed, "Many Israelis feel that the walls—and history—are closing in on their 60-year-old state. . . ." I like Benny. He smiles broadly, and frequently chuckles. He started out as a reporter for the *Jerusalem Post,* and he writes serious narrative-driven history. Like me, Benny grew up as an expatriate in London and New York, his father serving in the Israeli Foreign Service.

Over lunch I asked him if he had any Palestinian friends: did he socialize at all with Palestinian historians or journalists? "Not one," he answered quickly. He then went on to explain his astonishment that after having published several books that lend credence to the Palestinian narrative, he had not received even one invitation to speak at a Palestinian university. He resented this.

Later that same week, I asked the same question of one of my Palestinian friends from my year at the American University of Beirut. Rita Giacaman is now a professor at Bir Zeit University, just outside the West Bank town of Ramallah. Rita replies that "literally, some of my best friends are Israelis." She cites a few names, including Avi Shlaim, a prominent Israeli-British historian. But she hastens to add that these are Israelis who are "all on the side of justice" and actively call for the end of the Israeli military occupation. "Our family does not even bother to ask about whether someone is a Zionist or not; to us, this is irrelevant at this stage. What matters most is if they are for justice and the end of occupation or not. Notice that we do not even raise the issue of two states or one state, because neither is in the offing right now."

Stalemate.

But maybe not. As I write, both of my parents are in their mid-eighties, still working long hours to educate Americans about the Middle East conflict. They have their own nonprofit foundations. Mother's is Partners for Peace—which brings half a dozen or more women annually from Jerusalem and sends them around the country speaking to audiences at universities, synagogues and churches. Every three-member team consists of a Christian Palestinian, a Muslim Palestinian and a Jewish Israeli. They are always strangers to each other, and they all have to agree on only one thing: a vague but implicit vision that Jerusalem should somehow be "shared" among the three "faiths" and two nationalities.

Father's organization is called the Council for the National Interest. He leads a group of Americans about once a year on a "fact-finding" trip through the Middle East, where they usually meet with a very wide range of Israelis, Palestinians and other Arabs. They talk with Israeli officials, but they also see the leading lights of the Palestinian National Authority, Fatah, Hamas and even Lebanon's Hezbollah. They engage with everyone, and then they come back and talk to legislators and staff on Capitol Hill. It is a small, shoestring operation, funded by small donations from some 8,000 contributors across the country. They lobby Congress for a two-state solution. It's just my father, several full-time staffers and a handful of idealistic interns.

I sometimes think their efforts quixotic. Who realistically thinks today, after all that has happened, that a two-state solution is possible, let alone imminent? Who thinks peace lies just beyond that closed door?

But my parents insist, "If not now, when?" They point to my childhood neighbor Sari Nusseibeh, today the president of Al-Quds University in Jerusalem, and the cosigner of a simple one-page outline for a two-state solution to the conflict. As Sari described it in his 2007 memoir, *Once Upon a Country,* "An unusual visitor came to my office one day." As the head of Shin Bet, Israel's internal intelligence agency, it had once been Ami Ayalon's job to imprison Palestinian activists like Nusseibeh. But in retirement this once-feared intelligence chief had thought hard about the conflict. And he had come to the conclusion that time was not on the side of the Jewish state. That day he produced a single sheet of paper and placed it on Sari's desk. "I don't want to read it," Nusseibeh told him. "I want to hear it from you."

Ayalon explained that he thought any piecemeal, step-by-step approach would never resolve the conflict. It was necessary to lay out in full what a final peace agreement would give both the Palestinians and the Israelis. Every reasonable person could describe the outlines of a compromise, a two-state solution. The really difficult obstacle was getting the politicians to risk their lives and careers to get there. Ayalon had an answer: "The only way to force the leaders to finally sign a deal is by winning over both peoples." So Ayalon's one-page document was couched as a citizen's initiative, and he hoped to get a million signatures. But the first signature he wanted was Sari Nusseibeh's. Other Palestinians he had consulted said they liked Ayalon's proposal, but they would not be the first to sign it. "They thought you might be crazy enough to do it," Ayalon told Nusseibeh.

After hearing Ayalon outline seven simple points, Nusseibeh made a snap decision. He stood up, shook hands with the Shin Bet man and said, "Fine, I agree."

"Don't you want to read the paper first?" Ayalon asked.

"In due time."

Months passed. But eventually, in the late summer of 2002, Nusseibeh made a few small revisions in Ayalon's draft paper and then told him that he was ready to initial the document. It remains a simple one-page document:

- There will be two states for two nations.
- The permanent borders will be drawn on the basis of June 4, 1967, with the possibility of exchanging tracts of land, on a one-to-one basis.
- Jerusalem will be the capital of both states (the Arab neighborhoods under Palestinian sovereignty and the Jewish neighborhoods under Israeli sovereignty).

- Arab refugees will be able to return only to Palestinian territory and Jews only to Israeli territory.
- In cognizance of the suffering of the Palestinian refugees, an international fund will be established with the participation of Israel for compensating and rehabilitating Palestinian refugees.
- The Palestinian state will be demilitarized.
- Both sides will renounce all claims after a political agreement is signed.

In the years since 2002—in the midst of the horrific suicide bombings—the Nusseibeh-Ayalon plan has collected a quarter million Israeli signatories, and just slightly fewer Palestinian signatories. And nothing has happened. Recently, Nusseibeh challenged the Obama Administration to insist that the Israelis and the Palestinians submit the seven-point plan to referendums for each people. They think the polls show that a majority of average Israelis and Palestinians would endorse it. It's a worthwhile gamble.

There is much to commend in this "citizen's initiative." It possesses both clarity and simplicity. If enacted, it might usher in a permanent peace. Sharon's separation wall would surely disappear. Security. Peace. Prosperity. It promises much. If I were either Israeli or Palestinian, I would endorse it.

But I know Nusseibeh has been much criticized for having "given away" the Palestinians' cherished "right of return" to their homes inside Israel. I know for many Palestinians this is a pill too bitter to swallow. This—and the recognition of the "Jewish state"—is the core of the conflict. "Everybody here still insists on the right of return," says Rita, my feisty Palestinian friend from Ramallah. "But it means different things for different people." Rita knows that most Palestinians will not want to return to live in modern Israel. But for her and many Palestinians the principle matters deeply—that, and a simple apology. "People here, as we say in Arabic, have *nafas*—literally 'breath' [meaning endless patience]. They are willing to linger in misery until vindication comes, and an apology from the world is what is needed, then compensation and repatriation. . . . This is how the right of return is interpreted by most people."

Apologies are due all around. But before either camp can offer apologies, these peoples must acknowledge the history. No one should be expected to forgive and forget. Forgetting the history is not humanly possible. Quite the opposite, only by knowing the history is it possible to come to the kind of understanding that makes forgiveness possible. But first comes an acknowledgment of the history. The Israelis and Palestinians need to see each other, and acknowledge each other's historical narrative. The Palestinians need to acknowledge the Shoah and come to understand that their adversary is heavily burdened by a history of victimhood. Likewise, Jewish Israelis need to accept the Nakba as a core part of the Israeli-Palestinian experience. We're not there yet. We're not even close. But at least for the Palestinians, the Nusseibeh-Ayalon plan implicitly contains an Israeli apology insofar as it requires the explicit participation of the Israelis in the "compensation and rehabilitation" of the Palestinian refugees. Perhaps this is not enough for some Palestinians. Perhaps some symbolic quotient of "return" is also required. But Palestinians should realize that the Nusseibeh-Ayalon plan would open the door to all the hard questions asked by Hillel Kook and others over the last sixty years. Peace would eventually transform the "Jewish state" into the Hebrew Republic. Peace would be a highly contagious virus. Peace would be highly subversive to the notion that neighbors can be or should be separated.

My friends—Israelis, Palestinians—call me naïve. They say so in a generous spirit. "Kai means well." But he is naïve. I plead guilty. So does Nusseibeh. He once told an Israeli newspaper, "I am a naïve person. Most of my friends say that about me." But the realists have failed. So maybe the time has come for the naïveté of a child. The Mandelbaum Gate of my childhood memories is gone, physically destroyed. But it remains in a "virtual" sense, haunting a Jerusalem still divided. Mandelbaum Gate's barbed wire and tank barriers once divided people. But perhaps it is important to remember that it was also a meeting ground where on rare occasions the Israelis permitted brief family reunifications. Relatives and friends came to shout their news, and sometimes they got close enough to stretch out their arms and fingers through the barbed wire to touch each other. So perhaps Mandelbaum Gate also remains a symbol of hope, a place of reunion—and a reminder that these divisions cannot last forever.

Acknowledgments

The idea for this memoir came to me nearly two decades ago, during the 1990–91 Persian Gulf War. That war brought on such a rush of difficult childhood memories that I wrote about them in a short essay for the *Washington Post* titled "Intimate Hatreds: In the Holy Land the War Was a Reminder of Ties That Blind." I wrote about Jerusalem—and about my childhood friend who was both a Jewish and Muslim Palestinian. I wrote about living through the Suez War, the June 1967 War, the Black September hijackings and the Jordanian-Palestinian civil war of September 1970. I wrote about my Jewish American wife. I confessed my skepticism that Desert Storm had "ended the killing cycle."

In 1991 I had been a working journalist for nearly eighteen years, and I was about to publish my first biography, *The Chairman: John J. McCloy; The Making of the American Establishment*. But my wife, Susan Goldmark, bluntly told me that this essay about my childhood was the best writing I had ever produced. She's a tough, discerning critic, so sometimes I listen to her. Over the years, I wrote two more biographies, but all the while, Susan insisted I should be writing this book. Without her firm encouragement, I never would have attempted this project.

Once I embarked on this book, my parents, Eugene and Jerine Bird, graciously handed over hundreds of personal letters—many of them love letters dating back to the 1950s. Without these I could not have written this book. No doubt they will find much to argue about in my historical judgments, but I will forever be grateful that they allowed me to use their life stories in a book that is not theirs.

I have known Helma Blühweis Goldmark now for thirty-seven years. A decade ago I began interviewing her on tape, recording her Shoah survival story—much of which was unknown to Susan, her only child. Since then, we have uncovered scores of archival documents to complement her oral history. Having waited so long to tell her story, I am grateful that she has let me tell it in my own fashion.

Victor S. Navasky—the Editor Emeritus of *The Nation*—taught me the art of journalism. But Victor is also an eminent historian, and his books have been models for my own work. (I particularly recommend his last book, a wise and witty memoir, *A Matter of Opinion*.) It was Victor who insisted in 1978 on providing me with an introduction to Hillel Kook, and without the insights I acquired from Kook's remarkable life story I would not have had an ending to this book.

I am grateful to such childhood friends as Theresa Barger, Robert Bauer, Howard Blanning, Nick Bromell, Paul Chiramel, Aline Kalbian, Jeff Parker, Johnny Pendleton, Fred Rogers, Mona Wahba and Sheri Wahba for sharing their own memories of the Middle East. I cherish the friendship of "Dani Bahar"—who wishes to remain anonymous. Joy Riggs-Perla surely did not want to relive her memories of being hijacked. But she patiently answered my questions and allowed me to write about the Black September hijackings through her experience. I saved all her letters for nearly four decades. Now I know why.

Many friends and colleagues agreed to read portions of the manuscript. Eric Alterman and Arthur Samuelson read the entire manuscript and gave me many critical comments. So too did Keith Leslie, a friend from my new life in Kathmandu. All of us argued about some of the history, and sometimes I rewrote. More importantly, I am gratified that they can embrace the spirit with which I have tried to grapple with an inevitably contentious history.

Many more friends in America, Saudi Arabia, Italy, Jordan and Israel gave me comments on individual chapters, including Gabi Afram, Faiza Ambah, Eneo Baborsky, Neil Barsky, Maria Bauer, Stephen Frietch, Nick Goldberg, Peter Iseman, Brennon Jones, Dr. Vicken Kalbian, Tami Litani, Emily Medine, Duke Merriam, Zyg Nagorski, Paula Newberg, Nancy "Nicky" Nickerson, Ambassador Richard Parker, Caleb Rossiter, Michael Schwartz, Ellen Selonick Berick, Sol Stern, Nilgün Tölek, Amy Wilentz, Don Wilson and Adam Zagorin.

I imposed on some of my new friends in Kathmandu, where I wrote the bulk of the book, to read many chapters. These include the fabulous Barbara Adams (now at last a citizen of Nepal), the short-story writer Sushma Joshi, the fearless snowboarder Richard Ragan and his talented wife Marcela Sandoval, legal scholar Dave Sadoff and Ted Ricardi, Professor Emeritus in the Department of Middle East and Asian Languages and Cultures, Columbia University. The historian and novelist Manjushree Thapa and the journalists Kanak Dixit, Kunda Dixit and Vijay Panday encouraged me to think that I could sit in Kathmandu and write about Jerusalem.

I also showed individual chapters to historians who have written scholarly works on various issues addressed in the book. These include Professor Joseph Agassi (Tel Aviv University), Avner Cohen (Tel Aviv and Washington, DC), Professor Becky Kook (Ben-Gurion University), Professor Douglas Little (Clark University), Professor Saad Sowayan (King Abdul-Aziz University), and Professor Robert Vitalis (University of Pennsylvania), whose scholarly writings on Saudi Arabia have influenced my thinking about the Kingdom. Similarly, I am particularly grateful for the comments of the Israeli-American historian Bernard Avishai, whose important new book, *The Hebrew Republic,* helped to shape my own views about the future of Israel. And though my Palestinian friend Dr. Rita Giacaman is a professor of public health and not a historian, I want to acknowledge that our conversations and emails have contributed enormously to my understanding of the "conflict." Ronald Steel, the eminent biographer of Walter Lippmann and Robert F. Kennedy (among many other works), suggested an early version of what became the book's subtitle.

In addition, I wish to acknowledge the fine works of such other historians as Said K. Aburish, Fouad Ajami, Sadik al-Azm, Steve Coll, Robert Fisk, Sir Martin Gilbert, Charles Glass, David Grossman, Rashid Khalidi, Amin Maalouf, Benny Morris, Sari Nusseibeh, David Raab, the late Edward Said, Tom Segev, Avi Shlaim, Alexander Stille, Yaroslav Trofimov, Milton Viorst, Lawrence Wright, David S. Wyman and a host of other historians cited in the notes.

I am grateful for the archival research of Dr. Gerald Lamprecht, who located Nazi-era documents for me in the Graz archives related to the confiscation of the Blühweis estate. That is a story that remains in part a mystery. For this, I apologize to Adriano Endrizzi and my wife's other Italian cousins.

I also offer an apology to my sisters—Nancy Bird, Shelly Bird and Christina Macaya—who read the manuscript only to see how little of their stories is told. I can only plead that while they witnessed much of the same history, I experienced a different journey.

Martin J. Sherwin, my good friend and coauthor of *American Prometheus: The Triumph and Tragedy of J. Robert Oppenheimer,* did not want me to write this book because it would take me away from another fruitful collaboration. Now I hope he knows why I had to do it.

Gail Ross has been my literary agent for more than two decades. She is smart, bold and unabashedly frank with her opinions. She and Howard Yoon pushed me to write a lengthy proposal that made it possible to sell this book to Scribner.

My editor at Scribner, Nan Graham, saw instinctively the promise of a project that combined memoir with a deeply historical narrative. And when the manuscript arrived on her desk, she and her astute assistant, Paul Whitlatch, spent months doing the kind of page-by-page editing that every author deserves. When they were done, they turned the manuscript over to Mel Rosenthal—who must be one of the most gifted copy editors in the business. Nan, Paul and Mel are the best: old-fashioned editors in the twenty-first century.

Finally, this book is dedicated to my son, Joshua, who is old enough now to know why his father is obsessed with history.

A Note on Sources

Like any memoir, this book relies in part on the imperfect childhood memories of the author. Some of these memories were revived by a brief trip back to the Middle East in the spring of 2007. But I was also fortunate to be able to quote at length from the voluminous correspondence saved over the decades by my parents, Eugene and Jerine Bird. These letters are now in my possession, and I have not bothered to cite them by date in the notes. In addition, I interviewed some childhood friends—only one of whom wished to remain anonymous. Otherwise, I have relied on the splendid work of many other historians to inform me on what was taking place all around me as I came of age in the Middle East.

Notes

❦

Preface

xvii   "multiple allegiances": Amin Maalouf, *In the Name of Identity*. New York: Penguin, 1996, p. 5.

xvii   "'a stranger's wakefulness'": Leon Wieseltier, "Against Identity," *The New Republic,* November 28, 1994.

1: Jerusalem

7   "The American Colony": Bertha Spafford Vester, *Our Jerusalem: An American Family in the Holy City, 1881–1949.* Jerusalem: Ariel Publishing, 1988, p. 355.

8   "Stones to right": Amos Elon, *Jerusalem: City of Mirrors.* Boston: Little, Brown, 1989, p. 11.

8   "the knobbiest town": Mark Twain, *Innocents Abroad.* Hartford, CT: American Publishing Company, 1869, p. 558.

10   "A noble band": *Minneapolis Sunday Tribune,* 7/4/1920.

10   "self-segregation": Jane Fletcher Geniesse, *American Priestess: The Extraordinary Story of Anna Spafford and the American Colony in Jerusalem.* New York: Doubleday, 2008, p. 280.

10   "By the end of World War I": Ibid., p. 285.

11   "After the Deir Yassin": Vester, *Our Jerusalem,* pp. x and 354.

12   "Aboard were 112": Tom Segev, *One Palestine, Complete: Jews and Arabs Under the British Mandate.* New York: Henry Holt, 1999, p. 508.

12   "Seventy-seven Jews": Amos Oz, *A Tale of Love and Darkness: A Memoir.* New York: Harcourt, 2003, pp. 367–368; Benny Morris, *Righteous Victims: A History of the Zionist-Arab Conflict, 1881–2001.* New York: Alfred A. Knopf, 2001, p. 209.

12   "The adult males": Benny Morris, *Righteous Victims,* pp. 207–208.

15   "But, in violation": Bernard Wasserstein, *Divided Jerusalem: The Struggle for the Holy City.* New Haven, CT: Yale University Press, 2001, p. 204.

16   "the roar of a hungry lion": Dr. Vicken Kalbian interview, 1/27/07.

17   "Katy was naughty": Ibid.

17   "Katy Antonius was": Segev, *One Palestine, Complete,* p. 469.

18   "people are people": Mary Elizabeth King, *A Quiet Revolution: The First Palestinian Intifada and Nonviolent Resistance.* New York: Nation Books, 2007, p. 128.

18   "Evening dress, Syrian food": Segev, *One Palestine, Complete,* pp. 469–470.

19   "Katy, I love you": Ibid., pp. 480 and 499.

19   "Before the Jewish state": Howard M. Sachar, *A History of Israel: From the Rise of Zionism to Our Time*. New York: Alfred A. Knopf, 1979, p. 453.

19   "STOP! DANGER!": Martin Gilbert, *Jerusalem in the Twentieth Century*. New York: John Wiley and Sons, 1996, p. 268.

19   "Daddy, we have to win": Andrew Kilgore interview, 2/2/07.

22   "the ferocity of the Arab anger": Vincent Sheean, *Personal History*. New York: The Literary Guild, 1935, p. 367.

22   "The photographs were fake": Pierre van Paassen, *Days of Our Years*. New York: Hillman-Curl, 1939, p. 370.

22   "We found the twelve-foot-high": van Paassen, *Days of Our Years,* p. 371; http://smoothstone.blogspot.com/2004/02/1929-hebron-massacre.html.

23   *"Our hope is not"*: Sari Nusseibeh with Anthony David, *Once Upon a Country: A Palestinian Life*. New York: Farrar, Straus and Giroux, 2007, p. 31.

23   "The ensuing riots": Sheean, *Personal History,* pp. 354–370.

24   "I remember that day well": Chana Regev, "The Mandelbaum Gate: Home of the Mandelbaum Family," Nov. 3, 2004, http://chareidi.shemayisrael.com/archives5765/CHS65features.htm.

25   "By 1956 this figure": Morris, *Righteous Victims,* p. 269.

25   "Some 200 Israeli": Ibid., p. 271.

26   "persons from Beit Jalla": Commander E. H. Hutchison, USNR, *Violent Truce: A Military Observer Looks at the Arab-Israeli Conflict, 1951–1955*. New York: Devin-Adair, 1956, pp. 12–16.

26   "just in case": Eugene Bird phone interview, 3/10/09.

26   "2,700 Palestinian infiltrators": Morris, *Righteous Victims,* p. 274.

26   "In crossing the lines": Gilbert, *Jerusalem in the Twentieth Century,* p. 255.

31   "Just around the corner": Stuart W. Rockwell oral history interview, 7/8/76, Harry S Truman Presidential Library.

34   "I could also look down": Nusseibeh with David, *Once Upon a Country,* pp. 68–69.

35   "As the writer Robert Kaplan": Robert Kaplan, *The Arabists: The Romance of an American Elite*. New York: Free Press, 1995, pp. 7–8.

36   "If you read the book": Susan Silsby Boyle, *Betrayal of Palestine: The Story of George Antonius*. Boulder, CO: Westview, 2001, p. 2.

36   "The educational activities": George Antonius, *The Arab Awakening: The Story of the Arab National Movement*. Beirut: Librairie Du Liban, 1969, p. 43.

37   "No one that I have ever met": Boyle, *Betrayal of Palestine,* p. 94.

38   "a personal library of 12,000 books": Ibid., p. 294.

39   "an extremely level-headed": Sheean, *Personal History,* p. 372.

39   "They have no pity": Benny Morris, *One State, Two States*. New Haven, CT: Yale University Press, 2009, p. 106.

39   "had bewitched George Antonius": Freya Stark, *The Arab Island: The Middle East, 1939–1943*. New York: Alfred A. Knopf, 1945, p. 159.

39   "His intelligence never seemed": Sheean, *Personal History,* p. 338; Sheean, "Holy Land 1929," reprinted in Walid Khalidi, ed., *From Haven to Conquest: Readings in Zionism and the Palestine Problem Until 1948*. Washington, DC: Institute for Palestine Studies, 1987, p. 276.

39   "a bridge between": Martin Kramer, "Ambition, Arabism and George Antonius," an essay found in Mark Kramer, ed., *Arab Awakening and Islamic Revival: The Politics of Ideas in the Middle East*. New York: Transaction Publishers, 2008, pp. 112–23.

39   "believed the Zionist programme": Sheean, *Personal History,* p. 338.

39   "In 1918 the population": Morris, *Righteous Victims,* pp. 37 and 86.

40   "750,000 Arabs and 150,000 Jews": Sheean, *Personal History,* p. 341.

40   "goat by goat": Ibid.; Charles Glass, *The Tribes Triumphant*. London: HarperPress, 2006, p. 90.

40 "There is a fundamental conflict": Morris, *Righteous Victims,* p. 122.

40 "We will expel the Arabs": Nusseibeh, *Once Upon a Country,* p. 36.

41 "killing as many as 6,000 Palestinians": Morris, *Righteous Victims,* p. 159.

41 "Their policy has turned": Boyle, *Betrayal of Palestine,* p. 225.

41 "in the entire 18 years": Ibid., p. 228.

41 "There is no room for a second nation": Antonius, *Arab Awakening,* pp. 410–411.

42 "an eloquent advocate": P. W. Wilson, *New York Times Book Review,* 2/5/39.

42 "The treatment meted out": Antonius, *Arab Awakening,* p. 411.

42 "All the elements": Boyle, *Betrayal of Palestine,* p. 14.

43 "Arise, ye Arabs": Fouad Ajami, *The Dream Palace of the Arabs: A Generation's Odyssey.* New York: Pantheon Books, 1998, p. 24.

43 "the complete annihilation of the Jews": Martin Gilbert, *The Holocaust: A History of the Jews of Europe During the Second World War.* New York: Holt, Rinehart and Winston, 1985, p. 285.

43 "Antonius died at the moment": Boyle, *Betrayal of Palestine,* p. 290.

2: On the Road to Suez

47 "350,000 Holocaust survivors": Tom Segev, *The Seventh Million: The Israelis and the Holocaust.* New York: Henry Holt, 2000, p. 154.

49 "United States policy": Mohamed H. Heikal, *Cutting the Lion's Tail: Suez Through Egyptian Eyes.* New York: Arbor House, 1987, p. 38.

51 "We must assume": Mordechai Bar-On, *The Gates of Gaza: Israel's Road to Suez and Back, 1955–1957.* New York: Macmillan, 1994, pp. 4–5.

51 "The arms were purchased": Ibid., p. 7.

51 "Nasser was a pragmatist": Heikal, *Cutting the Lion's Tail,* pp. 91–92.

51 "throw the Jews into the sea": Kennett Love, *Suez: The Twice-Fought War.* New York: McGraw-Hill, 1969, p. 638. Love writes quite categorically that these charges "have never been substantiated by a single documented quotation from Nasser."

51 "Up until 1955": Bar-On, *Gates of Gaza,* p. 17.

52 "I think we must bring about": Ibid., p. 41.

52 "Again I asked myself": Ibid., p. 80.

53 "Let them die": Heikal, *Cutting the Lion's Tail,* p. 121.

54 "a paltry 800,000 pounds": Ibid., p. 99.

55 "He [Nasser] must be stopped": Love, *Suez: The Twice-Fought War,* p. 441.

55 "At all costs Israel": Ibid., p. 440.

56 "in the early phases": Ibid., pp. 465–466.

57 "On September 12 and 13": Ibid., p. 440.

57 "They knew their military": Ibid., p. 446.

59 "mobilizing 100,000 reservists": Ibid., p. 469.

60 "an opportunity to settle accounts": Ibid., p. 476.

62 "It was not exactly blackmail": Ibid., p. 625.

63 "We not only had": Ibid., p. 633.

63 "Our forces did not infringe": Ibid., p. 637.

64 "None of us knows": Ibid., pp. 639–640.

64 "We thought the American Jew": Ibid., pp. 639–641.

68 "There is going to be a war": Amos Oz, *My Michael.* Orlando, FL: Harcourt, 2005, pp. 153 and 167.

69 "Kai was not": F. Honore to Eugene Bird, 1/22/58.

69 "Mr. Albina, yesterday": Dr. Vicken Kalbian interview, 1/27/07.

70 "They gave King Abdullah": Roland Dallas, *King Hussein: A Life on the Edge.* New York: Fromm International, 1999, p. 21; Avi Shlaim, *Lion of Jordan: The Life of King Hussein in War and Peace.* New York: Alfred A. Knopf, 2008, pp. 143–144.

72 "deeply laid, cleverly contrived": Uriel Dann, *King Hussein and the Challenge of Arab Radicalism: Jordan, 1955–1967.* New York: Oxford University Press, 1989, p. 58.

72 "James Russell Barracks": Said K. Aburish, *A Brutal Friendship: The West and the Arab Elite.* New York: St. Martin's Press, 1997, p. 131.

72 "political parties were now banned": Bernard Wasserstein, *Divided Jerusalem: The Struggle for the Holy City.* New Haven, CT: Yale University Press, 2001, p. 191.

72 "The NOBEEF payments": Nigel Ashton, *King Hussein of Jordan: A Political Life.* New Haven, CT: Yale University Press, 2008, p. 62; Carl Bernstein, *Rolling Stone,* 10/20/77; Douglas Little, "Mission Impossible: The CIA and the Cult of Covert Action in the Middle East," *Diplomatic History,* Nov. 2004, p. 684; Bob Woodward, *Washington Post,* February 18, 1977. Woodward reported that the payments totaled millions of dollars. See also Dean Brown, "Jordan: A Case of CIA/Class Collaboration," a booklet published by *Counter-Spy,* 1977, p. 2; Shlaim, *Lion of Jordan,* pp. 148–151.

73 "the young King": Ashton, *King Hussein of Jordan,* p. 65.

73 "outnumbered the 'Transjordanians'": Dallas, *King Hussein,* p. 41.

77 "the Haganah sent trucks": Wasserstein, *Divided Jerusalem,* p. 134; Dr. Vicken Kalbian interview, 1/27/07.

77 "My father had a man stay": Dr. Vicken Kalbian interview, 1/27/07.

81 "Most expatriate diplomats": E. H. Hutchison, *Violent Truce: A Military Observer Looks at the Arab-Israeli Conflict, 1951–1955.* New York: Devin-Adair, 1956, pp. 18–19.

81 "Only eight years ago": Bar-On, *Gates of Gaza,* pp. 129–130.

82 "Flint, age forty-seven, was hit": "U.N. Aide Killed in Scopus Clash," *New York Times,* 5/27/58; and "Slain U.N. Truce Chief Was Wounded in 1956," *New York Herald Tribune,* 5/27/58.

83 "the underlying state of mind": Bar-On, *Gates of Gaza,* p. 128.

83 "Jerusalem is a remote city": Oz, *My Michael,* p. 82.

3: The Magic Kingdom

87 "I gather the Chiefs": Robert Vitalis, *America's Kingdom: Mythmaking on the Saudi Oil Frontier.* Stanford, CA: Stanford University Press, 2007, p. 228; Memorandum from the President's Special Assistant for National Security Affairs (Bundy) to the Chairman of the Joint Chiefs of Staff (Taylor), Washington, DC, January 11, 1963, Kennedy Library, National Security Files, Countries Series, Saudi Arabia, 1/63–3/63, Secret, printed in *Foreign Relations of the United States, 1961–1963,* vol. 18, Near East, 1961–1962, document 132.

88 "It was also the site": Wallace Stegner, *Discovery!: The Search for Arabian Oil.* Vista, CA: Selwa Press, 2007, p. 139.

88 "A quarter century": Peter Iseman, "The Arabian Ethos," *Harper's,* February 1978.

89 "The flames of Hell!": Kay Hardy Campbell, *The History of the United States Consulate General, Dhahran, Saudi Arabia,* p. 61 (unpublished manuscript, 30 Hancock Road, Hingham, MA, 1988).

90 "The oil town": Vitalis, *America's Kingdom,* p. 80.

91 "Dhahran was a utopia": Matthew Kuehn Miller and Todd Nims, directors, *Home: The Aramco Brats Story,* 2007, DVD.

91 "Aramcons called their home brew": Robert Lacey, *The Kingdom.* New York: Harcourt Brace Jovanovich, 1981, p. 388; Thomas W. Lippman, *Inside the Mirage: America's Fragile Partnership with Saudi Arabia.* Boulder, CO: Westview Press, 2004, p. 60.

92 "without booze there would be": Nora Johnson, *You Can Go Home Again: An Intimate Journey.* Garden City, NY: Doubleday, 1982, p. 49.

92 "With a population": Vitalis, *America's Kingdom,* p. 252. Vitalis says there were about 3,000 Americans in Dhahran, Abqaiq and Ras Tanura in 1963 and about 2,500 in 1966. But Lippman, *Inside the Mirage,* p. 68, reports that there were 10,000 residents in Dhahran in 1955 but a total of 6,400 Americans in the three camps in 1955. David

Holden, *Farewell to Arabia*. London: Faber and Faber, 1966, p. 129. Holden reports that there were 4,000 Americans living in the Senior Staff compound in 1965.

92 "anti-Semitic jokes": Johnson, *You Can Go Home Again*, p. 65.

92 "By 1963 Aramco": Ali M. Dialdin, Muhammad A. Tahlawi and Thomas A. Pledge, *Saudi Aramco and Its People: A History of Training*. Dhahran: Saudi Aramco, 1998, pp. 84–85.

93 "Saudis as 'coolies'": George Rentz memo to Tom Barger, 1/12/48, Mulligan Papers, Georgetown University, quoted by Robert Vitalis, "Aramco World," published in Madawi Al-Rasheed and Robert Vitalis, eds., *Counter-Narratives: History, Contemporary Society, and Politics in Saudi Arabia and Yemen*. New York: Palgrave, 2004, p. 160.

93 "water fountains for Americans only": Vitalis, *America's Kingdom*, p. 274.

93 "The intellectuals of Dhahran": Johnson, *You Can Go Home Again*, p. 42.

95 "They were a rough": Michael Sheldon Cheney, *Big Oil Man from Arabia*. New York: Ballantine Books, 1958, p. 59.

95 "the Americans as 'Nasranis' ": Vitalis, *America's Kingdom*, pp. 59 and 159.

95 "You Americans don't understand": Tim Barger email to Kai Bird, 3/25/08. The emir said this to Tom Barger.

96 "gave Aramco a monopoly": Daniel Yergin, *The Prize: The Epic Quest for Oil, Money, and Power*. New York: Simon and Schuster, 1991, p. 291.

97 "The decision to build": Vitalis, *America's Kingdom*, p. 54.

97 "pressed the point": Lippman, *Inside the Mirage*, p. 83.

99 "In his first letters home": Vitalis, *America's Kingdom*, p. 59.

100 "conscience of Aramco": Anthony Cave Brown, *Oil, God, and Gold: The Story of Aramco and the Saudi Kings*. New York: Houghton Mifflin, 1999, p. 135.

100 "Some Americans here": Tom Barger, *Out in the Blue: Letters from Arabia, 1937 to 1940*. Vista, CA: Selwa Press, 2000, p. 168.

100 "With the first light of dawn": Abdelrahman Munif, *Cities of Salt*. New York: Random House, 1987, p. 98.

101 "black-market copies": Peter Theroux, *Sandstorms: Days and Nights in Arabia*. New York: Norton, 1990, p. 177.

101 "Before the oil the desert man": Fouad Ajami, *The Dream Palace of the Arabs: A Generation's Odyssey*. New York: Pantheon Books, 1998, p. 126.

101 "Now it is not death": Ajami, Ibid., p. 129.

102 "The government is for princes": Cheney, *Big Oil Man from Arabia*, p. 225.

102 "William Eddy, a CIA asset": William Eddy memo, 12/29/53, as quoted by Vitalis, *America's Kingdom*, p. 153.

103 "expelled across the Iraqi border": Cheney, *Big Oil Man from Arabia*, p. 232; Vitalis, *America's Kingdom*, p. 154.

103 "the poor ignorant": Mildred Webster letter, October 21, 1953, http://www.aramcoexpats.com/Articles/Pipeline/In-Search-Of-Oil/Dear-Folks/3065.aspx.

103 "growing dislike for Americans": Tom Barger memo, 1955, cited by Vitalis, "Aramco World," Al-Rasheed and Vitalis, *Counter-Narratives*, p. 172.

103 "No matter what": Vitalis, *America's Kingdom*, p. 153.

104 "the Shi'ites as 'dogs'": David Holden and Richard Johns, *The House of Saud*. London: Sidgwick and Jackson, 1981, p. 250.

104 "emir arrested some two hundred workers": Ibid., p. 188; Peter Theroux, *Sandstorms*, p. 85.

104 "By the time we arrived": Holden and Johns, *House of Saud*, p. 169.

104 "complained that Mr. Barger": Lippman, *Inside the Mirage*, p. 92.

104 "While working on an FBI case": Ibid., p. 256.

104 "He was a diplomat": Ibid.

105 "American ambassadors to Saudi Arabia": Ambassador J. Rives Child cable to Washington, 2/13/47, quoted by Vitalis, "Aramco World," Al-Rasheed and Vitalis, *Counter-Narratives*, p. 152.

106   "William A. Eddy was one such": Vitalis, *America's Kingdom*, p. 79; Thomas W. Lippman, *Arabian Knight: Colonel Bill Eddy USMC and the Rise of American Power in the Middle East*. Vista, CA: Selwa Press, 2008, pp. 241–242. Lippman suggests that Eddy may have been on Aramco's payroll, but he writes that Eddy was nevertheless regularly reporting to the CIA. The biographic sketch that accompanies Eddy's papers at Princeton manuscript library states that "he served in the OSS and CIA for the remainder of his life, and was also a full-time consultant for the Arabian-American Oil Company" (Lippman, *Arabian Knight*, p. 242).

107   "Metz was suddenly called": Helen Metz interview, 7/2/2008.

113   "The very presence": Lippman, *Inside the Mirage*, p. 299.

114   "Pearl fishermen had earned": Sheikh Hafiz Wahba, *Arabian Days*. London: Arthur Barker, 1964, pp. 22–23.

114   "many Saudi Bedouin women drove": Lippman, *Inside the Mirage*, p. 193.

115   "liquid energy": Peter Iseman, "The Arabian Ethos," *Harper's*, February 1978.

115   "4,000 to 10,000 slaves": Lacey, *The Kingdom*, p. 345; Holden and Johns, *House of Saud*, p. 230.

115   "bought for $900": David Holden, *Farewell to Arabia*. London: Faber and Faber, 1966, p. 136. Three hundred English pounds was then worth about $900 U.S.

116   "The severed hand": Cheney, *Big Oil Man from Arabia*, p. 18.

116   "A police squad car arrives": Iseman, "The Arabian Ethos."

117   "Abdul-Wahhab's definition of Islam": Hamid Algar, *Abdul-Wahhabism: A Critical Essay*. Oneonta, NY: Islamic Publications International, 2002, pp. 16–17.

118   "stoned to death": Ibid., p. 18.

118   "His own brother": Ibid., pp. 6 and 78.

120   "We are talking about a place": Saad Sowayan, "Fresh Look at King Saud Marks Shift in Attitudes Towards Saudi Past," 12/5/06, ArabLife.org.

120   "When Abdul-Aziz died": Cheney, *Big Oil Man from Arabia*, p. 234.

121   "cost nearly $50 million": Ibid., p. 244; Lacey, *The Kingdom*, pp. 299–300.

121   "The royal family's personal finances": Lippman, *Inside the Mirage*, p. 105.

122   "women and alcohol": Holden and Jones, *House of Saud*, p. 182.

122   "will become a constitutional monarchy": Ibid., p. 210, and the *New York Times*, 6/4/58.

122   "no more than 18 percent": Lacey, *The Kingdom*, p. 324.

123   "believed Eddy was now working": Vitalis, *America's Kingdom*, p. 217. See also Lippman, *Arabian Knight*, pp. 241–242.

123   "the biggest political poker game": Vitalis, *America's Kingdom*, p. 220; Sarah Yizraeli, *The Remaking of Saudi Arabia: The Struggle between King Sa'ud and Crown Prince Faysal, 1953–1962*. Tel Aviv: Tel Aviv University, 1997, pp. 88–89.

124   "Aramco's Ron Metz reported": Vitalis, *America's Kingdom*, p. 221.

124   "He had been a leader": Yizraeli, *Remaking of Saudi Arabia*, p. 114.

124   "radical and emotionally unbalanced": Vitalis, *America's Kingdom*, pp. 168 and 309.

125   "By Tariki's calculations": Lacey, *The Kingdom*, p. 330.

125   "We are the sons": Vitalis, *America's Kingdom*, epigraph page.

126   "I was the first Arab": *Time*, April 27, 1959; Vitalis, *America's Kingdom*, p. 136; Madawi Al-Rasheed, *A History of Saudi Arabia*. Cambridge: Cambridge University Press, 2002, p. 111; Brown, *Oil, God and Gold*, p. 153; Lacey, *The Kingdom*, p. 329.

126   "Wahba told a consulate officer": Vitalis, *America's Kingdom*, p. 222.

127   "He had submitted evidence": Ibid., p. 234.

127   "the defeat of liberal reformers": Yizraeli, *Remaking of Saudi Arabia*, pp. 91–92; Alexei Vassiliev, *The History of Saudi Arabia*. New York: New York University Press, 2000, pp. 357–360.

127   "A small army detachment": Vitalis, *America's Kingdom*, p. 234.

127   "Saudi liberals were naïve": Yizraeli, *Remaking of Saudi Arabia*, p. 95.

128   "four slave girls": Holden and Johns, *House of Saud*, p. 218.

128   "Faisal compensated each slaveowner": Holden, *Farewell to Arabia*, p. 136.

129   "Metz described this group": Brown, *Oil, God and Gold,* p. 254.

129   "Barger alerted Washington": Ibid., p. 255.

129   "gently pleading with Faisal": Mike Ameen email to Kai Bird, 2/10/08.

129   "in excellent humor": Brown, *Oil, God and Gold,* p. 256.

130   "The CIA predicted": National Intelligence Estimate, NIE 30–64, *The Outlook for the Arabian Peninsula,* Washington, DC, June 24, 1964. Source: Johnson Library, National Security File, NIEs, 30, Middle East.

4: Arabia: "Progress Without Change"

132   "Faisal proved to be": Lacey, *The Kingdom,* p. 242.

133   "a quarter million girls": Ibid., pp. 366–368.

133   "could read and write": Jerine B. Bird, "Revolution for Children in Saudi Arabia," published in Elizabeth Warnock Fernea, ed. *Children in the Muslim Middle East.* Austin: University of Texas Press, 1995, p. 276.

133   "his deep-seated anti-Semitism": Lippman, *Inside the Mirage,* pp. 220–221.

134   "The appearance of beautiful homes": Brown, *Oil, God and Gold,* p. 284.

134   "Either you stop": Lacey, *The Kingdom,* p. 381.

134   "Forget your father": Vitalis, *America's Kingdom,* p. 251.

134   "ominous reminder to everyone": Ibid., p. 236.

134   "running the government by himself": Ibid., p. 250.

135   "It wasn't so much a family": Hume Horan oral history interview, 11/3/2000, Georgetown University.

136   "On June 5, 1969, Faisal's": Holden and Johns, *House of Saud,* pp. 277–280.

136   "Several hundred people were arrested": Lacey, *The Kingdom,* pp. 380–381.

137   "Saleh was most happy": Eugene Bird, memorandum of conversation, "The Return of a Prodigal," April 9, 1973, Yamamah Hotel, Riyadh, RG 59 Entry 1613, Box 2586, Sub Numeric Files 1970–73, Political Saud-A, National Archives.

137   "arm and leg manacles": Ambassador Herman Eilts, March 8, 1970, Secret Jidda 854 cable to Washington, "Subject: Ahmed Zaki Yamani," RG 59, Entry 1613, Box 2586, Sub. Numeric files 1970–73, Political-Saud-A, National Archives.

137   "number one enemy of the state": American Consulate cable to American Embassy Jeddah, Confidential Dhahran 1313, November 11, 1972, "Subject: Release of Dean Ambah," RG 59, Entry 1613, Box 2586, Sub. Numeric files 1970–73, Political-Saud-A, National Archives.

138   "too great a shock to the Saudi system": Eugene Bird, confidential memorandum of conversation, "The Return of a Prodigal," RG 59, Entry 1613, Box 2586, Subject Numeric Files 1970–73, Political-Saud-A, National Archives.

138   "He had allowed the students": Faiza Ambah email to Kai Bird, 2/15/09.

138   "Saudi Arabia would probably continue": Ambassador Thatcher to Washington, drafted by Eugene Bird, 4/18/73, "Subject: The Rehabilitation of Salah Ambah," RG 59, Entry 1613, Box 2586, Sub. Numeric files 1970–73, Political-Saud-A, National Archives.

138   "inspired by a new nationalism": Faiza Ambah email to Kai Bird, 2/15/09; Aisha al-Fassi email to Kai Bird, 2/10/09.

140   "presence of infidels": Yaroslav Trofimov, *The Siege of Mecca: The Forgotten Uprising in Islam's Holiest Shrine and the Birth of Al Qaeda.* New York: Doubleday, 2007, p. 20.

140   "Sheikh bin Baz rejected": Trofimov, *Siege of Mecca,* p. 28; Charles Allen, *God's Terrorists: The Wahhabi Cult and the Hidden Roots of Modern Jihad.* Cambridge, MA: Da Capo Press, 2006, pp. 276–280.

141   "America's complete support of Zionism": Lacey, *The Kingdom,* p. 400.

142   "The Saudi Spending Machine": Trofimov, *Siege of Mecca,* p. 23.

142   "progress without change": The phrase is Chas Freeman's, who served as the American ambassador to Saudi Arabia from 1989 to 1992. Lippman, *Inside the Mirage,* p. 313.

142   "innocent recreation": Lacey, *The Kingdom,* p. 344.

143   "What would a blind person": Lippman, *Inside the Mirage,* p. 113.

143   "A senior police officer": Holden and Johns, *House of Saud,* p. 261.

143   "King Faisal died": Lacey, *The Kingdom,* pp. 425–426.

144   "If Faisal was an enlightened man": Kai Bird, "Faisal's Legacy," *Worldview,* September 1975.

144   "hoped to have congressmen": Eugene Bird email, 4/24/08.

145   "Mohammed lost one eye": Steve Coll, *The Bin Ladens: An Arabian Family in the American Century.* New York: Penguin Press, 2008, p. 26.

145   "the king grounded him": Wright, *Looming Tower,* p. 91.

145   "he ate pork": Coll, *Bin Ladens,* p. 191.

148   "bolster corrupt rulers": Holden and Johns, *House of Saud,* p. 515.

148   "Juhayman wrote a series": Ibid., p. 518.

148   "worship of the riyal": Trofimov, *Siege of Mecca,* pp. 27–28 and 31–32.

148   "Juhayman's critique was not confined": F. M. Dickman cable from U.S. Embassy in Kuwait to Jeddah embassy, 12/16/88, declassified 6/22/06 by the State Department and published on website of Via Intelwire.com by J. M. Berger.

149   "The princes will corrupt the earth": Lacey, *The Kingdom,* p. 479.

149   "Recognize the Mahdi": Ibid., p. 478.

151   "public cinemas in Jeddah": Faiza Ambah email to Kai Bird, 3/12/09. Ambah recalls that she saw movies in the Attas Hotel in Obhur and in another downtown Jeddah cinema owned by the Jamjoon family.

151   "millions of petrodollars for the propagation": Trofimov, *Siege of Mecca,* p. 100.

151   "Salem arrived in Mecca": Wright, *Looming Tower,* p. 91.

151   "ought to be given a medal": Trofimov, *Siege of Mecca,* p. 162.

153   "took more than 1,000 lives": Ibid., pp. 224–225; Wright, *Looming Tower,* p. 94.

154   "On January 9, 1980, Juhayman": Holden and Johns, *House of Saud,* p. 527.

154   "If he [Juhayman] had attacked my palace": Lacey, *The Kingdom,* p. 512.

154   "turmoil in Saudi Arabia": Coll, *Bin Ladens,* pp. 227 and 232.

154   "The mosque thing": Lippman, *Inside the Mirage,* p. 210.

155   "who has fought in Afghanistan": Trofimov, *Siege of Mecca,* p. 248.

155   "The men who seized Mecca": Ibid., p. 247.

155   "As Steve Coll observes": Coll, *Bin Ladens,* p. 248.

155   "He [Osama bin Laden] had a strong relation": Ibid., p. 295.

156   "as a cane to strike": Trofimov, *Siege of Mecca,* p. 247.

156   "The Zionist-Crusader alliance": Fawaz A. Gerges, *The Far Enemy: Why Jihad Went Global.* New York: Cambridge University Press, 2005, p. 31.

156   "an empire without colonies": Engseng Ho, "Empire Through Diasporic Eyes: A View from the Other Boat," *Society for Comparative Study of Society and History,* 2004, p. 225.

158   "In the arc of coasts": Ho, "Empire Through Diasporic Eyes," p. 212.

159   "the fatwas included a blanket condemnation": Algar, *Wahhabism: A Critical Essay,* p. 66.

159   "Saudis have become hostages": Sulaiman al-Hattlan, "Homegrown Fanatics," *New York Times,* 5/15/03, quoted from Lippman, *Inside the Mirage,* p. 335.

161   "70 percent of the company's workforce": Ali M. Dialdin, Muhammad A. Tahlawi and Thomas A. Pledge, *Saudi Aramco and Its People: A History of Training, Saudi Aramco.* Dhahran, Saudi Arabia: Saudi Aramco, 1998, p. 199.

161   "a phenomenal $781 billion": Zvika Krieger, *Newsweek,* 5/26/08; *Financial Times,* 12/14/06.

162   "Saudi girls are going": Lippman, *Inside the Mirage,* p. 270.

162   "Most Powerful Businesswomen": *Forbes Arabia,* 3/25/06, Dubai, United Arab Emirates.

162   "Saudi women are denied": "Perpetual Minors: Human Rights Abuses Stemming from Male Guardianship and Sex Segregation in Saudi Arabia," *Human Rights Watch,* April 2008.

162   "Ultimately, that petition": www.ArabLife.org.

163   "With more than 60 percent": *New York Times,* 11/24/08.

163   "the Hamlet of our times": Sadik Al-Azm, "Time Out of Joint," *Boston Review,* October/November 2004.

5: Cairo and Nasser's Egypt, 1965–1967

167   "Nasser's greatest achievement": Max Rodenbeck, *Cairo: The City Victorious.* New York: Alfred A. Knopf, 1999, p. 70; Said K. Aburish, *Nasser: The Last Arab.* New York: St. Martin's Press, 2004, p. 215.

168   "5 million people": Rodenbeck, *Cairo,* p. 172.

169   "one-third of the population": Samir W. Raafat, *Maadi, 1904–1962: Society and History in a Cairo Suburb.* Cairo: Palm Press, 1994, p. 105.

170   "The pond contained frogs": Ibid., p. 69.

171   "The Turkish bath": Ibid., p. 232.

173   "What, are they crazy?": *Umm Kulthum: A Voice Like Egypt.* Director, Michal Goldman; Narrator, Omar Sharif. 1996. VHS. Arab Film Distribution, 1996.

175   "perpetual outsiders": Maria Bauer, *Beyond the Chestnut Trees.* Woodstock, NY: Overlook Press, 1984, p. 17.

175   "Bobby was always": Robert Bauer Jr. email to Kai Bird, 3/23/09.

176   "A hundred years later": Maria Bauer, "The Cats of Cairo," *Opera News,* May 1989, pp. 38–39.

177   "Hitler never died": Bernard Avishai, "You Can't Go Home Again," *The New York Review of Books,* November 10, 1977.

177   "Suave and articulate": Robert St. John, *The Boss: The Story of Gamal Abdel Nasser.* New York: McGraw-Hill, 1960, p. 232.

178   *"It's a Wonderful Life":* Aburish, *Nasser,* p. 128.

178   "a bulletproof vest": Douglas Little, "Mission Impossible: The CIA and the Cult of Covert Action in the Middle East," *Diplomatic History,* November 2004, p. 678.

179   "A young Palestinian engineer": Aburish, *Nasser,* p. 223.

179   "No one in our government": Little, "Mission Impossible," p. 678.

180   "He ordered Touhami": Aburish, *Nasser,* p. 95.

180   "Roosevelt's erection": Miles Copeland, *The Game of Nations.* London: Weidenfeld and Nicholson, 1969, pp. 149–151; Tim Weiner, *Legacy of Ashes: The History of the CIA.* New York: Doubleday, 2007, p. 127.

180   "Nasser never closed the door": Aburish, *Nasser,* p. 60.

181   "The Israelis replied": Howard M. Sachar, *A History of Israel.* New York: Alfred A. Knopf, 1979, p. 474.

181   "Operation Susannah": Aburish, *Nasser,* pp. 64–72; Richard Deacon, *The Israeli Secret Service.* New York: Taplinger, 1980, p. 66.

182   "Prime Minister Sharett publicly denied": David Hirst, *The Gun and the Olive Branch.* New York: Nation Books, 2003, p. 291.

182   "I would never have imagined": Livia Rokach, *Israel's Sacred Terrorism: A Study Based on Moshe Sharett's Personal Diary.* Belmont, MA: Association of Arab-American University Graduates, 1980, pp. 38–41.

183   "to carry out reprisal actions": Ibid., pp. 43–47, quoting Sharett's diary, 1/25/55; 2/10/55; 2/14/55.

184   "Sharett wrote in his diary": Ibid., quoting Sharett's diary, 3/1/55.

184   "he had had a personal contact": Ibid., quoting Sharett's diary, 3/12/55.

184   "The conclusions from Dayan's words": Ibid., quoting Sharett's diary, 5/26/55.

185   "Maadi's Jews": Raafat, *Maadi, 1904–1962,* pp. 105–106.

186   "only about 4,000 Jews": Rodenbeck, *Cairo,* p. 158; Michael B. Oren, *Six Days of War: June 1967 and the Making of the Modern Middle East.* New York: Ballantine Books, 2003, p. 307.

186   "He lied to me": Raafat, *Maadi, 1904–1962,* pp. 64–65.

186   "Moscow's man": Ibid., pp. 149–151 and 252.

187   "Dr. Hannes Eisele": Ibid., p. 246.

187   "Ayman's father used to take him": Lawrence Wright, *The Looming Tower: Al-Qaeda and the Road to 9/11.* New York: Alfred A. Knopf, 2006, p. 34.

188   "the wicked opposition of the Jews": Sayyid Qutb, "Ma'alim fi al-Tariq" (Milestones) quoted in Wikipedia; David Zeidan, "The Islamic Fundamentalist View of Life as Perennial Battle," *Middle East Review of International Affairs,* vol. 5, no. 4 (December 2001); Daniel Benjamin and Steven Simon, *The Age of Sacred Terror.* New York: Random House, 2002, p. 68.

189   "Our means didn't match": Wright, *Looming Tower,* pp. 37–38; Gerges, *Far Enemy,* p. 91.

192   "The Syrians rebelled": Mohamed Hassanein Heikal, *The Cairo Documents: The Inside Story of Nasser and His Relationship with World Leaders, Rebels, and Statesmen.* Garden City, NY: Doubleday, 1973, pp. 204–205.

193   "Yemen was 'my Vietnam'": Ambassador Lucius Battle oral history, 11/14/68, Association for Diplomatic Studies and Training Foreign Affairs Oral History Project, Georgetown University; Warren Bass, *Support Any Friend: Kennedy's Middle East and the Making of the US-Israeli Alliance.* New York: Oxford University Press, 2004, p. 141.

193   "protective war": Bass, *Support Any Friend,* p. 228.

193   "imprisoned some 18,000": Rodenbeck, *Cairo,* p. 176.

193   "Nasser was sometimes cross with me": Heikal, *Cairo Documents,* p. xxi.

193   "Politics, news of arrests and imprisonments": Naguib Mahfouz, *Karnak Café.* New York: Anchor Books, 2007, p. 26.

193   "When Heikal contradicted him": Heikal, *Cairo Documents,* 1973, p. xxi.

194   "You know, we made a serious effort": Richard Parker oral history, 4/26/89, Association for Diplomatic Studies and Training Foreign Affairs Oral History Project, Georgetown University.

195   "Cairo was a particularly bad place": Lucius D. Battle oral history, 7/10/91, Georgetown University.

195   "found him perfectly empathetic": Robert Dreyfuss, "Cold War, Holy Warrior," *Mother Jones,* January–February, 2006.

195   "$100 million on anti-Nasser operations": Wilbur Crane Eveland, *Ropes of Sand: America's Failure in the Middle East.* New York: Norton, 1980, pp. 244–245; Eveland interview with Kai Bird, 7/25/82.

195   "his expenditures are financed by the American side": Ian Johnson, "The Beachhead: How a Mosque for Ex-Nazis Became Center of Radical Islam," *Wall Street Journal,* 7/12/05, p. A1; Dreyfuss, "Cold War, Holy Warrior."

196   "The CIA arranged for Ramadan": Miles Copeland, *The Game Player.* London: Aurum Press, 1989, pp. 142–147; Aburish, *Nasser,* pp. 133 and 303; Georges Corm, *Abdel Nasser and the Muslim Brotherhood.* London, 1986, p. 109.

196   "King Hussein of Jordan allowed": Aburish, *Nasser,* p. 230; Aburish, *A Brutal Friendship,* p. 61.

196   "This is the worst attack": Bass, *Support Any Friend,* p. 139.

197   "It was an attempt to use aid": Richard Parker oral history, 4/21/89, Association for Diplomatic Studies and Training Foreign Affairs Oral History Project, Georgetown University.

197   "If they don't like our behavior": Aburish, *Nasser,* p. 251.

198   "All of these things cost very little": David G. Nes oral history, 4/28/92, Association for Diplomatic Studies and Training Foreign Affairs Oral History Project, Georgetown University.

199   "If they didn't shoot": Tom Segev, *1967: Israel, The War, and the Year That Transformed the Middle East.* New York: Metropolitan Books, 2007, p. 193; Richard B. Parker, *The Politics of Miscalculation in the Middle East.* Bloomington: Indiana University Press, 1993, pp. 47–49.

200   "in retaliation for Palestinian guerrilla raids": Clea Lutz Bunch, "Strike at Samu: Jordan, Israel, the United States and the Origins of the Six-Day War," *Diplomatic History,* January 2008, p. 55.

201   "50,000 troops in the Sinai": Roland Popp, "Stumbling Decidedly into the Six-Day War," *The Middle East Journal,* vol. 60, no. 2, Spring 2006, p. 302.

201   "only 117 Israeli ships passed": Eitan Barak, "Between Reality and Secrecy: Israel's Freedom of Navigation through the Straits of Tiran, 1956–1967," *The Middle East Journal,* vol. 61, no. 4, Autumn 2007. p. 678; Parker, *Politics of Miscalculation in the Middle East,* pp. 47–49.

202   "In response to Israel's protests": Parker, *Politics of Miscalculation in the Middle East,* p. 49.

202   "Nasser was astonished": Heikal, *Cairo Documents,* p. 245.

202   "If Israel embarks on an aggression": Patrick Seale, *Asad: The Struggle for the Middle East.* Berkeley: University of California Press, 1990, p. 131.

202   "no strike first": David Nes interview, the Association for Diplomatic Studies and Training Foreign Affairs Oral History Project, Georgetown University, interviewed by Dayton Mak, 4/28/92.

203   "140 American women and children": *New York Times,* 5/27/67.

204   "It looks to me": Eugene Bird interview, 1/6/94, Association for Diplomatic Studies and Training Foreign Affairs Oral History Project, Georgetown University, http://memory .loc.gov/ammem/collections/diplomacy/index.html.

204   "I read you loud and clear": Oren, *Six Days of War,* p. 147.

205   "break Nasser to pieces": Parker, *Politics of Miscalculation in the Middle East,* p. 120; Segev, *1967,* pp. 328–335.

205   "a search for compromise, at Israel's expense": Popp, "Stumbling Decidedly into the Six-Day War," p. 308.

205   "The only crisis was psychological": Segev, *1967,* p. 337; for a legal analysis of Israel's decision to strike, see: David A. Sadoff, "A Question of Determinacy: The Legal Status of Anticipatory Self-Defense," *Georgetown Journal of International Law,* vol. 40, no. 2, Winter 2009, pp. 566–568.

205   "Eshkol emerges as a statesman": Segev, *1967,* p. 334.

205   "Israel is approaching a decision": Popp, "Stumbling Decidedly into the Six-Day War," pp. 281–309. Popp draws his Israeli and Egyptian troop estimates from various declassified CIA estimates and vol. 19 of Foreign Relations of the United States, *Arab-Israeli Crisis and War, 1967.* Washington, DC, 2004.

206   "When Father stepped outside": Eugene Bird letter, 6/6/67; Slaytor Blackiston oral history, April 22, 1992, Association for Diplomatic Studies and Training Foreign Affairs Oral History Project, Georgetown University.

206   "turkey shoot": Parker, *Politics of Miscalculation in the Middle East,* p. 121.

207   "This became known as the 'Big Lie' ": Oren, *Six Days of War,* p. 226.

207   "return to the ranks of the masses": Joel Gordon, *Nasser: Hero of the Arab Nation.* Oxford: Oneworld, 2006, p. 98.

207   "shouting, 'Gamal, Gamal' ": Rodenbeck, *Cairo,* p. 174.

208   "A young man seized him": Nicholas Bromell, "Family Secrets: A Cold War boyhood, at the front," *Harper's,* July 1992, pp. 73–74.

209   "He accused the administration": *New York Times,* 6/30/67.

209   "Why am I languishing": *Umm Kulthum: A Voice Like Egypt.*

210   "Ambah refused to divulge": Faiza Ambah email to Kai Bird, 3/12/09.

210   "It was also a disaster for the Arab world's": Avraham Burg, *The Holocaust Is Over; We Must Rise From Its Ashes.* New York: Palgrave Macmillan, 2008, p. 25.

210   "7,000 Arab Jews were deported": Oren, *Six Days of War,* p. 307.

210   "Why should I go there": Edward Said, *Reflections on Exile: and Other Literary and Cultural Essays.* New Delhi: Penguin Books, 2001, p. 274.

210   "Victory is a much less profound": Charles Glass, *The Tribes Triumphant: Return Journey to the Middle East.* London: HarperPress, 2006, p. 50.

210   "an intense wave of self-criticism": Fouad Ajami, *The Arab Predicament: Arab Political Thought and Practice Since 1967.* Cambridge: Cambridge University Press, 1981, p. 24.

210   "The Imam came forward": Ibid.

211   "The Israelis don't want peace": Heikal, *Cairo Documents,* p. xxvii.

211   "a man walking in a desert": Gordon, *Nasser,* p. 107.

211   "Most of these hopes": Ghada Talhami, "An interview with Sadik Al-Azm," *Arab Studies Quarterly,* June 22, 1997, vol. 19, no. 3, pp. 113–114; Segev, *1967,* p. 509.

212   "Ayman al-Zawahiri wrote": Gerges, *Far Enemy,* p. 91.

212   "I was becoming very conscious": Talhami, "An interview with Sadik Al-Azm," pp. 113–114.

213   "from the Arab *thawra* (revolution)": Ajami, *Dream Palace of the Arabs,* p. 130.

214   "Tom Segev captures the triumphalist": Segev, *1967,* p. 546.

214   "We're waiting for the Arabs to call": Ibid., p. 500.

214   "Let this be said": Sachar, *History of Israel,* p. 673.

214   "Better Sharm al-Sheikh without peace": Bernard Avishai, *The Tragedy of Zionism.* New York: Farrar, Straus and Giroux, 1985, pp. 249 and 255.

215   "Though the Israelis denied": Abdullah Schleifer, *The Fall of Jerusalem.* New York: Monthly Review Press, 1972, pp. 180–181, 192–193 and 195. Schleifer, a Jewish-American convert to Sufi Islam, was an eyewitness to the battle for the Old City.

215   "It sounded as though": Dani Bahar email to Kai Bird 6/28/08.

215   "Two days into the war": Schleifer, *Fall of Jerusalem,* p. 192.

216   "The idea of occupation": Rita Giacaman email to Kai Bird, 2/23/09.

216   "or their homes would be shelled": Schleifer, *Fall of Jerusalem,* p. 208.

217   "Thus we have lost the victory": Ibid., p. 210.

218   "Once they took me out in the Sarafand area": Segev, *1967,* p. 499; United Nations Report of the Special Committee to Investigate Israeli Practices Affecting the Human Rights of the Population of the Occupied Territories, Nov. 13, 1979, A/34/631, UN General Assembly, 34th Session, Agenda Item 51.

218   "We have a moral obligation": Segev, *1967,* p. 525; *Ha'aretz,* 6/18/67.

219   "But Eshkol, Dayan and the other partners in the blunder": Segev, *1967,* pp. 520 and 542.

219   "A peace treaty": Henry Siegman, "Grab More Hills, Expand the Territory," *London Review of Books,* 4/10/08, p. 15.

219   "Most Israelis also wanted": Segev, *1967,* p. 551.

219   "No part of our land": Ibid., p. 543.

219   "some 2.5 million Jews": Amos Elon, *The Israelis: Founders and Sons.* New York: Holt, Rinehart and Winston, 1971, pp. 7 and 31.

220   "As Amos Elon wrote in 1971": Ibid., p. 334.

222   "Nasser has had his [military]": Kai Bird, *The Chairman: John J. McCloy; The Making of the American Establishment.* New York: Simon and Schuster, 1992, pp. 605–609.

222   "The Egyptians suffered 10,000 casualties": Parker, *Politics of Miscalculation in the Middle East,* p. 125.

223   "The whole concept": Bird, *The Chairman,* p. 609.

223   "Nasser is not dead": Rodenbeck, *Cairo,* p. 70; Aburish, *Nasser,* p. 215.

224   "In East Jerusalem": Peter Snow and David Phillips, *The Arab Hijack War.* New York: Ballantine Books, 1970, p. 173.

224   "He died with a modest bank account": Aburish, *Nasser,* p. 235.

6: "A Man Without a Country," 1967–1970

227   "I spent the month of August": Linda Bell, *Hidden Immigrants: Legacies Growing up Abroad.* Notre Dame, IN: Cross Cultural Publications, 1997, p. 114.

235   "Molly Ivins . . . wrote a story": Molly Ivins, *Minneapolis Tribune,* 4/28/70.

238   "The jail was really crappy": Kai Bird letter to Eugene and Jerri Bird, 5/8/70.

240   "taking myself too seriously": Ibid., 5/11/70.
240   "I still have a head": Ibid., 5/21/70.

7: Black September, 1970

244   "Lebanese civil war": Robert Fisk, *Pity the Nation: The Abduction of Lebanon*. New York: Atheneum, 1990, p. 147; James Craig, Donald Maitland and Paul Tempest, eds., *The Arabists of Shemlan, Volume 1*. London: Stacey International, 2006, pp. xi and 4.
245   "steer clear of the plane": "BOAC Jet Joins Others in Jordan," *New York Times,* 9/10/70.
247   "He was a gentle, nice man": Janet Shenk interview with Kai Bird, 1/24/06.
248   "Arguello agreed to participate": Arguello reportedly was paid an "advance" of 5,000 English pounds. See John Bulloch, *The Making of a War: The Middle East from 1967 to 1973*. London: Longman Group, 1974, p. 58.
248   "I was conscious": Leila Khaled, *My People Shall Live,* ed., George Hajjar. London: Hodder and Stoughton, 1973, p. 13, found at http://www.onepalestine.org/resources/articles/My_People_Shall_Live.html.
248   "Arabs killed Jews, Jews killed Arabs": Khaled, *My People Shall Live,* p. 13.
249   "My instinctive reaction": Ibid., p. 14.
249   "Leila was a bright student": *New York Times,* 11/27/70; Eileen MacDonald, *Shoot the Women First*. New York: Random House, 1991, p. 100.
250   "It was all nice, clean American fun": Khaled, *My People Shall Live,* p. 45.
250   "Judy was an imperial citizen": Ibid., p. 46.
251   "Mother fought back": Ibid., p. 59.
252   "arguments against Zionism": Ibid., p. 87.
253   "The 127 passengers": Leila Khaled, "This Is Your New Captain Speaking," as told to Godfrey Jansen, *Life,* 9/18/70, pp. 34–35; Philip Baum, "Leila Khaled in Her Own Words," *Aviation Security International,* 9/5/00, www.avsec.com/interviews/leila-khaled.htm.
253   "Who are the Palestinians?": MacDonald, *Shoot the Women First,* p. 110.
253   "She was feted": Ibid., p. 111.
254   "A breakaway faction": John K. Cooley, *Green March, Black September: The Story of the Palestinian Arabs*. London: Frank Cass, 1973, p. 108.
255   "Yankee doctor, the revolution will": Khaled, "My People Shall Live," excerpted in Isaac Cronin, *Confronting Fear: A History of Terrorism*. New York: Thunder's Mouth Press, 2002, pp. 175–176.
255   "Mossad's attempt to assassinate": Ian Black and Benny Morris, *Israel's Secret Wars: A History of Israel's Intelligence Services*. New York: Grove Weidenfeld, 1991, p. 272.
256   "Are you Queen Elizabeth?": Baum, "Leila Khaled."
256   "He let out a bellow": *Leila Khaled: Hijacker,* a film by Lina Makboul, 2006.
256   "Go ahead, I'll protect your back": Khaled, "My People Shall Live," excerpted in Cronin, *Confronting Fear,* p. 181.
256   "I saw the man hijacker": Snow and Phillips, *The Arab Hijack War,* pp. 10–13; David Raab, *Terror in Black September: The First Eyewitness Account of the Infamous 1970 Hijackings*. New York: Palgrave Macmillan, 2007, p. 19.
257   "As the bullets flew": *New York Times,* 10/9/70.
257   "In fact, one source suggests": Raab, *Terror in Black September,* p. 19.
257   "Khaled claims she had": Khaled, *My People Shall Live,* pp. 163–164.
257   "I saw everything": *New York Times,* 10/15/70.
257   "'Please stop the bloodshed'": Snow and Phillips, *Arab Hijack War,* p. 12; MacDonald, *Shoot the Women First,* p. 117. Khaled, "My People Shall Live," excerpted in Cronin, *Confronting Fear,* pp. 175–176. Also at http://www.onepalestine.org/resources/articles/My_People_Shall_Live.html, p. 166.
258   "I didn't intend to hurt": Snow and Phillips, *Arab Hijack War,* p. 17.
258   "lawful homicide": Ibid., p. 18.

258   "The two El Al security guards": David Raab reports that British Prime Minister Edward Heath's files contain a note suggesting that Arguello was shot dead "more probably after" the struggle (Edward Heath notes, Sept. 18, 1970, courtesy of David Raab. www .terrorinblackseptember.com/.../04_september_06_1970.doc). But Raab points out that at the time she was detained Khaled never said to British authorities that Arguello had been shot after being tied up. And finally, two experts at the inquest testified that Arguello had not been shot afterwards. I was unable to find a record of the inquest, and Arguello's autopsy report is sealed.

258   "310 hostages parked in two planes": Snow and Phillips, *Arab Hijack War*, p. 43.

258   "Walter Cronkite intoned": *CBS Evening News*, 9/6/70; *Hijacked!* A documentary film produced and directed by Ilan Ziv, aired on the PBS program *American Experience*, 2/26/06.

258   "If the world has become": "Drama of the Desert: The Week of the Hostages," *Time*, 9/21/70.

259   "They did not exist": *Sunday Times* (London), 6/15/69; David Hirst, *The Gun and the Olive Branch: The Roots of Violence in the Middle East*. New York: Thunder's Mouth Press, 2003, p. 392.

259   "He had obviously never heard": Bassam Abu-Sharif and Uzi Mahnaimi, *Best of Enemies*. Boston: Little, Brown, 1995, p. 83.

259   "The cabin was filling up": "Drama of the Desert: The Week of the Hostages."

260   "Now we will blow up the plane": Joy Riggs letter to Kai Bird, postmarked 9/14/70.

260   "No, we go to Tel Aviv": "G-ASGN," BOAC pamphlet published "as a small memento for the passengers and crew and their relatives who were so deeply involved in the happenings from 9–26 September 1970," published by BOAC, printed in Great Britain, undated; Raab, *Terror in Black September*, pp. 71–73.

260   "Revolutionary Airport": Snow and Phillips, *Arab Hijack War*, p. 39.

261   "The visibility was very poor": Raab, *Terror in Black September*, p. 73.

261   "like a lousy war movie": Joy Riggs letter to "Mom and Dad," 9/13/70.

261   "A plane has been hijacked just for me": MacDonald, *Shoot the Women First*, p. 122.

262   "Yellow Submarine": Snow and Phillips, *Arab Hijack War*, p. 54.

263   "waiting for them to shoot": Raab, *Terror in Black September*, p. 84.

263   "The commandos were usually friendly": Joy Riggs letter to "Mom and Dad," 9/13/70.

264   "We don't want to kill you": Snow and Phillips, *Arab Hijack War*, p. 52.

264   "We all got to know": Joy Riggs letter to Kai Bird, 10/1/70.

264   "The only time I argued": Kai Bird interview with Joy Riggs-Perla, 10/22/06.

266   "I lost four children by Hitler": "Drama of the Desert: The Week of the Hostages."

266   "When we hijack a plane": Hirst, *Gun and the Olive Branch*, p. 432.

266   "She will do it again": *Leila Khaled: Hijacker*, a film by Lina Makboul, 2006.

267   "At the press conference": Kai Bird interview with Joy Riggs-Perla, 10/22/06.

267   "Hot lights and stupid questions": Joy Riggs letter to Kai Bird, postmarked 9/14/70.

267   "But it didn't bother me a bit": Joy Riggs letter to "Mom and Dad," 9/13/70.

268   "please stay away from the Arabs": Joy Riggs letter to Kai Bird, postmarked 9/14/70.

268   "We fight Israel": Photo by Kai Bird, 1970.

268   "I just wrapped it around a bullet": www.myspace.com/135337792.

269   "They were completely mutilated": Loren Jenkins, *Newsweek*, 9/28/70.

270   "People's committees": Snow and Phillips, *Arab Hijack War*, p. 49.

270   "political and demographic minority": Avi Shlaim, *Lion of Jordan: The Life of King Hussein in War and Peace*. New York: Alfred A. Knopf, 2008, p. 342. The CIA Fact Book for Jordan estimates that today 60 to 80 percent of Jordan's population is Palestinian.

270   "we are all *fedayeen*": Nigel Ashton, *King Hussein of Jordan: A Political Life*. New Haven, CT: Yale University Press, 2008, p. 140.

271   "the king's nephew, Sharif Nasser": Shlaim, *Lion of Jordan*, p. 323.

271   "King Hussein was extraordinarily isolated": Hume Horan interview, 11/3/2000,

Foreign Affairs Oral History Collection of the Association for Diplomatic Studies and Training, Georgetown University; Raab, *Terror in Black September*, p. 7.

271 "I didn't think the King": Harrison M. Symmes oral history interview, 2/25/89, Foreign Affairs Oral History Collection of the Association for Diplomatic Studies and Training, Georgetown University.

271 "bugged the ambassador's phone": Shlaim, *Lion of Jordan*, p. 326.

271 "Kissinger later wrote": Ibid., p. 322.

272 "Jack O'Connell, now rushed to the palace": Douglas Little, "Mission Impossible: The CIA and the Cult of Covert Action in the Middle East," *Diplomatic History*, vol. 25, no. 5, November 2004, p. 23.

272 "It's we who are the women now": Snow and Phillips, *Arab Hijack War*, p. 41.

273 "Savages! Mere savages": Jean Genet, *Prisoner of Love*. New York: New York Review of Books, 2003, p. 195.

273 "40,000 armed *fedayeen*": Snow and Phillips, *Arab Hijack War*, pp. 94–95; Raab, *Terror in Black September*, p. 5.

273 "any advantages to be derived": Raab, *Terror in Black September*, p. 186.

273 "The Palestinian revolt strikes a very deep": Shlaim, *Lion of Jordan*, p. 333.

273 "It was pretty clear . . . Hume Horan": Hume Horan interview, 11/3/2000, Foreign Affairs Oral History Collection of the Association for Diplomatic Studies and Training, Georgetown University.

274 "The President's instincts are to crush": Document 214. Minutes of a Combined Washington Special Actions Group and Review Group Meeting 1, Washington, September 9, 1970, 11:40 a.m.–12:35 p.m. Foreign Relations of the United States, Nixon-Ford Administrations, vol. 24, *Foreign Relations, 1969–1976 Middle East Region and Arabian Peninsula, 1969–1972*; *Jordan, September 1970*. Washington, DC: Govt. Printing Office, 2004.

274 "We have just gotten word from the Palace": Raab, *Terror in Black September*, pp. 138–139; Hume Horan interview, November 3, 2000, Georgetown University.

274 "Then something totally unexpected happened": "Bloody King of Black September," *Revolutionary Worker #992*, 2/21/99.

275 "The fight goes on": Snow and Phillips, *Arab Hijack War*, pp. 104 and 141.

275 "some 360 subterranean bunkers": Shlaim, *Lion of Jordan*, p. 340.

275 "should Syria and Iraq enter the conflict": Snow and Phillips, *Arab Hijack War*, p. 107.

276 "asked for an air strike by Israel": "Black September Plea to Israel," BBC, Monday, January 1, 2001: http://news.bbc.co.uk/2/low/middle_east/1095221.stm. See also Ashton, *King Hussein of Jordan*, pp. 148–149.

276 "a panicked King Hussein": Document 284. Telegram from the Embassy in Jordan to the Department of State, September 21, 1970, 0124Z. Foreign Relations of the United States, Nixon-Ford Administrations, Vol. 24, *Foreign Relations, 1969–1976 Middle East Region and Arabian Peninsula, 1969–1972; Jordan, September 1970*.

276 "An Arab monarch was asking": "Black September Plea to Israel," BBC, Monday, January 1, 2001: http://news.bbc.co.uk/2/low/middle_east/1095221.stm. See also Ashton, *King Hussein of Jordan*, pp. 148–149.

276 "We could not allow Hussein": Shlaim, *Lion of Jordan*, pp. 333–334; Shlaim also cites Mahmoud Riad, *The Struggle for Peace in the Middle East*. London: Quartet, 1981, p. 162.

276 "Iraqi stab in the back": Cooley, *Green March, Black September*, p. 115.

277 "You can't fire into those refugee camps without killing": Document 267. Minutes of a Washington Special Actions Group Meeting, Washington, September 19, 1970, 9:25–10 a.m, Foreign Relations of the United States, Nixon-Ford Administrations, Vol. 24, *Foreign Relations, 1969–1976 Middle East Region and Arabian Peninsula, 1969–1972; Jordan, September 1970*.

277 "as high as 4,000": Shlaim, *Lion of Jordan*, p. 330; Christopher Dobson, *Black September: Its Short, Violent History*. New York: Macmillan, 1974, p. 34.

277   "I had no idea the army": Snow and Phillips, *Arab Hijack War,* p. 154; Shlaim, *Lion of Jordan,* p. 330.

277   "The good guys won": Hume Horan interview, November 3, 2000, Georgetown University.

277   "His sixteen-year-old daughter": Genet, *Prisoner of Love,* p. 67.

277   "I was indignant": Snow and Phillips, *Arab Hijack War,* p. 154.

278   "There are men, women and children dying": Joel Gordon, *Nasser: Hero of the Arab Nation.* Oxford: Oneworld Publications, 2006, p. 114.

278   "Full support for the Palestine revolution": Snow and Phillips, *Arab Hijack War,* p. 162.

278   "I'm very sad": Ibid., p. 175.

279   "Hussein told al-Tal": www.country-studies.com/jordan/hussein---the-guerrilla-crisis.html.

279   "2,300 were arrested": Cooley, *Green March, Black September,* p. 122.

279   "al-Fatah's charismatic one-eyed commander": Roland Dallas, *King Hussein: A Life on the Edge.* New York: Fromm International, 1999, p. 139. Dallas says the story about Abu Ali Iyad being dragged behind a tank is a "myth" peddled by the PLO. On the other hand, he says "some say 4,000" *fedayeen* were killed in the July assault. Christopher Dobson, an Arabic-speaking reporter for the *London Sunday Telegraph* asserts that Abu Ali Iyad's body was "certainly" dragged through the streets. See Dobson, *Black September,* p. 37.

279   "Hussein's secret police": Shlaim, *Lion of Jordan,* p. 340.

279   "a cancer operation": Ashton, *King Hussein of Jordan,* p. 157.

280   "King Hussein's close friend John Fistere": Said K. Aburish, *A Brutal Friendship: The West and the Arab Elite.* New York: St. Martin's Press, 1997, pp. 335–340; *Intelligence,* No. 94, 3/8/99, p. 7.

280   "The PLO is dead": Interview with a retired Foreign Service officer, who recalled hearing about this legendary cable years later. As I had known the late Hume Horan, it sounds to me like something he might have written. Horan was the Embassy's Deputy Chief of Mission during the Black September crisis. I was unable to find the actual cable in the archives.

280   "The President will never forget": Raab, *Terror in Black September,* p. 234; Douglas Little, *American Orientalism: The United States and the Middle East Since 1945.* Chapel Hill: University of North Carolina Press, 2002, p. 106.

280   "$1.15 billion in 1971–73": Martha Wenger, "US Aid to Israel: From Handshake to Embrace," *Middle East Report,* No. 164/165, May–Aug. 1990.

280   "his CIA stipend": Ashton, *King Hussein of Jordan,* p. 190.

281   "We are Black September": Dallas, *King Hussein,* p. 141.

281   "According to Christopher Dobson": Dobson, *Black September,* pp. 69–70.

283   "I knew violence would never work": Abu-Sharif and Uzi Mahnaimi, *Best of Enemies,* p. 101.

283   "I found their bodies": Dr. Mahdi Abdul Hadi, ed., *Palestinian Personalities: A Biographic Dictionary.* Jerusalem: Palestinian Academic Society for the Study of International Affairs, rev. ed., 2006, p. 111; MacDonald, *Shoot the Women First,* pp. 96 and 126; Rex A. Hudson (Project Manager: Helen C. Metz), "The Sociology and Psychology of Terrorism: Who Becomes a Terrorist and Why," A Report Prepared under an Interagency Agreement by the Federal Research Division, Library of Congress, September 1999, p. 75.

283   "All kinds of resistance": Leila Khaled interview, *The Electronic Intifada,* 7 January 2008, www.electronicintifada.net.

284   "If I am unable to return": http://www.onepalestine.org/resources/articles/My_People_Shall_Live.htm.

284   "That was an act of terror": Timur Moon, "Leila Khaled: Hijacked by Destiny," *The Friday Times,* 10/17/02.

284   "The opposing opinion": Shlaim, *Lion of Jordan,* p. 3; Ashton, *King Hussein of Jordan,* p. 154.

284 "Right-wing Israelis": Shlaim, *Lion of Jordan,* p. 344.
285 "Kissinger claims that he knew nothing": Document 281. Minutes of a Washington
     Special Actions Group Meeting 1, Washington, September 20, 1970, 7:10–9:15 p.m.
     Foreign Relations of the United States, Nixon-Ford Administrations, Vol. 24, *Foreign
     Relations, 1969–1976 Middle East Region and Arabian Peninsula, 1969–1972; Jordan,
     September 1970.*
285 "Foreign Minister Eban told": Document 325. Intelligence Memorandum Prepared in
     the Central Intelligence Agency, Washington, September 24, 1970, Foreign Relations
     of the United States, Nixon-Ford Administrations, Vol. 24, *Foreign Relations, 1969–
     1976 Middle East Region and Arabian Peninsula, 1969–1972; Jordan, September 1970.*
285 "any move to undermine Hussein": Ashton, *King Hussein of Jordan,* pp. 154 and 398.
286 "A basic change in Fatah ideology": Robert C. Ames to Ambassador Helms, July 18,
     1973, declassified CIA papers of Richard Helms, quoted by Amir Oren, "Top Secret,
     Eyes Only," *Ha'aretz,* March 10, 2008; David Ignatius, "In the End, CIA-PLO links
     weren't helpful," *Washington Post,* 11/12/04.
287 "the PLO would have been finished": Ashton, *King Hussein of Jordan,* p. 162.
287 "Bassam Abu-Sharif reports": Abu-Sharif and Mahnaimi, *Best of Enemies,* p. 75.
288 "I think things will get worse": Gerald McKnight, *The Terrorist Mind.* New York: Bobbs-
     Merrill, 1974, p. 78.
291 "killing seventeen Americans": Fisk, *Pity the Nation,* 480.

8: The Night of Broken Glass

298 "The Modern Age is the Jewish Age": Yuri Slezkine, *The Jewish Century.* Princeton, NJ:
     Princeton University Press, 2004, p. 1.
299 "Susan wore a maroon colored Tibetan": Kai Bird diary, 11/19/73.
300 "possessed by a history": Helen Epstein, *Children of the Holocaust: Conversations with
     Sons and Daughters of Survivors.* New York: G.P. Putnam's Sons, 1979, p. 14.
302 "Heil Hitler!": Helma Blühweis Goldmark interview, 3/3/99.
303 "Richard Gibiser, a secret Nazi Party member": I am indebted to Dr. Gerald Lamprecht
     of the Centrum für Jüdische Studien at the Karl-Franzens-Universität, Graz, for
     providing me with this information about Richard Gibiser from the Graz archives.
304 "No, that young man has emigrated": Helma Goldmark interview, 3/3/99.
306 "the black bread we bought": Ibid.
308 "Only 80 prisoners escaped": Martin Gilbert, *The Holocaust: A History of the Jews of
     Europe during the Second World War.* New York: Holt Rinehart and Winston, 1985, p.
     798.
308 "a man named Cabiglio": Notarized affidavit issued in Rome, January 21, 1947,
     notarized by Dr. Raoul Guidi and signed by Paul Urbach, Paul Kollman, Paolo
     Hertman, Fritz Citron and Viktor Goldmark, courtesy of Helma Goldmark.
308 "In Croatia less than 10 percent": Susan Zuccotti, *The Italians and the Holocaust:
     Persecution, Rescue, Survival.* New York: Basic Books, 1987, p. 77.
308 "So . . . on April 16, 1942, Helma": Emergency Identity Certificate No. 1866 for Helma
     Blühweis, issued by Displaced Persons and Repatriation Sub-Commission, Allied
     Commission, Central Mediterranean Forces, November 29, 1946. The document states
     that Helma Blühweis arrived in Italy on April 16, 1942.
309 "In my house you eat": Helma Goldmark interview, 3/16/99.
309 "more than 10,000 Jews": Alexander Stille, *Benevolence and Betrayal: Five Italian Jewish
     Families Under Fascism.* New York: Penguin Books, 1991, p. 22.
310 "Jews do not belong to the Italian race": Ibid., p. 70.
311 "The Germans are all over": Jane Scrivener, *Inside Rome with the Germans.* New York:
     Macmillan, 1945, p. 13.
311 "All Jews, regardless of nationality": Zuccotti, *Italians and the Holocaust,* p. 109.
313 "It was forbidden to ride": Stille, *Benevolence and Betrayal,* p. 190.

313   "6,746 of them were gassed": Gilbert, *The Holocaust,* p. 623.

315   "the Pensione Jaccarino": Fernande Leboucher, *Incredible Mission: The Amazing Story of Pére Benoît, Rescuer of the Jews from the Nazis.* Garden City, NY: Doubleday, 1969, pp. 136–137.

315   "he was assisting some 4,000": Gilbert, *The Holocaust,* p. 622; Zuccotti, *Italians and the Holocaust,* pp. 65, 115 and 209–210; Stille, *Benevolence and Betrayal,* p. 264.

315   "the Vatican funneled": Zuccotti, *Italians and the Holocaust,* p. 210. Zuccotti uses the figure of 25 million Italian lira, which in 1944 would have been worth about $1.5 million. Fernande Leboucher reports that the Vatican tapped one of its sources to funnel some $4 million to fund Father Benoît's various operations. See Leboucher, *Incredible Mission,* p. 143.

317   "proceed urgently with the arrest": Zuccotti, *Italians and the Holocaust,* p. 191.

317   "42 Germans lay dead": Robert Katz, *Death in Rome.* New York: Macmillan, 1967, pp. 73–76; Scrivener, *Inside Rome with the Germans,* p. 143.

317   "In retaliation, the SS rounded up": Zuccotti, *Italians and the Holocaust,* p. 192; Stille, *Benevolence and Betrayal,* p. 213; Scrivener, *Inside Rome with the Germans,* pp. 144–145.

322   "After the war ended, my aunt Frania": Sara Roy, "Living with the Holocaust: The Journey of a Child of Holocaust Survivors," *Journal of Palestine Studies,* vol. 32, no. 1, Autumn 2002, Issue 125.

324   "Some aspects of Willy's narrative": Victor Goldmark taped interview, circa 1985.

326   "another 5,000 were sentenced": Stille, *Benevolence and Betrayal,* p. 231; Susan Zuccotti, *Under His Very Windows: The Vatican and the Holocaust in Italy.* New Haven, CT: Yale University Press, 2000, p. 86.

327   "820 cases of malaria": Carlo Spartaco Capogreco, *Ferramonti.* Florence: Giuntina, 1987 (translated by Helma Goldmark); Simon Wiesenthal Center, Multimedia Learning Center, Annual 4, chapter 1, part 2.

327   "Ironically, Rabbi Pacifici would be deported": Stille, *Benevolence and Betrayal,* pp. 234 and 342.

327   "Ferramonti grew into a small village": Simon Wiesenthal Center, Multimedia Learning Center, Annual 4, chapter 1, part 2.

328   "baptized seventy-nine Jews": Zuccotti, *Under His Very Windows,* p. 83.

329   "A dreadful awe": Ibid., pp. 90–92.

330   "Willy was unaware of it": Carlo Spartaco Capogreco, *I Campi del Duce: l'internamento civile nell'Italia fascista (1940–1943),* editore Einaudi, Torino, 2004.

331   "Son Safe, Photo Shows": *New York Times,* 10/7/43. (The *Times* published the photo on October 4, 1943.)

333   "Please note . . . that restitution of my one-half share": Helma Blühweis letter to Graz State District Court, received on November 29, 1946.

334   "to be paid to Dr. Fritz Strassmann": Court Document of the Commission on Restitution for Styria at the District Court in Graz, February 5, 1949, Presiding Justice Dr. Felber. Also found in the Austrian archives is a December 31, 1948, document showing that Helma Blühweis and Dr. Leone Endrizzi were both represented by attorney Dr. Fritz Strassmann in a proceeding before the District Court. Helma Blühweis, of course, had left for New York in July 1947. Dr. Endrizzi was in Italy.

336   "Perhaps one cannot": Primo Levi, *Survival in Auschwitz and the Reawakening: Two Memoirs.* New York: Summit Books, 1986, p. 393.

337   "as a Freedom Rider": Eric Pace, "Henry Schwarzschild, 70, Opponent of Death Penalty," *New York Times,* 6/4/96.

338   "24,000 dead in a single day": Levi, *Survival in Auschwitz,* p. 388.

338   "They must learn love of the homeland": Tom Segev, *The Seventh Million: The Israelis and the Holocaust.* New York: Henry Holt, 2000, pp. 35 and 158–159.

339   "Among the survivors": Mordecai Richler, *This Year in Jerusalem.* London: Vintage, 1995, p. 89.

339   "by 1952 some 40,000": Epstein, *Children of the Holocaust,* pp. 96–97.

339   "800,000 Israelis had emigrated": Richler, *This Year in Jerusalem,* p. 65.

339   "Entire cities and hundreds of villages": Segev, *The Seventh Million,* pp. 161–162.

339   "Israel's security policy": Avraham Burg, *The Holocaust Is Over: We Must Rise From Its Ashes.* New York: Palgrave Macmillan, 2008, p. 23.

340   "In our eyes": Ibid., p. 78.

9: The Hebrew Republic

343   *"What am I?":* Louis Rapoport, *Shake Heaven and Earth: Peter Bergson and the Struggle to Rescue the Jews of Europe.* Jerusalem: Gefen, 1999, p. 192.

348   "Are you in favor": Ibid., pp. 195–196.

348   "raised a million dollars": Ibid.

348   "in fact the money": Victor S. Navasky, *A Matter of Opinion.* New York: Farrar, Straus and Giroux, 2005, pp. 280–281; Richler, *This Year in Jerusalem,* p. 26.

350   "he was dispatched to Poland": Rapoport, *Shake Heaven and Earth,* pp. 19–21 and 227–228.

350   "in every cabinet": Efraim Karsh, "Benny Morris's Reign of Error, Revisiting the Post-Zionist Critique," *Middle East Quarterly,* Spring 2005. Karsh is quoting from Jabotinsky's 1940 book, *The Jewish War Front* (London: Allen and Unwin), pp. 216–217.

350   "We are a people": Ze'ev Jabotinsky, "Instead of Excessive Apology," 1911, quoted in wikipedia.org/wiki/Jabotinsky.

351   "With Jabotinsky's death": Judith Tydor Baumel, *The "Bergson Boys" and the Origins of Contemporary Zionist Militancy.* Syracuse, NY: Syracuse University Press, 2005, p. 12.

351   "But then on November 25, 1942": Rapoport, *Shake Heaven and Earth,* p. 66.

351   "emergency committee to rescue": Joseph Agassi, *Liberal Nationalism for Israel: Towards an Israeli National Identity.* Jerusalem: Gefen, 1999, p. 149.

351   "We responded as a human": "Hillel Kook" entry at www.wikipedia.org.

352   "systematic extermination": Deborah E. Lipstadt, *Beyond Belief: The American Press and the Coming of the Holocaust, 1933–1945.* New York: Free Press, 1985, p. 157.

352   "But by the end of 1942": Ibid., p. 188.

352   "Representatives of the United States government": Ibid., p. 186.

352   "world's helplessness": Ibid.

353   "Guaranteed Human Beings": Ibid., p. 200.

353   *"We Will Never Die":* Baumel, *The "Bergson Boys,"* p. 116.

353   "to do the utmost to rescue": Lipstadt, *Beyond Belief,* p. 201. For an indictment of the New York Times's coverage of the Holocaust, see Laurel Leff, *Buried by the Times: The Holocaust and America's Most Important Newspaper.* New York: Cambridge University Press, 2006.

354   "only 21,000 Jewish refugees": Edwin McDowell, "New Book Criticizes U.S. Effort to Rescue Jews," *New York Times,* 11/6/84.

354   "The 1924 Immigration Act": David S. Wyman, *Paper Walls: America and the Refugee Crisis, 1938–1941.* New York: Pantheon, 1985, pp. 220–221.

354   "'sensationalist' and ineffectual": David S. Wyman, *The Abandonment of the Jews: America and the Holocaust, 1941–1945.* New York: Pantheon, 1984, p. 202.

354   "125,000 members": Baumel, *The "Bergson Boys,"* p 191.

355   "Meyer rejected the idea": Lipstadt, *Beyond Belief,* p. 228.

355   "Rabbi Abba Hillel Silver": Wyman, *Abandonment of the Jews,* p. 163; Aryeh Neier letter to the editor, *The Nation,* 1/26/85.

356   "guilty not only of gross procrastination": Bird, *The Chairman,* p. 203.

357   "The WRB was in effect buying Jews": Ibid.

357   "McCloy rejected the idea": Ibid., pp. 220–222.

358   "Jews could have been saved": Peter Bergson/Hillel Kook quotes come from Laurence Jarvik's 1982 documentary, *Who Shall Live and Who Shall Die?* Kino International (2006).

358   "terror attacks on British soldiers": For instance, in September 1944, a force of some 150 Irgunists attacked four British police stations, and on September 29, 1944, a senior British police officer in the Criminal Intelligence Department was assassinated in Jerusalem. [Martin Gilbert, *Churchill and the Jews.* New York: Holt, Rinehart, 2007, pp. 221 and 253.] The Irgun's most notorious attack took place on July 22, 1946, when it bombed the King David Hotel in Jerusalem, killing ninety-one people.

358   "The British must be driven out": Baumel, *The "Bergson Boys,"* p. 197.

359   "a 'post-Zionist' worldview . . . Bergson agrees with you": Rapoport, *Shake Heaven and Earth,* p. 183.

359   "The Jews must decide": Ibid., p. 181; Agassi, *Liberal Nationalism for Israel,* p. 179.

360   "They are a people": Linda Grant, *When I Lived in Modern Times.* New York: Plume/Penguin, 2002; see the epigraph at the beginning of Grant's novel about Israel.

361   "ascertained by J. Edgar Hoover's gumshoes": Rapoport, *Shake Heaven and Earth,* p. 185.

361   "This is not a quibble!": Ibid., p. 215.

362   "There is little doubt": Ibid., p. 186.

362   "I am a Hebrew": Ibid., pp. 190–191.

362   "My country is Palestine": Ibid., p. 192.

363   "placed a bounty on his head": Ibid., p. 193.

363   "The whole Jabotinsky family hated": Ibid., p. 208.

363   "a group of self-appointed people": Myrna Oliver, "Hillel Kook: As Peter Bergson, Led Campaign to Save Jews in WWII," *Los Angeles Times,* 8/22/01.

366   "So Ben-Gurion did the deal": Bernard Avishai, *The Hebrew Republic: How Secular Democracy and Global Enterprise Will Bring Israel Peace at Last.* New York: Harcourt, 2008, p. 43.

368   "If all the blood that is being shed": "Myths of the Middle East," A special issue of *The Nation,* 12/5/81.

369   "We are now in a society": Avishai, *Hebrew Republic,* pp. 92–93.

369   "A small majority openly opposes equal rights": Ibid., p. 97; Eric Alterman, "How Israel Failed Its Arab Minority," *Moment,* November/December 2008. Alterman is citing a poll conducted by Tel Aviv University's Jaffee Center for Strategic Studies.

369   "You cannot live in Hebrew": Avishai, *Hebrew Republic,* p. 117.

Epilogue

373   "could the fire that we lit": Fawaz A. Gerges, *The Far Enemy: Why Jihad Went Global.* New York: Cambridge University Press, 2005, p. 243.

373   "Despite current predictions": Ibid., p. 244.

373   "Neither Palestinians nor Israelis": Gershom Gorenberg, "The Missing Mahatma," *The Weekly Standard,* 4/6/09.

374   "nearly everybody in Israel": Avishai, *Hebrew Republic,* p. 212.

374   "To call this view 'marginal'": Alterman, "How Israel Failed Its Arab Minority."

374   "another quarter are Palestinian Israelis": Avishai, *Hebrew Republic,* p. 21.

375   "hundreds of thousands of Palestinians": Morris, *Righteous Victims,* p. 214.

375   "Many Israelis feel": Benny Morris, "Why Israel Feels Threatened," *New York Times,* 12/30/08.

377   "They thought you might be crazy enough": Sari Nusseibeh with Anthony David, *Once Upon a Country: A Palestinian Life.* New York: Farrar, Straus and Giroux, 2007, pp. 470–473.

377 "There will be two states": Nusseibeh with David, *Once Upon a Country*, p. 488. For a slightly revised version of the Nusseibeh-Ayalon initiative, see http://www .jewishvirtuallibrary.org/jsource/Peace/peoplesvoiceplan.html.
378 "People here, as we say in Arabic": Rita Giacaman email to Kai Bird, 4/13/09.
379 "I am a naïve person": Nusseibeh with David, *Once Upon a Country*, p. 469.

Index

Page numbers in *italics* refer to illustrations.

About the Author

Kai Bird is the coauthor with Martin J. Sherwin of the Pulitzer Prize–winning biography *American Prometheus: The Triumph and Tragedy of J. Robert Oppenheimer* (2005), which also won the National Book Critics Circle Award for Biography. He wrote *The Chairman: John J. McCloy; The Making of the American Establishment* (1992) and *The Color of Truth: McGeorge Bundy and William Bundy; Brothers in Arms* (1998). He is also coeditor with Lawrence Lifschultz of *Hiroshima's Shadow: Writings on the Denial of History and the Smithsonian Controversy* (1998). Bird is the recipient of fellowships from the John Simon Guggenheim Memorial Foundation; the Alicia Patterson Foundation; the John D. and Catherine T. MacArthur Foundation; the Thomas J. Watson Foundation; the German Marshall Fund; the Rockefeller Foundation's Study Center, Bellagio, Italy; and the Woodrow Wilson International Center for Scholars in Washington, DC. A member of the Society of American Historians and a contributing editor of *The Nation,* he lives in Kathmandu, Nepal, with his wife and son.

www.kaibird.com

DATE DUE